Jacob P. Panzarella

July 1985

THE HALSTEAD-REITAN NEUROPSYCHOLOGICAL TEST BATTERY

Theory and Clinical Interpretation

Ralph M. Reitan
Professor of Psychology
University of Arizona

Deborah Wolfson
Neuropsychology Laboratory
Tucson, Arizona

Neuropsychology Press

1985

Neuropsychology Press, 1338 East Edison Street, Tucson, Arizona 85719

Made in the United States of America

Library of Congress Catalog Card Number: 85-71561
ISBN 0-934515-02-6

Great care has been taken to maintain the accuracy of the information contained in the volume. However, Neuropsychology Press cannot be held responsible for errors or for any consequences arising from the use of the information contained herein.

PREFACE

In recent years there has been a tremendous growth in interest in human brain-behavior relationships. This interest is expressed in many ways, including both experimental studies and clinical assessment and evaluation. The Halstead-Reitan Neuropsychological Test Battery is reported to be the most extensively used method for clinical evaluation of brain-behavior relationships. More than half of the clinical psychology training programs in major universities give training in use of the Battery. Many institutions that offer clinical internships and postdoctoral fellowships include the Battery in their assessment program and offer training in administration and interpretation. There have been numerous publications concerning the Halstead-Reitan Battery, and additional research studies appear in the literature frequently.

The purpose of this book is to contribute further clinical knowledge of the neuropsychology of brain diseases or injuries as measured by the Halstead-Reitan Neuropsychological Test Battery. To accomplish this purpose we have presented a general statement of the theory and rationale of the Battery, a description of the tests included in the Battery, a manual for administering and scoring the test, and 28 case presentations, carefully selected as teaching cases, in which the neuropsychological test results were related to the independently identified neurological description of the patient's brain. We chose cases that represented the major categories of neurological disease and damage and, in addition, introduced each of these categories with a brief description and summary of the nature of the disease or damage represented. Thus, the categories of brain damage include brain tumors (included principally because of their excellent teaching potential), cerebral vascular disease, craniocerebral trauma, Alzheimer's disease, multiple sclerosis, alcoholism, effects of substance abuse, epilepsy, and aging. The interested reader will find a useful introduction to each condition and examples of how these conditions are expressed on the Halstead-Reitan Battery as well as pertinent references for further study. It is important to recognize that neuropsychological interpretation, with relation to independent neurological findings, is not a circular exercise merely duplicating the original diagnosis already established. Although neuropsychological testing is distinctly relevant to neurological diagnosis and can serve in many instances to identify the likely neurological condition that may be present, its principal purpose is to describe brain-related disorders that fall in the neuropsychological (as contrasted with the neurological) domain. Neuropsychological assessment describes the behavioral manifestations of brain damage or disorders in detail, including the higher-level aspects of brain functions. In this sense, neuropsychological evaluation represents a tremendously important aspect of assessment of impaired as well as normal brain functions. One's intelligence, verbal skills, visual-spatial abilities, abstraction, reasoning, and ability in basic understanding of complex situations contributes not only to occupational and professional capabilities, but, in a much broader sense, to the quality of living. A ready argument could be presented that such characteristics of human behavior, in fact, are much more important than specific capabilities in motor and sensory functions. Thus, there is no doubt that neuropsychological assessment represents an area of very important and significant contributions. However, in order for the interpretation of test results to be relevant and pertinent, it is necessary that the assessment procedures relate to the underlying biological condition of the brain in a valid and realistic way. Both neurology and neuropsychology are closely concerned with brain functions and complement each other in terms of the brain-related manifestations that each area emphasizes.

The relationship between neuropsychology and psychology concerns the degree of emphasis on brain-related manifestations of behavior. Assessment procedures in neuropsychology, documented by careful research, have a known relationship and dependence upon brain functions whereas in psychology, more generally, behavior is validly studied in its own right even though the biological bases are not of immediate concern. The relationship between these areas concerns the overlapping emphasis on behavior rather than a common focus on brain functions. The rapid growth of neuropsychology has attracted the interest and contributions of many psychologists, some of whom have a limited background in the biological sciences. Correspondingly, there has been a growing tendency in neuropsychology to presume that any type of measurement must be a manifestation of brain functions and thereby subject to inclusion in the area of neuropsychology, regardless of the procedure or instrument used, the content of the behavior, or the evidence that might link the behavior to brain functions. This tendency blurs the identification of neuropsychology as a separate discipline within psychology. Those investigators who have devised and validated procedures for assessment of brain function, thereby focussing directly on brain-behavior relationships, have learned through difficult experience that a host of problems may interfere with this type of "easy" presumption. Even among abilities clearly dependent on brain functions, the particular measurement technique, apparatus, or procedure may fail to correlate closely with underlying brain function. Also, some abilities are a reflection of immediate adaptive capabilities of the brain whereas others are deeply ingrained and are little affected, at least initially, by developing brain disorders. Still other skills and behaviors are insecurely established in terms of how they relate to brain functions. Thus, there is a definite need at the present time to communicate the relationship of neuropsychological measurements to identified conditions of brain disease or damage so that, as a practical matter, the clinical neuropsychologist can discern those aspects of measured behavior in the individual subject that relate in known ways to the underlying biological condition of the brain. One of the principal aims of this book is to provide such information.

A second goal is to provide a statement of the theory and rationale of the Halstead-Reitan Battery. The Battery was developed over a period of many years through study of thousands of patients with neurological disease or damage. Initially we found that patients with certain lesions, even though often quite significant, failed to show any significant deviation from expected results of normal subjects. Gradually we added testing procedures and learned to identify the aspects of the test results that reflected impaired brain functions in these patients as well as in many others. Finally, through study of correlations between independent neurological, neurosurgical, and neuropathological findings and the neuropsychological test results, we were able to identify nearly every patient having significant brain disease or damage by his/her corresponding deficits on the Halstead-Reitan Battery. There is probably no substitute for such a procedure in developing and validating the clinical usefulness of any neuropsychological test battery. As described in the section concerned with the theory and rationale of the Battery, many factors enter into the process, including the types of abilities measured, general versus specific tests of brain function, measurement strategies, and formal research efforts.

A final aim of this book is to provide a description of the actual tests used in the Halstead-Reitan Battery and a manual for administration and scoring of the tests. Examination procedures require that every effort be made to stress the subject's brain in an attempt to determine the best abilities that the person's brain can produce. First, it is necessary to learn how to elicit the patient's best performances. Second, it is extremely important that the test be given in a specified manner. Use of the Halstead-Reitan Battery represents a laboratory procedure rather than a casual or even clinical examination. Thus, we hope that the manual of instructions included in this book will be studied carefully by those who use the Battery and that the quality of data will thereby be upgraded.

This volume does not contain detailed information about neuroanatomy, neurology, and neuropathology but instead concentrates on the neuropsychological aspects of interpretation of results for individual subjects. A companion volume by Reitan and Wolfson entitled, *NEUROANATOMY AND NEUROPATHOLOGY: A Clinical Guide for Neuropsychologists (1985)* is intended to be used conjointly with this book. We would recommend that neuropsychologists who are not familiar with neuroanatomy and the clinical and neuropathological consequences of various neurological disorders initially study this companion volume. Together, these two books represent our conceptualization that the nervous system, and especially the brain, must be viewed from a number of vantage points, beginning with biological structure and extending through physiological and neurochemical aspects of function, clinical neurological signs and symptoms of brain disease or damage as well as neurological diagnostic techniques (all of which may have great significance with respect to treatment indications), and extending to higher level aspects of behavior (neuropsychology). In fact, the Halstead-Reitan Battery was deliberately devised to extend from primary aspects of motor and sensory functions, touching base with clinical neurology, to measurement of high level abstraction, reasoning, and logical analysis, language facility, spatial problem-solving, flexibility in thought processes, and other complex adaptive behavior.

We have tried to design this book to be useful to educators teaching the administration, scoring, and interpretation of the Halstead-Reitan Battery to clinical neuropsychology students. For example, the individual cases are deliberately presented in somewhat varied format. In some cases the history material and neurological findings are presented first so that the test results can be considered in light of the patient's problems and the clinical findings. In other cases the test results are presented first and a "blind" analysis of the data is done so that the reader can learn to appreciate the potential of the data for predicting the clinical and neurological findings. In some instances the neuropsychological interpretations refer quite specifically to results on individual tests as a basis for drawing conclusions but other times the conclusions are stated without specific reference to the individual test on which they were based. In these latter cases the reader is implicitly encouraged to review the test results and to draw personal conclusions about each test as it contributes to the total assessment. We encourage the interested student to re-study the cases presented from one approach or another, learning through deliberate effort to extract the full significance of the entire data set.

We also believe that our theoretical model of brain-behavior relationships, the manual for administration and scoring, and the detailed clinical interpretations will be useful for experienced clinical neuropsychologists. We hope that this information, particularly concerning administration and interpretation of the Battery, will clarify the misconceptions, incorrect instructions for administration of the tests, and errors in interpretation that have been communicated by various other authors in recent years.

Finally, we have included a comprehensive glossary of terms to facilitate understanding of the text by students and psychologists who do not have an extensive background in technical terminology relating to the brain and nervous system.

We are indebted to our many colleagues for their interest in the

Halstead-Reitan Battery as well as the much broader interest in human brain-behavior relationships. When Ward Halstead began systematic investigation in this area in 1935, even his close colleagues found his aims and aspirations to be difficult to comprehend (if not actually mysterious). As would be expected, there is still some lack of understanding of the extent to which the behavioral correlates of brain functions can be assessed and the scientific community is only gradually becoming aware of the importance of such measurements.

We are indebted to many teachers, colleagues and students who have contributed to our ability to write this book. We wish specifically to acknowledge the help of Jan Janesheski for reviewing and updating the instructions for administration of the tests, Jacquelyn Tarpy for proofreading the manuscript, and Sharon Russell for typing the manuscript.

CONTENTS

I
THEORY AND RATIONALE OF THE HALSTEAD-REITAN NEUROPSYCHOLOGICAL TEST BATTERY

Any battery of tests which assesses human brain-behavior relationships must have three components: (1) content, or measurement of the types of psychological functions represented by the brain; (2) measurement strategies which permit application of the results to individual subjects; and (3) validation of the measurements through formal research procedures, with respect to clinical evaluations and applications.

Types of Brain-Related Functions

A neuropsychological test battery must be able to measure the full range of behavioral functions subserved by the brain. This aim is probably impossible to achieve completely, but we can measure many appropriate brain-related abilities. Historically, the approach has been to evaluate persons with cerebral lesions, identify their deficits, and infer normal brain-behavior relationships by comparing persons with cerebral damage to persons who have presumably normal brains. The basic approach in neuropsychology, then, has been to relate consistent evidence of impairment to increasingly precise descriptions of underlying neuropathology.

In the early phases of such research the method generally used was to develop a "test" of brain damage. As more detailed investigations progressed, however, it became clear that the brain was a remarkably complex organ in terms of the behaviors that it subserved, and a series of tests would be necessary to even approximate the extensive range of strengths and weaknesses manifested by any single brain.

Another significant problem arose with the inferential procedure — comparisons of damaged and normal brains. First, there is undoubtedly a wide range of variation among normal brains in both level and structure of abilities. Imposed on this initial realization that normal brains vary considerably was the definite possibility that two brains sustaining similar damage may not demonstrate the exact same behavioral deficits. Finally, using brain damage as the starting point for determining the characteristics of normal brains required that "brain damage" be assessed in terms of what it constituted. Studies of persons with various types of lesions, placed in different locations, occurring at different times and at different ages, made it clear that brain lesions showed a great deal of variability.

Thus, researchers faced a very complicated situation and recognized the immense difficulties implicit in validly describing the behavioral correlates of an individual brain. It was apparent that procedures had to be standardized before any progress could be made. Since both normal and pathological brains were extremely variable, and since behavior was widely variable from one individual to another, scientists were unsure about which behaviors in a person should be measured. Some investigators, implicitly assuming that "brain damage is brain damage," elected to principally study only one type of lesion. This procedure allowed the researcher to vary the behavioral measurements and pursue initial findings in increasingly refined detail.

The alternative method was to develop a standardized neuropsychological test battery and administer that battery to patients with different types of brain lesions. In order to develop a valid and reliable neuropsychological test battery, certain procedures must be followed. Initially, many organizational problems must be solved, such as having patients with brain lesions available for testing; obtaining careful independent descriptions of the patient's brain lesion through the cooperation of neurologists, neurological surgeons, and neuropathologists; obtaining money and space to conduct examinations; and attending to the administrative details that are always present with large-scale research projects. We learned that it was necessary to study thousands of patients with brain lesions, correlate their test results with independent neurological data, and compare their performances to results obtained from control subjects. A standardized battery was developed and used so that the independent variables (brain lesions) could be varied while the dependent variables (neuropsychological test results) were held constant.

Another problem in developing a neuropsychological test battery concerned identifying *brain-related* variables as compared with behavioral manifestations that were principally dependent upon other types of influences. It is well-recognized that a person's chronological age, education, socioeconomic status, medical history, personality, specific skills, and the host of variables that determine human individuality are all factors that contribute to an individual's psychological performance. It is not necessary to review the arguments of the genetic-versus-environmental determinants of intelligence debate; we do, however, have to identify which aspects of psychological test results relate specifically to the biological condition of the brain. We have found that the best way to answer this question has been to carefully examine an individual's neuropsychological test data and, from that information, predict the neurological status. To implement this procedure we collected data on thousands of patients using a three-step process: (1) administer a comprehensive battery of neuropsychological tests to the patient without knowing any of the patient's neurological findings; (2) make a written prediction of the patient's neurological status based solely on his/her neuropsychological test results; and (3) compare the neurological diagnosis with the neuropsychological test results.

Using this procedure, we have learned that certain variables contribute little to neurological conclusions (even though they may serve as comparison variables in certain respects) whereas other combinations of test results are of unequivocal significance in identifying cerebral dysfunction. This method has permitted us to gradually refine clinical interpretation of results on individual subjects to a high degree of accuracy, as will be illustrated later in the discussion of test results of patients.

Certain neuropsychological test data are particularly helpful in determining whether or not brain damage is present; other test results are especially useful for lateralizing and localizing cerebral damage; certain patterns of results relate to generalized or diffuse cerebral damage; other test results (particularly as they reflect the entire configuration of data) are used to differentiate the chronic, static lesion from the recent, acutely destructive or rapidly progressive lesion; and still different findings aid the interpreter in deciding whether the cerebral damage was sustained during the developmental years or adulthood.

One can readily see that in addition to formal, controlled research studies (the type usually published in the literature) there were challenging questions involving the development of valid clinical interpretation of results for individual subjects. Answering these questions required the development of a test battery that represented at least a reasonable approximation of the behavioral correlates of brain function.

Conceptual Model of the Halstead-Reitan Battery

The efforts to design a comprehensive set of neuropsychological measures led to a conceptual model of brain functions represented by the Halstead-Reitan Test Battery. The Battery consists of tests in six categories: (1) input measures; (2) tests of attention, concentration and memory; (3) tests of verbal abilities; (4) measures of spatial, sequential and manipulatory abilities; (5) tests of abstraction, reasoning, logical analysis and concept formation; and (6) output measures. The tests cover a broad range of difficulty: both very simple and quite complex tasks are included. Attention, concentration, and memory are distributed throughout the tests in the Battery, just as they appear to occur in the tasks that people face in everyday living. Many of the tests require immediate problem-solving capabilities, others depend upon stored information and some require simple perceptual skills which focus principally upon the sensory modalities of vision, hearing, and touch. A conceptual model of the behavioral correlates of brain function is presented in Figure 1-1.

The first step in a neuropsychological response cycle requires input to the brain from the external environment via one or more of the sensory avenues. Although a neuropsychological battery can hardly be expected to include a thorough assessment of all sensory functions, there must be some provision in the battery to document any significant sensory impairment. This often can be done by merely observing

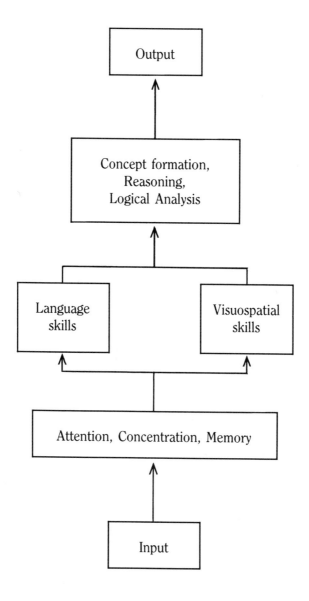

Fig. 1-1. *A conceptual model of the behavioral correlates of brain function.*

the subject carefully throughout the testing procedures and using appropriate instructions in test administration.

In giving the Speech-sounds Perception Test, for example, we begin with a sample of the test to be sure that the subject is able to see the response alternatives on the answer form and hear the auditory stimulus on the tape player. If the patient has a significant problem in either of these respects, we attempt to make proper adjustments (such as increasing the sound volume or asking the patient to wear his/her glasses). Most of the tests, however, have been developed in such a way that minor variations in sensory input do not affect the patient's scores.

The tests that provide information regarding sensory integrity have also been designed or selected to give information regarding cerebral functioning. For example, rather than performing a test of tactile sensitivity that depends exclusively on receptor structures, we use tests (e.g., Tactile Finger Recognition) which also require a degree of discrimination. Therefore, many of the measures in the Reitan-Kløve Sensory Perceptual Examination not only yield information regarding input to the brain but require judgments by the patient which give the investigator information about the integrity of the selected receptor area of the cerebral cortex.

To aid in understanding the various complexities of central processing, we have described a hierarchy of brain-related abilities (*See* Fig. 1-1). The first level of central processing represents attention, concentration and memory (the ability to scan a range of prior experiences for comparison with immediate input) and can be identified as the "registration phase."

Obviously, input stimuli must be registered in the brain before more complex and specialized processing can be performed. The limiting point occurs at this level in some patients who have severe deficits. If the patient is so seriously impaired that he/she cannot pay attention to incoming material, test performances will be marked by significant deficits regardless of either the sensory avenue involved or the content (verbal, non-verbal, etc.) of the tests. The clinician should be aware that limitations shown by a patient at an initial level may be differentially represented throughout the rest of the model. For example, a patient with left cerebral damage may have more difficulty paying attention, maintaining concentration, and remembering verbal input than performing visuospatial types of tasks.

After registering input material, the next step in central processing involves the specialized or differential functions of the cerebral hemispheres and depends upon the content of the test material. Some verbal tasks will stress the left cerebral hemisphere much less than others. Naming the capital of Italy, for example, is as much a verbal task as responding to an item on the Word Finding Test (Reitan, 1972). Nevertheless, many persons with significant left cerebral lesions who could name the capital of Italy have performed poorly on the Word Finding Test. The difference concerns the extent to which the particular test item or procedure permeates the entire model: If the verbal task does not require involvement at the highest level of central processing (abstraction, reasoning, logical analysis and concept formation), the damaged left cerebral hemisphere will be able to perform relatively well compared to normal expectations. If, however, the verbal task requires a substantial element of concept formation and reasoning skills, the compromised left cerebral hemisphere will perform poorly. Of course, the damage may be so severe or in such a location that it will cause obvious impairment in specific language functions (aphasia) and such information would aid the interpreter in localizing the lesion.

The same types of considerations apply to right cerebral damage and impairment in the area of spatial, sequential and manipulatory skills. Some patients with very serious or posteriorly located lesions in the right cerebral hemisphere will show evidence of constructional dyspraxia even when copying simple figures such as a square, cross and triangle. Other patients may not show striking deficits on such simple tasks but, when abstraction and reasoning are involved in the constructional process (as in the Block Design subtest of the Wechsler Scale), a distinctly deficient performance may be obtained.

A neuropsychological test battery must also include items which evaluate the highest level of central processing, namely, reasoning and concept formation. These skills may be relatively independent of specific content requirements. The best example of this type of measure in the Halstead-Reitan Battery is the Category Test, a test that requires complex abilities in the area of attention, concentration, immediate memory, recognition and differentiation of spatial configurations, use of numerical symbols as a response mechanism, and formation of concepts on the basis of observation of recurring similarities and dissimilarities in the test items. Thus, limited ability at any of the levels of central processing may be responsible for a poor performance on the Category Test. It is extremely important that a neuropsychological test battery evaluate this highest level of central processing in order to provide information relevant to the complexity of real-life situations.

Finally, output capabilities must be assessed. The effector organs of the body, the muscles and glands, are not evaluated in detail during neuropsychological assessment. However, motor functions on the two sides of the body are compared and often provide valuable information about the status of a patient's cerebral functioning.

General versus Specific Measures of Cerebral Status

Goodglass and Kaplan (1979) have cited the importance of including both general and specific measures of brain functions in a neuropsychological test battery. Most batteries, however, have concentrated heavily on specific measures and do not include tests which evaluate the highest level of central processing and the skills necessary to function in daily life. The neuropsychological response cycle shown in Figure 1-1 illustrates the complementary potential of general and specific tests. The Halstead-Reitan Battery was carefully designed to include both types of measures.

Specific tests often provide useful information about the localization of maximal cerebral damage. Positive findings on tests which are specific in nature are associated with more destructive types of lesions and therefore contribute valuable information regarding developing or focal lesions. We should also note, however, that these types of lesions are the kind that are most easily identified through use of conventional neurological methods (such as computed tomography) and patients with these types of lesions are rarely referred to a neuropsychologist for diagnosis.

General tests of cerebral functions, able to identify the impairment found in persons with diffuse or generalized cortical damage, are the unique contributions of neuropsychological evaluation. Although diffuse cerebral damage may sometimes be associated with structural deficits (such as cerebral atrophy) and be diagnosed by using imaging or contrast techniques, it is not infrequent that neuropsychological evaluation presents the only positive evidence in such cases.

Measurement Strategies

Evaluation of brain-damaged subjects has made it clear that it is necessary to have a number of inferential strategies to be able to draw valid conclusions about brain-behavior relationships for the individual person (Reitan, 1966a; Reitan, 1967b). These methods of inference, recently described as "time-honored" procedures in clinical neuropsychology, (Rourke, Bakker, Fisk & Strang, 1983) had never been systematically included in neuropsychological assessment before development of the Halstead-Reitan Battery. These measurement strategies have been described in detail elsewhere, and will be mentioned here only briefly.

First, it is necessary to determine how well the subject performs on each of the measures included in the Battery. This approach essentially refers to level of performance and, on most of the measures, is represented by a normal distribution for non-brain damaged subjects. Since some persons perform quite well and others perform more poorly, it clearly would not be possible to accept a level-of-performance strategy alone as a basis for diagnosing cerebral damage. In other words, there are some persons who demonstrate above-average ability levels despite having sustained cerebral damage and some persons with below-average ability levels who do not have cerebral damage. A level-of-performance approach represents an inter-individual inferential model. It is useful for comparing subjects, but offers relatively little direct information regarding the brain functions of the individual subject. (As the reader has probably noted, this is the model used in most research studies.)

A second approach, introduced by Babcock (1930), postulated that differences in levels of performance on various tests might denote impaired brain functions, or at least a loss of efficiency in psychological performances. This approach has also been used to compute the Deterioration Quotient based on comparison of scores from different subtests of the Wechsler Scale (Wechsler, 1955). This method represents an intra-individual comparison procedure (a comparison of the subject's own performances on various tests) and helps to identify the uniqueness of an individual's ability structure. Research with the tests included in the Halstead-Reitan Battery has produced a number of intra-individual patterns that are useful for assessing differential functions of the brain and identifying impaired areas within the brain.

A third approach incorporated into the Halstead-Reitan Battery is the identification of specific deficits on simple tasks of the type that occur almost exclusively among brain-damaged persons. Deficits in performance on these simple tasks may not only identify the presence of cerebral damage but also indicate areas of maximal involvement (Wheeler & Reitan, 1962). The reader should be aware, however, that this inferential strategy fails to identify a significant proportion of brain-damaged persons: those who do not show the specific deficit in question (false negatives).

The fourth measurement strategy used in the Halstead-Reitan Battery to identify cerebral damage is one which compares motor and sensory-perceptual performances of the same type on the two sides of the body, thus permitting inferences regarding the functional status of homologous areas of the two cerebral hemispheres. This method is also based on intra-individual comparisons, using the subject as his/her own control. When positive findings occur they may have unequivocal significance for cerebral damage. A more detailed discussion of these inferential methods can be found in a previous publication (Reitan, 1967a).

Brief Review of Research Findings

We will not attempt to present an exhaustive survey of published research concerned with validation of the Halstead-Reitan Battery, but a brief review may be helpful to the reader who wishes to have a general guide to this literature.

The Halstead-Reitan Battery has probably been researched in more detail than any other set of neuropsychological tests. Through the close cooperation among neuropsychologists, neurologists, neurological surgeons and neuropathologists it has been possible to compose groups of subjects with definite unequivocal evidence of cerebral damage and compare these persons with subjects who have no history or present evidence of cerebral damage or disease. This approach has a tremendous advantage over research oriented toward development of constructs such as intelligence, affective disorders, emotional maturity, etc. In attempting to validate psychological measures against such constructs, there has been the continual criterion problem of not having an unequivocal definition of the condition being evaluated. In neuropsychology, however, it has been possible to not only recognize the presence or absence of cerebral damage but also provide more detailed information regarding localization, type, duration of lesion and acuteness or chronicity.

The initial approach in developing the Halstead-Reitan Battery was to compare control subjects to persons known to have diversified cerebral damage (heterogeneous types of lesions in various locations) and, based on these comparisons, identify the tests which were sensitive to the general condition of the cerebral hemispheres. Numerous reports documenting the efficacy of the Halstead-Reitan Battery have appeared in the literature, including: Boll, Heaton and Reitan, 1974; Chapman and Wolff, 1959; Doehring and Reitan, 1961a; Doehring and Reitan, 1961b; Fitzhugh, Fitzhugh and Reitan, 1961; Fitzhugh, Fitzhugh and Reitan, 1962a; Fitzhugh, Fitzhugh and Reitan, 1960; Fitzhugh, Fitzhugh and Reitan, 1965; Heimburger, DeMyer and Reitan, 1964; Heimburger and Reitan, 1961; Matthews, Shaw and Kløve, 1966; Reed and Reitan, 1962; Reed and Reitan, 1963a; Reed and Reitan, 1963b; Reed and Reitan, 1963c; Reitan, 1955b; Reitan, 1955c; Reitan, 1958; Reitan, 1959a; Reitan, 1959b; Reitan, 1960; Reitan, 1964; Reitan, 1970a; Reitan, 1970b; Reitan and Boll, 1971; Reitan and Fitzhugh, 1971; Reitan, Reed and Dyken, 1971; Ross and Reitan, 1955; Shure and Halstead, 1958; Vega and Parsons, 1967; Wheeler, Burke and Reitan, 1963; Wheeler and Reitan, 1962; Wheeler and Reitan, 1963.

The above references refer to studies of adult subjects and do not include the many investigations that have been performed using the Halstead-Reitan Neuropsychological Test Battery for Older Children or the Reitan-Indiana Neuropsychological Test Battery for Younger Children.

A similar range of investigations had to be completed in order to evaluate the role of the Wechsler Scales concerning general intelligence in brain-behavior relationships. Studies with adult subjects include: Anderson, 1950; Doehring, Reitan and Kløve, 1961; Fitzhugh, Fitzhugh and Reitan, 1962b; Kløve, 1959; Matthews and Reitan, 1964; Reed and Reitan, 1963c; Reitan, 1955b; Reitan, 1960; Reitan, 1964; Reitan, 1970b; Reitan and Fitzhugh, 1971; Wheeler, Burke and Reitan, 1963; and Wheeler and Reitan, 1963.

These studies demonstrated that the Wechsler Scales were generally not as sensitive as the tests devised by Halstead. It has been shown, however, that persons with acutely destructive left cerebral lesions usually show significant impairment on the Verbal subtests and persons with acute right hemisphere damage will frequently have poor scores on the Performance subtests of the Wechsler Scale.

Positive correlations between the specialized or lateralized psychological correlates of brain functions and the Wechsler scales have been reported by Anderson, 1950; Reitan, 1955b; Doehring, Reitan and Kløve, 1961; Fitzhugh, Fitzhugh and Reitan, 1962b; Kløve and Reitan, 1958; Matthews and Reitan, 1964; and Meier and French, 1966. These studies with the Wechsler scale have been summarized by Matarazzo (1972) and Kløve (1974).

Other lateralization effects based on tests in the Halstead-Reitan Battery have been reported in a number of investigations, including Doehring and Reitan, 1961a; Doehring and Reitan, 1961b; Heimburger and Reitan, 1961; Heimburger, DeMyer and Reitan, 1964; Kløve and Reitan, 1958; Reitan, 1959b; Reitan, 1960; Reitan, 1964; Wheeler, 1964; Wheeler and Reitan, 1963; Kløve, 1959.

Reitan (1964) has also studied the effects of frontal versus posterior lesions in each cerebral hemisphere. In addition, several other variables have been investigated using data from the Halstead-Reitan Battery. Studies examining the differential effects of acute and chronic cerebral damage have shown that more severe and selective losses are usually present with acute damage, presumably because the brain has not had sufficient time to reorganize its functional status (Fitzhugh, Fitzhugh, & Reitan, 1961; Fitzhugh, Fitzhugh, & Reitan, 1962a; Fitzhugh, Fitzhugh, & Reitan, 1963).

Various types of cerebral deficits have also been studied in considerable detail. They include aphasia (Reitan, 1960; Doehring & Reitan, 1961b; Heimburger & Reitan, 1961); emotional problems and their influence on cognitive deficits (Fitzhugh, Fitzhugh, & Reitan, 1961; Dikmen & Reitan, 1974a; Dikmen & Reitan, 1974b; Dikmen & Reitan, 1977a; Dikmen & Reitan, 1977b; Reitan, 1970c; Reitan, 1977); epilepsy (Reitan, 1976); and sensory-perceptual losses as related to intelligence (Fitzhugh, Fitzhugh, & Reitan, 1962).

Other investigations have evaluated and compared various kinds of neurological disorders and types of lesions, including cerebral vascular disease (Reitan, 1970b; Reitan & Fitzhugh, 1971); brain tumors (Hom & Reitan, 1982; Hom & Reitan, 1984); multiple sclerosis (Ross & Reitan, 1955; Forsyth, Gaddes, Reitan, & Tryk, 1971; Reitan, Reed & Dyken,

1971); Huntington's chorea (Boll, Heaton, & Reitan, 1974); craniocerebral trauma (Reitan, 1973; Dikmen & Reitan, 1976; Dikmen & Reitan, 1977a; Dikmen & Reitan, 1977b; Dikmen & Reitan, 1978; Dikmen, Reitan, & Temkin, 1983); alcoholism (Fitzhugh, Fitzhugh, & Reitan, 1960; Fitzhugh, Fitzhugh, & Reitan, 1965); drug abuse (Grant, Mohns, Miller, & Reitan, 1976); mental retardation (Matthews & Reitan, 1961; Matthews & Reitan, 1962; Matthews & Reitan, 1963; Davis & Reitan, 1966; Davis & Reitan, 1967; Davis, Hamlett, & Reitan, 1966; Reitan, 1967); and aging effects (Reitan, 1955d; Reitan, 1962; Reitan, 1967; Reitan, 1970a; Fitzhugh, Fitzhugh, & Reitan, 1963; Fitzhugh, Fitzhugh, & Reitan, 1964; Reed & Reitan, 1962; Reed & Reitan, 1963a; Reitan & Wolfson, in press).

Although it is not possible to review these various studies in detail, the reader may note that extensive research has been performed to establish the validity of neuropsychological measurements in a number of clinical conditions. For the interested researcher, there is a considerable amount of data published in the recent literature to serve as a guide for developing clinical expertise.

II
DESCRIPTION OF TESTS
IN THE HALSTEAD-REITAN
NEUROPSYCHOLOGICAL
TEST BATTERY

The individual neuropsychological tests included in the Halstead-Reitan Battery have long and varied histories. They were selected or adapted from many sources: several of the tests were devised or developed by Halstead; Wechsler's Scale for measurement of general intelligence has been included as part of the Battery since 1951; and a number of the tests were adapted or developed by Reitan and Kløve. This chapter will give a description of the various tests in the Halstead-Reitan Battery and discuss the theoretical, methodological, and practical factors that make this set of tests a "battery" rather than simply an extensive collection of individual tests. Detailed and specific instructions for administration and scoring of the tests in the Halstead-Reitan Battery are given in a separate chapter of this book. Instructions for administering the Wechsler Scales and Minnesota Multiphasic Personality Inventory can be found in other publications (Wechsler, 1955; Hathaway and McKinley, 1967). Three overlapping test batteries have been developed: (1) Adults, ages 15 and older; (2) Older Children, ages 9 through 14; and (3) Younger Children, ages 5 through 8 (Reitan & Davison, 1974). Only the Adult Battery is described in this volume.

HALSTEAD'S TESTS

Category Test

This test uses a projection apparatus to present the subject with a series of 208 stimulus figures on a 10″ x 10″ screen. An answer panel, containing four levers numbered from 1 to 4, is attached to the test apparatus at a convenient level below the screen. The subject is told that he will be asked to inspect each stimulus figure when it appears on the screen and depress the lever corresponding to the answer he thinks is correct. (Fig. 2-1). Depressing a lever will cause either a bell (if the answer is correct) or a buzzer (if the answer is incorrect) to sound. The subject is allowed to make only one response for each stimulus item.

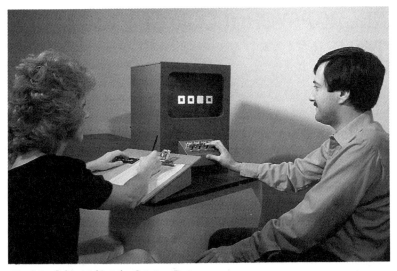

Fig. 2-1. Subject taking the Category Test.

Before the test begins, the subject is told that the test is divided into seven groups of items and a single principle or theme runs through each entire group from beginning to end. The subject is instructed to try to figure out the principle for each group. As he responds to each item by depressing one of the four levers on the answer panel, the bell or buzzer indicates whether his choice was correct or incorrect. In this way, the test procedure permits the subject to test one possible principle after another; a correct hypothesis is positively reinforced by the bell. Regardless of the difficulty he might encounter, the subject is never told the principle for any group.

The first and second groups are nearly always easily performed, even by persons with serious brain lesions. The first group requires matching Arabic numerals above each of the answer levers with individual Roman numerals shown on the screen.

In the second group, the subject must learn to press the lever corresponding to the number of items appearing on the screen. For example, the answer would be "2" if two squares appeared, "4" if four letters of the alphabet were displayed, etc.

The examiner announces the end of each group as it occurs. At the beginning of each group of items the examiner tells the subject that the principle might be the same as it has been or it might be different. The subject's task is to discern the principle of each group.

The principle of the third group of items is based on the concept of uniqueness. Each stimulus item is composed of four figures, and the subject must learn to depress the lever corresponding with the figure which is most different from the others. Although this group begins rather simply, it progresses to items in which one figure may differ from the others in three or more respects (such as size, shape, color, or solidness of figure) while the rest of the figures differ from each other in only two respects. For example, a stimulus item appearing in the beginning of the group may be made up of a row of four equilateral triangles; the first, second and fourth triangles are the same size and the third triangle is about 50 percent larger. In this case the "correct" answer would be "3," with size being the determinant of uniqueness. On a later item, all four figures, differing in shape and color, are the same size. The first figure is solid and the other three figures are formed only by an outline. In this instance, uniqueness could not be determined by shape, color, or size, since these determinants were entirely variable or entirely constant. The answer would be "1," since the first figure was the only one that was solid.

The fourth group uses identification of one of the four quadrants of a figure as the basis for the correct response. The upper left quadrant is associated with "1" as the correct answer and "2," "3" and "4" correspond with a clock-wise progression of quadrants. In each of the first six items in this group, one of the quadrants is omitted; each of the three quadrants present is identified by its proper Roman numeral. The relationship between number and quadrant is, of course, constant throughout the entire group of items. After the first six items, one of the quadrants continues to be omitted, but, in addition, the Roman numerals identifying each quadrant have been removed. At this point the subject is told that the principle remains the same, even though the numbers are no longer present. Some normal subjects do not remember the correct answer for each quadrant, and frequently confuse quadrants 3 and 4. However, the bell and buzzer soon provide them with the information necessary to revise their hypothesis. Subjects with cerebral lesions, however, often persist in misidentifying quadrants (especially 3 and 4) even though the buzzer makes it perfectly clear that their answers are wrong.

The fifth group of items is organized according to a principle based on the proportion of the figure that is composed of solid (versus dotted) lines. If one-quarter of the figure is solid, the answer is "1," progressing to an answer of "4" for a completely solid figure. The principle remains constant throughout the group even though various types of stimulus figures are used. As with other groups, the examiner announces when the end of the group occurs and states that the next group may be based upon the same principle or it may use a new principle.

Group six is based on the same principle as group five. This is the only instance in the test where use of the same principle is repeated in an ensuing group.

The seventh group is not based on any single principle; it is a review group that uses items and principles which have previously been shown to the subject. The subject is told this information and instructed to try to remember the correct answer for each item.

The Halstead Category Test has several characteristics that make it different from many tests. It is a relatively complex concept formation test which requires ability to (1) note recurring similarities and differences in stimulus material; (2) postulate reasonable hypotheses about these similarities and differences; (3) test these hypotheses by receiving positive or negative reinforcement (bell or buzzer); and (4) adapt hypotheses based on the reinforcement following each response. The Category Test is not particularly difficult for most normal subjects, but since the subject is required to postulate possible solutions in a structured (rather than permissive) context, it appears to require special competence in abstraction ability. In effect, the test presents each subject with a learning experiment in concept formation. This is in contrast to the usual situation in psychological testing, which requires solution of an integral problem situation.

The essential purpose of the Category Test is to determine the subject's ability to use both negative and positive experiences as a basis for altering his performance. The precise pattern and sequence of negative and positive reinforcement in the Category Test is probably never exactly the same for any two subjects (or for the same subject upon repetition of the test). Since it can be presumed that every item in the test affects the subject's response to ensuing items, the usual approaches toward determination of reliability indices may be confounded. Nevertheless, the essential nature of the test, as an experiment in concept formation, is fairly clear.

Tactual Performance Test

The Tactual Performance Test utilizes a modification of the Sequin-Goddard formboard. The subject is blindfolded before the test begins and is not permitted to see the formboard or blocks at any time. His first task is to fit the blocks into their proper spaces on the board using only his preferred hand (Fig. 2-2). After completing this task (and without having been given prior warning) he is asked to perform the same task using only his non-preferred hand. Finally, and again without prior warning, he is asked to do the task a third time using both hands.

The amount of time taken to perform each of the three trials is recorded. This provides a comparison of the efficiency of performance of the two hands. The total time score for the test is based on the amount of time needed to complete all three trials. After the subject has completed the third trial, his blindfold is removed only after the board and blocks have been removed from his field of vision. The subject is then asked to draw a diagram of the board with the blocks in their proper spaces. This drawing is scored according to Memory and Localization components. The Memory score is the number of shapes correctly remembered. The Localization score is the number of blocks correctly identified by both shape and position on the board.

In terms of its requirements, the Tactual Performance Test is undoubtedly a complex task. Ability to correctly place the variously

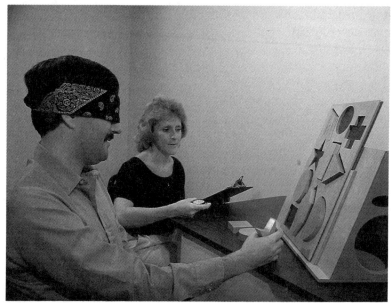

Fig. 2-2.   *Subject taking the Tactual Performance Test.*

shaped blocks on the board depends upon tactile form discrimination, kinesthesis, coordination of movement of the upper extremities, manual dexterity, and an understanding of the relationship between the spatial configuration of the shapes and their location on the board.

Halstead had observed that many people with biologically compromised cerebral functions were deficient in performing relatively simple tasks, especially if required to perform the task in an unusual way or under unusual circumstances. Placing the blocks in their proper spaces is a relatively simple task; the novel aspect is requiring the subject to use only haptic sensitivity. At no time during the test is the subject allowed to use vision, the usual sensory avenue.

Halstead postulated that this task would be much more difficult for the brain-damaged person than for the normal person when performance under unusual conditions was required. The person with brain damage, suffering from a general impairment of adaptive capabilities, would not be able to adapt to these more difficult circumstances as efficiently as persons with normal brain functions. In fact, on the average, persons with cerebral lesions require about twice as much time to complete the three trials of the Tactual Performance Test as control subjects.

Halstead also believed that persons with brain lesions would not be able to reproduce as much of the content as persons with normal brain functions. In other words, he postulated that both control and brain-damaged subjects could complete the task but the brain-damaged subject would learn less from the experience than the control subject — even though the brain-damaged subject had been exposed to the stimulus material about twice as long. In order to test this hypothesis Halstead decided to have the subject draw a picture of the board and blocks. Of course, since subjects are never allowed to actually see the test, they are dependent upon the information gained through standard exposure to the task. Halstead's postulate was confirmed by the experimental results. The mean number of remembered shapes and the mean number of properly localized shapes was strikingly less for brain-damaged than control groups. Thus, the results indicate that the Tactual Performance Test has very definite meaning in describing the nature of psychological impairment in persons with brain lesions.

Another important aspect of the design and procedure used in this test relates to the neurological model. The test's design allows comparison of the functional efficiency of the two cerebral hemispheres (right hand versus left hand) and supplies information regarding the general efficiency of brain functions (total time for three trials). During the first trial, when the subject uses his preferred hand, information is being transmitted from the preferred hand to the contralateral cerebral hemisphere (usually the right hand to the left cerebral hemisphere). The time required to complete the task indicates the efficiency of brain functioning under these circumstances. Of course, because of the connections between the two cerebral hemispheres through the anterior and the posterior commissures and the corpus callosum, the information sent to the left cerebral hemisphere is not restricted to that hemisphere. Therefore, although information is first delivered to the left cerebral hemisphere, the whole brain receives the information that is being brought in through sensory channels. If the left cerebral hemisphere were damaged, it is likely that the information would not be registered very well initially and the rest of the brain would be impaired in its ability to contribute to the solution of the task. More specifically, the input area of the cerebral cortex for this task is probably mainly the parietal area and distinct impairment in performance might well be principally related to the parietal lobe if the deficit were a function of input limitations. It is possible that motor or expressive aspects of the task may also limit the performance on a trial of the Tactual Performance Test, but motor measures which are not strongly influenced by sensory input (such as finger tapping and grip strength) can provide comparative information regarding motor function.

In the second trial the subject is required to perform the task using only his non-preferred (usually left) hand and the information is sent to the right cerebral hemisphere. The efficiency of performance is measured by the time required to complete the task. If the right cerebral hemisphere (particularly the parietal area) was damaged, the performance on the second trial would be deficient.

One additional aspect of the neurological model must be considered. Obviously, there would be positive practice-effect, or bilateral transfer, from the first to the second trial. Thus, for a right-handed subject, we would expect the left hand to perform the task better than the right hand because the entire brain has had the advantage of experiencing solution of the problem when the right hand was performing during the first trial.

The neurological basis for bilateral transfer is represented by the commissures between the two cerebral hemispheres. Although the concept of bilateral transfer is discussed in nearly every introductory psychology textbook, its neurological basis is rarely considered. Developing an understanding of bilateral transfer, as manifested in the procedure in the Tactual Performance Test, was a relatively simple matter. The test had to be administered to a large number of control subjects to determine the magnitude of bilateral transfer among persons with normal brain functions. The data indicated a rather consistent relationship: the second trial usually requires about two-thirds of the time required for the first trial and the third trial (using both hands) usually requires about two-thirds of the time of the second trial. In other words, the expected pattern and relationship among the results for the three trials is that the time required for a particular trial is reduced by about ⅓ in each ensuing trial. By considering this pattern as the normal set of relationships, it is possible to compare the functional efficiency of the two cerebral hemispheres. For example, it would not be unusual to find the following pattern in a person with a right cerebral lesion: right hand — 7.0 minutes; left hand — 10.0 minutes; both hands — 5.0 minutes. Such a pattern would suggest impaired functioning of the second trial (left hand) and provide a basis for inferring right cerebral hemisphere dysfunction.

Rhythm Test

The Rhythm Test is a subtest of the Seashore Tests of Musical Talent. In this test the subject is required to differentiate between thirty pairs of rhythmic beats. The stimuli are presented to the subject from a standardized tape recording. After listening to a pair of stimuli the subject writes "S" on his answer sheet if he thinks the two stimuli sounded the same, "D" if he thinks they were different. This test requires alertness to non-verbal auditory stimuli, sustained attention to the task, and the ability to perceive and compare different rhythmic sequences.

It is interesting to note that many psychologists presume that the Rhythm Test is dependent upon the integrity of the right cerebral hemisphere. This presumption stems from the observation that the test is nonverbal in nature. We have analyzed results on the Rhythm Test in groups of subjects with left and right cerebral damage (Reitan, unpublished data) and found that both groups were significantly impaired when compared with a control group. However, since the brain-damaged groups showed no differences between themselves, the Rhythm Test seems to be an indicator of the general adequacy of cerebral functioning and has no lateralizing significance. In the presence of serious generalized impairment, a good score on the Rhythm Test may be an indication of a relatively stabilized (as contrasted with progressive) condition of brain damage. This point will be illustrated later in this book when individual cases are presented.

Speech-sounds Perception Test

The Speech-sounds Perception Test consists of sixty spoken nonsense words which are variants of the "ee" sound. The stimuli, presented in multiple-choice form, are played from a tape recording with the volume adjusted to the subject's preference. The subject responds by underlining one of the four alternatives printed for each item on the test form.

For example, on the answer form in front of the subject, the following appears:

1. theeks   zeeks   theets   zeets

The voice on the tape player says, "The first word is theets." The subject must listen closely and underline the alternative he thinks is correct. This test requires the subject to (1) maintain attention through 60 items; (2) perceive the spoken stimulus sound through hearing; and (3) relate the perception through vision to the correct configuration of letters on the test form.

As might be expected, research results (Reitan, unpublished data) show that in general, persons with left cerebral lesions are considerably more impaired on this test than persons with right cerebral lesions. Brain-damaged subjects average about 14 errors on the Speech-sounds Perception Test whereas control subjects average only about 7 errors (Reitan, 1955a). Thus, the test serves as a good indicator of the general integrity of cerebral cortical functions. However, when the score is particularly poor in terms of the overall intra-individual distribution of results, the result may reflect special impairment of left cerebral functions. Although we have not demonstrated precise localization of the brain area involved in processing the visual and auditory information required by this test, we would postulate that the most important area is in the posterior part of the left cerebral hemisphere, especially involving the posterior left temporal-parietal area. Precise localization is difficult to demonstrate because this test is a good general indicator (apparently relating to the requirement of alertness and concentration) as well as a reflection of the adequacy of receptive language functions through the auditory and visual avenues.

Finger Oscillation Test

This test is a measure of finger-tapping speed using a specially adapted manual tapper. Precise characteristics of this apparatus (tension of the arm, angle of the arm, position of the board, etc.) have been maintained to ensure comparability of data between subjects and between various investigators. Measurements are made first with the subject using the index finger of the preferred hand. Next, a comparable set of measurements are obtained with the non-preferred hand. Five consecutive 10-second trials are given to each hand with the hand held in a constant position in order to require movements of only the finger rather than the whole hand and arm. Every effort is made to encourage the subject to tap as fast as possible. This test would appear to be rather purely dependent upon motor speed.

Halstead Impairment Index

The Impairment Index is a summary value initially based upon Halstead's 10 tests. Three of these tests have been omitted from the Battery, and the Impairment Index is presently computed from the results of seven tests: (1) Category Test; (2) Tactual Performance Test — Total time; (3) Tactual Performance Test — Memory score; (4) Tactual Performance Test — Localization score; (5) Rhythm Test; (6) Speech-sounds Perception Test; and (7) Finger Tapping speed.

The Impairment Index for an individual subject is the proportion of tests which have results in the range characteristic of brain-damaged subjects. Customarily, normal subjects obtain Impairment Indices that range between 0.0 and 0.3; 0.4 is a borderline score; and 0.5 to 1.0 characterizes subjects with impaired brain functions. Using independent neurological findings as the criteria, the Halstead Impairment Index has been shown to be very sensitive to impaired brain functions; however, to obtain a comprehensive understanding of brain-behavior relationships for the individual person, more extensive measurements are necessary.

WECHSLER'S SCALE

The Scales developed by Wechsler are generally recognized as the most widely used individual tests for evaluating general intelligence. Wechsler's tests were developed for use with normal subjects and standardized on samples presumed to be normal. Therefore, it is probably not surprising that, in general, the results from Wechsler's tests are much less sensitive to the effects of cerebral damage than Halstead's tests (Reitan, 1959a). Nevertheless, we have found that Wechsler's tests provide important information regarding the comparative status and specialized functions of the left and right cerebral hemispheres (Reitan, 1955b) and, in some instances, specific information about localization of a lesion.

Wechsler's tests are well known and have been described in detail by others (Wechsler, 1955; Matarazzo, 1972) so we will provide only brief descriptions here. The Scales are divided into groups of Verbal subtests and Performance subtests. The Verbal subtests include measures of general information (Information); questions concerning the proper course of action in a variety of situations that have some judgmental or social significance (Comprehension); performance of arithmetic problems without the use of paper or pencil (Arithmetic); repetition in forward and reverse sequence of increasingly long series of digits following the example of the examiner (Digit Span); stating what pairs of words have in common (Similarities); and giving the definition of individual words (Vocabulary).

In order to respond correctly to the questions or instructions of the examiner, most of the Wechsler tests require previously acquired skill or knowledge. There is little immediate or direct problem-solving required on the Verbal subtests. In the case of the Arithmetic subtest it is necessary for the subject to solve the particular problems presented, but his ability to do so is obviously dependent upon having previously developed these skills over an extended period of time. Even the Similarities subtest probably depends largely upon vocabulary skills, or a full understanding of the meaning of each of the words, as a basis for correct performance. Although the Similarities subtest has been proposed to measure abstraction, Reitan (1956a) did not find that this test had a higher correlation with the Category Test than did tests such as Information and Vocabulary. Thus, we suspect that the Similarities Test is more closely related to vocabulary skills than abstraction ability.

In contrast to the Verbal subtests, the Performance subtests of the Wechsler Scale do require immediate problem-solving capabilities. This may be the reason that the Performance subtests have long been recognized as being more generally sensitive to the biological integrity of the brain than the Verbal subtests. The Performance subtests include a task that requires the subject to arrange pictures in the proper sequence to tell the most meaningful story (Picture Arrangement); identify the missing part in each of a series of pictures (Picture Completion); arrange colored blocks in a spatial relationship that reproduces a design depicted on a card (Block Design); arrange variously shaped pieces to complete a whole figure, in the format of a jig-saw puzzle (Object Assembly); and, using a pencil and working as quickly as possible, to reproduce different shapes corresponding to numbers given in a conversion code (Digit Symbol).

Most of our research results were based upon the Wechsler Bellevue Scale. The Wechsler Adult Intelligence Scale, the successor to the Wechsler-Bellevue Scale, appears to give similar results. Our experiences, as well as those of a number of other investigators, suggest that results obtained with the Wechsler Adult Intelligence Scale are essentially comparable (in terms of their meaning for brain functions) to the results obtained with the Wechsler-Bellevue Scale. Of course, since the content of the two Scales is very similar, this is not particularly surprising. We believe that it is possible to use the results of the Wechsler Adult Intelligence Scale in essentially the same way as the results of the Wechsler-Bellevue Scale have been used. The current version, the Wechsler Adult Intelligence Scale-Revised (WAIS-R) has a number of changes and has not been adequately tested or validated in regard to brain-behavior assessment.

TRAIL MAKING TEST FOR ADULTS

The Trail Making Test is composed of two parts, A and B. Part A consists of 25 circles printed on a white sheet of paper. Each circle contains a number from 1 to 25. The subject is required to connect the circles with a pencil line as quickly as possible, beginning with the number 1 and proceeding in a numerical sequence (Fig. 2-3). Part B also consists of 25 circles. The circles are numbered from 1 to 13 and lettered from A to L. The subject is required to connect the circles, in sequence, alternating between numbers and letters (Fig. 2-4). The scores represent the number of seconds required to finish each part.

This test requires immediate recognition of the symbolic significance of numbers and letters, ability to scan the page continuously to identify the next number or letter in sequence, flexibility in integrating the numerical and alphabetical series, and completion of these requirements under the pressure of time. It seems likely that the ability to deal with the numerical and language symbols (numbers and letters) is sustained by the left cerebral hemisphere, the visual scanning task necessary to perceive the spatial distribution of the stimulus material is represented by the right cerebral hemisphere, and speed and efficiency of performance may be a general characteristic of adequate brain functions. Thus, it is not surprising that this test is one of the best measures of general brain functions (Reitan, 1955f; Reitan, 1958).

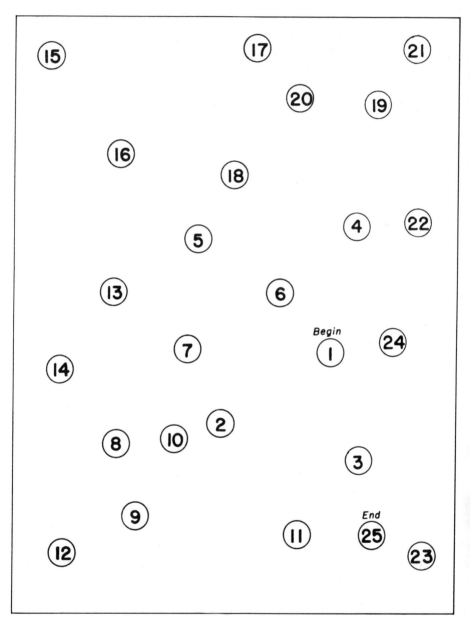

Fig. 2-3. Trail Making Test — Part A.

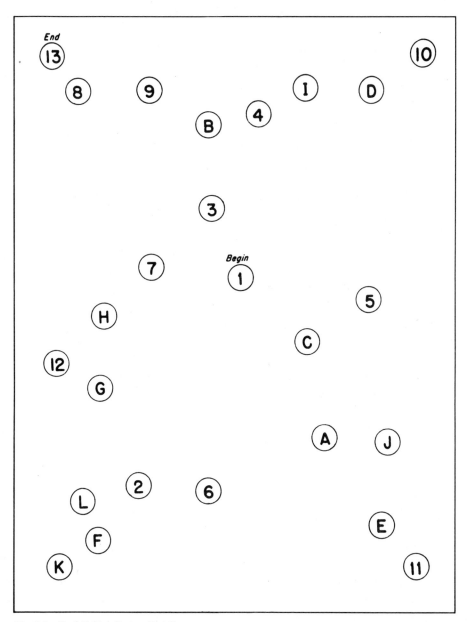

Fig. 2-4.   *Trail Making Test — Part B.*

GRIP STRENGTH

The subject's grip strength of each upper extremity is measured twice, in an alternating sequence beginning with the preferred hand. To obtain standard results it is necessary for the subject to extend his arm with the dynamometer pointed toward the floor as he registers his strongest grip. Normally, the preferred hand is about 10% greater than the non-preferred hand. Obviously, this measure of motor strength complements the finger tapping measure (motor speed) included among Halstead's Tests.

REITAN-INDIANA APHASIA SCREENING TEST

This test represents Reitan's modification of the Halstead-Wepman Aphasia Screening Test (Halstead & Wepman, 1949). A comprehensive review of aphasia and illustrations of the interpretation of this test have recently been published (Reitan, 1984). The Aphasia Test was not devised to provide continuous distributions that reflect a range of responses on the individual items but, instead, to identify failures of performance and specific deficits. Therefore, we do not score the results; we observe them for any indications of brain-related deficiencies or abnormalities in performance. This procedure is in accordance with an approach intended to identify pathognomonic signs.

Although only a few procedures are used to evaluate each kind of ability, the Reitan-Indiana Aphasia Screening Test provides an extensive survey of possible aphasic and related deficits. In fact, research has shown that the performances on this test are strongly correlated to the status of each cerebral hemisphere and actually appear to contain almost as much diagnostic information as the tests in the rest of the Battery (Wheeler & Reitan, 1962; Wheeler & Reitan, 1963). This latter conclusion is based on discriminant function analyses of the Aphasia and Sensory-perceptual Examination (to be described below) which permitted classification of normal subjects and persons with right, left, and generalized cerebral lesions into their appropriate groups with essentially the same degree of accuracy as achieved using the rest of the Battery (Wheeler, Burke, & Reitan, 1963). One must remember, however, that the major purpose of neuropsychological examination is to provide an adequate set of psychological measures that correlate with brain functions rather than to generate neurological diagnoses.

The rest of the Battery yields much more *neuropsychological* information than the Aphasia Screening Test and this additional information is necessary for understanding the neuropsychology of the individual subject.

The tasks involved in the Aphasia Screening Test are simple and the presumption is that it should be possible for any normal adult with an elementary education to perform the items satisfactorily. Adequate responses are anticipated and deficient performances take on definite significance. A testing strategy of this type, intended to elicit specific pathognomonic signs of brain damage, necessarily produces many cases of "false negatives": persons with cerebral lesions who do not show deficits. Thus, the examiner is able to draw meaningful conclusions regarding brain impairment only when deficits in performance occur. Such a strategy places a special burden on the person who interprets the results — he/she must be able to (1) identify a defective performance; and (2) judge whether or not it is the type of deficit that is characteristic of persons with cerebral damage. The strength of this testing strategy, and the factor that makes it such a valuable complement to test data scaled on a continuous distribution, is that specific deficits of known cerebral significance may be discerned. The weakness of this format is that considerable experience and competence is required of the examiner to judge whether or not the performances represent brain-related deficits. Because of the need for further instructional material of this kind, Reitan (1984) has recently completed a volume providing detailed illustrations of brain-related deficits on the Aphasia Test.

The Aphasia Screening Test requires the subject to perform a series of tasks: name common objects; spell simple words; identify individual numbers and letters; read, write, enunciate, and understand spoken language; identify body parts; calculate simple arithmetic problems; differentiate between right and left; and copy simple geometric shapes. The Test is so organized that these various performances are examined, to some extent, in terms of the particular sensory modalities through which the stimuli are perceived. In addition, the receptive and expressive components of the test (as differentially required by various items) provide an opportunity to judge whether the limiting deficit for a particular subject is principally receptive or expressive in character.

REITAN-KLØVE
SENSORY-PERCEPTUAL EXAMINATION

Tests for Perception of Bilateral Sensory Stimulation

These procedures attempt to determine how accurately the subject can perceive bilateral simultaneous sensory stimulation after it has been established that perception of unilateral stimulation of each side is essentially intact.

To examine tactile function, each hand is first touched separately to determine that the subject is able to respond correctly to unilateral stimulation. Next, unilateral stimulation is interspersed with bilateral simultaneous stimulation. The normal subject is able to accurately recognize stimulation of the right hand, left hand, and both hands. Subjects with lateralized cerebral lesions are often able to identify unilateral stimulation correctly but sometimes fail to respond correctly to bilateral simultaneous stimulation; the stimulus to the hand contralateral to the damaged hemisphere is often not perceived. Contralateral face-hand combinations are also used with unilateral and bilateral simultaneous tactile stimulation as part of the standard procedure.

In testing for auditory perception the subject is required to identify which side of the body an auditory stimulus is heard. The examiner administers the stimulus by rubbing his thumb and index fingers together lightly, very quickly and sharply, next to the subject's ear.

A similar procedure is used in the visual examination. The examiner executes discrete movements of his fingers while the subject focuses on the examiner's nose. The standard procedure is to use as minimal a stimulus as necessary to achieve consistently correct responses to unilateral stimulation.

A test for perception of bilateral simultaneous stimulation is, of course, precluded if the patient has a serious lateralized tactile, auditory, or visual loss and is not able to respond correctly to unilateral stimulation on the affected side. Such unilateral impairment is rarely encountered in the tactile and auditory modalities but not infrequently is seen in the visual modality (homonymous hemianopia). Lateralized deficiencies, of course, may have significant implications for nervous system disorders even though they obviate use of a test for perception of bilateral stimuli. The score for each modality is recorded as the number of errors.

Valuable historical background information regarding sensory-perceptual losses in persons with cerebral lesions is given in Bender's book (1951), *Disorders of Perception* and Critchley's book (1953), *The Parietal Lobes*. The neurological model being investigated with such tests is relatively simple: even a damaged hemisphere can adequately subserve perception of a simple stimulus when there is no functional involvement of other brain areas. Therefore, if the left hand is lightly touched, the stimulus is perceived by the right cerebral hemisphere; perception can occur even if the right cerebral hemisphere is damaged. However, when the left cerebral hemisphere is required to perform exactly the same task simultaneously, the damaged right cerebral hemisphere sometimes is no longer able to perceive the stimulus. A damaged hemisphere is not able to perform its function as well when the homologous area of the other cerebral hemisphere is processing information at the same time.

We have experimented informally with alterations of the input (stimulus) characteristics to give the damaged hemisphere a better competitive status when functioning simultaneously with the unimpaired cerebral hemisphere. This can be done by administering a more intense stimulus on the side contralateral to the damaged hemisphere. When stimulus intensity is increased, it is possible to elicit recognition that both sides were touched. Birch, Belmont and Karp (1967) performed this type of experiment by altering the temporal relationships of the stimuli to the sides of the body rather than the intensity of the stimuli. They found that it was possible to elicit recognition that both sides were touched when the stimulus was given slightly sooner to the side across from the damaged cerebral hemisphere.

In summary, then, if the damaged cerebral hemisphere is given an advantage (a stronger stimulus or a stimulus that occurs slightly before the competing input from the other side) it is able to be competitive with the intact cerebral hemisphere. Obviously, this kind of information is of great importance concerning administration of the tests: under normal testing conditions, it is necessary to maintain approximate equivalence of the intensity and the timing of the stimuli to the two sides of the body.

Although we have not done research specifically examining areas of the cerebral cortex that are involved in subserving perception of the stimuli used in testing for sensory perception, our impressions are that (1) tactile perception is a function of the parietal cortex; (2) auditory perception is subserved by the temporal cortex; and (3) visual perception is a function of the more posterior parts of the cerebral hemispheres.

Tactile Finger Recognition

This procedure tests the subject's ability to identify the individual fingers on each of his hands following tactile stimulation of each finger. Before the examination begins, the examiner must work out a system with the patient for reporting which finger was touched. Customarily, the patient will report by number, but sometimes patients prefer to identify their fingers in other verbal terms. Although the test itself is given without the subject's use of vision for identification, it is sometimes necessary to give the patient practice with his eyes open ensure that he is able to give a reliable verbal report. The subject is given a total of twenty trials on each hand. The score is recorded as the number of errors for each hand.

This test is relatively easy for most normal subjects and few, if any, errors are expected. Occasionally, a normal subject will find his attention wandering on one or two trials and not be quite sure which finger was touched. However, we generally expect a perfect score. Parietal lobe lesions, contralateral to the hand on which defective responses are found, definitely impair the performance on this test. Of course, many lesions are sufficiently large to involve more than just the parietal lobe and, in general, posterior cerebral lesions are principally responsible for defective responses in tactile finger recognition.

Finger-tip Number Writing Perception

This procedure requires the subject to report numbers written on the fingertips of each hand without the use of vision. The numbers (3, 4, 5, and 6) are written on the fingertips in a standard sequence with a total of four trials for each finger. The score represents the number of errors for each hand.

Some practice is required for the examiner to develop skill in writing numbers on the fingertips with constant and steady pressure. The numbers are written slowly and carefully and are sufficiently large to cover most of the pad at the end of the finger.

Errors in finger-tip number writing perception are more common than errors in tactile finger recognition. Apparently finger-tip number writing perception requires more concentrated attention. Since research has shown that finger-tip number writing perception is more closely correlated with I.Q. than tactile finger recognition (Fitzhugh, Fitzhugh, & Reitan, 1962), it is not particularly surprising when a person makes more mistakes on Finger-tip Number Writing Perception than Tactile Finger Recognition. A number of mistakes in Finger-tip Number Writing Perception is usually expected in persons of lower general intelligence.

The primary information gained from this test is based upon differences in performance on the two sides of the body. Inferences regarding contralateral parietal lobe damage or dysfunction can be drawn when one hand is definitely deficient compared to the other hand.

REITAN-KLØVE
TACTILE FORM RECOGNITION TEST

In this evaluation of tactile form recognition ability the subject is asked to identify flat, plastic shapes (cross, square, triangle and circle) as they are individually placed in one of his hands which is held out of his range of vision. The subject feels the plastic shape in his hand and, with the other hand, points to one of the four plastic shapes mounted on a board in front of him which he thinks corresponds to the shape in his hand (Fig. 2-5). The response element of this task is deliberately minimized and the input sensory (afferent) aspect, together with central processing, predominates. This test has been found to be suitable for use with subjects five years of age and older.

Response time measurements are made for each trial and the total time required for four trials for each hand is determined. The total number of errors for each hand is recorded as a separate score.

REITAN-KLØVE
LATERAL DOMINANCE EXAMINATION

This test is given to determine handedness and footedness. Lateral dominance can be evaluated either in terms of the side used for a task or the comparative skill on the two sides of the body, but these two

Fig. 2-5. Subject taking the Tactile Form Recognition Test.

methods should not be confused. Asking the subject to perform a unimanual task (such as throwing a ball) demonstrates which hand he prefers for this task. Finger tapping can be done with either hand and the results obtained relate much more to assessment of cerebral function contralateral to each hand. Therefore, if the examiner wishes to determine hand (or peripheral) preference, he should use tasks that can be performed with only one hand or one foot in order to determine the subject's preference. Usually these would be well-practiced tasks for which preference had been established. If one wishes to assess brain functions, the performances on the two sides of the body should be compared, preferably using relatively nonpracticed tasks that may range from simple to complex performances.

The set of procedures in this Battery for determining lateral dominance (or preference) utilizes only tasks that can be performed with one side of the body or the other. Other tests in the Battery — such as the Halstead Finger Oscillation Test, Grip Strength, and the Halstead Tactual Performance Test — provide information on the comparative functional efficiency of the upper extremities as they reflect brain functions.

Handedness is determined by having the subject perform a series of simple unimanual tasks. First, he is asked to write his name in his usual manner. The hand he uses, as well as the time required, is recorded. Then he is asked to write his name in the same manner using his other hand. The subject is next requested to perform a series of other tasks which include throwing a ball, hammering a nail, cutting with a knife, turning a door knob, using a pair of scissors, and using a pencil eraser. The examiner records which hand the subject uses to perform each task.

Footedness is briefly evaluated by having the subject show how he would (1) kick a football and (2) step on an imaginary bug on the floor. Results are recorded by indicating which foot is used.

III
INSTRUCTIONS FOR ADMINISTERING THE HALSTEAD-REITAN NEUROPSYCHOLOGICAL TEST BATTERY FOR ADULTS

This section includes instructions for administering and scoring the Category Test, Tactual Performance Test, Seashore Rhythm Test, Speech-sounds Perception Test, Finger Oscillation (Tapping) Test, Trail Making Test, Tactile Form Recognition Test, measurement of Grip Strength, Aphasia Screening Test, Sensory-perceptual Examination, and Lateral Dominance Examination. The Battery routinely includes administration of the Wechsler Adult Intelligence Scale (WAIS). The reader should be aware that the revised version of this test, the WAIS-R, has not yet been validated as a substitute for the WAIS, either as an instrument for evaluation of brain functions or for interpretation in conjunction with other tests as an integral part of the HRNB.

The Minnesota Multiphasic Personality Inventory is also frequently administered with the HRNB, not as a neuropsychological procedure for evaluation of brain functions, but to provide information regarding any emotional distress or personality disturbance the patient may be experiencing.

Throughout the HRNB the principal effort is aimed at eliciting the best performance of which the subject is capable without giving the subject any actual help with the tasks. No comments that would give the subject even procedural help are permitted (e.g., "Why don't you try another block?"; "Have you noticed the position of the figure that is different?"). Every effort is made to encourage the subject to perform as well as his/her brain will permit (e.g., During the demonstration the examiner may say, "I think you can tap faster than that — here, let me show you"). Competence in administration of the Battery may be gained by practice and experience in testing a large number of subjects as well as by direct supervision and training by highly-skilled examiners. The entire HRNB for Adults, including the WAIS, can be completed in about four hours by an experienced examiner who knows the instructions and procedures thoroughly. The instructions should be memorized and given in the exact form presented on the following pages.

Finally, we should warn the reader that many altered and abbreviated versions of the tests in the HRNB are being sold by numerous individuals and firms. Anyone using these versions should be aware that they have NOT been adequately validated either through experimental studies or in clinical practice. (The Booklet Category Test is an example.) Such validation is absolutely necessary to provide reliable and meaningful data for interpretation.

Over the years we have made a determined effort to maintain standardization of each test, down to the last detail, so that the published research results and clinical interpretations may serve validly. We feel that this point must be emphasized because the clinical responsibility implicit in drawing conclusions about a subject's brain is of a different order than many of the more typical evaluations done by psychologists. The only authorized version of the HRNB is the one that duplicates the tests *exactly* as they were when the validation studies were done.

THE CATEGORY TEST

General Instructions

The purpose of the Category Test is to determine the subject's abstraction or concept formation abilities. To achieve this, it is necessary that the examiner elicit the subject's best possible performance. We insist that the subject observe each item carefully before making a response. Usually he/she is very interested in the tests and makes a serious effort to answer correctly. Occasionally a subject will answer apparently at random, and in such instances the examiner must attempt to get the patient to make a serious effort to solve the problems. If this is not possible, the examiner should declare the test invalid.

Since the purpose of the test is to measure ability in concept formation (without the adverse influence of the patient's lack of interest, etc.), a variety of techniques may be used as necessary. Some patients need to be told repeatedly to observe the items carefully (in some instances they must be asked to describe the figures before being permitted to answer), or to state the reason for selecting a particular response. If a patient says that he was only "just guessing," the subject must be encouraged to not "just guess" but figure out the principle. As a general rule, any part of the instructions may be repeated or elaborated upon when the examiner believes it to be necessary. Our purpose is to give the subject a perfectly clear understanding of the problem he is facing and the rules involved in its solution. The principles themselves are never given to a subject, but, for subjects who are extremely impaired in their ability to form concepts, it may become necessary for the examiner to urge them to study the picture carefully, ask them to describe the stimulus material (followed by questions directed to the subject such as, "Does that give you any idea of what might be the right answer?"), encourage them to try to notice and remember how the pictures change since this often provides clues to the underlying principle, and try to think of the possible reason when a correct answer occurs.

In conversation such as that described above, it is possible that an unwary examiner may give unwarranted reinforcement to certain hypotheses voiced by the subject. The examiner should always remember that his/her questions and advice should be pertinent and consistent with the aims of the formal instructions rather than provide any information relevant to the solution of the problems presented by the test; the only information of this kind comes from the bell or buzzer following each response.

Most subjects are able to take the Category Test with little additional information or direction than provided in the formal instructions. Impaired subjects sometimes find the test very trying and frustrating. The examiner should always encourage the subject to continue working at the task, although any direct comment or response related to the underlying principle should never be made. If a subject shows no sign of making progress on any one of subtests III through VI in the first twenty items *and also* shows extreme frustration with the task, it is better to discontinue the subtest at that point and pro-rate the error scores (linear extrapolation) than to risk not being able to complete the test.

Some additional points should be mentioned briefly:

1. Although speed is not a factor and subjects should not be hurried, neither should they be permitted to sit and daydream or to take an unduly long time to respond. Some subjects would impair the continuity of the test if not encouraged to make reasonably prompt decisions. If excessive delays occurred between items, some subjects might be placed at a disadvantage in remembering previous items and thereby in discerning the principle underlying the items in the group as a whole.

2. The examiner should always be alert to the slide on the screen, not only to keep in touch with the subject's performance but also to make sure the answer switch is set appropriately.

3. Although it would be possible to automate the testing procedure and eliminate the need for the examiner to set the controls for the bell or buzzer for each item, we have always felt that it is quite important for the examiner to be present, actively involved, alert to the test content and the subject's efforts at all times, and actually "giving" the test. In this way the subject is more readily motivated to pay attention and do his best as contrasted with the possible reaction to an automated or impersonal situation.

4. The testing room should be somewhat darkened, but light enough for the examiner to record errors.

5. The subject should sit directly in front of the screen. The colored stimulus figures may be difficult to see from an angle (*See* Fig. 2-1).

Specific Instructions

ON THIS SCREEN YOU ARE GOING TO SEE DIFFERENT GEOMETRICAL FIGURES AND DESIGNS. SOMETHING ABOUT THE PATTERN ON THE SCREEN WILL REMIND YOU OF A NUMBER BETWEEN ONE AND FOUR. ON THE KEYBOARD IN FRONT OF YOU (*indicate to subject*) THE KEYS ARE NUMBERED 1, 2, 3, AND 4. FIRST LOOK AT THE SCREEN AND DECIDE WHICH NUMBER THE PICTURE SUGGESTS. THEN PRESS DOWN ON THE KEY THAT HAS THAT SAME NUMBER. FOR

EXAMPLE, WHAT NUMBER DOES THIS REMIND YOU OF? *Project the first picture. If the subject says, "One," ask him which key he should press. After he has pressed the number 1 key, say:* THE BELL YOU JUST HEARD TELLS YOU THAT YOU GOT THE RIGHT ANSWER. EVERY TIME YOU HAVE THE RIGHT ANSWER YOU WILL HEAR THE BELL RING. NOW, TRY ANOTHER KEY YOU KNOW IS WRONG. *After the buzzer sounds, say:* THE BUZZER IS WHAT YOU HEAR WHEN YOU HAVE THE WRONG ANSWER. IN THIS WAY YOU WILL KNOW EACH TIME WHETHER YOU ARE RIGHT OR WRONG. HOWEVER, FOR EACH PICTURE ON THE SCREEN YOU GET ONLY ONE CHOICE. IF YOU MAKE A MISTAKE WE JUST GO RIGHT ON TO THE NEXT PICTURE.

Project the second slide. NOW, WHICH KEY WOULD YOU CHOOSE FOR THIS PICTURE? *Continue with slides in Subtest I.*

After Subtest I, say: THAT WAS THE END OF THE FIRST SUBTEST. THIS TEST IS DIVIDED INTO SEVEN SUBTESTS. IN EACH SUBTEST THERE IS ONE IDEA OR PRINCIPLE THAT RUNS THROUGHOUT THE SUBTEST. ONCE YOU HAVE FIGURED OUT WHAT THE IDEA OR PRINCIPLE IN THE SUBTEST IS, BY USING THIS IDEA YOU WILL GET THE RIGHT ANSWER EACH TIME. NOW WE ARE GOING TO BEGIN THE SECOND SUBTEST AND THE IDEA IN IT MAY BE THE SAME AS THE LAST ONE OR IT MAY BE DIFFERENT. WE WANT YOU TO FIGURE IT OUT. *Proceed with Subtest II.*

When you reach the first slide in subtest II that has circles, say: YOU WILL NOTICE THAT WE FIRST SAW SQUARES, THEN LINES, AND NOW CIRCLES. EVEN THOUGH THE PATTERNS CHANGE, YOU SHOULD CONTINUE TO USE THE SAME IDEA TO GET THE RIGHT ANSWER. *Continue with slides in Subtest II.*

After Subtest II, say: THAT WAS THE END OF THE SECOND SUBTEST AND AS YOU PROBABLY NOTICED, YOU DON'T NECESSARILY HAVE TO SEE A NUMBER TO HAVE A NUMBER SUGGESTED TO YOU. YOU SAW SQUARES, CIRCLES, AND OTHER FIGURES. ALSO, YOU PROBABLY NOTICED THAT THERE WAS ONLY ONE IDEA OR PRINCIPLE WHICH RAN THROUGHOUT EACH OF THESE SUBTESTS. ONCE YOU FIGURED OUT THE IDEA YOU CONTINUED TO APPLY IT TO GET THE RIGHT ANSWER EACH TIME.

NOW WE ARE GOING TO START THE THIRD SUBTEST AND THE IDEA IN IT MAY BE THE SAME AS THE LAST ONE OR IT MAY BE DIFFERENT. I WANT TO SEE IF YOU CAN FIGURE IT OUT AND USE IT TO GET THE RIGHT ANSWER. REMEMBER, THE IDEA REMAINS THE SAME THROUGHOUT THE SUBTEST. I WILL TELL YOU WHEN WE COMPLETE ONE SUBTEST AND ARE READY TO BEGIN A NEW ONE. *Proceed with Subtest III.*

After Subtests III, IV, and V say: THAT WAS THE END OF THAT SUBTEST, NOW WE ARE GOING TO BEGIN THE NEXT ONE. THE IDEA IN IT MAY BE THE SAME AS THE LAST ONE OR IT MAY BE DIFFERENT. WE WANT YOU TO FIGURE IT OUT.

In Subtest IV, after slide #6 (first slide without numbers), say: THIS IS STILL THE SAME GROUP, BUT NOW THE NUMBERS ARE MISSING. THE PRINCIPLE IS STILL THE SAME.

After Subtest VI, say: IN THIS LAST SUBTEST THERE IS NO ONE IDEA OR PRINCIPLE THAT RUNS THROUGHOUT THE GROUP BECAUSE IT IS MADE UP OF ITEMS YOU HAVE SEEN BEFORE. TRY TO REMEMBER WHAT THE RIGHT ANSWER WAS THE LAST TIME YOU SAW THE PATTERN AND GIVE THAT SAME ANSWER AGAIN.

Scoring

The score on the Category Test is the total number of errors on all seven tests (Fig. 3-1). The criterion score on this test is 50 or more errors. At the bottom of the test sheet, the examiner should write a description of any unusual behavior observed, help given that is more than usually required, or any other comments which would assist in clarifying the test performance.

HALSTEAD CATEGORY TEST
Adult Form

Name: _____ Date: _____ Examiner: _____ Total Number of Errors: _____

Item	Subtest I	Subtest II	Subtest III	Subtest IV	Subtest V	Subtest VI	Subtest VII
1	1	1	1	1	1	1	1
2	3	3	3	3	3	3	3
3	1	1	1	1	1	1	1
4	4	4	4	4	4	4	4
5	2	2	2	2	2	2	2
6	4	4	4	4	4	4	4
7	1	1	1	1	1	1	1
8	2	2	2	2	2	2	2
9	E=	3	3	3	3	3	3
10		2	2	2	2	2	2
11		3	3	3	3	3	3
12		1	1	1	1	1	1
13		4	4	4	4	4	4
14		3	3	3	3	3	3
15		4	4	4	4	4	4
16		2	2	2	2	2	2
17		1	1	1	1	1	1
18		4	4	4	4	4	4
19		1	1	1	1	1	1
20		3	3	3	3	3	3
21		E=	2	2	2	2	E=
22			1	1	1	1	
23			2	2	2	2	
24			4	4	4	4	
25			3	3	3	3	
26			2	2	2	2	
27			4	4	4	4	
28			3	3	3	3	
29			1	1	1	1	
30			4	4	4	4	
31			2	2	2	2	
32			1	1	1	1	
33			3	3	3	3	
34			1	1	1	1	
35			3	3	3	3	
36			2	2	2	2	
37			4	4	4	4	
38			3	3	3	3	
39			4	4	4	4	
40			2	2	2	2	
			E=	E=	E=	E=	

(The right-hand column for each subtest is used to check correct responses and the left-hand column to record each incorrect response by number. The middle column merely separates the columns in which the results are recorded.)

Fig. 3-1. Answer sheet for the Category Test.

TACTUAL PERFORMANCE TEST

General Instructions

The subject must never see the formboard, either before, during, or after the test. Adequate precautions must be taken to ensure that no other subject comes into the room while the test is being given. The standard procedure is to have the subject do the test three times while blindfolded: first, using the dominant hand; second, using the non-dominant hand; and third, using both hands. Then, after placing the board out of the patient's field of vision and removing the blindfold, the patient is asked to draw what he remembers of the board.

The patient is seated squarely facing and close to a table. Two gauze pads are placed over his eyes and a blindfold tied over them. Ask the subject if he can see, especially downwards. When you are certain the subject cannot see, bring out the board.

Set up the board about six or eight inches in front of the patient and lay the blocks in a row between the board and the subject (*See* Fig. 2-2). Although the blocks are put down essentially in random order, do not place blocks adjacent on the board next to each other on the table. Start the stopwatch when the subject first touches the board or blocks and stop it when he has correctly placed the last piece. Record the time for each hand in minutes and seconds.

If the subject appears anxious or is having a difficult time, it is permissible for the examiner to express pleasure when a subject places a block correctly, especially at the beginning of the test. Some subjects become apprehensive when blindfolded and many find this task quite difficult. It is important for the examiner to offer encouragement if there is any sign that such verbal reinforcement is necessary to elicit the subject's best possible performance.

As the subject places blocks correctly, the examiner should move other blocks in front of the subject to keep a supply ready at hand.

When the subject has finished the first trial, immediately warn him not to remove the blindfold and suggest that he relax for a minute or two. Then, after laying out the blocks again in the same manner described above, proceed with the second trial. After the third trial, place the test out of the patient's line of vision, remove the blindfold, and place a sheet of white, unlined paper and pencil in front of the subject and proceed with the instructions.

Once a block has been properly placed by the subject it is the responsibility of the examiner to keep it there. If a block that had previously been placed correctly is accidentally knocked out, the examiner replaces it and informs the subject that this is being done.

Although it rarely happens, sometimes a subject forces a block into an incorrect space. If this occurs, the examiner should have the subject feel the block and space and explain to him that the block was not correctly placed and must be removed. Some patients seem to forget the size of the board and tend to ignore the top row of spaces. If this occurs (generally after most of the other blocks have been placed), remind the subject to "feel the entire board." It may become necessary to have him run his hand around the board again, the same way he did at the beginning of the trial. Some subjects "wander" from the board to the stand or even the table-top. Always tell the subject when he is working off the board. Some subjects would spend a great deal of time feeling the sections of the stand if the examiner did not redirect their attention to the board.

Some patients could spend hours trying to complete this test. If the patient seems to be getting discouraged and is making very slow progress, it is permissible to discontinue each trial after 15 minutes of working time. The trial should not be discontinued if the patient appears capable of completing it. The trial should continue until it is completed if most of the blocks have been placed. In some instances, though, only a 5- or 10-minute trial is possible; if this is the case, the second trial should not be discontinued until the same amount of time as used in the first trial has elapsed. This is also true with the third trial unless, of course, the patient completes the trial before this time is reached.

An important part of the information derived from this test concerns the comparative performances of the two hands. The timing procedure described above permits collection of data relevant to such comparisons even if the test is not completed. Although we always try to obtain at least a 15-minute sample on each trial, it would be better to limit each trial to 10 minutes than deplete the patient's emotional or physical resources on the first trial. In cases in which the subject can use only one of his hands, all three trials should be done with the one useable arm. Such an instance would occur, for example, in patients with a complete right or left hemiplegia. If the patient has partial paralysis, he may be able to handle the blocks and feel the board well enough to do the task. Even though the patient has some impairment of an upper extremity, it is advisable to have him try to do the test using the standard testing procedure in order to get an actual comparison of the performances with the two hands. If a patient has used only *one* extremity for the first two trials, *only* this same extremity should be used on the third trial.

Subjects may get extremely tired while working on this test and need rest periods. The watch is stopped during these periods and the length of the rest period should be noted on the test form. Occasionally a patient (such as one with intracranial hypertension) may become dizzy or nauseated during the test. If it is necessary to remove the patient's blindfold, be sure that the board and blocks are first put out of his line of vision. The examiner should record the time stopped, length of rest period and number of blocks in place up to that point.

After completing the part of this test that requires placement of the blocks, the subject is given a sheet of unlined, white paper and asked to draw a picture of the board, reproducing as many blocks in their correct positions as he can remember. This drawing is scored for the number of shapes remembered (Memory component) and the number correctly placed (Localization component).

Specific Instructions

Blindfold the subject as the first step in preparing to administer this test. While putting out the board and blocks, say: ON THE TABLE IN FRONT OF YOU I AM PUTTING OUT A BOARD. THE BOARD IS SITTING ON A STAND SO THAT IT WILL BE UPRIGHT AND WILL NOT FALL OVER. ON THE BOARD ARE SPACES OF VARIOUS SIZES AND SHAPES. ON THE TABLE I AM PUTTING

OUT BLOCKS OF VARIOUS SIZES AND SHAPES. THE BLOCKS WILL FIT INTO THE SPACES ON THE BOARD. THERE IS A BLOCK FOR EACH SPACE AND A SPACE FOR EACH BLOCK. YOU'RE GOING TO TRY TO PLACE THE BLOCKS INTO THEIR PROPER SPACES. WHEN YOU HAVE PLACED THE BLOCK IN ITS PROPER SPACE, IT WILL FIT AND WILL NOT FALL OUT. *After the board and blocks are in position, say:* THIS IS WHAT THE BOARD FEELS LIKE. *While running subject's preferred hand around board say:* HERE IS ONE SIDE, HERE IS THE TOP, AND HERE IS THE OTHER SIDE. THIS IS THE STAND THAT YOU FEEL OUT HERE AT THE SIDES. *Guide subject's hand to the two sides of the stand.* AS YOU RUN YOUR HAND OVER THE BOARD, YOU CAN FEEL THE VARIOUS SPACES. *Run the subject's hand quickly over the entire board.* HERE ARE THE BLOCKS. *Guide subject's hand over the span of blocks.* NOW USING ONLY YOUR RIGHT HAND (*or left hand if the subject is left-handed; always have the subject use his preferred hand on the first trial*) I WANT YOU TO FIT THE BLOCKS INTO THEIR PROPER SPACES ON THE BOARD. DO YOU HAVE ANY QUESTIONS? (*Pause.*) REMEMBER TO DO IT AS QUICKLY AS YOU CAN. ALL RIGHT — READY? BEGIN! *Start timing.*

After the subject has finished the task with his preferred hand, say: THAT WAS THE LAST BLOCK THAT YOU JUST PUT IN. NOW I WOULD LIKE YOU TO DO THE SAME THING OVER AGAIN, BUT THIS TIME USING ONLY YOUR LEFT HAND (*or right hand if the subject is left-handed*). *Immediately warn the subject that he is not to remove the blindfold, and suggest that he relax for a minute or two before beginning the second trial. Guide the subject's nonpreferred hand quickly over the board and blocks again before beginning the second trial, reminding him that it is the same board and the same blocks and that he is to do the same task again as quickly as possible but using only his left hand.*

After he has completed the task with his left hand, say: THAT WAS THE LAST BLOCK YOU JUST PUT IN. NOW KEEP THE BLIND-FOLD ON BECAUSE I WANT YOU TO DO THIS STILL ANOTHER TIME. THIS TIME YOU GET TO USE BOTH HANDS. (*Again, a short rest period is permissible, especially if the patient appears tired.*) REMEMBER, PUT THE BLOCKS IN THEIR PROPER SPACES AS

QUICKLY AS YOU CAN USING BOTH HANDS. READY, BEGIN! *After the third trial the examiner must be especially alert to be sure that the subject does not remove his blindfold before the blocks and board have been removed. The examiner then removes the blindfold and says:* NOW I WOULD LIKE YOU TO DRAW A PICTURE OF THE BOARD THAT YOU WERE JUST WORKING WITH. MOST PEOPLE FIND IT HELPFUL FIRST TO DRAW AN OUTLINE OF THE SHAPE OF THE BOARD AND THEN FILL THE BLOCKS IN.

Instruct the subject, if necessary, that the outline of the board should be large enough to permit him to draw the shapes. If he starts with a very small outline, have him start over again. If he has gone ahead but finds that he is not able to include the figures he remembers, have him start over again but permit him to use his original drawing as a guide. If the subject is confused, point out that the outside shape should represent the board but not the stand.

If you have any reason to believe that a shape drawn by the subject, which is not definitely recognizable as a correct figure, is meant to represent one of the blocks, ask him if he can name the shape in his drawing. If he names the shape correctly (even though the drawing is done inaccurately or poorly), he is given credit. For example, if the subject has drawn a pointed type of figure but identifies it as a star, he is given credit for a correct response.

DRAW IN AS MANY OF THE BLOCKS AS YOU CAN REMEMBER AND TRY TO PUT THEM IN THEIR PROPER PLACES AS WELL AS YOU CAN REMEMBER. IF YOU REMEMBER A CERTAIN BLOCK BUT DON'T REMEMBER WHERE IT GOES, PUT IT IN AS BEST YOU CAN. THINK CAREFULLY, AND PUT DOWN ALL OF THE BLOCKS YOU CAN REMEMBER AND ALSO TRY TO PUT THEM IN THEIR CORRECT LOCATIONS.

Scoring

This test is scored by (1) determining the total time for the three trials; (2) counting the number of blocks correctly reproduced; and (3) counting the number of blocks properly located in the drawing. For the total time, the seconds should be expressed to the nearest tenth of a minute.

In scoring the drawing for the number of blocks remembered usually it is necessary only to count those shapes which are fairly accurately drawn and indicate that the subject had a true concept of the block. A star of four or five points is accepted as correct. However, if you suspect that the subject had a correct shape in mind but could not draw it properly, be sure to question him about it. If he identifies the shape verbally, give him credit for remembering the shape.

The Localization score is obtained by counting the number of correctly drawn shapes located approximately in the right place in the drawing and in relation to the other blocks. For example, if the circle was drawn near the top of the board and the cross and diamond placed to each side of it, but another shape drawn in above the circle, then the circle would not count as correctly localized. A useful procedure to follow in scoring Localization is to divide the drawing into nine segments. If the major portion of a block fits in its appropriate division, it is given credit for localization. No localization credit is given unless memory credit for the block has already been given.

Scores are recorded as follows:

Time

Dominant Hand: _____

Non-dominant Hand: _____

Both Hands: _____

Total Time: _____

Memory (# of blocks): _____

Localization (# of blocks): _____

If the subject is not able to complete the test and has worked for a standard time period (usually 15 minutes) on each trial, both the time and the number of blocks successfully placed should be recorded.

SEASHORE RHYTHM TEST

General Instructions

The Rhythm Test measures the ability to discriminate variations in rhythmical patterns. The test consists of 30 pairs of rhythmical patterns presented on a standardized tape recording. The subject is asked to determine whether the two stimuli in each pair are the *same* or *different.*

The first three items of the Rhythm Test are presented as a sample. After giving the instructions, these items should be played for the subject and the examiner should be alert to the following conditions: (a) that the volume is at the optimal level for the subject; (b) that the subject understands the meaning of "S" and "D" in his response (it is helpful to write "S = same" and "D = different" on the answer form when explaining the procedure to the subject); (c) that the items proceed down Column A, then B, and then C; and (d) that the subject understands the silent interval which separates the two patterns of each item. During the sample the examiner should have the subject tell the examiner his answer; however, incorrect responses are not corrected. In this way the examiner can determine whether the subject has comprehended the instructions.

The sample may be replayed as often as necessary for subjects having difficulty understanding instructions. However, after the test is started there cannot be any interruption for further help.

Specific Instructions

YOU WILL HEAR TWO RHYTHMIC PATTERNS, ONE AFTER THE OTHER. THE SECOND PATTERN IS EITHER THE SAME AS THE FIRST OR DIFFERENT FROM IT. NOW I AM GOING TO PLAY THE SAMPLE. LISTEN CLOSELY AND TELL ME WHETHER THE TWO PATTERNS SOUND THE SAME OR DIFFERENT. LISTEN CAREFULLY SO YOU WILL BE SURE TO UNDERSTAND WHAT TO DO. *Present sample using tape player.*

When a subject has difficulty understanding the instructions, the nature of the difficulty usually relates to a failure to realize that the patterns are presented in "pairs." Some subjects do not appreciate the time intervals either between patterns or between pairs. Stopping the tape at appropriate times (during the sample only) is often all that is necessary to overcome these difficulties. However, some persons need additional instructions. This can be accomplished by the examiner "tapping" out simple rhythmic patterns on the test table.

It is permissible to stop the sample at any place. The test itself is never stopped during any column. However, if further instruction, encouragement, etc. is needed, the test can be stopped between columns. (Part of the requirement of this task is that the patient maintain immediate attention as well as discriminate auditory-nonverbal stimuli.) The sample may be repeated as many times as necessary.

Give the subject an answer sheet after presenting the sample. Then say: IF THE TWO PATTERNS ARE THE SAME, PRINT "S" IN THE PROPER PLACE ON YOUR TEST BLANK. *Show patient the proper space.* IF THEY ARE DIFFERENT, PRINT "D." *Write* "S = same" *and* "D = different" *on the side of the paper, explaining that this shows the type of responses to be given.*

REMEMBER, "S" IF THEY ARE THE SAME, AND "D" IF THEY ARE DIFFERENT. PUT YOUR FIRST ANSWER IN THE SQUARE OPPOSITE NUMBER 1 AND GO DOWN COLUMN A *(indicate to subject)*. REMEMBER TO LISTEN FOR TWO PATTERNS EACH TIME BEFORE PUTTING DOWN AN ANSWER. A VOICE WILL TELL YOU WHEN TO START COLUMN B AND COLUMN C, BUT HE WILL NOT SAY ANY NUMBERS TO LET YOU KNOW WHAT SQUARE YOU SHOULD BE WORKING IN. THE TEST MOVES RAPIDLY SO BE SURE TO PUT YOUR ANSWER DOWN RIGHT AWAY.

Scoring

The raw error score is translated into a rank score. The criterion score is a rank score of greater than five (25 or less correct).

For subjects who have difficulty controlling a pencil, the answers can be written in by the examiner. However, in such cases, the examiner can write an answer only when spoken by the subject. If the subject is behind or ahead of the tape, the examiner is not permitted to tell him; standard procedure requires that the subject coordinate his responses with the speed of the tape without any assistance.

Correct responses for the 30 items are shown in Fig. 3-2. The raw score may be translated into ranked scores from 1 to 10 as indicated by the conversion table on page 54.

SEASHORE RHYTHM TEST

Name_____ Date_____ Examiner_____ Raw Score_____

Ranked Score_____

	Column A	Column B	Column C
1.	S	S	D
2.	D	D	S
3.	S	S	S
4.	D	D	D
5.	S	D	S
6.	D	D	D
7.	S	S	S
8.	D	D	D
9.	D	S	D
10.	S	S	S

Fig. 3-2.   Answer sheet for the Seashore Rhythm Test.

	Ranked Score
Raw Score	Conversion Table
No. Correct	**Rank**
29-30	1
28	2
27	3
26	5
25	6
24	8
23	9
15-22	10

SPEECH-SOUNDS PERCEPTION TEST

General Instructions

This test measures the subject's ability to match a spoken sound to the correct alternative among a group of similar printed sounds. The double vowel, "ee," is in the middle part of every syllable spoken. An accurate performance is determined by discriminating and matching the consonant or combination of consonants at the beginning and end of each syllable.

The subject should be seated comfortably at the opposite end of the table from the tape player, with his head about four feet from the speaker. Care should be taken to make sure that the subject faces the speaker and does not move his head excessively. This is done so that the sound comes equally to both of the subject's ears.

The first three items presented on the tape are samples. As the subject listens to these items, have him point to the word he selects as his answer. Wrong selections are not corrected by the examiner. This procedure is to permit the examiner to be certain that the subject understands the instructions. If the subject does not understand the instructions, the sample can be replayed as many times as the examiner feels it is necessary. However, once the test begins, no further help can be given. The only help the examiner can give is to make sure that the subject is working in the correct column. Make certain the tape player's tone and volume are adjusted for the subject, and that the room is as free from distracting noises as possible.

Specific Instructions

THIS IS A HEARING TEST. YOU ARE GOING TO HEAR A MAN'S VOICE SAYING, "THE FIRST WORD IS _____" AND THEN HE WILL SAY ONE OF THE FOUR NONSENSE WORDS OPPOSITE NUMBER ONE ON YOUR ANSWER SHEET. *Point to this place on subject's answer sheet.* THEN HE WILL SAY, "THE SECOND WORD IS _____," AND GIVE ONE OF THE FOUR WORDS LISTED OPPOSITE NUMBER TWO. WE ARE GOING TO START WITH A SAMPLE, SO THAT YOU CAN SEE WHAT THE TEST WILL BE LIKE, AND SO THAT YOU CAN TELL ME HOW LOUD YOU WANT THE RECORDING TO BE. YOU JUST

SIT BACK AND LISTEN. DON'T WRITE ANYTHING YET. TELL ME IF THIS IS LOUD ENOUGH OR IF IT IS TOO LOUD. DURING THE SAMPLE DO NOT WRITE DOWN ANY ANSWERS, BUT LOOK AT EACH WORD CAREFULLY AND POINT TO THE WORD YOU THINK IS SAID. *Play the sample on the tape player.*

NOW WE ARE GOING TO BEGIN THE TEST. THE VOICE ON THE RECORDING WILL SAY ONE OF THE FOUR WORDS EACH TIME, AND YOU ARE TO UNDERLINE THE WORD THAT YOU THINK HE SAYS. IF YOU ARE NOT SURE OF WHAT HE SAYS, THEN MAKE A GUESS. UNDERLINE ONE WORD EVERY TIME. IF YOU MAKE A MISTAKE, DON'T BOTHER TO ERASE IT; JUST CIRCLE YOUR MISTAKE AND UNDERLINE THE RIGHT ANSWER. WORK DOWN COLUMN "A," FROM ONE TO TEN, THEN START COLUMN "B" OVER HERE, *(indicate place to the subject on his answer sheet)* THEN "C," AND THEN DO "D," "E," AND "F" DOWN HERE.

Scoring

The score is the number of errors or omissions among the 60 items. The criterion level, according to Halstead's data, falls between seven and eight errors. Reitan's data, however, yielded a mean score of seven errors for control subjects and 14 errors for subjects with cerebral lesions. The realistic expectation for persons without cerebral damage or dysfunction is that they may make 10 errors or less.

Correct responses for the 60 items on the Speech-sounds Perception Test are underlined on the answer form (Fig. 3.3).

Adult Form

Speech-sounds Perception Test

Name_____Date_____Examiner_____Score_____

Directions: Underline the syllable which you hear.

Series A	Series B	Series C

1. theeks zeeks <u>theets</u> zeets   1. peem beem <u>peen</u> been   1. deeld <u>deel</u> beeld beel

2. weech yeech <u>weej</u> yeej   2. theez <u>theerz</u> feez feerz   2. weev heev·<u>weef</u> heef

3. leeg bleeg <u>leeng</u> bleeng   3. sheesh <u>sheez</u> zeesh zeez   3. thee fee <u>theer</u> feer

4. peez <u>peest</u> teez teest   4. veef weef <u>veeth</u> weeth   4. neeld <u>neel</u> meeld meel

5. freeb fleeb <u>freep</u> fleep   5. theel feel <u>theeld</u> feeld   5. seed zeed <u>seet</u> zeet

6. pleeb preeb <u>pleed</u> preed   6. peet <u>peent</u> beet beent   6. yeeg <u>yeek</u> heeg heek

7. seek <u>seech</u> sheek sheech   7. treep <u>treeb</u> teep teeb   7. meen <u>meem</u> neen neem

8. neek <u>neenk</u> meek meenk   8. steets speets <u>steeks</u> speeks   8. theerd <u>theer</u> teerd teer

9. wheech heech <u>wheesh</u> heesh   9. beert <u>beerd</u> peert peerd   9. heez wheez <u>heev</u> wheev

10. preet <u>preekt</u> peet peekt   10. sheed zeed <u>sheend</u> zeend   10. neep teep <u>neet</u> teet

Series D	Series E	Series F

1. heep <u>heet</u> wheep wheet   1. seeng sheeng <u>seen</u> sheen   1. yeem <u>yeen</u> heem heen

2. keev <u>keem</u> feev feem   2. geerd keerd <u>geer</u> keer   2. leern theern <u>leer</u> theer

3. neek <u>neeg</u> meek meeg   3. keen geen <u>keem</u> geem   3. feeth <u>fees</u> theeth thees

4. cheem <u>cheen</u> sheem sheen   4. ween weeng <u>heen</u> heeng   4. reeg treeg <u>reek</u> treek

5. feep theep <u>feet</u> theet   5. teed <u>teet</u> peed peet   5. yeed <u>yeet</u> weed weet

6. heeld weeld <u>heel</u> weel   6. keets <u>keez</u> teets teez   6. meep <u>meet</u> deep deet

7. deed teed <u>deend</u> teend   7. theet <u>theent</u> zeet zeent   7. deez <u>dees</u> beez bees

8. teesh peesh <u>teez</u> peez   8. beep peep <u>beet</u> peet   8. teeld <u>teel</u> peeld peel

9. <u>weef</u> veef weev veev   9. tee pee <u>teer</u> peer   9. meel <u>meer</u> feel feer

10. leen heen <u>leeng</u> heeng   10. beeb <u>beed</u> deeb deed   10. ween wheen <u>weem</u> wheem

Fig. 3-3. Answer sheet for Speech-sounds Perception Test. Correct answers are underlined.

FINGER OSCILLATION (TAPPING) TEST

General Instructions

The purpose of this test is to measure the maximal tapping speed of the index finger of each hand. Five 10-second trials are given for each hand except when the results are too variable from one trial to another. Specifically, the standard test procedure calls for five consecutive trials within a five-point range with each hand. This procedure is used in order to avoid single deviant scores from unduly influencing the total performance.

Clinically, it sometimes is very difficult to achieve this criterion for certain subjects because their finger may slip off the lever or invalidate the trial in some other way and thus not represent the subject's maximal performance. These invalid trials may be deleted and therefore do not interrupt a "consecutive series" of trials, provided that the examiner is conservative in his interpretation and only deletes trials in which some obvious factor has occurred that prevented the attempt from representing the subject's best performance.

Fatigue may definitely be a factor in limiting the performance on this test. A brief rest period should be given after each trial. The examiner should be alert to the development of fatigue (such as obvious slowing toward the end of a trial) and require the subject to take rest periods as necessary in order to give him a full chance to do his best. Even when no sign of fatigue is apparent, a rest period of one to two minutes is required after the third trial. A practice period is given before the test begins so that the subject may get a "feel" for the apparatus, but do not let the subject practice so much that he becomes fatigued before the first trial.

The heel of the subject's hand should rest firmly on the board during each trial. An attempt is made in this test to record isolated movement of the index finger. Although some accompanying movement of other fingers may occur, do not permit movement of the whole hand or arm.

Some subjects will aim for the score achieved on a preceding trial, slowing down or even stopping when that score is reached. In such instances the examiner may elect to place her fingers over the dial so the subject will not see his score. In other cases the subject may make such an effort to exceed a previous score that his arm (in addition to just his finger) will begin to move. If it seems to be distracting to the subject, the dial should be covered and the examiner should comment that it is better for the subject only to try to do his absolute best on each trial and not pay attention to the score obtained.

It is important that exactly 10 seconds be given for each trial. Some subjects do not start immediately when told to begin. Do not begin timing until the subject begins tapping. The examiner should say "STOP!" to coincide with the end of the 10-second period. Some subjects do not stop tapping immediately and the examiner should deduct "extra" taps beyond the 10-second period. A little practice may be necessary to develop skill in identifying the number of "extra" taps that have occurred. The examiner should encourage the subject to tap as fast as he possibly can. The physical arrangement should be optimal regarding chair and table height in relation to body size; usually, though, no special arrangements are needed for adults.

During the practice period the examiner should be sure that the subject finds a comfortable position for his hand and arm with relation to the apparatus (Fig. 3-4). He should be encouraged to move the position of the apparatus as necessary in order to achieve his best performance.

Do *not* alternate hand trials. The dominant hand is tested first, then the non-dominant hand is evaluated.

We cannot emphasize strongly enough that the Finger Tapping Test is *not* a reaction-time test. We want to measure how many times an individual can tap each of his index fingers in a 10-second time period. GIVE THE SUBJECT 10 SECONDS OF TIMING. In other words, do not begin timing until you hear the first "click" of the manual counter. In addition, listen for extra taps after the subject is told to stop.

Test energetically and vigorously. Convey to the subject both directly and indirectly that you want him to tap as fast as he can:

demonstrate tapping as fast as you are able to tap; keep the stopwatch clearly in view; give active verbal encouragement.

Specific Instructions

NOW WE ARE GOING TO DO A TEST TO SEE HOW FAST YOU CAN TAP. WE WILL USE THIS LITTLE KEY HERE (*show the key to the subject*) AND I WANT YOU TO TAP JUST AS FAST AS YOU CAN, USING THE FOREFINGER (*point to the subject's index finger*) OF YOUR RIGHT (*or left, if the subject is left-handed*) HAND. WHEN YOU DO IT, BE SURE TO USE A FINGER MOVEMENT: DO *NOT* MOVE YOUR WHOLE HAND OR YOUR ARM. WHEN YOU TAP THIS KEY, YOU WILL HAVE TO REMEMBER TO LET THE KEY COME ALL THE WAY UP AND CLICK EACH TIME, OR ELSE THE NUMBER ON THE DIAL WON'T CHANGE. (*Demonstrate to the subject how the key operates and how it should be allowed to "click," etc. Also demonstrate actual tapping, for a five- or six-second period, going as fast as possible*).

NOW YOU MOVE THE BOARD TO A COMFORTABLE POSITION FOR YOUR HAND AND TRY IT FOR PRACTICE. *After a brief practice period, say*: REMEMBER TO TAP AS RAPIDLY AS YOU POSSIBLY CAN. *Be sure that the subject knows what to do and is properly challenged to tap as fast as possible. Then say*: ALL RIGHT. READY! GO!

At the end of 10 seconds, say: STOP! *The subject may rest his hand after any trial, but always suggest resting after the third trial for each hand. After completing the test with the preferred hand, finger tapping speed for the index finger of the non-preferred hand is determined. Do not alternate between right and left hand trials.*

Scoring

The number of taps for each trial is recorded. The score is the mean for five consecutive valid trials, i.e., trials within a five-point range in which no obvious procedural disadvantage has occurred. If five consecutive valid trials within a range of five points cannot be elicited, give no more than 10 trials. In such a case, the score is the mean score for the total number of trials.

Fig. 3-4. Subject taking the Finger Oscillation (Tapping) Test.

THE TRAIL MAKING TEST

General Instructions

It is important for the subject to understand that he is to work as quickly as possible and avoid making errors. The most common error in administering this test occurs when a subject becomes confused; correct administration procedure requires that the subject be stopped when he makes an error and returned to his last correct position. This must be done quickly and efficiently, as the stopwatch is kept running during this time. The subject should not be penalized in his time score because of the examiner's verbalizations/corrections. Errors count against the subject's performance because the stopwatch continues to run until the test is completed (or discontinued).

Specific Instructions

When ready to begin the test, place the Part A test sheet, sample side up, flat on the table directly in front of the subject. The bottom of the test sheet should be approximately six inches from the edge of the table. Give the subject a pencil and say: ON THIS PAGE (*point*) ARE SOME NUMBERS. BEGIN AT NUMBER 1 (*point to 1*) *AND DRAW A LINE FROM 1 TO 2 (point to 2)*, 2 TO 3 (*point to 3*), 3 TO 4 (*point to 4*), AND SO ON, IN ORDER, UNTIL YOU REACH THE END (*point to the circle marked "END"*). DRAW THE LINES AS FAST AS YOU CAN. READY! BEGIN!

If the subject completes the sample item correctly in a manner demonstrating that he understands what to do, say: GOOD! LET'S TRY THE NEXT ONE. *Turn the paper over and give Part A of the Test.*

If a subject makes a mistake on Sample A, point out the error and explain it. The following explanations of mistakes serve as illustrations.

1. YOU STARTED WITH THE WRONG CIRCLE. THIS IS WHERE YOU START (*point to number 1*).

2. YOU SKIPPED THIS CIRCLE* (*point to the circle omitted*). YOU SHOULD GO FROM NUMBER 1 (*point*) TO 2 (*point*), 2 TO 3 (*point*), AND SO ON, UNTIL YOU REACH THE CIRCLE MARKED "END"(*point*).

If it is clear that the subject intended to touch a circle but missed it, do not count it as an omission. Remind the subject, however, to be sure to touch the circles.

If the subject still cannot complete Sample A, take his hand and guide his pencil (using the eraser end) through the trail. Then say: NOW YOU TRY IT. *Return the pencil to the subject with the point down and say*: REMEMBER, BEGIN AT NUMBER 1 (*point*) AND DRAW A LINE FROM 1 TO 2 (*point to 2*), 2 TO 3 (*point to 3*), 3 TO 4 (*point to 4*) AND SO ON, IN ORDER, UNTIL YOU REACH THE CIRCLE MARKED "END" (*point*). DO NOT SKIP AROUND BUT GO FROM ONE NUMBER TO THE NEXT IN THE PROPER ORDER. REMEMBER TO WORK AS FAST AS YOU CAN. READY! BEGIN!

If the subject succeeds this time, go on to Part A. If not, repeat the procedure until he does succeed, or it becomes evident that he cannot do the task.

After the subject has completed the sample, turn the paper over to Part A and say: ON THIS PAGE ARE NUMBERS FROM 1 TO 25. DO THIS THE SAME WAY. BEGIN AT NUMBER 1 (*point*) AND DRAW A LINE FROM 1 TO 2 (*point to 2*), 2 TO 3 (*point to 3*), 3 TO 4 (*point to 4*) AND SO ON, IN ORDER, UNTIL YOU REACH

THE END (*point*). REMEMBER, WORK AS FAST AS YOU CAN. READY! BEGIN!

Start timing as soon as the instruction is given to begin. The examiner must watch closely in order to catch any errors as soon as they are made. If the subject makes an error, call it to his attention immediately and have him proceed from the point the mistake occurred. Do not stop timing.

After the subject completes Part A, take the test sheet from him and record the time in seconds. Errors count only by increasing the performance time.

Next, tell the patient: THAT'S FINE. NOW WE'LL TRY ANOTHER ONE. *Proceed immediately to Part B, Sample.*

Place the test sheet for Part B, sample side up, flat on the table in front of the subject, in the same position as the sheet for Part A was placed. Point to the sample and say: ON THIS PAGE ARE SOME NUMBERS AND LETTERS. BEGIN AT NUMBER 1 (*point*) AND DRAW A LINE FROM 1 TO A (*point*), A TO 2 (*point to 2*), 2 TO B (*point to B*), B TO 3 (*point to 3*), 3 TO C (*point to C*), AND SO ON, IN ORDER, UNTIL YOU REACH THE END. (*Point to circle marked "END".*) REMEMBER, FIRST YOU HAVE A NUMBER (*point to 1*), THEN A LETTER (*point to A*), THEN A NUMBER (*point to 2*), THEN A LETTER (*point to B*), AND SO ON. DRAW THE LINES AS FAST AS YOU CAN. READY! BEGIN!

If the subject completes the sample correctly, say: GOOD. LET'S TRY THE NEXT ONE. *Proceed immediately to Part B.*

If the subject makes a mistake on Sample B, point it out and explain it. The following explanations of mistakes serve as illustrations:

1. YOU STARTED WITH THE WRONG CIRCLE. THIS IS WHERE YOU START (*point to number 1*).

2. YOU SKIPPED THIS CIRCLE* (*point to the circle omitted*). YOU SHOULD GO FROM 1 (*point*) TO A (*point*), A TO 2 (*point to 2*), 2 TO B (*point to B*), B TO 3 (*point to 3*), AND SO ON UNTIL YOU REACH THE CIRCLE MARKED "END" (*point*).

*If it is clear that the subject intended to touch a circle but missed it, do not count it as an omission. Remind the subject, however, to touch the circles.

If the subject still cannot complete Sample B, take his hand and guide the pencil (using the eraser end) through the circles. Then say:

NOW YOU TRY IT. REMEMBER, YOU BEGIN AT NUMBER 1 (*point*) AND DRAW A LINE FROM 1 TO A (*point to A*), A TO 2 (*point to 2*), 2 TO B (*point to B*), B TO 3, (*point to 3*), AND SO ON UNTIL YOU REACH THE CIRCLE MARKED "END" (*point*). READY! BEGIN!

If the subject succeeds this time, go on to Part B. If not, repeat the procedure until he does succeed, or it becomes evident that he cannot do the task.

After the subject has completed the sample, turn the paper over to Part B and say: ON THIS PAGE ARE BOTH NUMBERS AND LETTERS. DO THIS THE SAME WAY. BEGIN AT NUMBER 1 (*point*) AND DRAW A LINE FROM 1 TO A (*point to A*), A TO 2 (*point to 2*), 2 TO B (*point to B*), B TO 3 (*point to 3*), 3 TO C (*point to C*), AND SO ON, IN ORDER, UNTIL YOU REACH THE END (*point to circle marked "END"*). REMEMBER, FIRST YOU HAVE A NUMBER (*point to 1*), THEN A LETTER (*point to A*), THEN A NUMBER (*point to 2*), THEN A LETTER (*point to B*), AND SO ON. DO NOT SKIP AROUND, BUT GO FROM ONE CIRCLE TO THE NEXT IN THE PROPER ORDER. DRAW THE LINES AS FAST AS YOU CAN. READY! BEGIN!

Start timing as soon as the subject is told to begin. Again, remember to be alert for mistakes. If the subject makes an error, call it to his attention immediately and have him proceed from the point the mistake occurred. Do not stop timing.

After the subject completes Part B, take the test sheet from him and record the time in seconds. Errors count only by increasing the performance time.

Scoring

The score for each part is the number of seconds required to complete the task. In a study of normal and brain-damaged adult subjects, approximately 23 percent were misclassified by scores on Part A and 15 percent were misclassified by scores on Part B. The cut-off score for Part A fell between 39 and 40 seconds and between 91 and 92 seconds for Part B.

TACTILE FORM RECOGNITION TEST

General Instructions

The purpose of this examination is to test tactile form discrimination ability in each of the patient's hands. The right hand is tested first (regardless of the patient's handedness) using all four figures; then the left hand is tested, followed by the right hand again, and finally the left hand. The order of presentation of the figures is as follows: Right hand: circle, square, triangle, cross. Left hand: triangle, cross, circle, square. Right hand: cross, circle, square, triangle. Left hand: square, triangle, cross, circle. To indicate his response, the patient points with the hand not being tested to one of the four figures displayed on the face of the board (*See* Fig. 2-5).

The subject is permitted to feel the figure as long as necessary in order to identify it, but he is encouraged to respond as quickly as possible because each response is timed. The time required for each response as well as the total time for the eight trials and number of errors for each hand is recorded. In giving the test, do not allow the subject to remove the hand being tested from the board until all four trials have been completed and be sure that the subject does not see the figure when it is placed in his hand. Place the figure toward the subject's finger tips rather than in the middle of his palm.

Specific Instructions

Have the subject place his right hand through the hole in the board and tell him: I AM GOING TO PLACE AN OBJECT IN YOUR HAND. FEEL IT CAREFULLY, THEN POINT WITH YOUR LEFT HAND TO THE FIGURE ON THE BOARD (*point to the row of figures on the front of the board*) WHICH IS JUST LIKE THE ONE IN YOUR HAND. BE SURE TO SHOW ME THE RIGHT FIGURE AS QUICKLY AS YOU CAN. *Place the first figure (circle) in the subject's right hand. After the subject's response, remove the figure from his hand and place the next figure (square) in the same hand. The sequence of the first series, using the right hand, is circle, square, triangle, and cross. After each response, record the time in seconds required for the response and, if the response is incorrect, note the figure mistakenly identified. If the subject makes an incorrect response that is clearly due to carelessness, poor motor control, or other similar factor, it should not be counted as an error. However, even an immediate correction by the patient of a genuine error should not overrule the fact that the error occurred, and the examiner should make a note of the spontaneous correction. Verbal responses are permissible only if the patient is too handicapped to make the required motor response.*

After completing the first series with the right hand, say: YOU MAY TAKE THAT HAND OUT NOW, AND PUT IN YOUR LEFT HAND. WE WILL DO THE SAME THING USING YOUR LEFT HAND. FEEL THE OBJECT WITH YOUR LEFT HAND, AND POINT TO THE CORRECT FIGURE WITH YOUR RIGHT HAND. BE SURE TO SHOW ME THE RIGHT FIGURE AS QUICKLY AS YOU CAN.

Place the figure (triangle) in the subject's left hand and proceed as above. The sequence is triangle, cross, circle, and square. Next, the right hand is tested again (cross, circle, square, triangle) followed by a second series with the left hand (square, triangle, cross, circle). The total number of mistakes and the total time required for each hand is recorded.

Scoring

As noted above, the score represents (1) the time required to identify the figures; and (2) the errors made with each hand (Fig. 3-5).

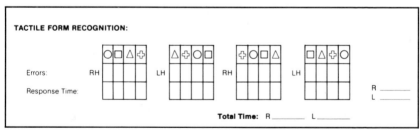

Fig. 3-5.   Form for recording subject's responses to the Tactile Form Recognition Test.

MEASUREMENT OF GRIP STRENGTH

General Instructions

This test measures motor strength of each of the patient's upper extremities. In our laboratory we use a Smedley Hand Dynamometer for this purpose. Because of the variability in hand sizes, an adjustment must be made for each subject. We restrict the range to settings between 3 (small hand) and 5 (large hand) and attempt to find a comfortable position within that range for the individual subject. During the test it is important for the subject to keep his arm extended with the dynamometer pointed toward the floor (Fig. 3-6).

Two trials are given to each hand, beginning with the preferred hand and alternating to the non-preferred hand on the second and fourth trials. The subject should be encouraged to take rest periods between the trials if he feels that they would help his performance. If either an increase or decrease of more than five kilograms occurs on the second trial for either hand, the examiner should have the patient wait for a few moments and then administer a third trial.

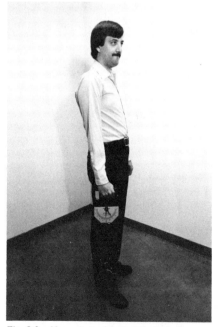

Fig. 3-6. Measuring subject's grip strength.

Specific Instructions

NOW I WANT TO FIND OUT HOW STRONG YOU ARE. WE WILL USE THIS INSTRUMENT AND HAVE YOU GRIP IT WITH YOUR HAND AS HARD AS YOU POSSIBLY CAN. BEFORE GOING AHEAD, I WANT TO BE SURE THAT THE INSTRUMENT IS ADJUSTED SO THAT IT WILL BE COMFORTABLE FOR YOU. *With a little experience the examiner will be able to estimate the approximate position that will suit the subject, but in each case it should be checked with the subject to be sure that it feels comfortable.*

NOW, POINT THE INSTRUMENT TOWARD THE FLOOR, BE SURE TO KEEP YOUR ARM STRAIGHT, AND SQUEEZE AS HARD AS YOU POSSIBLY CAN.

After recording the results for the first (preferred hand) trial, the same instructions are given for the next trial using the non-preferred hand. Trial #3 measures the preferred hand again and trial #4 measures the non-preferred hand.

Scoring

Two measurements within five kilograms of each other are recorded for each hand. A mean value for the two trials of each hand is recorded.

APHASIA SCREENING TEST

General Instructions

The Aphasia Screening Test is simple to administer but it is important for the examiner to follow the instructions explicitly. Because of the nature and purpose of the test (to determine abnormal performances) the examiner should repeat items or amplify instructions whenever necessary in order to elicit the patient's best performances. Although the examiner should carefully avoid giving actual help with any item, she should elaborate on the instructions if necessary to be sure the subject understands exactly what is required from him in each instance. Sometimes it is difficult to communicate the instructions because a subject demonstrates a receptive language abnormality and impaired ability to understand the instructions (auditory-verbal dysgnosia). Such problems should be noted and considered part of the test results.

Brief instructions for each item are given on the back of the flip-card that can be seen by the examiner at the same time the corresponding stimulus (on the front of the card) is seen by the subject. These very brief instructions are intended to be only a cue to the examiner, rather than a substitute for the actual instructions used in administering the test. It is recommended that the examiner follow the recording form (Fig. 3-8) rather than depend on the instructions on the back of the stimulus cards. (The cross-hatched instructions indicate items that have no visual stimulus for the subject.)

The most likely type of deficit associated with a defective performance on each item is also noted on the back of the stimulus card. The reader should be aware, however, that the deficit may be receptive, expressive, or possibly a combination of both. A subject may not be able to name an object because of an expressive naming difficulty (dysnomia) or, alternatively, because of a deficit such as visual-form dysgnosia.

There is no absolute way to resolve whether the deficit is expressive

Fig. 3-7. Subject taking the Reitan-Indiana Aphasia Screening Test.

REITAN-INDIANA APHASIA SCREENING TEST

Form for Adults and Older Children

Name: _____ Age: _____ Date: _____ Examiner: _____

Copy SQUARE	Repeat TRIANGLE
Name SQUARE	Repeat MASSACHUSETTS
Spell SQUARE	Repeat METHODIST EPISCOPAL
Copy CROSS	Write SQUARE
Name CROSS	Read SEVEN
Spell CROSS	Repeat SEVEN
Copy TRIANGLE	Repeat/Explain HE SHOUTED THE WARNING.
Name TRIANGLE	Write HE SHOUTED THE WARNING.
Spell TRIANGLE	Compute 85 − 27 =
Name BABY	Compute 17 X 3 =
Write CLOCK	Name KEY
Name FORK	Demonstrate use of KEY
Read 7 SIX 2	Draw KEY
Read MGW	Read PLACE LEFT HAND TO RIGHT EAR.
Reading I	Place LEFT HAND TO RIGHT EAR
Reading II	Place LEFT HAND TO LEFT ELBOW

Fig. 3-8. Recording form for the Reitan-Indiana Aphasia Screening Test.

or receptive. Even the most simple type of response requires input, central processing and output in order for the cycle to be completed. The subject's limitation may occur on the input or receptive side (dysgnosia) or on the output or expressive side (dyspraxia). The particular responses of the subject may make the nature (receptive or expressive) quite obvious. In other instances the interpreter may need to consider recurring difficulties on separate items of the test to gain additional insight. A confident judgment regarding a preponderance of expressive or receptive aphasic problems can often be made by reviewing similar types of difficulties on various items of the test.

Before beginning with instructions for administering the test itself, we will review some general information regarding the procedure that should be followed. As with all of the neuropsychological testing procedures in the Halstead-Reitan Battery, the examiner should make every effort to elicit the best performance of which the subject is capable. (This is in contrast to recommendations for some testing procedures, such as Wechsler's Scale.) Since we are interested in learning how well the subject's brain is able to perform, the instructions should be given so that the subject understands that a formal test is being administered and he is expected to do as well as possible. This approach may cause a certain amount of stress in many brain-damaged persons. The examiner should be aware, however, that the neuropsychological testing is intended to stress the subject's brain in order to find out what it can and cannot do.

It is not uncommon for a subject to be taken by surprise by a deficient performance on a task. He may not know that he has this kind of problem and may have been entirely unaware of it. This is true even in some instances of patients with definite aphasia. In casual, everyday situations the patient may think that he has some type of difficulty with verbal communication, but uses various devices (such as circumlocution) to avoid the problem. In a formal testing situation, however, the patient must follow the examiner's instructions and these compensatory mechanisms are no longer functional. The preciseness of the required response often reveals specific deficits. If the subject obviously feels stressed, it is permissible to give him some general support and verbal reassurance, but the examiner may neither give the subject any specific information regarding how to do the individual tasks nor do the tasks for the subject.

The examiner should provide the subject the best possible opportunity to perform correctly *on his first attempt.* Although additional trials may be given for the same item, consecutive trials permit some positive practice-effect which is often difficult to evaluate. Therefore, the examiner should be sure that the subject does not perform carelessly on the first trial. If the subject has difficulty on tasks such as drawing the square, cross, or triangle, standard practice requires that at least one additional trial be given to determine whether the subject is able to show improvement or, as sometimes occurs, has even more serious difficulties. Although it is rarely necessary, the examiner may give three (or more) trials if there seems to be variability in the performance.

When the subject has difficulty on an item, it is important that he is given an opportunity to correct this difficulty. The examiner should make neutral requests such as, "Would you try that again?" or "Are you sure that is right?". More specific verbal suggestions may be given later, but only after the subject has had an opportunity to correct his error.

The fact that an error occurred initially is not "excused" by a correct performance on the second trial. Since the tasks on the Aphasia Screening Test are quite simple, most persons who make a serious attempt to do well are able to perform adequately. In other words, if the subject was able to perform correctly on the second trial, he should not have made the mistake in the first place. Since the material used is relatively simple and the examiner uses careful and deliberate testing techniques, frequently a *correct* response on the second trial merely documents the evidence of brain dysfunction that was manifested on the first trial.

It is important that the examiner record the actual responses of the subject for each individual item on which deficits occur. If the responses are without error, the appropriate space on the recording form is customarily left blank. However, if there is hesitation, apparent confusion, or some difficulty in responding, this should be noted even though the response is correct. Self-corrections, whether spontaneous or prompted, should also be noted. Sometimes a verbatim response is difficult to record, but the examiner should make an attempt to record exactly what was said so that full details are available for interpretation.

For example, when the subject is asked to repeat METHODIST EPISCOPAL, it is not satisfactory for the examiner to merely write down that the subject had difficulty. The examiner should listen very carefully to the exact sounds said by the subject and write the subject's response phonetically.

It is also important for the examiner to influence the subject to attempt to perform each task. The examiner should not accept responses such as, "I don't know," since such responses do not yield any significant information. Because this test depends upon the "sign" approach, it is important to determine whether or not the subject demonstrates a *sign* of brain damage. In addition, unless the subject makes an actual attempt on each task, the examiner in effect has deleted some of the items from the test. Under such circumstances it may be difficult to interpret the results and determine, in terms of the overall pattern of responses, whether the deficit is expressive, receptive, or both.

In reaching a judgment regarding this problem it is often important for the examiner to have made notes regarding the subject's ability to understand the instructions. A subject who is continually confused about the instructions demonstrates an important indication of auditory receptive difficulties in the language area.

It is imperative that the subject *not* be permitted to cross out performances or erase. Persons who have difficulty with the tasks frequently want to delete their incorrect performance. Obviously, this may destroy the evidence of cerebral disease or damage.

Finally, we should state that it is not uncommon for inexperienced examiners to fail to observe errors in performances. The examiner must make a special effort to listen closely. In our training procedures we have found that novice examiners frequently accept spellings such as T-R-I-A-N-G-A-L-E as correct until they have learned to listen closely to the subject's response.

Specific Instructions

A piece of unlined, white paper is placed on the table in front of the patient and he is given a pencil without an eraser. The instructions begin quite simply: I HAVE A NUMBER OF THINGS THAT I WANT TO ASK YOU TO DO. SOME OF THEM ARE VERY SIMPLE. BUT EVEN IF THEY ARE EASY FOR YOU I WANT YOU TO DO THEM CAREFULLY AND BE SURE TO DO YOUR BEST.

If the subject has obvious difficulty drawing any of the figures in the test, encourage him to proceed until it is clear that he can make

Fig. 3-9. Stimulus figures in the Reitan-Indiana Aphasia Screening Test. The number in the right-hand corner of each card corresponds to the instructions for administration beginning on page 75.

no further progress. If he has not accomplished the task reasonably well on the first trial, ask him to try again, and instruct him to be particularly careful to do it as well as he can. Refer to Fig. 3-9 for stimulus figures for Aphasia Test.

1. (Square) FIRST, DRAW THIS (*point to the square*) ON YOUR PAPER. I WANT YOU TO DO IT WITHOUT LIFTING YOUR PENCIL FROM THE PAPER. MAKE IT ABOUT THIS SAME SIZE (*pointing to the square*).

The purpose of asking the subject to avoid lifting the pencil is to keep him from skipping around in the drawing. The task is to make steady progress in drawing the figure until it is finally completed at the original starting point. Although subjects are allowed to begin the drawing at whatever point they wish, the requirement of a continuous line brings about some standardization of the problem of "closing" the drawing. If the subject shows concern about making a heavy or double line, point out that only a reproduction of the shape is required.

2. (Square) WHAT IS THAT SHAPE CALLED? Or, WHAT IS THE NAME FOR THAT FIGURE?
3. (Square) WOULD YOU SPELL THAT WORD FOR ME?

If the subject has not been able to name the figure, tell him the name so that an attempt can be made to spell the correct name.

4. (Cross) DRAW THIS (*point to the cross*) ON YOUR PAPER. GO AROUND THE OUTSIDE LIKE THIS (*quickly draw a finger-line around the edge of the stimulus figure*) UNTIL YOU GET BACK TO WHERE YOU STARTED. MAKE IT ABOUT THIS SAME SIZE (*point to the cross*).

Additional instructions, if necessary, should be similar to those used with the square.

5. (Cross) WHAT IS THAT SHAPE CALLED?
6. (Cross) WOULD YOU SPELL THE NAME OF IT?

Again, if the subject cannot name the figure or gives a wrong name, tell the subject, SOME PEOPLE CALL THIS A CROSS. WOULD YOU SPELL "CROSS" FOR ME?

7. (Triangle) NOW I WANT YOU TO DRAW THIS FIGURE. (*Point to the triangle.*)
8. (Triangle) WHAT WOULD YOU CALL THAT FIGURE?
9. (Triangle) WOULD YOU SPELL THE NAME OF IT FOR ME?
10. (Baby) WHAT IS THIS?

The stimulus figure is deliberately presented in a sideways position in order to make the problem of visual form perception slightly more difficult.

11. (Clock) NOW I AM GOING TO SHOW YOU ANOTHER PICTURE BUT DO *NOT* TELL ME THE NAME OF IT. I DON'T WANT YOU TO SAY ANYTHING OUT LOUD. JUST *WRITE* THE NAME OF THE PICTURE ON YOUR PAPER.

If the subject prints, let him finish and then ask him to do it again in cursive writing.

12. (Fork) WHAT IS THIS?

13. (7 SIX 2) I WANT YOU TO READ THIS.

If the subject has difficulty, attempt to determine whether he can read any part of the stimulus figure.

14. (M G W) READ THIS.

15. (See the black dog.) NOW I WANT YOU TO READ THIS.

16. (He is a friendly animal, a famous winner of dog shows.) CAN YOU READ THIS?

Listen carefully for omissions, additions, transposition, or mispronunciations.

17. NOW I AM GOING TO SAY SOME WORDS. I WANT YOU TO LISTEN CAREFULLY AND SAY THEM AFTER ME AS CAREFULLY AS YOU CAN. SAY THIS WORD: "TRIANGLE."

18. THE NEXT ONE IS A LITTLE HARDER BUT DO YOUR BEST. SAY THIS WORD: "MASSACHUSETTS."

19. NOW REPEAT THIS ONE: "METHODIST EPISCOPAL."

20. (Square) DON'T SAY THIS WORD OUT LOUD. (*Point to the stimulus word* "SQUARE.") JUST WRITE IT ON YOUR PAPER.

If the patient prints the word, ask him to write it.

21. (Seven) WOULD YOU READ THIS WORD?

21A. *Remove the stimulus card and say:* NOW, I WANT YOU TO SAY THIS AFTER ME: "SEVEN."

22. I AM GOING TO SAY SOMETHING THAT I WANT YOU TO SAY AFTER ME, SO LISTEN CAREFULLY: "HE SHOUTED THE WARNING." NOW YOU SAY IT.

TELL ME IN YOUR OWN WORDS WHAT THAT MEANS.

Sometimes it is necessary to amplify by asking about the kind of situation to which the sentence might refer. An adequate understanding brings the concept of impending danger into the explanation or illustration given.

23. NOW I WANT YOU TO WRITE THAT SENTENCE ON THE PAPER.

Sometimes it is necessary to repeat the sentence so the patient understands clearly what he is to write.

24. (85–27 =) HERE IS AN ARITHMETIC PROBLEM. COPY IT DOWN ON YOUR PAPER ANY WAY YOU LIKE AND TRY TO WORK IT OUT.

If the patient does not perform subtraction, ask him to do the problem again, and to be very careful to do it right. If the subject still does not recognize the meaning of the minus sign, question him to determine the degree of his confusion.

25. (17 X 3) NOW DO THIS ONE IN YOUR HEAD. WRITE DOWN ONLY THE ANSWER.

If the patient has difficulty with these problems, use some simple problems in addition, subtraction, and possibly multiplication. The purpose is not to see if the patient has developed skill in dealing with complex arithmetic problems but to determine whether or not he has specific losses in his understanding of arithmetical processes. The drawback in using extremely simple problems is that the patient may respond correctly through rote memory rather than through immediate use of arithmetical processes, but some patients have such limited formal training in arithmetic that it is necessary to use very simple problems.

26. (Key) WHAT IS THIS?

27. (*Still presenting the picture of the key*): IF YOU HAD ONE OF THESE IN YOUR HAND, SHOW ME HOW YOU WOULD USE IT.

28. (Key) NOW I WANT YOU TO DRAW A PICTURE THAT LOOKS JUST LIKE THIS. TRY TO MAKE YOUR KEY LOOK ENOUGH LIKE THIS ONE (*pointing to the picture of the key*) SO THAT I WOULD KNOW IT WAS THE SAME KEY FROM YOUR DRAWING. MAKE IT ABOUT THE SAME SIZE.

Tell the patient that he may lift his pencil (but that he may not erase). If he makes a serious mistake, he may start a new drawing, but may not erase the original error, as it may be important for interpretation of the results. It is not necessary for the subject to put the shading in his drawing; in fact, attempts to reproduce the shading sometimes conceal errors that would be important to observe.

29. (Place left hand to right ear.) WOULD YOU READ THIS?
30. (Place left hand to right ear) NOW, WOULD YOU DO WHAT IT SAID?

Be sure to note any false starts or even mild expressions of confusion.

31. NOW I WANT YOU TO PUT YOUR LEFT HAND TO YOUR LEFT ELBOW.

Confusion on this item often reveals minimal or subtle difficulties in right-left orientation even though the patient does not make mistakes in responding to direct requests that are within the realm of possibility. Sometimes this item elicits evidence of a very serious problem — confusion of body parts (body agnosia). This would be manifested by confusion, for example, between the shoulder and the elbow and might be evident even though right-left confusion was not demonstrated.

Scoring

Despite the tendency of some investigators to score each item as pass/fail and then total the failures, we do not recommend that this test be scored. It is more important to interpret the failures and use this test as intended, namely, to identify specific deficits on simple tasks that should be performed satisfactorily by persons with normal brain functions.

THE SENSORY-PERCEPTUAL EXAMINATION

General Instructions

The procedure for administering the Sensory-perceptual Examination is relatively simple but requires practice on the part of the examiner and close attention to detail. With sufficient experience, many examiners are able to proceed quite quickly with the examination, mentally tabulating any errors made by the subject and recording them when a natural break occurs in the testing procedure. However, if the examiner has not had sufficient experience with administration of the test, it is necessary to record errors as they occur. As with any standardized and formal testing procedure, it is important that the instructions be given to the subject in an exact and precise manner. In other words, the examiner must memorize the instructions. The instructions should be given in a standard form initially but may be restated or elaborated upon whenever necessary so that the subject understands exactly what is expected from him.

For a person who has never given these tests, it would be advisable for her to memorize the specific instructions, obtain "dry run" experience with practice subjects, and give the tests to an experienced and knowledgeable person in order to be sure that all aspects of the procedure are followed correctly. If the test is routinely administered by a person who does not have any background and experience in the area of human brain-behavior relationships, supervision should be provided by a person who is knowledgeable regarding the purpose of the test and the neuroanatomical and neuropathological background for interpretation of the results. In general, however, the tests can be given by any intelligent person who has been trained in the administration.

In administering the tests for perception of bilateral simultaneous stimulation, it is important that a minimal stimulus be given. The stimulus is given with the examiner's own finger, not a pencil or other object. The examiner should determine how minimal a stimulus will still elicit a correct response. The examiner should continue to use this same degree of pressure when stimuli are given to both sides simultaneously, even though one side may initially have been determined to require more pressure than the other.

The same general rule is followed with auditory stimulation. Use as minimal a sound as necessary to elicit correct responses to unilateral stimulation. A loud finger-snap is not necessary. In fact, the examiner is usually not even able to hear the stimulus although the subject is able to respond correctly.

A very minimal movement with only one finger is frequently sufficient to elicit correct unilateral responses with visual stimulation. It is not necessary to wave at the subject.

The Sensory-perceptual Examination is concerned principally with evaluating the intactness of input (receptive) avenues to the brain rather than response (expressive) capabilities. Sometimes an individual has intact input avenues but has difficulty giving appropriate responses. This occurs particularly in persons with right-left confusion or serious impairment of the ability to pay attention. Therefore, the examiner must be alert to errors in responding that are due to the subject's general confusion or specific errors in identifying the right and left sides.

If a person is confused by responding "right" or "left," a different response procedure should be used. In some instances, it is necessary for the subject to point to the side stimulated. With tactile stimulation it is not satisfactory to have the subject merely move the hand that was stimulated; more reliable responses are obtained when the subject is instructed to point to the location of the stimulus, even though it is may be necessary to point to both sides.

Homonymous visual field defects and lateralized instances of visual imperception generally have similar significance; however, the two findings may definitely be complementary and should not be considered as identical manifestations. Of course, if a person has a complete homonymous hemianopia, the test for visual imperception is precluded; the subject would not be able to respond to the stimuli presented on the affected (blind) side. In many instances, though, visual imperception occurs without a corresponding visual field deficit.

Instances of unilateral impairment of tactile or auditory perception are important to note but do not constitute a test for sensory imperception any more than mapping of the visual fields does. The principal purpose for giving unilateral stimulation initially is to determine that the individual has the capability to respond to stimulation on each side of the body. The term "imperception" refers to a failure to report the stimulus to one side when in competition with a stimulus given to the other side. Thus, bilateral simultaneous stimulation is necessary in order to elicit a manifestation of imperception as defined by this test. Of course, unilateral impairment of tactile perception (hypesthesia) may be of definite significance with respect to lateralization of a cerebral lesion. This may possibly be true of unilateral auditory impairment as well, although unilateral auditory deficiencies are more common (in association with peripheral rather than central hearing losses) than deficits in tactile perception.

The Tactile Finger Recognition Test is an evaluation for finger agnosia (impairment of tactile finger localization). The least perceptible stimulus should be used. Stimuli should be administered to the fingers in random order, but adjacent fingers should not be tested consecutively. The examiner should always be sure that both the examiner and the subject understand the reporting system that the subject is going to use. Any reporting system is satisfactory, provided that it is unambiguous. Remember that this is a test of tactile perception rather than a test of the subject's adequacy in reporting. The stimulus is applied to the fingers by giving a distinct, light touch rather than a brushing motion.

On the Finger-tip Number Writing Perception Test, the numbers are administered in the prescribed order indicated on the recording form. The numbers should be written on the palmar aspect of the hand (palm up) at the distal part of the finger. The examiner should use an instrument such as a stylus or ballpoint pen that has run out of ink. The numbers should be written clearly, slowly, and distinctly, in a form that might resemble "first grade" instruction. In this test the examiner does not use the "least stimulus possible" but, instead, uses a steady pressure that is sufficient to leave a "trail of white" where the pen has been.

Specific Instructions

SENSORY IMPERCEPTION

A) Tactile: PUT YOUR HANDS ON THE TABLE LIKE THIS (*demonstrate with palms down*). I AM GOING TO TOUCH YOUR RIGHT HAND (*touch the subject's right hand*) OR YOUR LEFT HAND (*touch the subject's left hand*). *The place that should be touched is the back of the hand, just proximal to the middle knuckle.*

I WANT YOU TO CLOSE YOUR EYES SINCE I WANT YOU TO DEPEND ONLY ON YOUR FEELING TO TELL ME WHICH HAND I TOUCH. IF I TOUCH YOUR RIGHT HAND (*touch the subject's right hand*), YOU SAY, "RIGHT." THAT WAY I WILL KNOW YOU FELT IT. IF I TOUCH YOUR LEFT HAND (*touch the subject's left hand*) YOU SAY LEFT." BE SURE YOU DO NOT MAKE A MISTAKE IN TELLING ME WHICH HAND I TOUCHED. DO YOU HAVE ANY QUESTIONS?

Repeat or elaborate the instructions as necessary to be sure that the patient understands the procedure.

First, touch the right hand or left hand in random sequence approximately four times each in order to determine the lightest pressure needed to obtain consistent and correct responses to unilateral stimulation. Then, touch right hand, left hand, or both hands simultaneously in random sequence until each has been tested at least four times. If the patient has more difficulty feeling the stimulus on one side or the other, this should be recorded. The important point of this test, however, is to determine whether or not the patient fails to respond to one side consistently with bilateral simultaneous stimulation even though he responded correctly on the same side with unilateral stimulation. Never warn the patient that both hands will be simultaneously touched on some trials, and do not give bilateral stimuli on consecutive trials. Although it happens only rarely, some patients have so much difficulty keeping their eyes closed that it may be necessary to use a blindfold. Be sure that the responses are based upon tactile perception alone. Record errors on the form.

Using the above procedure as a model, proceed with:
NOW I'M GOING TO TOUCH EITHER YOUR HAND OR YOUR FACE, AND I WANT YOU TO TELL ME WHICH ONE I'M TOUCHING. YOU DON'T HAVE TO TELL ME "RIGHT" OR "LEFT." JUST SAY "HAND" OR "FACE." ALL RIGHT, CLOSE YOUR EYES.

Touch the right hand, left face, and both face and hand simultaneously in random sequence until each has been done at least four times. Then repeat with left hand, right face, and both.

B) Auditory: NOW I'M GOING TO STAND BEHIND YOU AND MAKE A NOISE LIKE THIS: (Demonstrate auditory stimulus)

Make a barely audible finger snap by rubbing two fingers (thumb and another finger) together lightly. Once should be sufficient. Be careful not to touch the subject or his hair.

I WANT YOU TO TELL ME IF THE SOUND IS BY THIS EAR (touch the subject's right ear) OR THIS EAR (touch the subject's left ear). YOU CAN TELL ME WHICH EAR JUST BY SAYING "RIGHT" OR "LEFT." BE SURE TO KEEP YOUR EYES CLOSED.

Use the instructions for tactile stimulation as a model for completing this test, interspersing unilateral with bilateral stimulation.

C) Visual: I'M GOING TO SIT IN FRONT OF YOU AND HOLD MY HANDS OUT LIKE THIS.

Place yourself about three feet in front of the patient so that you and the patient are at equal eye level; extend your hands about two feet away from your body. Both the examiner and the subject should use binocular vision (both eyes open).

I WANT YOU TO LOOK DIRECTLY AT MY NOSE AND TELL

ME IF I AM MOVING THIS HAND (*move the fingers of your right hand obviously*) OR THIS HAND (*move the fingers of your left hand obviously*). TELL ME WHICH HAND I MOVE BY SAYING "RIGHT" IF IT IS OVER TO *YOUR* RIGHT SIDE OR BY SAYING "LEFT" IF IT IS OVER TO *YOUR* LEFT SIDE. BE SURE TO LOOK DIRECTLY AT MY NOSE ALL THE TIME — DON'T LOOK AT MY HANDS.

Administer four unilateral stimuli interspersed with four bilateral simultaneous stimuli above, at, and below patient's eye level.

It is very difficult for some patients to fixate their vision on one point. However, the test is invalidated if the patient's vision is not fixated in the center of his visual field. The examiner must be alert to give the stimulus only when the subject's vision is properly fixated. First proceed with unilateral stimuli because correct responses to unilateral movement must be determined before possible failure to respond to one side or the other with bilateral simultaneous stimulation has any special significance. If the examiner suspects a possible limitation of visual fields, gross confrontation procedures or more exact methods (perimetry or use of a tangent screen) may be used to map the visual fields. In the event of homonymous hemianopsia, bilateral simultaneous visual stimulation is meaningless, but the homonymous visual field loss may have given the lateralizing information sought. Homonymous quadrantanopsia may not invalidate the test provided that the intact quadrants are used for presenting the stimulus. The test may be given at eye level, but many examiners give the test in the upper parts of the visual field, at eye level, and in the lower parts of the visual field in order to deal with partial homonymous visual field losses.

TACTILE FINGER RECOGNITION (FINGER AGNOSIA)

Ask the subject to place his right hand, palm down, on the table in front of him with his fingers extended and spread slightly apart. Ask the subject to close his eyes, or shield the subject's hand with a piece of paper.

Say, I'M GOING TO NAME (NUMBER) YOUR FINGERS. WE'LL CALL THIS FINGER #1 (*touch the subject's thumb*) THIS ONE #2 (*touch the subject's index finger*), THIS ONE #3 (*touch the subject's* middle finger), THIS ONE #4 (*touch the subject's ring finger*) AND THIS ONE #5 (*touch the subject's little finger*).

Touch each finger with a distinct but light touch (using your own finger to control the intensity of the stimulus), just proximal to the nail bed of the subject's finger.
NOW, KEEP YOUR EYES CLOSED AND TELL ME, BY NUMBER, WHICH FINGER I TOUCHED.

It is usually helpful initially to give a single trial to each of the fingers in a consecutive order. In this way the examiner ensures that the subject understands the reporting system and that the intensity of the stimulus (light touch) is sufficient. Then, the examiner should touch each finger in a random sequence, touching each finger a total of four times. Avoid delivering a stimulus to two adjacent fingers consecutively. It is often necessary to remind the subject that he should pay close attention and tell the examiner exactly which finger was touched.

Most persons can adapt to this numbering/reporting system, but it is sometimes necessary for the examiner to adapt to the limitations of individual subjects. For example, some persons prefer to name the thumb as "thumb" and then consecutively number the fingers 1 through 4 beginning with the index finger.

FINGER-TIP NUMBER WRITING

I AM GOING TO WRITE SOME NUMBERS ON YOUR FINGER-TIPS. I WANT YOU TO PAY CLOSE ATTENTION SO THAT YOU WILL BE ABLE TO TELL ME THE NUMBERS THAT I WRITE.
Illustrate on the subject's palm how the numbers will be written. Tell him: THIS IS THE WAY I WILL MAKE A "3"; THIS IS THE WAY I WILL MAKE A "4"; THIS IS THE WAY I WILL MAKE A "5"; AND I WILL MAKE A "6" LIKE THIS.

If the subject gives any indication that he makes the numbers differently than the examiner, the examiner's method should be adapted to the subject's method for writing the numbers. In some instances it is worthwhile to have the subject write the numbers 3, 4, 5, and 6 on paper before the illustrations are given on the subject's palm, so that the numbers can be made in the way most familiar to the subject. This illustration should not be used as a guide for the patient during administration of this procedure.

BE SURE TO KEEP YOUR EYES CLOSED BUT PAY CLOSE ATTENTION SO THAT YOU WILL BE ABLE TO TELL WHAT NUMBERS I WRITE. SINCE I AM FACING YOU, REMEMBER THAT I WILL BE WRITING THE NUMBERS UPSIDE DOWN.

Shield the patient's finger as you write each number so that he will not be able to see what is written even if he should open his eyes. Use a different finger for each trial (proceeding in order from finger #1 through #5) until four trials have been given (using the numbers indicated on the test form) for each finger of the right hand (Fig. 3-10). Repeat the procedure for the left hand. Record errors only.

Fig. 3-10. *Subject taking the Finger-tip Number Writing Perception Test.*

Scoring

Aside from totaling errors for each task, Tactile Finger Recognition and Finger-tip Number Writing Perception are not scored (Fig. 3-11). The purpose is to elicit abnormalities of sensory perception rather than derive a score along a scaled continuum.

REITAN-KLØVE SENSORY-PERCEPTUAL EXAMINATION
(Instance indicated where stimulus was not perceived or was incorrectly perceived.)

TACTILE: **Error Totals**

Right Hand-Left Hand – RH ☐☐☐ LH ☐☐☐ Both: RH ☐☐☐ LH ☐☐☐   RH ___ LH ___

Right Hand-Left Face – RH ☐☐☐ LF ☐☐☐ Both: RH ☐☐☐ LF ☐☐☐   RH ___ LF ___

Left Hand-Right Face – LH ☐☐☐ RF ☐☐☐ Both: LH ☐☐☐ RF ☐☐☐   RF ___ LH ___

AUDITORY:

Right Ear-Left Ear – RE ☐☐☐ LE ☐☐☐ Both: RE ☐☐☐ LE ☐☐☐   RE ___ LE ___

VISUAL:

Above eye level
Eye level   RV ⊞ LV ⊞ Both: RV ⊞ LV ⊞
Below eye level

TACTILE FINGER RECOGNITION:

Right: 1 ⊞ 2 ⊞ 3 ⊞ 4 ⊞ 5 ⊞   R ___/___
Left: 1 ⊞ 2 ⊞ 3 ⊞ 4 ⊞ 5 ⊞   L ___/___

FINGER-TIP NUMBER WRITING PERCEPTION:

Right: | 4 | 6 | 3 | 5 | | 3 | 5 | 4 | 6 | | 6 | 5 | 4 | 3 | | 5 | 4 | 6 | 3 | | 6 | 3 | 5 | 4 |
Left: ⊞   ⊞   ⊞   ⊞   ⊞   R ___/___
                                                                           L ___/___

Fig. 3-11. Form for recording subject's responses to the Sensory Perceptual Examination.

LATERAL DOMINANCE EXAMINATION

General Instructions

The Lateral Dominance Examination is performed in order to obtain information regarding the subject's handedness and footedness. There has been a great deal of interest about the relationships of these variables to cerebral dominance, or the extent to which the left and right cerebral hemispheres subserve specific and differential functions.

Lateral dominance can be approached in two different ways: (1) Determination of the preferred side in performance of tasks that can be done using only one side or the other (lateral preference); and (2) Comparison of the level of performance on one side versus the other in evaluating the efficiency or adequacy of performance on the two sides (lateral skill). The Lateral Dominance Examination to be described here relates to the first type of criterion. Several other tests in the Battery (such as the Finger Tapping Test, the Strength of Grip Test, and the Tactual Performance Test) provide information on the comparative functional efficiency of the upper extremities.

One element of the Lateral Dominance Examination determines

which hand is used by the subject for writing. This information serves as the criterion with respect to the hand used for the first trial on the Tactual Performance Test. Therefore, the information regarding the hand used for writing should be obtained before the Tactual Performance Test is administered. Generally, the Lateral Dominance Examination is given relatively early in the administration of the Battery.

Specific Instructions

1. The first item in this test is included principally to demonstrate that the subject is sufficiently intact to be able to understand the instructions that follow for additional items. The instructions are as follows:

SHOW ME YOUR RIGHT HAND. *Record the patient's response.*

SHOW ME YOUR LEFT EAR. *Record the patient's response.*

SHOW ME YOUR RIGHT EYE. *Record the patient's response.*

2. This item provides a comparison of the time required for the patient to write his full name using each hand. The subject is not told to write quickly; instead, he is asked to write his full name, first with his preferred hand, and then in the same form (printing or cursive) with his non-preferred hand, using his normal speed or tempo. In each instance, the time required in seconds is recorded.

NOW I WANT YOU TO WRITE YOUR FULL NAME ON THE PAPER.

Note the hand used by the patient but give him no further direction concerning the hand that is used. The hand used spontaneously by the patient is considered to be the preferred hand.

NOW I WANT YOU TO WRITE YOUR NAME IN THE SAME WAY, USING YOUR OTHER HAND.

Again, no mention should be made that the patient should write quickly or in any other way alter his conventional manner of writing his name. The difference in time required provides an additional indication of hand preference for this task.

3. This item requires the subject to perform a number of unimanual tasks. Do not try to influence the subject to use one hand or the other; present the stimulus material in such a way that it is equally available to either hand. Except for writing, the tasks have been selected in such a way that they probably are not heavily influenced by social pressures. The material necessary for this test can easily be obtained at any novelty store. Items included are a small rubber ball, a toy hammer, a toy knife, a small pair of scissors, and a pencil with an eraser. Instructions are as follows:

SHOW ME HOW YOU WOULD THROW A BALL.

Be sure that the ball is presented so that it is equidistant and equally available to both hands. Record the hand used. Essentially the same instructions should be used with the remaining items.

SHOW ME HOW YOU WOULD HAMMER A NAIL.

SHOW ME HOW YOU WOULD CUT WITH A KNIFE.

SHOW ME HOW YOU WOULD TURN A DOOR KNOB. Take the patient to a door, stand him directly before the knob, and have him actually perform the task.

SHOW ME HOW YOU WOULD USE SCISSORS.

SHOW ME HOW YOU WOULD USE THE ERASER ON YOUR PENCIL.

Also record which hand the patient initially used when he was asked to write his name. The results obtained on this item are summarized by indicating the number of times the right hand and the left hand were used in performing the seven items.

4. Information regarding footedness is obtained as follows:

SHOW ME HOW YOU WOULD KICK A FOOTBALL. An actual football is not used for this item, because of the possibility that kicking it would cause some type of damage such as broken windows. However, the examiner records the foot that the patient would use.

PRETEND THAT THERE IS A BUG ON THE FLOOR AND SHOW ME HOW YOU WOULD STEP ON IT. Record the foot that is used.

In each of these items it is necessary to have a patient stand when the instructions are given. If a patient is in a wheelchair and is unable to stand it is still possible to have him demonstrate to you which foot he would use if he were able to do the task.

In the past we have used the Miles ABC Test of Ocular Dominance to provide information regarding eyedness. However, we were never able to relate the results to cerebral damage or dysfunction. In addition, these test materials no longer seem to be available for purchase.

Scoring

The results are recorded as described above (Fig. 3-12). No formal scoring is done.

LATERAL DOMINANCE EXAMINATION

Name: _____ Date: _____ Examiner: _____

1. Show me your right hand _____; left ear _____; right eye _____.

2. Show me how you:
   throw a ball   _____
   hammer a nail   _____
   cut with a knife   _____
   turn a door knob   _____
   use scissors   _____
   use an eraser   _____
   write your name   _____

3. Write your full name

   preferred hand (_____)   _____ seconds
   non-preferred hand (_____) _____ seconds

4. Show me how you look through a telescope. _____ eye

   Aim this gun at the tip of my nose. _____ shoulder _____ eye

5. Show me how you kick a football. _____ foot

   step on a bug. _____ foot

6. Strength of grip. (Hold dynamometer at arm's length, point to the floor, and squeeze as hard as you can.)

   1. preferred (_____) _____ kgs.   2. non-preferred (_____) _____ kgs.
   3. preferred   _____ kgs.   4. non-preferred   _____ kgs.

              Total _____ kgs.   Total _____ kgs.

   _____ Hand Mean: _____ kgs.   _____ Hand Mean: _____ kgs.

7. ABC Test for Ocular Dominance

   (1) _____   (6) _____   Right: _____
   (2) _____   (7) _____
   (3) _____   (8) _____   Left: _____
   (4) _____   (9) _____
   (5) _____   (10) _____

Fig. 3-12. *Form for recording subject's responses to the Lateral Dominance Examination.*

IV
GUIDELINES TO INTERPRETATION
OF THE HALSTEAD-REITAN
NEUROPSYCHOLOGICAL
TEST BATTERY

General aspects of the approach and procedure in interpretation of results for individual subjects varies somewhat from one neuropsychologist to another, but there are commonalities that can be reviewed. There are distinct differences in interpretation of results for children compared with adults (Reitan, 1984; Reitan, 1985), and the present comments will be restricted to adult interpretations.

The general procedure is to first refer to results from the Wechsler Scale to determine the subject's previous intellectual abilities. If relatively normal neuropsychological development has occurred during the developmental years, most persons (including those who have sustained significant neuropsychological impairment) will show relatively good scores on some of the Wechsler subtests.

The Wechsler subtests most useful in this respect are Information, Comprehension, Similarities, and Vocabulary. If these subtest scores are low, one cannot use them as a contrast for poor scores on neuropsychological (brain-sensitive) tests. If these scores are relatively good, one can presume that circumstances in the past have been adequate to permit development of these abilities; poorer scores on tests which are more specifically sensitive to the biological condition of the brain may be subject to interpretation as evidence of impairment. The

Wechsler subtests may be used for more specific aspects of interpretation as well, but only after reviewing the results obtained with the remaining tests of the Halstead-Reitan Battery.

The next step in interpretation is to review the subject's scores on the four most sensitive measures of the Battery: Halstead's Impairment Index, the Category Test, Part B of the Trail Making Test, and the Localization component of the Tactual Performance Test. If these tests were performed poorly and Wechsler's scores suggest that the person had developed relatively normal abilities in the past, a presumption may be made that the person has suffered some neuropsychological deficit resulting from brain damage.

Each of these four measures is a general indicator and does not have significance for localization of cerebral damage. Focal lesions (regardless of localization) and generalized or diffuse damage may have pronounced effects on the general indicators. Poor scores on the four general indicators, particularly when coupled with relatively good I.Q. values, may also indicate the severity of loss of pre-existing abilities. In most instances, persons with cerebral damage will have at least some degree of impairment on the four most sensitive general indicators when contrasted with certain of the better scores on the Wechsler scale.

The third step in interpretation is to evaluate the measures that relate to lateralization and localization of cerebral damage. The inferential approaches of value in this regard concern patterns and relationships among test results, the occurrence of specific signs of cerebral damage, and comparisons of performances on the two sides of the body. The tests and findings most useful for this part of the interpretation include (1) the Wechsler Scale (Verbal versus Performance scores; selective deficits on individual subtests with relation to better scores on other subtests); (2) deviant performances on one hand as compared with the other on the Tactual Performance Test; (3) disparities in finger tapping speed of the two hands; (4) the presence of dysphasia; (5) evidence of constructional dyspraxia; (6) lateralized deficits on the Sensory-perceptual Examination (bilateral tactile, auditory, and visual stimulation; tactile finger recognition; and finger-tip number writing perception); and (7) the presence of homonymous visual field losses.

The above listing may not be entirely complete, depending upon the individual pattern of test scores. For example, in some instances, an extremely poor score on the Speech-sounds Perception Test, with relation to other scores, may be an indicator of left cerebral damage even though this test usually is more closely related to the subject's ability to pay attention to explicit stimulus material and maintain concentrated attention over time.

Because these results constitute arrays for individual subjects that are extremely variable, it is not possible to offer a simple set of rules for evaluation of the indications of lateralization and localization. Competent ability in interpretation must necessarily be gained by studying results of a large number of individual subjects.

The next step in the interpretation is to discern the course of the lesion. Some brain lesions are progressive in nature, others are relatively static, and some are on a course of spontaneous recovery. Inferences regarding these possibilities can be drawn from the test results. The basic approach is to effect comparisons of certain tests with others, complemented by the extent to which the test results point toward a focal cerebral lesion. Most focal lesions tend to be progressive and cause serious generalized deficits as well as specific pathognomonic signs. It is possible, of course, for a lesion to be focal and relatively static, but such a lesion would be accompanied by specific focal signs and relatively better scores on at least some of the tests which are general indicators. In persons with static conditions, we have found that the Speech-sounds Perception Test and the Seashore Rhythm Test are frequently done fairly well compared to some of the tests more sensitive to brain damage (e.g., the Category Test). Part B of the Trail Making Test is also helpful in this respect: the results on this test are often comparatively good in persons who are in a recovery phase.

The final step in diagnostic neuropsychological interpretation involves compiling all of the data and drawing inferences about the type of lesion or neurological disorder that may have produced the findings. Skill in this area obviously requires knowledge of neurology, neuroanatomy and neuropathology, and the neuropsychologist should be familiar with the major categories of neurological disease and damage. Reviews of the specific neuropsychological characteristics of various types of lesions have been published (e.g., Hom & Reitan, 1982; Hom & Reitan, 1984) and in many instances it is possible clinically to not only differentiate between categories of lesions (such as intrinsic tumors, vascular lesions, and head injuries) but to even differentiate within categories (fast vs. slowly growing intrinsic tumors).

In interpreting any neuropsychological data, though, the general guidelines supported by research results must be supplemented by clinical experience with individual cases. Many comprehensive publications in the area of neuropsychology have included illustrations of neuropsychological principles through individual cases. This procedure is particularly helpful in permitting the reader to gain knowledge that can be applied practically (Rourke, Bakker, Fisk & Strang, 1983; Reitan & Davison, 1974).

Although the above comments refer particularly to inferences regarding the neurological condition of the brain based upon neuropsychological measurements, inferences concerning the psychological significance of behavioral deficits are equally important. In fact, neuropsychological evaluation constitutes the only rigorous method of identifying impairment of *adaptive behavior* resulting from cerebral damage. The major areas of behavior related to impaired brain functions have already been reviewed, and the Halstead-Reitan Battery has been developed and organized to reflect these major areas. The unique value of neuropsychological interpretation is the assessment and evaluation of intra-individual ability patterns as they relate to the condition of the brain.

Although neurological diagnosis can validly be established using many other techniques and methods, the psychological consequences of cerebral damage are uniquely represented by neuropsychological evaluation. It is difficult to make absolute statements about selected behaviors in everyday living for all subjects, but the test results frequently indicate general areas in which the individual is probably experiencing difficulty. For example, a physician who retained high I.Q. values but was severely impaired in abstraction and reasoning processes as a result of brain damage showed significant problems in performing his work. In the case of another physician who worked as a general surgeon, scores on the Tactual Performance Test were worse than those of the average brain-damaged person. For this individual (who also showed evidence of distinct constructional dyspraxia) it was not difficult to recommend that he make immediate plans to disengage from his responsibilities as a general surgeon.

In other cases, disparities in performances on the two sides of the body may be of special significance. If the preferred hand is specifically defective, the affected individual may have special problems in a number of tasks. If the non-preferred hand is especially involved, tasks that involve bimanual performances may be impaired. For example, a woman who had sustained a closed head injury and had significant impairment of her left (non-preferred) upper extremity had difficulty with bimanual tasks such as driving a car with both hands or typing. Inferences of brain damage depend, at this point, largely on evaluation of the details of results for the individual subject.

Finally, in cases of static or recovering brain lesions, the potential for brain retraining is an important issue. There is a great deal of interest in this concept that represents the spirit of the present times. Promising results have been obtained with individual subjects. In fact, during the past several years a formal training program, REHABIT, has been developed by Reitan and, in many instances, results with individual subjects have far exceeded the degree of improvement seen in persons who were undergoing only spontaneous recovery (Reitan & Sena, 1983). The area of brain retraining is not only an immensely complex issue but a recent development in neuropsychology as well; detailed knowledge, beyond the fact that it is possible to facilitate recovery in certain individual persons, is relatively limited at this time.

V
NORMATIVE DATA

The Halstead-Reitan Battery can skillfully be interpreted with knowledge of only general normative score ranges; exact percentile ranks corresponding with each possible score are hardly necessary, because the other methods of inference are used to supplement normative data in clinical interpretation of results for individual subjects.

These complementary methods of inference are: (1) patterns and interrelationships of scores as they relate to the function of various parts of the cerebral cortex; (2) specific deficits (pathognomonic signs) that occur almost exclusively in persons with cerebral disorders and have lateralizing and localizing value; and (3) comparisons of performances on the two sides of the body, reflecting the functional status of the two cerebral hemispheres.

Integration of these approaches in clinical interpretation (which represents the essence of neuropsychological evaluation) is illustrated in this volume by patients with various cerebral lesions. We recognize that the reader must have general guidelines to evaluate the adequacy of a subject's performances on the various tests and these are provided in Table 5-1.

The score ranges under the first column (Perfectly Normal) are better-than-average scores that are well within the range of normality. Scores in the second column (Normal) are still within the normal range but not quite as good as they could be. A major shift in evaluation occurs between the second and third columns, because the latter (Mildly Impaired) represents some degree of deficit. Scores under the final column (Seriously Impaired) are significantly deviant from normal and may represent severe impairment.

Adult Severity Ranges

Test	Perfectly Normal	Normal	Mildly Impaired	Seriously Impaired
		Severity		
Impairment Index	.0–.2	.3 (.4)	.5–.7	.8–1.0
Category Test (errors)	0–25	26–45	46–65	65 +
Tactual Performance Test:				
Total Time (minutes)	0–9.0	9.1–15.0	15.1–25.0	25.1 +
Memory	8–10	7	4–6	0–3
Localization	7–10	6	3–5	0–2
Seashore Rhythm Test (correct)	28–30	25–27	20–24	0–19
Speech Sounds Perception Test (errors)	0–6	7–10	11–15	16 +
Finger Oscillation Test:				
Dominant Hand	55 +	50–54	44–49	0–43
Non-dominant Hand	Should be about 10% less than dominant hand.			
Trail Making Test (Part B)	0–60	61–72	73–105	106 +
Strength of Grip	Dominant hand should be 10% more than non-dominant hand			
Tactile Form Recognition Test	Total score for each hand should be 8-10". Look for differences between the two hands. No errors are expected.			
Sensory Perceptual Exam	No errors are normally expected.			
Total errors on both hands	0–1	2	3–4	5 +
Right–left difference	0–1	2	3	4 +
Tactile Finger Recognition	Look for differences between the two hands.			
Errors/both hands	0–2	3–4	5–8	9 +
Right-left difference	0–1	2	3–4	5 +
Finger-tip Number Writing	Look for differences between the two hands.			
Errors/both hands	0–3	4–6	7–11	12 +
Right-left difference	0–1	2	3–4	5 +

Finger Oscillation and Grip Strength differences:

Normally, the differences should be about 10 percent in favor of the preferred hand. Deviations that go substantially beyond this guideline should be considered with regard to lateralizing significance.

Tactile Form Recognition:

In general, the two hands are equivalent, but some subjects are slow on the first trials (right hand). When more than a 4-second discrepancy is validly present (considering the first four trials), the results may have lateralizing significance.

Tactual Performance Test:

Typically, a ⅓ faster performance is expected from the nonpreferred hand in relation to the preferred hand. Deviations from this may have lateralizing significance.

Table 5-1. Normative guide to tests in the Halstead-Reitan Neuropsychological Test Battery.

Means and standard deviations for both neurologically normal and heterogeneous brain-damaged groups are given in Table 5-2 below.

	Controls		Brain-Damage	
	Mean	S.D.	Mean	S.D.
Category	32.38	12.62	61.98	21.82
TPT — Time	12.59	5.20	25.19	12.67
TPT — Memory	7.65	1.41	5.92	1.75
TPT — Localization	5.29	2.12	1.88	1.74
Seashore Rhythm	5.20	3.45	8.46	2.62
Speech-sounds				
Perception	7.08	5.31	14.06	8.48
Finger Oscillation	50.74	7.29	45.58	7.32

Table 5-2. Means and standard deviations for non-brain damaged and brain-damaged groups (N = 50 in each group; matched in pairs on sex, age and education). (Reitan, 1955b.)

These values, determined by Reitan (1955b), were based on 50 subjects in each group. Some investigators (e.g., Vega and Parsons, 1967) have reported poorer scores for both control and brain-damaged groups and the exact reason(s) for this are unknown. Regional normative differences may exist. It is also imperative that the tests are given by an examiner who is capable of eliciting each subject's best perform-ance. In practice it is probably necessary for each clinician to develop a sensitivity to the score ranges that apply best in his/her individual setting, and Tables 5-1 and 5-2 will provide general guidelines.

Finally, the reader will need cut-off scores for the tests that are used to compute the Halstead Impairment Index (Halstead, 1947). These are given in Table 5-3.

	Normal Range	Brain-Damaged Range
Category Test	0–50 errors	51 or more errors
Tactual Performance Test		
Total Time	15.6 and below	15.7 and above
Tactual Performance Test		
Memory	6 and above	5 and below
Tactual Performance Test		
Localization	5 and above	4 and below
Seashore Rhythm Test		
(ranked score)	5 and below	6 and above
Speech-sounds Perception Test	7 and below	8 and above
Finger Oscillation Test	51 and above	50 and below
IMPAIRMENT INDEX	0.4 and below	0.5 and above

Table 5-3. Cut-off points recommended by Halstead (1947) for use in determining the Impairment Index.

The computational procedure for the Impairment Index is very simple: the number of tests that have scores in the brain-damaged range is divided by the total number of tests that were administered. The Halstead Impairment Index is based on 7 of the tests in the Battery. Therefore, the Impairment Index would be 0.4 if 3 of these tests had results in the impaired range (3 ÷ 7 = 0.4). Some clinicians compute the Impairment Index to two decimal points, but this practice may imply a degree of precision that is not justified.

The reader may notice that Halstead's cut-off scores do not correspond exactly with the cutting scores between the Normal and Mildly Impaired ranges given in Table 5-1.

It must be recalled that Halstead's cut-off scores were published in 1947 and Table 5-1 is based upon considerably more experience than was available at that time. Halstead's data were generally accurate except for the cut-off score on the Speech-sounds Perception Test. Normal subjects make up to 10 errors on this test. The Speech-sounds Perception Test has a high correlation (−0.73) with Verbal I.Q. and Halstead's more stringent requirement on this test may have reflected the verbal intelligence of his subjects.

ILLUSTRATIVE INTERPRETATIONS OF INDIVIDUAL CASES

The cases to be presented will emphasize the significance and validity of the Halstead-Reitan Battery in inferring the neurological nature of cerebral damage. It is well known that neurological diagnostic techniques have developed rapidly during the past 15 years and definitive identification (diagnosis) of cerebral lesions can be achieved through computed tomography (CT), positron emission tomography (PET) and nuclear magnetic resonance (NMR). There is little need for neuropsychological methods to diagnose the presence of an intrinsic brain tumor.

On the other hand, there is a tremendous need for valid information regarding the behavioral deficits associated with brain lesions, including intrinsic tumors, and neuropsychological examination is the best resource for filling this need. Identification of the behavioral correlates of such lesions is also a powerful manifestation of the validity of neuropsychological data. This is particularly true if the neuropsychological characterization of the lesion is sufficiently specific to provide unequivocal identification of the lesion in an individual case using *only* the test results.

The cases presented in this volume illustrate interpretation of the entire Halstead-Reitan Battery. We would recommend Reitan's recent (1984) book entitled *Aphasia and Sensory-perceptual Deficits in Adults* for those persons who wish to gain further information regarding research findings and clinical interpretation of the Reitan-Indiana Aphasia Screening Test. We believe that development of further clinical expertise with this test, which can be gained only by studying individual cases, represents a critical area for many neuropsychologists in improving their overall skill in interpreting the Halstead-Reitan Battery.

The cases presented in this volume were independently evaluated by neurologists, neurosurgeons, and neuropathologists, and the reader will have an opportunity to consider in detail the neuropsychological data with relation to the neurological findings. Little can be gained in fundamental knowledge of brain-behavior relationships unless this approach is used. It is not satisfactory, as a starting point, to present a series of neuropsychological interpretations of cases for which corresponding neurological findings and diagnoses are not included. Thus, we hope that the following cases will provide the reader with improved insight and understanding of the complex but consistent interactions of variables in the Halstead-Reitan Battery as they relate to cerebral disease and damage.

We have included some cases in which the patient was tested during the developmental phase of the Halstead-Reitan Battery. Many of the patients tested during this time demonstrated the need for additional formal tests in order to fully evaluate brain functions. Therefore, some cases do not have results for all of the tests in the Battery as it exists today; we have included these cases so that the reader can recognize the value that the results of these yet-to-be developed tests contribute to the understanding of the brain-behavior relationships for each individual.

All drawings done by patients were originally drawn on 8½″ x 11″ paper and were reduced in size for inclusion in this book.

VI
TUMORS OF THE BRAIN

Before presenting a brief description of the neurobiology of brain tumors and case illustrations, it would be advantageous to briefly discuss the usefulness of studying the behavioral correlates of tumors as an initial step in developing skill in neuropsychological interpretation. First, it must be recognized that individuals with brain lesions are drawn from the entire population, representing variable and unique psychological characteristics in many respects. In other words, any set of psychological tests (whether they are called neuropsychological or have some other designation) will show a great deal of variability from one individual to another. Given such circumstances, it is difficult for the novice clinician to discern which aspects of the test results are distinctly and definitely brain-related from those principally influenced by other factors (including chance). Patients with brain tumors frequently show distinct and definite manifestations of brain dysfunction, permitting an obvious differentiation from normal performances. Thus, in teaching the interpretation of brain-behavior relationships, it is tremendously important that the learner discover first how to identify brain-related manifestations as contrasted with normal variation, educational influences, occupational skills, personality factors, etc.

A second, and probably more fundamental reason for presenting tumor cases initially is that the neuropsychological manifestations of this condition tend to pervade the entire framework of interpretation of the Halstead-Reitan Battery. Tumors may show highly discrete focal effects in some instances, focal effects involving relatively large areas of brain tissue in other cases, and sometimes bilateral focal effects. This provides the opportunity to study the localization of brain lesions and to learn how to interpret the differential effects of lateralized lesions as well as the correlates of more specifically focal lesions within each cerebral hemisphere.

Study of brain tumors also provides an important advantage in assessing losses of previously developed skills. When a child has sustained brain damage early in life the damage has a striking influence on development of brain-behavior relationships; the resulting ability structure is often quite different from that of the person who has had the opportunity for normal development (Reitan, 1985a). Whenever the brain lesion has limited the childhood abilities and restricted the potential for development of normal brain-behavior relationships, a special situation exists that does not permit a satisfactory basis for generalization to normal brain function. However, most adult subjects with brain tumors have developed brain-behavior relationships normally and the deficits associated with the developing tumor present a basis for assessment. Of course, this advantage is equally true with many other conditions of brain damage that may occur after normal development has been completed, but the acute and relatively recent onset of many brain tumors provides an opportunity to assess intraindividual deficits in ability structure and contrast these deficits with the remaining, and relatively unimpaired, abilities.

The rapid onset and development of brain damage in tumor cases is correlated with striking deficits and deviations from normality of function in many instances. In other cases, depending upon the rate of growth and degree of malignancy of the tumor, a picture of slower progression of deterioration may be observed. In so-called benign tumors (such as meningiomas), chronic-static manifestations are likely to be present. This range of variability in both the onset of the lesion and its rate of deterioration provides an excellent opportunity to observe the interaction of various lateralizing and localizing findings both in terms of their complementary significance as well as their meaning when they do not appear simultaneously.

Since brain tumors are focal lesions it is obviously necessary to study additional material in order to gain a neuropsychological understanding of diffuse or generalized conditions of brain damage. Beginning with the study of brain tumors provides an excellent background for developing advanced understanding. In addition, certain neuropsychological manifestations are associated with rapidly developing and destructive types of lesions that require medical and surgical evaluation; it is important for neuropsychologists to be able to recognize the signs associated with medically significant brain lesions and to direct the patient to appropriate evaluation. Studying patients with brain tumors and cerebral vascular lesions probably constitutes the best approach to gaining this type of knowledge.

In terms of the significance of brain tumors to the overall framework of interpretation of the Halstead-Reitan Battery, we should note that rapidly growing intrinsic tumors frequently provide some of the most striking patterns of variation on the Verbal and Performance subtests of the Wechsler Scale. As observed many years ago (Reitan, 1955b), tumors in the left cerebral hemisphere tend to lower Verbal intelligence and tumors in the right cerebral hemisphere impair Performance intelligence. Obviously, normal subjects show some degree of variability in Verbal and Performance I.Q. values, and it is important for the neuropsychologist to be able to recognize pathological deviations, in the context of additional neuropsychological findings, as a basis for valid interpretation.

In persons with brain tumors, the four most sensitive indicators in the Battery (Halstead Impairment Index, Category Test, Part B of the Trail Making Test, and Localization component of the Tactual Performance Test) also consistently show striking deviations from some of the better scores. The acutely destructive nature of many brain tumors frequently causes pronounced lateralization effects. Comparisons of differential losses of anterior versus posterior lesions within each hemisphere are also manifested. Finally, despite certain generalized or "distance" effects that may be present, more specific localization within each cerebral hemisphere may also be studied because many tumors involve one particular area.

We recognize that patients with brain tumors are usually seen only in specialized settings of neuropsychological practice and research rather than in the independent practice of neuropsychology. Although few neuropsychologists will see a large number of patients with brain tumors in the course of their careers, studying the neuropsychological profiles of such patients illustrates many of the important principles that appear in more subtle form in other conditions and lays a groundwork for assessing the behavioral correlates of other types of brain lesions.

Overview of the Nature and Neurobiology of Brain Tumors

Tumors arise from tissues distributed throughout the body and about 10 percent of these lesions occur within the central nervous system, its meninges, and related bony structures. Eighty percent of these tumors are in the cranial cavity and 20 percent involve the area of the spinal cord. Tumors of the nervous system may be primary or metastatic. Primary tumors arise from tissue of the brain and spinal cord as well as the meninges and blood vessels. In addition, primary tumors may also arise from the pituitary and pineal glands and residual embryonic tissue. Metastatic tumors account for about 20 percent of intracranial tumors. The most common primary sites of metastatic tumors are (in order): lungs, gastrointestinal tract, breasts, and kidneys. The lesions are multiple in 70 percent of metastatic tumors to the brain.

Little is known about the etiology of most brain tumors. In general, hereditary factors seem to be significant for a limited category of tumors but the familial occurrence of brain tumors is rare. There have been occasional reports of tumors developing after brain trauma, but, in general, trauma is not considered to be a significant predisposing factor. Radiation may damage and impair tissues in the brain and lead to delayed degenerative changes, but there is no evidence that radiation produces intrinsic cerebral tumors. Some reports have suggested that delayed effects of radiation may be associated with development of meningiomas.

Viral infections may have some relationship to the development of certain rare brain tumors, such as lymphoma, but, in general, viruses appear to have little role in the development of most brain tumors. Chemical carcinogens have been used to produce experimental brain tumors in animals, and it has been suggested that carcinogens may play a role in the development of human brain tumors. However, there is little direct evidence or support of this hypothesis. Thus, although much is known about the types of cells from which tumors arise, little has been determined about factors that give rise to their development.

Brain tumors have been classified as intrinsic and extrinsic. Extrinsic brain tumors arise from tissues outside of the brain (such as the meninges) and intrinsic brain tumors arise principally from supporting cells in the brain tissue (although some tumors arise from nerve cells, glandular tissue, and blood vessels). The principal categories of brain tumors, in order of the frequency with which they occur, are:

gliomas, arising from neuroglia and ependymal tissue; (2) meningiomas, arising from the meninges; (3) pituitary adenomas, arising from the pituitary gland; (4) neurolemmomas, including neurofibromas and acoustic neuromas; (5) metastatic tumors from various primary sites throughout the body; and (6) blood vessel tumors (which may also be classified under categories of cerebral vascular disease).

It is customary to distinguish between benign and malignant tumors. However, the division of tumors of the brain, as compared with tumors involving other parts of the body, is nowhere nearly as clear in this respect. Gliomas customarily demonstrate characteristic features of malignancy, although some gliomas are slow-growing. It must be recognized that any tumor of the brain, including those that are classified as benign, may gradually increase in size and produce damage that is eventually fatal. The particular location of a tumor may also have considerable influence on the consequences. For example, a tumor near the aqueduct of Sylvius may obstruct cerebrospinal fluid circulation and result in a fatal increase in intracranial pressure.

Tumors may be classified according to their degree of malignancy. This applies particularly to gliomas because a number of other tumors do not show a sufficient degree of growth to be characterized as malignant. Gliomas, however, are classified according to the number of differentiated (as contrasted with embryonically immature) cells into Grades I, II, III, and IV. From a practical and therapeutic point of view, this grading of malignancy is more important than the predominant cell-type of the tumor, although the type of cell from which the tumor arises is related to the degree of malignancy. Gliomas classified as Grade I have 75 to 100 percent of differentiated cells, Grade II falls from 50 to 75 percent, Grade III ranges from 25 to 50 percent, and in Grade IV (the most malignant), 0 to 25 percent of the predominant glial cells are differentiated.

Intracranial tumors, due to their growth and the resultant increase in the content of the skull, frequently show signs of increased intracranial pressure, compression of tissue, and edema or swelling. Intracranial pressure may increase not only due to the growth of the lesion, but because of infarction or hemorrhage within the tumor, swelling due to metabolic factors and possibly an inflammatory response following infarction or venous obstruction caused by the tumor, or obstruction of the flow of cerebrospinal fluid by the tumor. Increased intracranial pressure may be particularly apparent in the eye grounds (a condition called papilledema). The patient may have congestion of veins, edema, elevation of the optic disc, and in later stages, the presence of venous hemorrhages around the optic disc.

An increase in pressure above the tentorium may also result in a range of symptoms due to herniation of brain tissue through the tentorium with consequent damage to the midbrain, pons, and medulla oblongata. In fact, chronic increases in intracranial pressure may actually cause damage of the skull, and may sometimes be observed on plain skull films. In such instances there may be spontaneous repair of the bone damage, leading to new bone formation in the area overlying damage, referred to as hyperostosis. Such changes, not exclusively due to intracranial hypertension but apparently associated with the proximity of the tumor to the bone, occur especially among meningiomas.

Clinical Symptoms Associated with Intracranial Tumors

Headache is usually associated with brain tumors and is usually worse upon arising in the morning. It is often exacerbated by coughing, sneezing, straining at the stool, lifting, or sudden exertion, and may be relieved by lying prone. Headache is thought to be the first symptom of brain tumor in about 20 percent of patients, although, of course, headaches occur with many other conditions as well.

Vomiting may also occur in patients with brain tumors and is associated with increased intracranial pressure. The vomiting occurs more frequently on awakening in the morning.

Epileptic seizures appear as the first symptom of a brain tumor in about 15 percent of patients. A cause for particular concern is the initial onset of an epileptic seizure in adult subjects, and most neurologists and neurological surgeons feel that unexplained epilepsy in an adult should be regarded as a possible symptom of brain tumor until proven otherwise. Seizures may be of a variety of types, depending upon the area of the brain that is principally involved. Seizures occur with benign and slowly growing tumors as well as with more malignant tumors.

Additional symptoms may include drowsiness (or even somnolence or stupor), various clinical manifestations of dementia, impaired judgment, memory loss, etc., and complaints of abnormal or strange sensations in the head which are usually vaguely described.

Brain tumors may give rise to a great number of physical signs that are quite variable from one patient to another. These signs include papilledema, motor deficits, sensory abnormalities or losses, and other manifestations. However, the presence or absence of a brain tumor is best determined through use of contrast radiography or computed tomography rather than clinical evaluation.

Treatment of Brain Tumors

Surgical removal of brain tumors is generally the treatment of choice. However, in many instances, it is not possible to effect a complete removal of the tumor and re-growth will occur. Surgery is frequently followed by radiation therapy, given in conjunction with high doses of corticosteroids. Treatment may result in increased survival time for the patient, particularly in cases of more slowly growing intrinsic tumors. Radiation therapy is an important factor in survival time of patients with rapidly growing gliomas, even though the survival period is generally shorter.

Although much research has been done with chemotherapy of brain tumors, the results have not been particularly successful. The use of various drug combinations, together with chemotherapy and radiation therapy, is currently a topic of active investigation.

Nonmalignant tumors, such as meningiomas, can usually be removed surgically without difficulty. The recurrence rate is low, and the prognosis for recovery is good.

Classification of Brain Tumors

Tumors are presently classified most often according to the cell type from which they arise; occasionally they are named for their location or the structure involved. An attempt has been made by the World Health Organization to develop an internationally acceptable classification. This effort classifies tumors under the headings of neuroepithelial tissue, tumors of nerve sheath cells, meningeal and related tumors, primary malignant lymphomas, tumors of blood vessel origin, tumors originating from germ cells, vascular malformations, tumors of the anterior pituitary body, metastatic tumors, tumors that represent local extensions from tumors of specific regions, a broad range of malformations that are space-occupying and fall under the general tumor category, and unclassified tumors. These various subdivisions, in turn, have a great number of more specific classifications and subclassifications. More detailed information regarding this classification system of the World Health Organization may be found in an article by Cobb and Youmans (1982) and a system of classification, quite popular in the United States, also has been devised by Russell and Rubinstein (1977).

Finally, the basic classification system proposed by Bailey and Cushing (1926) and the grading system proposed by Kernohan and his associates (Kernohan, Mabon, Svien, and Adson, 1949; Kernohan and Sayre, 1952) are frequently used. Thus, we should direct our attention briefly to a correlation of these systems of terminology.

Bailey and Cushing referred to astrocytomas as relatively slowly growing gliomas arising from astrocytes. Kernohan et al. referred to these lesions as astrocytomas, Grades I and II. The glioblastoma multiforme by Bailey and Cushing is referred to by Kernohan et al. as astrocytoma, Grades III and IV. Oligodendrogliomas are included in both systems, but Kernohan et al. grade them from I to IV, even though there are few that qualify as grades III and IV. Ependymomas are listed in each classification system without grading, as are medulloblastomas and pinealomas. The principal difference in the two systems is that Kernohan et al. used a Roman numeral I to IV grading system whenever possible. This translates into grading principally of astrocytomas and oligodendrogliomas, with astrocytomas in the Bailey-Cushing system being astrocytomas Grade I and II in the Kernohan system and glioblastoma multiforme in the Bailey-Cushing system being astrocytomas Grade III and IV. Grading is not relevant in the case of oligodendrogliomas because most of them are slowly growing and do not fall into grades III and IV.

CASE #1

Name:	P.H.	Sex:	Male
Age:	67	Handedness:	Right
Education:	16	Occupation:	Salesman

Following the procedure previously described, the first step in interpretation will be to inspect results obtained on the Wechsler Scale. The patient earned a Verbal I.Q. (104) that was in the upper part of the Average range and a Performance I.Q. (88) that was in the upper part of the Low Average range. These values yielded a Full Scale I.Q. (90) that was at the lower limit of the Average range. (The reader may note that the Performance I.Q. seems to be quite high considering the limited credit that the patient was able to obtain on the individual Performance subtests. The inordinate age adjustment for older persons on the Wechsler-Bellevue Scale accounts for this apparent disparity.)

Referring to the four Verbal subtests that generally provide the most valid information regarding the subject's prior intellectual development, we find that this man performed at the average level or above on three of them: Information, Comprehension and Vocabulary. Considering the fact that the patient was a college graduate, it is likely that his score of 8 on Similarities, the fourth subtest in this group of indicators, reflects some degree of impairment.

Of the Verbal subtests, Arithmetic is probably the most valid indicator of cerebral damage; however, compared with many of the other individual tests in the Battery, it is not a particularly good index of brain dysfunction. In view of P.H.'s other deficient scores, it is not surprising to see that he earned a poor score on Arithmetic as well.

The Digit Span subtest is often impaired in both brain- damaged and control subjects who are under the stress of illness and hospitalization. Therefore, this patient's score of 7 on Digit Span is not significant and does not contribute to the overall impression of his abilities that we have formulated so far.

Summarizing the results of the Verbal subtest scores, then, we can say that this man has had a relatively good intellectual level in the past, as demonstrated by his performances on measures that are

HALSTEAD-REITAN NEUROPSYCHOLOGICAL TEST BATTERY

Patient _____ P.H. _____ Age __67__ Sex __M__ Education __16__ Handedness __R__

__x__ WECHSLER-BELLEVUE SCALE (FORM I)

___ WAIS

VIQ	104
PIQ	88
FIS IQ	90
VWS	43
PWS	9
Total WS	52
Information	13
Comprehension	11
Digit Span	7
Arithmetic	4
Similarities	8
Vocabulary	13
Picture Arrangement	3
Picture Completion	4
Block Design	1
Object Assembly	0
Digit Symbol	1

HALSTEAD'S NEUROPSYCHOLOGICAL TEST BATTERY

Category Test   Discontinued

Tactual Performance Test

Dominant hand: _____ 10.0 (1 block in)

Non-dominant hand: _____ 10.0 (0 blocks in)

Both hands: _____ 8.0 (0 blocks in)

         Total Time __28.0__

         Memory __unable to do__

         Localization __unable to do__

Seashore Rhythm Test

Number Correct __15__   __10__

Speech-sounds Perception Test

Number of Errors   __34__

Finger Oscillation Test

Dominant hand: __52__   __52__

Non-dominant hand: __37__

TRAIL MAKING TEST

Part A: __120__ seconds

Part B: __227__ seconds Discontinued

Impairment Index __0.9__

REITAN-KLØVE SENSORY-PERCEPTUAL EXAM

				Error Totals	
RH____ LH.____	Both:RH____ LH _4_			RH____ LH _4_	
RH____ LF____	Both:RH____ LF _2_			RH____ LF _2_	
LH____ RF____	Both:LH _4_ RF____			RF____ LH _4_	
RE____ LE____	Both:RE____ LE _4_			RE____ LE _4_	

                  not   not

RV____ LV _4_ Both:RV __done__ LV __done__

      _4_   RV____ LV____

      _4_

TACTILE FINGER RECOGNITION

R 1__ 2__ 3__ 4__ 5__   R _0_ / 20

L 1__ 2__ 3_4_ 4_ 5__   L _4_ / 20

FINGER-TIP NUMBER WRITING — Bilateral mistakes — Patient confused

R 1__ 2__ 3__ 4__ 5__   R___ /___

L 1__ 2__ 3__ 4__ 5__   L___ /___

Visual Field Examination: Left homonymous hemianopia.

REITAN-INDIANA APHASIA SCREENING TEST

Form for Adults and Older Children

Name: P.H.   Age: 67

Copy SQUARE See	Repeat TRIANGLE
Name SQUARE	Repeat MASSACHUSETTS
Spell SQUARE	Repeat METHODIST EPISCOPAL
Copy CROSS See	Write SQUARE
Name CROSS	Read SEVEN
Spell CROSS	Repeat SEVEN
Copy TRIANGLE See	Repeat/Explain HE SHOUTED THE WARNING.
Name TRIANGLE	Write HE SHOUTED THE WARNING.
Spell TRIANGLE	Compute 85 – 27 =
Name BABY	Compute 17 X 3 = "54" then corrected.
Write CLOCK	Name KEY
Name FORK	Demonstrate use of KEY
Read 7 SIX 2	Draw KEY See
Read MGW	Read PLACE LEFT HAND TO RIGHT EAR. Place right hand to right ear.
Reading I	Place LEFT HAND TO RIGHT EAR RH to left ear - self-corrected.
Reading II	Place LEFT HAND TO LEFT ELBOW LH to right elbow - self-corrected.

he shouted the warning

Square

Clock

85 − 27
27
——
58

most reflective of past intellectual acquisitions. P.H.'s scores on subtests requiring more immediate utilization of problem-solving skills suggest that he has experienced some diminution of these cognitive abilities. Next, we will consider the Performance subtests of the Wechsler Scale. P.H. was able to make little progress on this section, although he did manage to score 3 points on the Picture Arrangement subtest and 4 points on the Picture Completion subtest.

On the Wechsler Scale, the Digit Symbol subtest is probably the measure most sensitive to the general effects of cerebral damage (regardless of lesion location). Picture Arrangement and Block Design are the subtests most sensitive to right cerebral damage. Not uncommonly, a person with a right cerebral lesion will have his highest Performance score on the Picture Completion subtest, demonstrating this test's low sensitivity to cerebral dysfunction.

Comparing P.H's pronounced deficits on the Performance subtests to the fairly good scores on the Verbal subtests, one could certainly raise a question of right cerebral damage in this man. Although not yet demonstrated in the literature, clinical experience suggests that involvement of the posterior part of the right cerebral hemisphere causes greater deficit on Performance intelligence measures than do lesions of the right frontal lobe. In the case of this patient, results from the Wechsler Scale alone would be sufficient to question the integrity of the right cerebral hemisphere; as a general rule, though, scores on the Wechsler Scale considered by themselves are of equivocal significance.

The next step in the process of interpretation is evaluating the results on the most sensitive measures in the Halstead-Reitan Battery. This man was severely impaired on all four of these tests: Impairment Index — 0.9; Category Test — unable to do; Trails B — worked for 227 seconds before the test was discontinued due to the patient's confusion; Tactual Performance Test, Localization component — unable to do. It is apparent from these results that this man was severely impaired in tasks that call for immediate adaptive abilities, despite his above-average Vocabulary score.

Considering this patient's results on these general indicators of cerebral status, it would not be surprising to find poor scores on measures that require close attention and concentration, indicating that even the first level of central processing (*See* Fig. 1-1) is significantly impaired. In such a case it is likely that any lateralizing indicators will be derived from rather simple and discrete procedures and the patient will have great difficulty with more complex tests that require continuing attention, organization of integral components, and memory of one aspect of the test as compared with another (e.g., Category Test and Tactual Performance Test). In fact, the patient was scarcely able to make any progress at all on the Tactual Performance Test. When a patient performs so poorly on all three trials of the test, no hypotheses regarding lateralization of damage can be made by comparing the performances of the two hands.

The lateralizing indicators of the Battery are the next factors to be considered. P.H. demonstrated relatively few deficits related specifically to the status of the left cerebral hemisphere. He initially made an error when he responded to the arithmetic problem, 17 X 3. Research has documented that dyscalculia occurs about three times more frequently with left cerebral lesions than with right. Based on this mistake alone, though, it would be difficult to conclude that this patient had dyscalculia.

The patient became confused in reading PLACE LEFT HAND TO RIGHT EAR, demonstrated this confusion when asked to perform the task, and responded incorrectly when asked to place his left hand to his left elbow. In this case one could question whether these mistakes actually constituted evidence of dyslexia and right-left confusion, or whether P.H.'s general state of confusion was sufficiently disabling to account for these errors. Although this question may not be answered unequivocally, it is clear that specific signs of left cerebral involvement were not very abundant. One might wonder whether the poor score on the Speech-sounds Perception Test represents a specific loss in the language area (particularly considering some of the good Verbal subtest scores on the Wechsler Scale), but it is more likely that the requirement for close attention and continued concentration was the basis for the 34 errors on this measure. Thus, so far, the findings are not sufficient to support a hypothesis of a specific lesion of the left cerebral hemisphere.

However, a number of right cerebral deficits were identified. Besides the low Performance I.Q. as compared with the Verbal I.Q., this patient showed distinct and definite evidence of constructional dyspraxia. He was not able to complete either the square or triangle correctly. He made fairly good progress with the cross, but when he reached the lower line of the left arm he became completely confused, did not know which way to turn, and refused to continue drawing the figure. He also had definite difficulty with the key, particularly on the left side.

Another significant sign of right cerebral damage was the finding of a left homonymous hemianopia, indicating involvement of the visual pathway on the right side at some point posterior to the optic chiasm. One can confidently infer that the geniculostriate tract (rather than the optic tract) was involved because of the additional right cerebral indicators.

Among the findings most suggestive of right cerebral involvement were the results from the Sensory-perceptual Examination. Even though P.H. made no mistakes in perceiving unilateral stimuli on either side, he had great difficulty perceiving either a tactile or auditory stimulus to the left side when it was given in competition with a stimulus to the right side. Testing of perception of bilateral simultaneous visual stimuli was precluded by the left homonymous visual field loss. Although the patient did not have a great deal of difficulty on the left hand on tactile finger recognition, his only errors did occur on that side. Actually, it is quite surprising that P.H. could concentrate well enough to complete all 20 trials on his right hand without making a single error. On the more complex task of finger-tip number writing perception the patient was so confused that he could not respond correctly to stimuli given to either hand.

It is especially important to note that results of tests of bilateral simultaneous stimulation were positive only on the left side of the body and that not a single error, either with unilateral or bilateral simultaneous stimulation, occurred on the right side. In terms of cerebral damage, then, the lateralizing findings were quite convincing for right hemisphere dysfunction. The fact that the patient did not have difficulty in tactile finger localization on the left hand (except for one finger) should not be used to attenuate the significance of the pronounced lateralized deficit obtained with tests of bilateral simultaneous sensory stimulation. A general rule in neuropsychological interpretation is to depend upon distinct positive findings to infer brain damage and recognize that negative results, or the relative retention of premorbid abilities, may be due to many factors.

Finally, this man had normal finger tapping speed in his right hand

(52) but was comparatively slow with his left hand (37). He was still able to tap an average of 3.7 times/second with his left hand, but, expecting only about a 10 percent difference in favor of the preferred hand, we would have postulated that this man should have been able to tap about 4.7 times/second with his left hand.

It is important to note that when using the Halstead-Reitan Test Battery all information is recorded and organized with relation to its pre-determined significance. No aspect of the data is ignored. Every test must be considered because the Battery, as a whole, has been organized to represent cerebral functions generally and the entire cerebral cortex must be evaluated in order to gain a total picture of the individual's comparative strengths and weaknesses. The "battery" approach has a great advantage over other methods of evaluation because it provides a balanced evaluation of the functional status of the entire cerebral cortex for the individual subject.

Others (e.g., Christenson, 1975; Lezak, 1976) have argued that composing a battery appropriate for each individual subject, based upon the subject's complaints and the clinical judgment of the neuro-psychologist, will provide an assessment for each patient which is pertinent and as economical as possible. However, if we had followed this method of evaluation and had examined the patient P.H. with only right hemisphere tests, we would never have known about the compelling nature of the right cerebral indicators as compared with the relative absence of left cerebral indicators. More importantly, perhaps, we would have never been aware of the severe generalized impairment this man was experiencing.

At this point we will summarize our findings on this patient. Considering the data from the entire Battery, it is apparent that the right cerebral hemisphere was involved and the lesion was of such a destructive nature that intellectual and cognitive functions were significantly deficient. It is also clear that the lesion principally involved the posterior part of the right cerebral hemisphere. Because of the slow finger tapping speed with the left hand, we know that the right posterior frontal area was also affected. The principal deficits on the Sensory-perceptual Examination involving tactile and auditory input suggest that the temporal and parietal lobes were areas of focal involvement. This inference was also supported by evidence of involvement of the right geniculostriate pathway, severe constructional dyspraxia, and pronounced deficits on the Performance subtests of the Wechsler Scale.

Thus, there is evidence that P.H. had a large focal lesion involving the posterior part of the right cerebral hemisphere. The right cerebral deficits as well as generalized confusion can be produced by a lesion of this type. It did not appear that the left cerebral hemisphere was specifically involved; the overall general confusion may have been responsible for the small number of left cerebral indicators.

As a final step in interpretation, one must consider the types of lesions that could have been responsible for these findings. A critical item of information to keep in mind is that this man was not hemiplegic on his left side: he was still able to tap 3.7 times/second with his left hand. We had initially considered finger tapping speed to be impaired on the left side; in light of the entire set of test results suggesting right cerebral damage, though, one might be amazed to find that P.H. had any finger tapping speed at all on his left side. Persons who have suffered strokes causing severe lateralized deficits nearly always have severe motor impairment across from the damaged hemisphere (Hom & Reitan, 1982). Therefore, if this man had experienced a stroke involving the right middle cerebral artery, he almost certainly would have had more severe motor impairment of the left upper extremity.

Patients with intrinsic tumors sometimes have severe motor impairment corresponding with other indications of lateralized cerebral damage, but they often experience only a milder degree of deficit (Hom & Reitan, 1982; Hom & Reitan, 1984). The relative retention of finger tapping speed with the left hand, despite some impairment, is a crucial finding in this case: it leans the diagnostic conclusion toward a rapidly growing intrinsic tumor of the posterior part of the right cerebral hemisphere. On autopsy, it was confirmed that this man had a large astrocytoma, grade III, involving the right parietal-temporal occipital area.

CASE #2

Name:	E.E.	Sex:	Male
Age:	42	Handedness:	Right
Education:	7	Occupation:	Carpenter

E.E. did poorly on the Wechsler-Bellevue Scale, earning a Verbal I.Q. that fell in the range of Borderline intelligence (73) and a Performance I.Q. that was in the lower part of the Low Average range (82). The Verbal subtests most useful for indicating premorbid intelligence (Information, Comprehension, Similarities and Vocabulary) all had weighted scores of 5 or 6. On the basis of these results one might question whether this man ever had general intelligence levels that were in the normal range.

We also note that E.E. had low scores on Digit Span (0) and Arithmetic (3). Digit Span has been found to be of limited value in identifying the effects of cerebral damage (Reitan, 1959a) because performances may be adversely affected by many factors other than brain damage. However, a score of 0 cannot be ignored and probably has some significance. The Arithmetic score (3) is of equivocal significance with respect to brain-related impairment. If we were to presume that this man had limited verbal intellectual skills all of his life, it might not be unusual to find that the Arithmetic score was somewhat lower than scores for the other Verbal subtests.

The scores for the Performance subtests were also low and showed minimal variability. The score of 7 on Picture Completion has relatively little neuropsychological meaning, principally because this test does not contribute much reliable information regarding brain-behavior relationships. In this case, then, results from the Wechsler Scale are not particularly helpful in gaining an understanding of possible impairment of brain functions. Our best presumption would be that the patient may have some deficits (based on the Digit Span and possibly Arithmetic scores), but that his general intellectual level has always been limited.

The four most sensitive indicators in the Halstead-Reitan Battery all yielded poor performances. The patient earned a Halstead Impairment Index of 1.0 (all of the tests had results in the brain-damaged

HALSTEAD-REITAN NEUROPSYCHOLOGICAL TEST BATTERY

Patient _____E.E._____ Age ___42___ Sex ___M___ Education ___7___ Handedness ___R___

_x_ WECHSLER-BELLEVUE SCALE (FORM I)
___ WAIS

VIQ	73
PIQ	82
FIS IQ	75
VWS	20
PWS	25
Total WS	45
Information	6
Comprehension	6
Digit Span	0
Arithmetic	3
Similarities	5
Vocabulary	6
Picture Arrangement	4
Picture Completion	7
Block Design	4
Object Assembly	5
Digit Symbol	5

HALSTEAD'S NEUROPSYCHOLOGICAL TEST BATTERY

Category Test	98

Tactual Performance Test
Dominant hand: 14.9
Non-dominant hand: 13.7
Both hands: 4.6

Total Time___33.3___
Memory___1___
Localization___1___

Seashore Rhythm Test
Number Correct___13___   10

Speech-sounds Perception Test
Number of Errors   33

Finger Oscillation Test
Dominant hand: 36   36
Non-dominant hand:___31___

TRAIL MAKING TEST
Part A: _105_ seconds
Part B: _379_ seconds

Impairment Index___1.0___

Miles ABC Test of Ocular Dominance
Right eye: _1_ Left eye: _9_

TACTILE FINGER RECOGNITION
R 1_0_ 2_0_ 3_0_ 4_0_ 5_0_   R _0_ / 20
L 1_0_ 2_0_ 3_0_ 4_0_ 5_0_   L _0_ / 20

REITAN-INDIANA APHASIA SCREENING TEST

Form for Adults and Older Children

Name: _____ E.E. _____ Age: 42

Copy SQUARE	Repeat TRIANGLE
Name SQUARE	Repeat MASSACHUSETTS
Spell SQUARE	Repeat METHODIST EPISCOPAL
	"Mestacul Epistacul" Central dysarthria
Copy CROSS	Write SQUARE
Name CROSS	Read SEVEN
Spell CROSS	Repeat SEVEN
Copy TRIANGLE	Repeat/Explain HE SHOUTED THE WARNING.
Name TRIANGLE	Write HE SHOUTED THE WARNING.
	See – Dysgraphia
Spell TRIANGLE	Compute 85 – 27 =
Spelling dyspraxia – See attempt at writing.	Dyscalculia & Visual number dysgnosia
Name BABY	Compute 17 X 3 =
	Cannot do.
Write CLOCK	Name KEY
Name FORK	Demonstrate use of KEY
Read 7 SIX 2 Visual letter	Draw KEY
"7.X.2" "7.SIX.X.2" dysgnosia	
Read MGW	Read PLACE LEFT HAND TO RIGHT EAR.
Reading I	Place LEFT HAND TO RIGHT EAR
Some dyslexia	
Reading II	Place LEFT HAND TO LEFT ELBOW
Some dyslexia	

▢

✚

△ crayon

clock

Square

cross

~~seven~~

~~(scribbled out)~~

8 5
2 4
6 1

He should the warrant

range). He did not do well on the Category Test, earning a score of 98. The score of 379 seconds on Trails B demonstrates an even worse comparative performance. On his drawing of the Tactual Performance Test board the subject was able to localize only one of the ten shapes.

At this point the reader may question whether these tests were merely reflecting the information already shown by the Wechsler Scale, namely, that this man has quite limited abilities. His overall ability limitations are probably part of the reason for the poor scores, but the deficits shown on the Category Test and Trails B go beyond allowances for persons with this man's I.Q. values and we would judge that the test results indicate the possibility of significant impairment of higher brain functions. The patient performed poorly on all measures in the Battery and did not have a single score in the normal range.

Many psychologists who are strongly oriented toward a level-of-performance approach may wonder how inferences regarding brain-related impairment can be discerned in persons whose general ability level is (for whatever reason) distinctly limited. As we will illustrate in several cases, an approach which considers only how well the subject has performed on the tests is inadequate for understanding brain-behavior relationships.

There can be many reasons why psychological tests (including neuropsychological tests) may be performed poorly. Besides considering the level of performance, it is necessary to evaluate the test results in terms of patterns and relationships, specific pathognomonic deficits, and comparative performances on the two sides of the body. In this case, patterns and relationships and comparative performances on the two sides of the body were of limited value. However, this man showed definite dysphasia and these pathognomonic signs were unequivocal in indicating the presence of left cerebral damage. This case was specifically selected to illustrate how pathognomonic signs contribute to the interpretation of test results.

Any relationships and patterns among higher level functions tended to be obscured by the generally poor performances of this patient. Although the Verbal I.Q. was nine points lower than the Performance I.Q., one could not postulate left cerebral damage from this finding alone. As noted previously, even the patient's poor performances on the four most sensitive indicators of the Halstead-Reitan Battery might be attributed to his overall low level of general intelligence.

Comparisons of performances on the two sides of the body also yielded little useful information. The patient performed poorly with his left hand (13.7 minutes) compared with his right (14.9 minutes) on the Tactual Performance Test, a finding that might suggest right cerebral damage; however, there were no other specific indications of damage to the right cerebral hemisphere.

Except for the key, the patient's figure drawings were adequate. The key was drawn in such a limited fashion that it is difficult to evaluate. Only one notch was made on the stem but the overall depiction, including the handle and the details of the teeth of the key, was so primitively drawn that the effort appears to be in the category of a generally poor performance rather than indicative of the types of problems in dealing with spatial relationships that characterize right cerebral damage.

Finger tapping speed was slow with both hands, and perhaps just a little slow with the left hand (31) as compared with the right (36). However, the difference was not sufficient even to use as a basis for postulating right cerebral damage.

Surprisingly, on the Tactile Finger Recognition Test the patient was able to identify all fingers on each hand without a single error. Although this finding would not contraindicate the presence of cerebral damage, it might be used as a basis for hypothesizing that the damage was not principally in the parietal areas. This patient was examined before tests of tactile, auditory, and visual perception and finger-tip number writing perception were done as a standard part of the Halstead-Reitan Battery. It is apparent that an insufficient number of procedures for comparison of the two sides of the body was available, but no significant evidence was derived from the tests that were used.

Results on the Aphasia Test, however, were of distinct and definite significance. The patient was able to perform a number of the tasks but the errors he made were quite typical of persons with left cerebral lesions. Even though not a formal part of the test, he was asked to write the word "triangle." His effort, which did not even come close to being correct, is shown in the figure next to the drawing of the triangle. One might wonder whether the man was making a serious effort, since it is obvious that he was able to write other words satisfactorily. In some patients with acutely destructive lesions, occasional instances of absolutely inadequate and suddenly confused performances occur. This extremely poor performance is probably indicative of such an episode and most likely represents an acutely destructive left hemisphere lesion rather than a deliberately uncooperative attitude. The patient was just not able to get started writing the word and could not manage to get the letters to come out correctly. This type of manifestation represents both spelling dyspraxia and dysgraphia.

Another instance of dysgraphia, and one that is considerably more typical, was shown in the patient's confusion with the word "warning." Again, he was just not able to get the letters written in a manner that would represent the word. One could offer the patient's limited educational background and low level of general intelligence as a basis for this problem, but it is much more likely that dysgraphia is the proper explanation.

The patient also had difficulty in reading simple symbolic material. In his first attempt to read 7 SIX 2, he failed to recognize that SIX represented a word. When asked to do the task again and be sure to get it right, E.E. responded by including the word SIX, but demonstrated his confusion again by adding the letter "X." This deficit suggests that the patient has a degree of visual letter dysgnosia as well as dyslexia. On the specific reading items the patient again had difficulty, but the examiner did not record the problem specifically. Thus, at this point we do not know exactly what the errors were, and, as a result, cannot evaluate them. We have made a point of noting carefully in the instructions for the Aphasia Test (in this volume and Reitan, 1984) that the examiner should try to record exactly what the patient says or does.

Although the patient was able to repeat "TRIANGLE" and "MASSACHUSETTS" correctly, he became confused with METHODIST EPISCOPAL. The type of error he made was a substitution of syllables, even though the enunciation was fairly distinct. Omission, addition, or substitution of syllables in enunciation is characteristic of persons with left cerebral damage (Wheeler and Reitan, 1962).

E.E. also had difficulty comprehending and dealing with the symbolic significance of numbers. In attempting to work the problem $85-27=$, he initially copied down the numbers incorrectly and, unfortunately, was able to cross them out before the examiner could stop him. He proceeded to attempt to solve the problem again, and, even though subtracting correctly, wrote "24" instead of "27." It was apparent that this man was significantly confused in dealing with numbers and arithmetical procedures, even though his difficulty might have been at least partly related to his limited educational background.

The type of confusion this man showed in dealing with numbers and arithmetical processes occurs about four times as frequently with left cerebral damage than with right cerebral damage (Wheeler & Reitan, 1962). Whether one calls this kind of confusion dyscalculia or visual number dysgnosia is probably of little significance in terms of evaluating the individual patient; that the difficulty did occur is the most important element.

In summary, the Aphasia Examination yielded evidence of spelling dyspraxia, dysgraphia, visual letter dysgnosia, reading difficulty that probably represented a degree of dyslexia, central dysarthria, and confusion of numerical symbols which may have represented visual number dysgnosia and dyscalculia. These findings were unequivocal in identifying significant damage of the left cerebral hemisphere.

The next question the examiner must consider concerns the type of lesion that could have produced these deficits and its location. In addition to a relatively low general ability level, brain-sensitive tests indicate that this man has a very significant degree of generalized cerebral impairment. Such a degree of impairment is often associated with relatively serious brain lesions. The patient has definite dysphasia, which implicates the left cerebral hemisphere. He did not show corresponding deficits involving the right upper extremity, and, in fact, made no errors on either hand in tactile finger localization. This finding suggests that the lesion probably does not specifically involve the parietal areas.

Given this information, it may be helpful to review the nature of the aphasic difficulties. This man had distinct receptive difficulties (visual letter dysgnosia and dyslexia) as well as pronounced expressive problems. His most distinct manifestation of an abnormal performance occurred in his attempt to write "triangle." It is the rule rather than the exception that patients with aphasic deficits have both expressive and receptive losses. Expressive losses are commonly associated with damage to the anterior part of the speech area. Receptive losses (except for auditory verbal dysgnosia) are frequently present with involvement of any part of the language area. Auditory verbal dysgnosia is almost always associated with damage of the posterior part of the language area (posterior temporal-parietal area). We also note that this man did not have any lateralizing deficits involving the right side of the body, in sensory-perceptual functions, finger tapping speed or complex manipulatory skills (Tactual Performance Test).

Considering all of this information, we would postulate the presence of a lesion in the left temporal area. In the absence of any motor or sensory deficits (the visual fields were full), it is entirely unlikely that this lesion is vascular in nature. Vascular lesions, particularly when they have caused significant lateralized impairment (such as the aphasia in this case), would almost certainly have produced contralateral motor and sensory-perceptual losses (Hom & Reitan, 1982). Aphasic symptoms may be produced by any serious structural damage, but the diagnostic clue in this case relates to the severe general impairment, aphasic symptoms, and relative absence of lateralized motor and sensory-perceptual skills. This particular combination characterizes intrinsic tumors. Perhaps as the tumor grows it is able to infiltrate neurons and thereby spare certain functions, despite involving higher level abilities. This particular pattern of symptoms has been confirmed by empirical observation. Although this would be a difficult case to diagnose blindly on the basis of neuropsychological data alone, it does appear that an intrinsic tumor, principally involving the left temporal lobe, would be the most likely possibility.

To briefly summarize the history and neurological findings, this patient was hospitalized on a psychiatric ward with a diagnosis of paranoid schizophrenia until shortly before this neuropsychological examination. An extensive work-up had been done, the patient's language and communicational problems were noted, and a detailed report had been written in which his language difficulties (which were variable over the course of time) were imaginatively related to his paranoid condition. Despite this pre-disposition to psychiatric diagnosis, a resident psychiatrist became suspicious of brain disease. In fact, he believed that he saw evidence of papilledema bilaterally in his examination of the patient's eye grounds. Referral of the patient to neurological surgeons led to a more appropriate history and it became apparent that the patient had experienced numbness of his right leg and arm for about three to four months, had what probably was a convulsion involving turning of the head and eyes to the right side one month before, and had experienced nausea and vomiting one week before the examination.

Neurological evaluation was normal and no papilledema could be seen, but the patient was thought to be confused. Cerebral angiography revealed a large mass in the left frontal-temporal area and surgery was done for partial removal of a left fronto-temporal glioma. The neuropsychological testing was done just prior to surgery.

CASE #3

Name:	K.H.	Sex:	Male
Age:	36	Handedness:	Right
Education:	9	Occupation:	Auto Inspector

Current Complaints and Pertinent History

K.H. was admitted to the hospital seven months prior to this neuropsychological examination. For three weeks before admission he had been experiencing severe headaches which were becoming progressively worse and not relieved by medication. At the time of admission, physical neurological examination revealed no abnormalities.

The day after admission the patient began vomiting and became stuporous. He was taken to surgery where occipital burr holes were made and his brain was visualized as being under obvious increased pressure. An angiogram showed a right frontal mass. A craniotomy and at least partial removal of a tumor of the right frontal lobe was performed. Histological examination identified the tumor as glioblastoma multiforme.

The patient did well post-operatively and his headaches subsided the day after surgery. X-ray therapy was instituted and K.H. was relatively free of symptoms and getting along quite well until he had a major motor seizure about 6½ months after the operation. A second seizure followed within hours and again three days later. His medication was changed and the seizures were more controlled.

About a month later K.H. was admitted to the hospital because of irregular breathing. His wife thought that he stopped breathing for long intervals when he was sleeping. She also indicated that the patient was having headaches again and since the operation (about seven months earlier), had been quick-tempered, nervous, irritable, and difficult to get along with in interpersonal relations.

At the time of admission, physical neurological examination revealed some impairment of the olfactory sense on the right side and equivocal reduction of pin-prick and touch sensitivity on the left face, left hand, and dorsal area of the left foot. K.H. also showed a possible Babinski response on the left side. An impression of memory impair-

HALSTEAD-REITAN NEUROPSYCHOLOGICAL TEST BATTERY

Patient ___K.H.___ Age __36__ Sex __M__ Education __9__ Handedness __R__

_x_ WECHSLER-BELLEVUE SCALE (FORM I)
___ WAIS

VIQ	96
PIQ	87
FIS IQ	92
VWS	42
PWS	32
Total WS	74
Information	8
Comprehension	11
Digit Span	7
Arithmetic	7
Similarities	9
Vocabulary	9
Picture Arrangement	7
Picture Completion	8
Block Design	9
Object Assembly	4
Digit Symbol	4

HALSTEAD'S NEUROPSYCHOLOGICAL TEST BATTERY

Category Test ___123___

Tactual Performance Test
Dominant hand: ___15.0 (2 blocks)___
Non-dominant hand: ___15.0 (4 blocks)___
Both hands: ___12.0 (10 blocks)___
Total Time __42.0 +__
Memory __6__
Localization __0__

Seashore Rhythm Test
Number Correct ___13___ ___10___

Speech-sounds Perception Test
Number of Errors ___8___

Finger Oscillation Test
Dominant hand: ___42___ ___42___
Non-dominant hand: ___32___

TRAIL MAKING TEST
Part A: __73__ seconds
Part B: __289__ seconds

STRENGTH OF GRIP
Dominant hand: __29.0__ kilograms
Non-dominant hand: __21.0__ kilograms

REITAN-KLØVE TACTILE FORM RECOGNITION TEST
Dominant hand: __—__ seconds; __0__ errors
Non-dominant hand: __—__ seconds; __0__ errors

REITAN-KLØVE SENSORY-PERCEPTUAL EXAM

				Error Totals	
RH___ LH___	Both:RH___ LH___			RH___ LH___	
RH___ LF___	Both:RH___ LF___			RH___ LF___	
LH___ RF___	Both:LH _2_ RF___			RF___ LH _2_	
RE___ LE___	Both:RE___ LE___			RE___ LE___	
RV___ LV___	Both:RV___ LV___			RV___ LV _4_	

__4__ __4__

TACTILE FINGER RECOGNITION
R 1___ 2___ 3 _2_ 4___ 5___ R _2_ / 20
L 1___ 2 _1_ 3 _2_ 4 _2_ 5 _1_ L _6_ / 20

FINGER-TIP NUMBER WRITING
R 1 _1_ 2 _1_ 3 _2_ 4 _2_ 5 _2_ R _8_ / 20
L 1 _3_ 2 _1_ 3 _2_ 4 _2_ 5 _2_ L _10_ / 20

Miles ABC Test of Ocular Dominance
Right eye: __10__ Left eye: __0__

Visual Field Examination: Lower left homonymous quadrantanopsia.

Impairment Index ___0.9___

MINNESOTA MULTIPHASIC
PERSONALITY INVENTORY

?	50	Hs	93
L	43	D	70
F	66	Hy	73
K	46	PD	62
		MF	51
		Pa	47
		Pt	69
		Sc	74
		Ma	65

REITAN-KLØVE
LATERAL-DOMINANCE EXAM
Show me how you:

throw a ball	R
hammer a nail	R
cut with a knife	R
turn a door knob	R
use scissors	R
use an eraser	R
write your name	R

Show me how you:

kick a football	R
step on a bug	R

REITAN-INDIANA APHASIA SCREENING TEST

Form for Adults and Older Children

Name: ___K. H._____ Age: ___36___

Copy SQUARE	Repeat TRIANGLE "Trianglar"
Name SQUARE	Repeat MASSACHUSETTS "Massachusess"
Spell SQUARE "S-Q-U-A-R"	Repeat METHODIST EPISCOPAL "Methodist Episcobal"
Copy CROSS	Write SQUARE
Name CROSS	Read SEVEN
Spell CROSS	Repeat SEVEN
Copy TRIANGLE	Repeat/Explain HE SHOUTED THE WARNING.
Name TRIANGLE "Diangular"	Write HE SHOUTED THE WARNING.
Spell TRIANGLE	Compute 85 – 27 = Patient said he divided. Examiner then gave 12-3.
Name BABY	Compute 17 X 3 =
Write CLOCK	Name KEY
Name FORK	Demonstrate use of KEY
Read 7 SIX 2	Draw KEY In spite of distraction by "shading", note "nose" of key.
Read MGW	Read PLACE LEFT HAND TO RIGHT EAR. "Place left hand on right ear". Immediately corrected.
Reading I	Place LEFT HAND TO RIGHT EAR
Reading II	Place LEFT HAND TO LEFT ELBOW

Clock Square

He ~~shouted~~ the warning

$$85$$
$$27$$
$$\overline{35}$$

$$51$$

$$12$$
$$-9$$
$$\overline{3}$$

ment and some difficulty in following instructions were also recorded on the basis of the physical neurological examination, but no other significant results were noted and the neurological examination was judged to show no remarkable findings.

Electroencephalographic tracings showed Delta waves, Grade II and Dysrhythmia, Grade II, particularly in the right frontal-temporal area. The full examination, however, suggested that there was no clinical evidence to support a hypothesis of re-growth of the tumor and that the seizures experienced by the patient probably represented some type of post-surgical irritation. Neuropsychological examination was performed two weeks after the current admission in order to provide additional information regarding the patient's status.

Neuropsychological Test Results

This 36-year-old man had completed nine grades in school and was employed as an inspector at an automobile assembly plant. He earned a Verbal I.Q. that fell in the Average range (96) and a Performance I.Q. that was in the Low Average range (87).

The weighted scores for the individual subtests of the Wechsler Scale suggested that the patient had not experienced any striking impairment of any aspect of Verbal intelligence. However, his poor score on the Digit Symbol subtest (4) may indicate that some deterioration from premorbid levels of intelligence has occurred.

In evaluating the Performance scales of the Wechsler Scale, we note that K.H. earned a comparably poor score on Object Assembly (4) but we have found that this subtest yields rather variable scores and does not, in general, have the reliability of the Digit Symbol subtest in reflecting impaired brain functions. The conclusion from the Wechsler-Bellevue Scale alone certainly could not be one of significant structural cerebral damage.

As is frequently observed among persons with cerebral lesions, K.H. performed very poorly on Halstead's Tests, despite not showing any gross impairment on the Wechsler Scale. The Halstead-Reitan Battery's four most sensitive indicators of the biological condition of the brain all had scores suggesting impaired cerebral functioning: Impairment Index — 0.9 (90 percent of the test results were in the brain-damaged range); Category Test — 123; Tactual Performance Test, Localization component — 0; and Trail Making Test, Part B — 289 seconds. The only score in the Battery in the normal range was the Tactual Performance Test, Memory Component (6). Considering the results of these general indicators, there is no doubt that this patient has serious neuropsychological deficits.

The next step in interpretation is to determine whether there is any lateralizing information. The subject's finger tapping speed with his non-preferred (left) hand was somewhat reduced compared to his preferred hand (32 vs. 42). A 10 percent reduction in speed with the non-preferred hand is generally anticipated. We also note that K.H.'s grip strength in the left hand is reduced more than the 10 percent we would expect: 21 vs. 29 kg.

At this point the interpreter should question whether the deficits in finger tapping speed and grip strength are due to a peripheral dysfunction or actually reflect impairment of the right cerebral hemisphere. Results on the Sensory-perceptual Examination give substantiation to a hypothesis of cerebral involvement: the patient had two instances of imperception on the left hand when in competition with the right face, and considerably more errors on the left hand than the right in Tactile Finger Recognition.

One of the most convincing signs for damage to the right hemisphere is found in the visual fields examination: the subject demonstrated a distinct lower left homonymous quadrantanopsia, suggesting right parietal involvement.

Next we will examine the test results for evidence of left hemisphere dysfunction. Looking at the responses on the Aphasia Screening Test, we find that K.H. spells SQUARE as "SQUAR." This response is not uncommon in persons with limited formal education and, in this case, cannot be considered spelling dyspraxia. When asked to name the shape of the triangle K.H. responded "diangular." This is a very unusual response and has to be considered evidence of a naming difficulty (dysnomia). The patient repeated "Massachusetts" and "Methodist Episcopal" with some mild slurring but in a still acceptable manner. He had more difficulty with "triangle," saying "trianglar." This substitution of syllables in the final syllable is a sign of central dysarthria.

The patient seemed to be a little confused when solving the arithmetic problem, 85–27 = . Although he came close to getting the right answer, K.H. told the examiner that he had divided.

Looking at the sample of his writing, we see that K.H. was also somewhat confused about the formation of the letters in the word "shouted."

On the Rhythm Test the subject performed very poorly. In fact, his score of 13 correct responses is less than would be expected from a chance performance. It is important to remember that the Rhythm Test is a general indicator of cerebral functioning, and does not have lateralizing significance for either hemisphere.

Although the Speech-sounds Perception Test score (8) is considered to be in the brain-damaged range, the interpreter should be aware that eight errors represents just one error over the cut-off point for normal subjects. Therefore, for K.H., this test was performed better than most of the other tests in the Battery. Since the Speech-sounds Perception Test is particularly sensitive to the integrity of the left cerebral hemisphere, the reader may wonder how to integrate the good score on the Speech-sounds Perception Test with the indicators of left hemisphere dysfunction demonstrated on the Aphasia Screening Test. The data is not contradictory; rather, it is complementary and helps the investigator localize the lesion to a frontal location. The good score on the Speech-sounds Perception Test suggests some remaining integrity in the posterior part of the left cerebral hemisphere.

The scores on the Minnesota Multiphasic Personality Inventory indicate that the patient had a deviant profile, particularly on the first three clinical scales (neurotic triad) and on the Schizophrenia Scale. Although one could offer a clinical interpretation of this profile, it is difficult to be confident regarding the validity of the MMPI findings in a patient who has a brain tumor and has undergone the types of difficulties experienced by this patient.

The overall results (especially the left lower homonymous quadrantanopsia) clearly implicate right cerebral damage. It is not unusual for a lesion classified as being frontal to have crossed into the adjacent parietal area, interrupting some fibers in the geniculostriate radiation, and thereby producing a homonymous defect of the contralateral lower quadrant of the visual fields. With definite evidence of a right cerebral lesions, one may wonder why the figure drawings of this patient were not done worse. The answer would necessarily require placement of the lesion more anteriorly, particularly involving the right frontal lobe (although the tactile losses shown by the patient point toward some implication of the right parietal lobe as well).

The remaining problem is to account for the indications of left cerebral dysfunction. We see no particular explanation for these results on the basis of the neurological findings. The initial blind interpretation of the results had postulated some type of structural damage in the right fronto-parietal area together with possible generalized impairment including the left cerebral hemisphere. We were reluctant, however, to postulate that the lesion had invaded the left cerebral hemisphere, although such a possibility is suggested by the neuropsychological findings.

CASE #4

Name:	E.H.	Sex:	Male
Age:	57	Handedness:	Right
Education:	16	Occupation:	Manufacturing Engineer

Current Complaints and Pertinent History

This patient experienced a major motor seizure four years before this neuropsychological examination. At that time the neurological examination was negative and EEG was normal. About a year later E.H. had a partial focal motor seizure involving his right upper extremity and was hospitalized. A pneumoencephalogram showed cortical atrophy with an enlarged ventricle on the left side of the brain. Despite taking antiepileptic medication, the patient continued to have Jacksonian seizures involving his right upper extremity.

About six months later E.H. was again re-admitted to the hospital. On the morning of admission he had a series of five right-sided seizures, beginning in the right forearm, and became somewhat stuporous. Physical and neurological examination, done after recovery, was entirely within the normal range. An EEG showed Dysrhythmia, Grade I in the left Sylvian area. The patient was again discharged and advised to continue antiepileptic medication.

The seizures involving the right side persisted and increased in frequency over the next two years. The patient maintained a log and recorded up to 90 seizures a month. The seizures began to involve more of the body; they still started in the right arm, then spread to the right face and the left arm. At the time of the current admission to the hospital the physical and neurological examination was still normal but EEG showed Delta waves Grade II in the right temporal area. Neuropsychological examination was done at this time.

Neuropsychological Test Results

The test results indicate that this man had a Verbal I.Q. that was well in the Superior range (129), but his Performance I.Q. was only in the upper part of the Average range (104). The scores on the Wechsler tests that best reflect intellectual background — Similarities

HALSTEAD-REITAN NEUROPSYCHOLOGICAL TEST BATTERY

Patient _____E.H._____ Age __57__ Sex __M__ Education __16__ Handedness __R__

_x_ WECHSLER-BELLEVUE SCALE (FORM I)
___WAIS

VIQ	129
PIQ	104
FIS IQ	116
VWS	69
PWS	33
Total WS	102
Information	15
Comprehension	17
Digit Span	10
Arithmetic	16
Similarities	11
Vocabulary	17
Picture Arrangement	6
Picture Completion	8
Block Design	8
Object Assembly	6
Digit Symbol	5

HALSTEAD'S NEUROPSYCHOLOGICAL TEST BATTERY
Category Test _____52_____

Tactual Performance Test
Dominant hand: _____12.9_____
Non-dominant hand: _____12.2 (7 blocks; disc.)_____
Both hands: _____—_____

Total Time__25.1 +__
Memory___5_____
Localization___0_____

Seashore Rhythm Test
Number Correct___27_____ _____3_____

Speech-sounds Perception Test
Number of Errors _____4_____

Finger Oscillation Test
Dominant hand: _____45_____ _____45_____
Non-dominant hand:___39_____

Impairment Index__0.7 (est)__

TRAIL MAKING TEST
Part A:___67__seconds
Part B:__149__seconds

Miles ABC Test of Ocular Dominance
Right eye:_10_ Left eye:_0_

REITAN-KLØVE SENSORY-PERCEPTUAL EXAM

					Error Totals	
RH____LH____	Both:RH____LH_1_				RH____LH_1_	
RH____LF____	Both:RH____LF____				RH____LF____	
LH____RF____	Both:LH____RF____				RF____LH____	
RE____LE____	Both:RE____LE____				RE____LE____	
RV____LV____	Both:RV____LV____					
____ ____		____			RV____LV____	
____ ____		____ ____				

MINNESOTA MULTIPHASIC
PERSONALITY INVENTORY

?	50	Hs	72
L	46	D	82
F	53	Hy	69
K	66	PD	57
		MF	59
		Pa	53
		Pt	79
		Sc	73
		Ma	48

TACTILE FINGER RECOGNITION
R 1___2___3___4___5 2_ R 2 / 20
L 1___2___3___4 1 5 1_ L 2 / 20

FINGER-TIP NUMBER WRITING
R 1_2_2_3 3_1 4___5 1_ R 7 / 20
L 1_1_2_2 3 2 4 1 5 2_ L 8 / 20

REITAN-INDIANA APHASIA SCREENING TEST

Form for Adults and Older Children

Name: _E. H._ Age: _57_

Copy SQUARE	Repeat TRIANGLE
Name SQUARE	Repeat MASSACHUSETTS
Spell SQUARE	Repeat METHODIST EPISCOPAL
Copy CROSS	Write SQUARE
Name CROSS	Read SEVEN
Spell CROSS	Repeat SEVEN
Copy TRIANGLE	Repeat/Explain HE SHOUTED THE WARNING.
Name TRIANGLE	Write HE SHOUTED THE WARNING.
Spell TRIANGLE	Compute 85 – 27 =
Name BABY	Compute 17 X 3 =
Write CLOCK	Name KEY
Name FORK	Demonstrate use of KEY In spite of the care used in the drawings, note the error in connecting the stem to the handle.
Read 7 SIX 2	Draw KEY
Read MGW	Read PLACE LEFT HAND TO RIGHT EAR.
Reading I	Place LEFT HAND TO RIGHT EAR
Reading II	Place LEFT HAND TO LEFT ELBOW

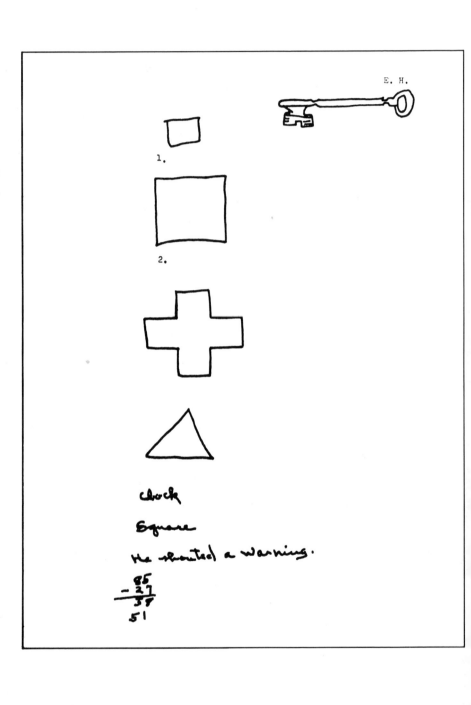

E. H.

1.

2.

clock

Square

He shouted a warning.

$$
\begin{array}{r}
85 \\
- 27 \\
\hline
58 \\
51
\end{array}
$$

(11), Information (15), Vocabulary (17) and Comprehension (17) — were consistently above average. Even so, the Similarities subtest may be somewhat depressed, suggesting that the patient may have experienced some degree of deficit on this measure.

The most significant finding was that the scores on all of the Performance subtests were much lower than the scores on the Verbal subtests. Results of this kind can conceivably occur in persons whose occupations require excellent verbal abilities, but using occupational status to predict either intelligence measurements or neuropsychological findings is hazardous. Nevertheless, one might possibly have expected E.H., a manufacturing engineer, to have had somewhat higher Performance subtest scores.

Each of the four most sensitive indicators in the Halstead-Reitan Battery yielded a poor score. Despite his excellent Verbal I.Q. the patient had an Impairment Index of 0.7 (about 70 percent of the tests in the brain-damaged range). His score on the Category Test (52) was not particularly poor; but considering the fact that there is a correlation of about .5 to .6 between Category score and either Verbal or Performance I.Q., one might postulate that this man had done poorly in relation to his own expected levels. His performance was definitely deficient on Trails B (149 seconds) and the Localization component of the Tactual Performance Test (0).

One might wonder how a person who did fairly well on Wechsler's tests could demonstrate such deficiencies on other ability measurements. Such results do not commonly occur among normal individuals. This patient deviated significantly from normal expectations (or the expected correlation between variables) on measures that were specifically related to the integrity of cerebral functioning. Thus, results in which there is a deviation from expected correlation are of particular significance in identifying the presence of brain-related deficits. The investigator must be familiar with the expected correlations (Reitan, 1956a; Reitan 1956b) to be able to recognize the deviation from these expectations in individual cases; this is one manner in which neuropsychological patterns of pathology are identified. In this case, the four most sensitive indicators definitely point toward the presence of impaired cerebral functions.

The next step in the analysis of the test results concerns organization of the test data in terms of good performances, average performances, and poor performances. This man performed very well on the Speech-sounds Perception Test (4), obtained an acceptable score on the Seashore Rhythm Test (27), and showed no difficulties on the Aphasia Test. The good scores on Speech-sounds Perception Test and the Rhythm Test indicate that E.H. has the capability to pay attention to stimulus material and maintain attention over time. Therefore, impairment at the first level of central processing cannot be offered as an explanation for his deficient scores on other measures.

E.H. performed at a mediocre level (although perhaps impaired with respect to his background abilities) on the Category Test (52), the Memory component of the Tactual Performance Test (5), finger tapping speed (45), and Tactile Finger Recognition. He demonstrated very poor performances on the Tactual Performance Test — Total Time (25.1 minutes), Part B of the Trail Making Test (149 seconds), the Localization component of the Tactual Performance Test (0), Finger-tip Number Writing Perception and drawing of the key (despite the generally good appearance).

This patient had particular difficulty on the Tactual Performance Test, finding the task to be extremely difficult and frustrating. When E.H. was using his left hand, he became so upset that the examiner had to discontinue the test. Thus, despite retaining certain abilities, the overall results point toward a considerable degree of impairment.

The Minnesota Multiphasic Personality Inventory showed that E.H. experienced a degree of emotional and affective distress. The elevated score on the Depression Scale strongly suggests some of the problems he was having in this area. He also was concerned about his physical condition, felt some degree of general anxiety, had lost a considerable degree of confidence in himself and was perhaps a little unrealistic in terms of his overall assessment of himself and others in his environment. The outstanding clinical impression, however, would be one of depressive tendencies.

A question could be raised as to whether the patient's depression could be responsible for his poor performances. Based on our study of many patients with depression, impaired performances on neuropsychological measures of the Halstead-Reitan Battery are rarely due to depression, and depression (as contrasted with cerebral damage) is usually of limited significance concerning interpretation of the results. This man may well have many reasons for emotional difficulties of adjustment, but past findings do not support a hypothesis that emotional stresses of this kind adversely affect neuropsychological measurements to any significant extent. Conversely, however, neurological problems are probably frequently reflected in MMPI results (Reitan, 1955a). Next, the interpretation concerns evaluation of the test findings with respect to lateralizing indications. As noted previously, the patient showed no evidence of aphasia. Right-left comparisons indicated comparable difficulties on both sides of the body in finger tapping speed, Tactile Finger Recognition and Finger-tip Number Writing Perception. However, the patient performed considerably worse with his left hand than his right hand on the Tactual Performance Test. He required about 12.2 minutes (placing only 7 blocks) with his left hand compared with 12.9 minutes (placing all 10 blocks) using the right (dominant) hand.

The patient also had some difficulty perceiving a tactile stimulus to his left hand when it was given in competition with the right hand. Single errors of this kind can sometimes occur because the subject's attention wanders during the test. The disparity between Verbal and Performance Wechsler scores is worth noting again here, and may have possibly gained some support, in the context of other results, for a hypothesis of right cerebral dysfunction.

A more specific positive indication of right cerebral dysfunction was the patient's drawing of the key. At first glance it would appear that the key is very well done. Obviously, the patient took great care, just as he did when drawing his other figures (as might be expected from an engineer). However, he made a type of error in drawing the handle of the key that is rarely, if ever, seen in persons with normal brain functions: He "closed off" the lower part of the handle. This kind of error does not occur among persons who are attempting to do a careful drawing. In addition, although less specifically diagnostic, the teeth of the key show a type of imbalance that is fairly characteristic of right cerebral dysfunction.

In summary, then, the overall set of test results suggests definite impairment of brain functions in a person who previously had excellent abilities (and still does in a number of respects). The right cerebral hemisphere is involved to a considerably greater extent than the left. In this instance, it would be difficult to specify the type of lesion involved. If one were considering a focal lesion, it would be impressive to see such little difficulty in tactile finger recognition and no disparity in finger tapping speed. These factors might incline the interpretation toward the possibility of an intrinsic tumor; we could not suggest though, that such a lesion could be implicated solely on the basis of these neuropsychological findings.

Finally, attention should be given to the apparent disparity between the history information and the neuropsychological findings. The reader will recall that this patient had a longstanding pattern of seizure involvement of the *right* upper extremity. The right upper extremity, obviously, is across from the left cerebral hemisphere and the lesion of this patient was finally identified as being an astrocytoma, Grade I, in the medial portion of the middle of the right temporal lobe. According to Falconer (1961) lesions in this location often cause ipsilateral epileptic manifestations. It is interesting to note that interpretations of diagnostic procedures, including the pneumoencephalogram and EEG, were apparently influenced by clinical evidence of right-sided seizures and interpreted as indicating a left cerebral disorder. There does not appear to be this type of prejudice with the Halstead-Reitan Battery. Identification of a small, slowly growing tumor does constitute something of a problem in interpretation, although the test results were accurate with respect to lateralization of the lesion and, in fact, showed general impairment on the most sensitive measures and implicated the right cerebral hemisphere rather than the left.

CASE #5

Name: M.F.   Sex: Male
Age: 52   Handedness: Right
Education: 8   Occupation: Radio News Announcer

Although this patient, M.F., also had a brain tumor, his test results were remarkably different from the previous cases. He performed extremely well on both Verbal and Performance I.Q. measures, showing no significant difference between the two. In addition, he had a Halstead Impairment Index of 0.4, completed Part B of the Trail Making Test in only 58 seconds, and performed well on both the Speech-sounds Perception Test and the Seashore Rhythm Test. Finally, the Sensory-perceptual Examination was done without a single error.

With this information, then, one might ask, "What kind of tumor, and in what location, could possibly be associated with such good neuropsychological test results?" The answer to this question depends upon identification of the positive indications of impairment and requires the neuropsychologist to be able to integrate the good results with the indications of deficit. A procedure of this kind obviously goes beyond a "level of performance" orientation. It would not be satisfactory to merely select the poorest scores for interpretation; every individual is going to have scores represented along a continuum, from best to worst, when an extensive number of tests has been given. Therefore, to understand the brain-behavior relationships in this case, it will be necessary to completely understand the organization of the Halstead-Reitan Neuropsychological Test Battery in terms of the various methods of inference.

We will begin by inviting the reader to consider the test results. Please take a moment at this point to review the data in detail and draw a conclusion concerning whether or not cerebral damage is indicated. If there is unequivocal evidence of impairment of cerebral functions, try to postulate the type of lesion, its lateralization and localization. If there is evidence of a brain lesion, decide whether its consequences are sufficiently devastating to impair even basic alertness and ability in concentration. Does the lesion have differential

HALSTEAD-REITAN NEUROPSYCHOLOGICAL TEST BATTERY

Patient ___M.F.___ Age __52__ Sex __M__ Education __8__ Handedness __R__

___x___ WECHSLER-BELLEVUE SCALE (FORM I)
_____ WAIS

VIQ	130
PIQ	136
FIS IQ	135
VWS	70
PWS	65
Total WS	135
Information	16
Comprehension	17
Digit Span	9
Arithmetic	13
Similarities	15
Vocabulary	16
Picture Arrangement	12
Picture Completion	15
Block Design	14
Object Assembly	13
Digit Symbol	11

HALSTEAD'S NEUROPSYCHOLOGICAL TEST BATTERY

Category Test	69

Tactual Performance Test

Dominant hand:	5.6
Non-dominant hand:	12.6
Both hands:	3.6
Total Time	21.8
Memory	7
Localization	1

Seashore Rhythm Test

Number Correct___27___ 3

Speech-sounds Perception Test

Number of Errors 5

Finger Oscillation Test

Dominant hand:	62	62
Non-dominant hand:	54	

TRAIL MAKING TEST

Part A: __43__ seconds
Part B: __58__ seconds

Impairment Index ___0.4___

Miles ABC Test of Ocular Dominance

Right eye: _7_ Left eye: _3_

TACTILE FINGER RECOGNITION

R 1___2___3___4___5___ R _0_ / 20
L 1___2___3___4___5___ L _0_ / 20

FINGER-TIP NUMBER WRITING

R 1___2___3___4___5___ R _0_ / 20
L 1___2___3___4___5___ L _0_ / 20

REITAN-INDIANA APHASIA SCREENING TEST

Form for Adults and Older Children

Name: M. F.   Age: 52

Copy SQUARE	Repeat TRIANGLE
Name SQUARE	Repeat MASSACHUSETTS
Spell SQUARE	Repeat METHODIST EPISCOPAL
Copy CROSS Note mild disparity of lateral extremities.	Write SQUARE
Name CROSS "C-R-O-I-S", immediately corrected.	Read SEVEN
Spell CROSS	Repeat SEVEN
Copy TRIANGLE	Repeat/Explain HE SHOUTED THE WARNING.
Name TRIANGLE	Write HE SHOUTED THE WARNING.
Spell TRIANGLE	Compute 85 – 27 =
Name BABY	Compute 17 X 3 =
Write CLOCK	Name KEY
Name FORK	Demonstrate use of KEY
Read 7 SIX 2	Draw KEY Note failure to connect inside of handle.
Read MGW	Read PLACE LEFT HAND TO RIGHT EAR.
Reading I	Place LEFT HAND TO RIGHT EAR
Reading II	Place LEFT HAND TO LEFT ELBOW

Clock

SQUARE

Square

He shouted the warning

$$85 \quad 51$$
$$- \frac{27}{58}$$

significance with regard to the specialized functions of the two cerebral hemispheres? Is the third and highest level of central processing (abstraction, reasoning, and logical analysis) involved? Are there any definite sensory-perceptual findings which would help with lateralization? What are the conclusions that the test findings require?

In referring to the test results, it is apparent that this 52-year-old man has high I.Q. values despite the fact that he finished only eight grades in school. M.F. had previously been a high-ranking U.S. Army officer. Both his Verbal I.Q. (130) and Performance I.Q. (136) values exceeded 98 percent of his age peers. It is apparent then that M.F. was exceptionally intelligent in terms of the criteria (tests) developed by Wechsler for this purpose.

One can inspect the subtest scores more specifically to discern possible impairment in particular areas. This man performed somewhat poorly on the Digit Span subtest (9) compared with his other scores. However, many people have difficulty on Digit Span when under stressful circumstances (and this man was hospitalized because of his difficulties). Our prior findings have indicated that Digit Span scores are not specifically relevant to organic impairment of cerebral functions. M.F. also did a little worse on Arithmetic (13) than he did on other Verbal subtests, but his score was still a standard deviation above the average. Thus, from the distribution of the Verbal subtests, there would scarcely be any reason to infer that this man had any significant brain-related impairment.

On the Performance subtests M.F. also showed a mild degree of variability, with scores ranging from 11 to 15. It might be considered significant that the lowest of these scores occurred on Digit Symbol, the subtest most sensitive to cerebral damage. However, the five Performance subtests were in adjacent order with respect to their levels of scoring, and it would appear that selecting the two lowest scores for attribution of deficit might well be considered to be a matter of convenience in interpretation. At least, it would be debatable that the Digit Symbol score was a reliable indication of cerebral damage.

Summarizing up to this point in our interpretation, then, we would note that this man performed extremely well on Wechsler's measures of general intelligence and would not be considered to have cerebral damage on the basis of these performances.

The Halstead-Reitan scores showed greater variability. One might well expect this if the patient had impairment of certain neuro-psychological functions and no impairment of others. M.F. earned a Halstead Impairment Index of 0.4, a borderline score with respect to cerebral impairment. It is important for the investigator to be aware that the Impairment Index must be attenuated to I.Q. values in its significance (Reitan, 1985). In other words, if a patient has excellent I.Q. values, we expect his Impairment Index to be low (even though some impairment of cerebral functions may be present). Therefore, in this case, the Impairment Index of 0.4 must be considered more suspicious than in the case of the average person. Furthermore, the tests contributing to the 0.4 Impairment Index — Category Test, Tactual Performance Test, Total Time and Tactual Performance Test, Localization Component—are especially sensitive measures. In fact, among the four most sensitive measures in the Halstead-Reitan Battery, the only one of M.F.'s test scores that clearly fell in the normal range was Part B of the Trail Making Test (58 seconds).

Although the literature has not selectively related the scores on the Category Test and the Localization component of the Tactual Performance Test to I.Q. values, coefficients of correlation have been reported both for normal and for brain-damaged groups. A substantial and significant correlation occurs (generally in the vicinity of .5 to .6), and the poorer scores on these two measures must be given even additional significance in consideration of this man's I.Q. values. Thus, the general indicators suggest that this man may have some impairment of higher-level aspects of brain functions. It is obvious that M.F. is generally alert. He performed better than the average control subject on the Speech- sounds Perception Test (5) and earned a satisfactory score on the Seashore Rhythm Test (27). It therefore appears that any deficits he may have shown were not attributable to primary aspects of attention and concentration.

The patient had no difficulty on the Aphasia Screening Test except for a very unusual spelling of the word CROSS: C-R-O-I-S. This particular mistake can hardly be considered a normal response, but in the complete absence of any other indications of left cerebral dysfunction it would be difficult to postulate a left cerebral lesion based on this answer alone. Conversely, the patient showed a striking deficiency with his left upper extremity on the Tactual Performance Test. Although he completed the task with his right hand (first trial) without difficulty and within normal time limits, he required more than twice as much time when using his left hand. It was apparent from the good perform-ance on the third trial, using both hands, that the impaired second (left hand) performance was not due to a diminution of motivation or fatigue. In fact, the relatively long total time required to complete the Tactual Performance Test was obviously due to the extremely poor performance on the second trial (left hand). This finding deviates from the range of normal variation and must be considered an indication of impairment.

The critical question, therefore, would concern whether the impairment of the left upper extremity was due to right cerebral hemisphere damage or peripheral involvement (such as childhood poliomyolitis). The test results provide an unequivocal answer to questions such as this. It is clear that the patient does not have any significant primary motor impairment of the left upper extremity. M.F.'s finger tapping speed was within the normal range, though it may have been slightly slow with the left hand as compared with the right. The patient's ability to tap 5.4 times/second with his left hand demonstrated that the extremely poor performance with the same hand on the Tactual Performance Test cannot be attributed to primary motor deficit.

It must also be noted that M.F. did not show any significant impairment in tactile finger recognition or finger-tip number writing perception on either hand. If the patient had demonstrated motor impairment we would have been inclined to attribute the poor left-handed performance on the Tactual Performance Test to involvement of the motor area. Conversely, if he had shown specific difficulty in tactile-receptive functions we would have been inclined to implicate the parietal area.

With these findings, then, there may be a question concerning the specific cerebral area involved. We would postulate that the tactile-receptive deficits were of principal importance and have leaned our interpretation to a parietal cortical deficit. Because of the rather strong indications of deficit from the general tests of cerebral functioning (Impairment Index, Category Test, and Localization component of the Tactual Performance Test), we would be inclined to judge that the left-handed deficit on the Tactual Performance Test was not due to peripheral involvement.

However, the patient performed quite well on a number of tests.

If we were to postulate a lesion of the right cerebral hemisphere, one could question why the Performance I.Q. value was not impaired. Also, the patient did not show the type of impairment in general alertness and concentrational ability frequently seen in persons with serious and destructive lateralized cerebral lesions (Speech-sounds Perception Test and Seashore Rhythm Test). A positive interpretation of the test results would require a lesion that (1) had certain general effects; (2) was chronic and static in nature (and thereby not impairing alertness and concentration); and (3) was probably in the parietal area of the right cerebral hemisphere. In a blind interpretation of these test results we postulated such a lesion and, in addition, suggested that it probably was epileptogenic in nature. This latter inference is not based upon the test results directly; however, when the test results suggest that a lesion is strictly focal and static, it frequently causes epileptic manifestations.

Neurological evaluation revealed that this man had a meningioma located on the upper convexity of the right parietal area. In fact, the location of the underlying lesion was apparent from plain skull films which showed a "sunburst" effect in the location of the lesion.

The conclusions to be drawn from the neuropsychological test results are quite clear: certain localizing findings will be present even if the lesion only compresses and does not actually invade brain tissue. Thus, the results for M.F. were quite different from those in persons with intrinsic brain tumors; in this case the brain tissue itself had not been invaded. Instead of being from direct cerebral involvement, neuropsychological manifestations of this lesion were a result of the gradual growth of the tumor and pressure effects on the underlying brain tissue. Further, it is particularly important to note that prior research has shown no consistent impairment of the I.Q. value corresponding with the impaired side of the brain in the case of meningiomas. In other words, although the right hemisphere was involved, the Performance I.Q. value was not depressed. This finding, which has been noted in many other instances of extrinsic tumors, expresses a dissociation between Verbal and Performance I.Q. differences and certain other manifestations of cerebral damage (e.g., left hand on the Tactual Performance). The selective nature of cerebral lesions, with respect to neuropsychological deficits, affords the opportunity of learning more rather than less when some deficits are found and others are spared.

CASE #6

Name:	W.M.	Sex:	Male
Age:	44	Handedness:	Right
Education:	14	Occupation:	Sales Engineer

Current Complaints and Pertinent History

This 44-year-old man developed a malignant melanoma in the area of the right scapula about 10 months before this neuropsychological examination was done. The lesion was removed surgically, but cancer cells were found in the right axillary nodes about four months later. For several weeks prior to the current hospital admission the patient had suffered severe frontal headaches which had been increasing in severity. During this period of time he had been bumping into things on his left side and, when driving his car into a small garage, had hit the left side of the car on the garage door. It is probable that these difficulties may have been related to a left homonymous hemianopia discerned during the neuropsychological examination. The only findings on neurological examination included this visual field defect and hypesthesia of the right ulnar area. However, EEG showed Delta waves, Grade III, in the right parietal area. Metastatic carcinoma was discovered in various parts of his body.

Neuropsychological Test Results

Neuropsychological examination yielded a Verbal I.Q. in the upper part of the Average range (109) and a Performance I.Q. that was 10 points lower, falling almost exactly at the Average level (99). The weighted scores for the individual Verbal subtests made it clear that this man had developed relatively adequate intelligence levels in the past. This would also be inferred from the fact that he had completed two years of college.

On the Performance subtests he performed more poorly. Even though the Verbal and Performance I.Q. values were only 10 points apart, the total weighted score for the Verbal subtest was considerably greater than the corresponding score for the Performance subtest. In fact, the distribution for the Performance subtest was strongly suggestive

HALSTEAD-REITAN NEUROPSYCHOLOGICAL TEST BATTERY

Patient _____W.M._____ Age __44__ Sex __M__ Education __14__ Handedness __R__

<u>_x_ WECHSLER-BELLEVUE SCALE (FORM I)</u>
___WAIS

VIQ	109
PIQ	99
FIS IQ	104
VWS	53
PWS	39
Total WS	92
Information	9
Comprehension	15
Digit Span	7
Arithmetic	9
Similarities	13
Vocabulary	15
Picture Arrangement	6
Picture Completion	9
Block Design	7
Object Assembly	10
Digit Symbol	7

<u>HALSTEAD'S NEUROPSYCHOLOGICAL TEST BATTERY</u>
Category Test _____72_____

Tactual Performance Test
Dominant hand: _____5.4_____
Non-dominant hand: _____10.7_____
Both hands: _____7.2_____
Total Time_23.3_
Memory__5___
Localization__0____

Seashore Rhythm Test
Number Correct___28____ _____2___

Speech-sounds Perception Test
Number of Errors _____12_____

Finger Oscillation Test
Dominant hand: _____61_____ ____61___
Non-dominant hand:___55____

TRAIL MAKING TEST
Part A:__51__seconds
Part B:_183__seconds

Impairment Index___0.7____

REITAN-KLØVE SENSORY-PERCEPTUAL EXAM

				Error Totals	
RH____LH____	Both:RH____LH____			RH____LH____	
RH____LF____	Both:RH____LF____			RH____LF____	
LH____RF____	Both:LH____RF____			RF____LH____	
RE____LE____	Both:RE____LE_1_			RE____LE_1_	
RV____LV_4_	Both:RV____LV_4_				
___4_	___4_			RV____LV_12_	
___4_	___4_				

TACTILE FINGER RECOGNITION
R 1___2___3 4 4___5___ R_4 / 20_
L 1___2___3 3 4 4 5 3 L_10 / 20_

FINGER-TIP NUMBER WRITING
R 1_1 2 2 3 0 4 2 5 1_ R_6 / 20_
L 1_1 2 1 3 2 4 0 5 1_ L_5 / 20_

Visual Field Examination: Left homonymous hemianopia.

REITAN-INDIANA APHASIA SCREENING TEST

Form for Adults and Older Children

Name: ___W. M._____ Age: __44__

Copy SQUARE	Repeat TRIANGLE
Name SQUARE	Repeat MASSACHUSETTS
Spell SQUARE "S-Q-U-A-I-R"	Repeat METHODIST EPISCOPAL
Copy CROSS Note the imbalance of the lateral extremities on the second day of testing.	Write SQUARE Note the initial error and correction when asked to do it again.
Name CROSS	Read SEVEN
Spell CROSS	Repeat SEVEN
Copy TRIANGLE	Repeat/Explain HE SHOUTED THE WARNING.
Name TRIANGLE	Write HE SHOUTED THE WARNING.
Spell TRIANGLE Note the errors in writing the word.	Compute 85 – 27 =
Name BABY	Compute 17 X 3 =
Write CLOCK	Name KEY
Name FORK	Demonstrate use of KEY
Read 7 SIX 2 "7 S-I-X 2"	Draw KEY Note the difficulties with the stem and "nose" of the key.
Read MGW	Read PLACE LEFT HAND TO RIGHT EAR.
Reading I	Place LEFT HAND TO RIGHT EAR Placed left hand to left ear - self-corrected.
Reading II "He is a friendly animal, a mouse winner of dog shows." Read it again the same way.	Place LEFT HAND TO LEFT ELBOW

Trimgae

Clock.

squair

square

he shouted the worn ing

85 - 27 = 58

REPEATED THE NEXT DAY

1.

2.

of right cerebral damage. The patient did poorly on the Digit Symbol subtest, a finding which might suggest cerebral damage. The other low scores among the Performance subtests were Picture Arrangement (6) and Block Design (7). This particular pattern is rather impressive and lends weight to a postulate of right cerebral damage because the difference between the Verbal and Performance subtest scores was mainly due to Digit Symbol (a general indicator of cerebral damage) and the two Wechsler tests that are most specifically sensitive to the biological status of the right cerebral hemisphere (Picture Arrangement and Block Design).

The four tests in the Halstead-Reitan Battery most sensitive to brain damage all yielded strong indications of impairment. The Halstead Impairment Index was 0.7 (about 70% of the tests in the brain-damaged range). There were only two tests that did not fall in the brain-damaged range — finger tapping speed and the Seashore Rhythm Test — and neither is among the tests most sensitive to cerebral damage with respect to level of performance. Despite apparently adequate premorbid intelligence the patient did not do well on the Category Test (72). W.M. had very poor scores on Trails B (183 seconds) and the Localization component of the Tactual Performance Test (0). Based on these results, there would be good reason to be concerned about the presence of serious brain disease.

Reviewing the general adequacy of performances, we see that W.M. performed poorly on most of the tests in the Battery. His scores were either approximately at the average level or below for brain-damaged persons. In addition to demonstrating poor performances on the tests of higher brain functions, this man also had significant sensory-perceptual losses (tactile finger recognition and finger-tip number writing perception) and a left homonymous hemianopia. The patient demonstrated constructional dyspraxia and certain aphasic signs that will be reviewed below. His only good scores occurred on certain Verbal subtests of the Wechsler Scale, finger tapping speed, and the Seashore Rhythm Test.

Thus, the results suggest that W.M. has sustained a significant and rather generalized impairment of the behavioral correlates of brain functions. He showed losses in verbal and language functions, visual-spatial and manipulatory skills, concept formation and abstraction, input and manipulatory skills, concept formation and abstraction, input measures and output measures (Tactual Performance Test). His best performances certainly were on pure motor output measures.

The lateralizing indicators showed involvement of both sides of the brain, although the more serious deficits implicated the right cerebral hemisphere. We will first review the indicators of left cerebral damage. On the Aphasia Test this patient had difficulties which were incompatible with his educational background and general verbal intelligence. When he was first asked to spell SQUARE, he responded "s-q-u-a-i-r." This spelling is so unusual for a person who had completed two years of college that we would consider it a possible demonstration of spelling dyspraxia.

W.M. was asked to write TRIANGLE after he had drawn the figure, and his response again indicated left cerebral dysfunction. He had difficulty getting the "r" started, omitted the "a," and confused the sequence of the "l" and "e." These findings deviate from normal expectancy. One could postulate that this man had never been able to spell adequately, but the particular kinds of mistakes that he made were more characteristic of errors made by persons with left cerebral lesions than persons with inadequate training in spelling.

The next error on the Aphasia Test was even more unequivocal. In reading 7 SIX 2, he responded to the letters individually, failing to recognize that they represented a word. He also became somewhat confused on the second reading item, but the type of error he made is extremely rare and of unknown significance with respect to impaired brain functions. Regardless, the error probably suggests some difficulty dealing with language material.

Finally, when asked to PLACE LEFT HAND TO RIGHT EAR, the patient placed his left hand to his left ear and then spontaneously corrected himself. This suggests some degree of right-left confusion, a manifestation more common in persons with left cerebral damage than right.

The patient also had some difficulty copying simple spatial configurations. W.M. was tested before we required patients to draw continuously around the square, cross, and triangle until getting back to the starting point. At first W.M. began to draw in the double lines on the square, but the examiner told him that this was not necessary.

The cross and the triangle were done fairly well. This man was examined on two successive days. The examiner asked the patient to draw the cross again when he returned for additional testing and these figures have been inserted at the bottom of the page showing the drawings done the first day. These drawings demonstrate definite distortion of the left lateral extremity and it would appear not only that the patient had some difficulty copying the cross, but that the difficulty may have been progressive from one day to the next.

The drawing of the key was definitely indicative of right cerebral damage. At first glance one might conclude that the key was carefully and painstakingly drawn; close inspection shows that there are several manifestations that rarely, if ever, occur among normal individuals. First, the patient did not draw corresponding indentations in the stem of the key near the handle. The indentations drawn on the stem near the teeth of the key were not mirror images. This kind of loss of symmetry in the drawing is characteristic of persons with right cerebral damage. Second, the patient had some problems with the teeth of the key, again failing to achieve symmetry. Finally, the nose of the key was not properly positioned with relation to the rest of the figure. Thus, a careful inspection of the drawing reveals deficits that are essentially pathognomonic for right cerebral damage. Failure to have closed the inside of the handle is a type of error that not infrequently occurs among normal subjects and does not represent a pathognomonic performance.

W.M. demonstrated other evidence of right cerebral damage, the most unequivocal finding being the presence of a left homonymous hemianopia. He also performed poorly with his left hand as compared with his right on the Tactual Performance Test and had considerably more difficulty in tactile finger recognition on his left hand than his right. The fact that he had equivalent difficulty in finger-tip number writing perception on both hands does not detract from the significance of the lateralized findings on the Tactile Finger Recognition Test. As we have already mentioned, the patient also performed poorly on the two Wechsler subtests most specifically sensitive to right cerebral damage, Picture Arrangement and Block Design.

The conclusion, then, is that the lateralizing indicators point toward more significant right than left cerebral damage. In making a comparison of this kind it is important to give some additional weighting to highly specific signs (such as left homonymous hemianopia) and to consider the comparative performances on identical tasks on the two sides of the body. In these respects W.M. consistently showed evidence of more serious right cerebral damage.

Finally, it is necessary to consider all of these results simultaneously and to reach a conclusion regarding the pathological involvement of the brain that would produce such behavioral deficits. It is clear that both cerebral hemispheres are involved. Evidence for damage of the left cerebral hemisphere was supported by dysphasic manifestations and the inability to recognize the third finger of the right hand when it was stimulated. The findings indicating right cerebral damage were reviewed above. The damage in the left cerebral hemisphere would be somewhat difficult to localize, but the selective loss in tactile recognition of the third finger of the right hand suggests that a rather discrete lesion in the left parietal area must have been present. Such a lesion could also have been responsible for the difficulty in dealing with language and related symbols.

The area of involvement of the right cerebral hemisphere can be inferred in somewhat more detail. First, it should be noted that the patient did not have any difficulty whatsoever in finger tapping speed with either hand; therefore, it is unlikely that primary motor functions were involved. The positive evidence gained from comparing performances on the two sides of the body related to tactile and visual stimulation. (W.M. did have one error on the left side with bilateral simultaneous auditory stimulation, but we are reluctant to accept a single error as an indication of cerebral damage). The left homonymous hemianopia clearly indicates that the geniculostriate pathway in the right cerebral hemisphere was interrupted. In addition, left-handed errors in tactile finger recognition and definite impairment on the Tactual Performance Test suggest that the right parietal lobe was involved.

A neoplastic, relatively posterior lesion in the right cerebral hemisphere would account for all of the findings. A neoplasm might be suggested not only on the basis of the considerable number of positive findings implicating the right cerebral hemisphere, but also because the patient had such definite right cerebral indicators without any significant motor impairment on the left side. A neoplastic involvement in the right hemisphere would also suggest the possibility of a smaller lesion, also neoplastic, in the parietal area of the left cerebral hemisphere.

The likelihood of two, independent, primary intrinsic tumors of the brain is highly unlikely. A more reasonable hypothesis would be the presence of a metastatic carcinoma. If the patient did have bilateral tumors of the brain, we must explain the patient's good scores on certain measures. In most patients with multiple metastatic lesions involving both cerebral hemispheres, we see very severe impairment of both left and right cerebral functions. This man, however, performed fairly well on some of the Verbal subtests of the Wechsler Scale and did extremely well on the Seashore Rhythm Test. (Adequate finger tapping speed is frequently retained in many persons with neoplastic damage.)

It might be an over-interpretation to suggest that the lesions were well-encapsulated and not having a devastating wide-spread effect on brain functions. Nevertheless, it must be observed that metastatic carcinoma of the brain, with lesions in both cerebral hemispheres, would rarely permit such a good score on the Seashore Rhythm Test.

Because the patient had evidence of multiple metastases throughout his body, surgery was not indicated; therefore, we were not able to obtain surgical verification of the type of lesion or its location. However, a cerebral angiogram clearly indicated a lesion in the parietal-occipital area of the right cerebral hemisphere. The left cerebral angiogram did not demonstrate a lesion. Various studies of cerebral angiography, however, have indicated that small lesions are sometimes not shown and, considering that this man had many metastatic lesions, it is possible that his left cerebral hemisphere also was involved. This patient expired about six months after this testing was done and we were able to attend the autopsy. We were not able to get confirming information regarding the location of cerebral damage at the time of neuropsychological testing because metastatic carcinoma pervaded almost all of this man's brain by the time of his death.

CASE #7

Name:	A.C.	Sex:	Male
Age:	61	Handedness:	Right
Education:	5	Occupation:	Saw Operator

Current Complaints and Pertinent History

This 61-year-old man had apparently been well until he started to show behavior changes about nine months prior to his admission to the hospital. His family reported that he did not converse as readily as he had previously, and, on occasions such as family gatherings, he would hardly speak at all; he would just sit and listen and then go to sleep. When he did speak his comments were unrelated to the topic of the conversation and he seemed to be more argumentative than usual.

Five months before his admission to the hospital A.C. had been told by his supervisor at the stone quarry where he worked that his work had been unsatisfactory because he had been forgetting so many things. He was warned that his work must either improve or he would be laid off because the work of other people was being delayed by his inefficiency. A.C.'s performance did not improve and two months later he was laid off.

At about this time the patient's family also noticed that he was having other serious difficulties. For example, he would sometimes sit in his car for 5-15 minutes before starting the engine, forget to stop at his intended destination, and go to wrong places. Family members also noted that the patient had difficulty remembering recent events, although he could remember things that had occurred long in the past. The family was concerned about his forgetfulness but tended to attribute his difficulties essentially to "memory" problems.

And the patient showed other problems as well. For example, his gait was not as straight and steady as it had been; he would sometimes stagger but had not fallen. He had difficulty picking up things from the floor after having dropped them, especially with his right (preferred) hand. The patient himself complained only of headaches and one episode of forgetfulness. He had lost 25 pounds within a one-month period prior to admission.

HALSTEAD-REITAN NEUROPSYCHOLOGICAL TEST BATTERY

Patient_____A.C._____Age___61___Sex___M___Education___5___Handedness___R___

| x WECHSLER-BELLEVUE SCALE (FORM I) | HALSTEAD'S NEUROPSYCHOLOGICAL TEST BATTERY |

___WAIS

Category Test   66

VIQ	69
PIQ	103
FIS IQ	81
VWS	10
PWS	30
Total WS	40

Tactual Performance Test
Dominant hand: 22.3 (10 blocks)
Non-dominant hand: 22.3 (5 blocks)
Both hands: 20.6 (10 blocks)

Total Time__65.2 +
Memory___1___
Localization___0___

Information	4
Comprehension	5
Digit Span	0
Arithmetic	0
Similarities	1
Vocabulary	2
Picture Arrangement	7
Picture Completion	4
Block Design	6
Object Assembly	11
Digit Symbol	2

Seashore Rhythm Test
Number Correct___17___   10

Speech-sounds Perception Test
Number of Errors   46

Finger Oscillation Test
Dominant hand: 22   22
Non-dominant hand: 22

TRAIL MAKING TEST
Part A:___79___seconds
Part B:_____seconds — **Discontinued at 300″ (9-I)**

Impairment Index___1.0___

STRENGTH OF GRIP
Dominant hand: 35.0 kilograms
Non-dominant hand: 31.5 kilograms

Miles ABC Test of Ocular Dominance
Right eye:__8__
Left eye: __2__

REITAN-KLØVE TACTILE FORM RECOGNITION TEST
Dominant hand: — seconds; __0__errors
Non-dominant hand: __—__ seconds; __0__errors

REITAN-KLØVE SENSORY-PERCEPTUAL EXAM

				Error Totals	
RH___LH___	Both:RH__1__LH___			RH__1__LH___	
RH___LF___	Both:RH___LF___			RH___LF___	
LH___RF___	Both:LH___RF___			RF___LH___	
RE___LE___	Both:RE___LE___			RE___LE___	
RV___LV___	Both:RV___LV___				
___ ___	___			RV___LV__2__	
___ ___	__2__				

REITAN-KLØVE LATERAL-DOMINANCE EXAM
Show me how you:

throw a ball	R
hammer a nail	R
cut with a knife	R
turn a door knob	R
use scissors	R
use an eraser	R
write your name	R

Show me how you:

kick a football	R
step on a bug	R

TACTILE FINGER RECOGNITION
R 1_1_2___3_2_4_3_5___ R_6_/ 20
L 1_1_2_1_3_3_4_3_5___ L_8_/ 20

FINGER-TIP NUMBER WRITING
R 1_2_2___3_3_4_2_5_1___ R_8_/ 20
L 1_1_2_2_3_3_4_3_5_3___ L_12 / 20

REITAN-INDIANA APHASIA SCREENING TEST

Form for Adults and Older Children

Name: _____ A. C. _____ Age: __61__

Copy SQUARE	Repeat TRIANGLE
Name SQUARE "Paste board"	Repeat MASSACHUSETTS
Spell SQUARE "S-q-u-e-l-e"	Repeat METHODIST EPISCOPAL "Methodist apisopal."
Copy CROSS	Write SQUARE
Name CROSS	Read SEVEN
Spell CROSS "C-l-o-r-s--double C"	Repeat SEVEN
Copy TRIANGLE	Repeat/Explain HE SHOUTED THE WARNING. Explained meaning of sentence poorly.
Name TRIANGLE "Cross"	Write HE SHOUTED THE WARNING.
Spell TRIANGLE "T-r-a-i-n-g-s"	Compute 85 − 27 = Patient asked if he was to "add or what?"
Name BABY	Compute 17 X 3 = Patient unable to perform. Examiner gave 6 X 2. See
Write CLOCK	Name KEY
Name FORK	Demonstrate use of KEY
Read 7 SIX 2 "6-2; 6 & 2; 6 & 2". Examiner pointed; OK	Draw KEY
Read MGW	Read PLACE LEFT HAND TO RIGHT EAR.
Reading I "See the black clock"	Place LEFT HAND TO RIGHT EAR Placed right hand to right ear.
Reading II "He is a friendly animal, a former winner of your dog shows."	Place LEFT HAND TO LEFT ELBOW Tried to place left hand to left elbow. Then left hand to right elbow after repetition of instructions.

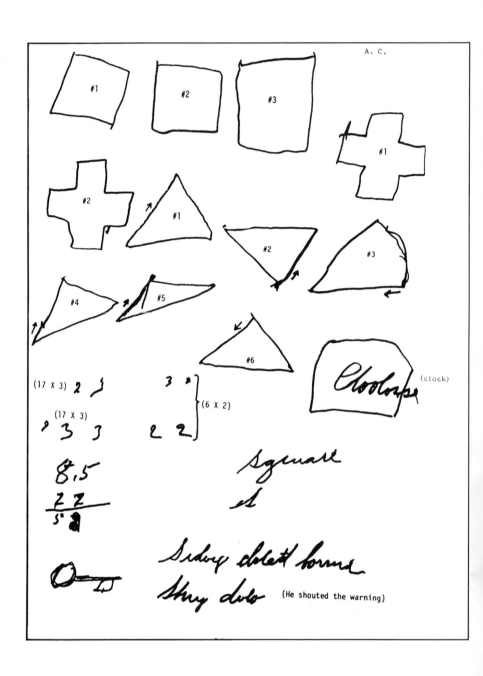

#1 #2 #3

#1 #2

#1 #2 #3

#4 #5

#6

(clock)

(17 X 3) 2

3

(6 X 2)

(17 X 3)

3 3 2 2

8.5

7 7
———
5· 2

square

(He shouted the warning)

A.C. seemed quite confused and was not oriented to time or place when he was brought to the hospital. He showed some hesitation in speech and a perseverative tendency. He was impaired in his ability to name common objects, showed a slight right central facial palsy, and slight weakness of the right upper extremity. Inspection of his eye grounds showed no papilledema. An x-ray of the chest showed a 3 x 5 centimeter mass in the left upper lobe compatible with bronchogenic carcinoma. Bilateral carotid angiograms showed a shift of the anterior cerebral arteries to the right and some shifting and straightening of the candelabra vessels on the left. A pneumoencephalogram showed a definite shift of the third and lateral ventricles to the right with the left lateral ventricle being pushed beneath the falx. Electroencephalographic tracings at this time showed Delta waves, Grade I, and Dysrhythmia, Grade II, which appeared to be located maximally in the left fronto-temporal area.

The patient had surgery six days after the neuropsychological examination was done and a cystic malignant tumor (a metastasis from the left upper lobe lung carcinoma) was found in the left fronto-parietal area.

Neuropsychological Test Results

This 61-year-old man completed only five grades in school. Nevertheless, this deficiency in his educational background was not sufficient to account for the striking disparity between his Verbal and Performance I.Q. values.

The patient earned a Verbal I.Q. (69) which falls in the Mentally Retarded range and a Performance I.Q. (103) which is in the Average range. (It should be noted that older persons receive an inordinate amount of credit for items in the Performance subtests of the Wechsler-Bellevue Scale. Undoubtedly, this accounts for at least part of A.C.'s score.)

The Verbal subtests which reflect the patient's premorbid abilities — Vocabulary, Information, Comprehension and Similarities — had scores ranging from 1 to 5 and suggest that the patient may never have acquired many of the skills tested by Wechsler's scales. The patient was unable to earn any points at all on Arithmetic, the subtest most dependent upon immediate problem-solving skills. In other case interpretations in this book we have noted that Digit Span scores are often low in persons under stress and do not necessarily indicate the presence of brain damage; however, A.C.'s score of 0 on this measure must be considered a significant deviation.

The patient also earned variable scores on the Performance subtests. It is interesting to note that he earned his highest score, 11, on a subtest that is not very reliable as an indicator of the biological condition of the brain (Object Assembly) and his lowest score, 2, on the subtest most sensitive to impaired cerebral functioning (Digit Symbol). The score of 11 on Object Assembly contributed significantly to the Performance I.Q. of 103.

At this point in the interpretation it appears that the patient has impairment of both Verbal and Performance intelligence.

Results on the four most sensitive indicators in the Halstead-Reitan Battery also suggest that A.C. has sustained significant impairment of adaptive abilities. He earned an Impairment Index of 1.0, signifying that 100 percent of the test results were in the brain-damaged range. The Category Test score of 66 indicates that he has some difficulty dealing with situations that require abstraction, reasoning and analytical abilities. He could not remember the location of any of the shapes on the Tactual Performance Test board, despite working on the test for over an hour. The examiner discontinued Part B of the Trail Making Test; in 300 seconds the patient had made six errors and only reached I-9. The poor results on these four general indicators of cerebral functioning denote serious impairment of adaptive abilities.

The test scores also yielded results that have distinct lateralizing significance. The patient performed poorly with his left (non-preferred) hand on the Tactual Performance Test, a finding pointing toward right cerebral dysfunction. Conversely, his finger-tapping speed, while slow with both hands, was no faster with the right (preferred) hand than the left. Thus, the results up to this point indicated severe impairment of cerebral functions with certain findings implicating left cerebral damage and others pointing toward right cerebral damage. It should be noted that the patient's grip strength measurements were in the expected relationship.

Next to be considered in the interpretation will be the Aphasia Test results. These findings indicate that the patient showed deficits that go beyond educational deficiency and are characteristic of cerebral damage.

The only name A.C. could give for the square was "pasteboard." He began spelling the word "square" correctly but then lost the ability to relate the letters to the sound of the word. Although he named the cross correctly, he demonstrated definite confusion between appropriate letters and the sound of the word during his attempt at spelling. He showed a verbal perseverative tendency in his naming of the triangle as a "cross." In his attempt to spell the word "triangle" he showed further spelling difficulty typical of left hemisphere damage.

The next error occurred on the 7 SIX 2 item. In this case A.C. showed a tendency to ignore the left side of the stimulus configuration; the patient finally responded correctly when the examiner pointed to the "7." It is difficult to interpret this response as an indication of language difficulty. Instead, it appears to be a genuine failure to perceive the "7" (even though the patient's visual fields were full), and thereby suggests right cerebral dysfunction.

Confusion in reading was demonstrated on both of the reading items. The first item, in which the patient substituted the word "clock" for the word "dog," probably represents another instance of verbal perseveration; A.C. had previously been exposed to the clock and had attempted to write the word. This type of verbal perseveration is a manifestation of left cerebral damage. It is difficult to determine whether this man had central dysarthria; his mistake in enunciation involved the word "Episcopal," but the error was more a slurring of the word rather than a loss of the appropriate sounds.

It is sometimes difficult to evaluate the explanation of the sentence, "He shouted the warning." A notation by the examiner indicated that this patient explained the meaning of the sentence poorly, but it would have been more helpful to have had an actual quotation of the patient's verbalization. Therefore, whether the poor explanation of the sentence merely represents generalized cognitive impairment and confusion or actually indicates auditory-verbal dysgnosia is hard to determine. Even though it is often difficult to record a patient's complete verbalization, it is worthwhile to try to write down as much as possible so that a judgment of the specific nature of the deficiency can be made.

This man was definitely impaired in his ability to do arithmetical computations; it is possible, though, that the problems in this test were too difficult for someone with only a fifth grade education. However, when A.C. asked if he was to "add or what?" on the 85–27 = problem, it is clear that he had some confusion about arithmetical processes and this constitutes evidence of dyscalculia. Almost certainly this man would normally have known the meaning of the minus sign. It is possible that 17 X 3 was too difficult for him, and the examiner was correct to give him a simpler problem. As seen on the page showing the patient's written efforts, he was grossly confused even with this problem.

On the last two items of the test the patient showed right-left confusion and may also have demonstrated some degree of auditory-verbal dysgnosia. Right-left confusion was shown when the patient placed his right hand to his right ear. Even though A.C. responded correctly on the last item, the examiner repeated the instructions (because the patient asked to hear the instructions again) and then the patient responded incorrectly. This could have been another manifestation of right-left confusion or it may also have represented confusion in comprehension through the auditory avenue of the verbal instructions.

The patient's writing and drawing indicate that he had a number of problems. The examiner asked A.C. to draw the figures several times because the patient was having difficulties. The most significant deficiency probably related to the second triangle. In this case the patient became quite confused and drew the figure upside down. He also had difficulty closing the third triangle. These drawings were not as bad as one might expect from a person with a right hemisphere lesion and such a generalized degree of impairment. The deficits might even be partially explained by the patient's poor educational level, but it seems more likely that they represent constructional dyspraxia.

It is not uncommon for persons with left cerebral lesions to attempt to respond to the instruction to write the name for the clock by drawing a picture of the clock. This patient began to draw the outside of the figure and was probably stopped by the examiner after the outside line had been drawn. He was then asked to write the name and his confusion (probably with both spelling and writing) was apparent. Even when he had the printed letters SQUARE directly in front of him, he showed some degree of confusion in his writing. The writing itself suggests that this man probably had never developed much skill in writing; however, he still seemed to have some particular difficulty in forming individual letters (dysgraphia) as well as in spelling (spelling dyspraxia). This was particularly apparent in his attempt to write the sentence, "He shouted the warning."

Finally, although the patient drew the key very poorly in terms of detail, it is clear that he had turned the key in the wrong direction. Many clinicians are inclined to interpret this type of finding as a definite sign of brain damage. We have reviewed thousands of cases and the key is drawn in the wrong direction with equal frequency by control subjects and brain-damaged persons; therefore, drawing the key in the "wrong" direction cannot be used as a specific sign of cerebral disease or damage. So, although "reversals" of this type are interpreted by many persons as definite evidence of cerebral damage (perhaps on the basis of "scientific hearsay"), one must remember the need for empirical verification of hypotheses and resist the tendency to presume that one's interpretation must be valid merely because it came to mind. Examples of this kind emphasize the importance of studying individual cases quite carefully in order to gain an understanding of the types of deficits that actually do represent impaired brain functions as contrasted with the types of deviations in performance that are not directly related to pathological involvement of the brain.

We find, then, that this patient showed evidence of dysnomia, spelling dyspraxia, dyslexia, possible mild central dysarthria, possible auditory verbal dysgnosia, dyscalculia, dysgraphia, and right-left confusion. These signs point definitely toward damage of the left cerebral hemisphere. The patient also showed a distinct tendency in one instance to fail to respond to the left side of a stimulus configuration and demonstrated constructional dyspraxia. These findings suggest right cerebral damage.

Results on the Sensory-perceptual Examination also yielded a number of positive findings. The patient did not show any significant tendency toward sensory imperception except on visual stimulation. Although the one error in tactile stimulation on the right side probably should be noted, it is difficult to count a single error as being significant. However, the patient made two errors in the left lower quadrant with bilateral simultaneous visual stimulation, and this finding probably implicates a mild degree of right cerebral dysfunction.

The patient had considerable difficulty in both tactile finger recognition and finger-tip number writing perception. The errors were nearly evenly distributed in tactile finger recognition, but the total of 12 errors on the left hand and only 8 errors on the right hand in finger-tip number writing perception probably has some lateralizing significance. In fact, the frequency of impaired function implicates both cerebral hemispheres, though the results lean in the direction of more serious involvement of the right cerebral hemisphere than the left. In summarizing the results from the Sensory-perceptual Examination, there are indications of bilateral involvement. The results suggest that the right cerebral hemisphere is somewhat more dysfunctional. The reader may wonder if only one of the hemispheres could be responsible for these results; there seems to be no support for such a hypothesis.

It is difficult to be specific about the area of involvement. Despite the indications of serious damage to both cerebral hemispheres, the fact that the visual fields were full would tend to argue in favor of neoplastic involvement rather than a vascular lesion. Since there is evidence for bilateral cerebral damage, a postulate of neoplastic involvement would require consideration of metastatic carcinoma of the brain to account for lesions of both hemispheres. These results definitely indicate serious damage of the cerebral hemispheres that would require neurological evaluation.

This man's medical and neurological history indicates that he had surgery for a malignant tumor in the left fronto-parietal area six days after our examination was done. The lesion was a metastasis from the lung carcinoma. Even though bilateral cerebral angiography had been done, only the left cerebral lesion was noted. Although it is not uncommon for cerebral metastases to be multiple and invade both cerebral hemispheres, no lesion of the right cerebral hemisphere was diagnosed in this case. However, results from the Aphasia Screening Test and the Sensory-perceptual Examination as well as the rest of the Battery provided evidence of right as well as left cerebral damage.

VII
CEREBRAL VASCULAR DISEASE

The cerebral cortex has a high metabolic rate and is dependent upon a continuous supply of oxygen and glucose through blood circulation. Because of this, cerebral vascular disease can have a pronounced influence upon basic aspects of brain function and, correspondingly, neuropsychological and behavioral correlates. A number of disorders of the cerebral vascular system can occur, including lesions (or interruption of blood supply) from the major arteries that feed the brain; various disorders relating to cerebral blood flow and cerebral vascular insufficiency; generalized deteriorative changes that may affect the cerebral vessels; emboli and infarcts of the cerebral vessels that may produce focal lesions; congenital lesions represented by weaknesses of vessel walls or malformations of arteries and veins eventually resulting in subarachnoid or cerebral hemorrhages; and impairment of brain functions associated with chronic hypertension.

Many disorders of cerebral vascularization may occur and these conditions essentially cover the full range of neuropsychological impairment, including mild and severe cerebral damage; focal and diffuse involvement; acutely destructive and gradually progressive involvement; and diversified age-range distributions. It is important for the clinician to have an understanding of cerebral vascular disease and its variability in order to fully appreciate the neuropsychological correlates and deficits associated with it.

Cerebral vascular disease affects about two million persons in the United States. It is a major cause of chronic disability and a common cause of death.

We will not attempt to provide a detailed description of the anatomy of the vascular system as it relates to the brain, but we will note that the principal sources of blood supply are the right and left internal carotid arteries and the right and left vertebral arteries. Occlusion or damage to these arteries may cause significant impairment of brain functions. Each cerebral hemisphere has three major arteries: anterior cerebral artery, middle cerebral artery, and posterior cerebral artery. The anterior and middle cerebral arteries arise from the internal carotid artery on the same side. The vertebral artery arises from the subclavian artery. The posterior cerebral arteries are terminal branches of the basilar artery and have a connection with the internal carotid artery through the posterior communicating artery. The circle of Willis provides a connection between the carotid system and the vertebral-basilar system at the base of the brain. A great number of specific symptoms and syndromes are associated with lesions of the cerebral vasculature and careful clinical examination is often accurate in suggesting the particular nature or location of the lesion. Of course, cerebral angiography and computed tomography are also useful in diagnosis.

A considerable number of diagnostic conditions and vascular lesions occur, and we shall provide a brief characterization of them. Cerebrovascular insufficiency is a frequent cause of clinical manifestations of cerebrovascular disorder. Almost all cases of cerebrovascular insufficiency result from atherosclerosis of the cerebral vessels, a chronic degenerative process of the internal linings of the blood vessels which may begin at an early age, usually is present to some degree in middle age, and progresses through the latter stages of life. Cerebral atherosclerosis can be accelerated by hypertension, heart disease, and diabetes mellitus. The initial factor giving rise to atherosclerosis may be damage to endothelial tissue resulting from stress associated with hypertension or turbulence of blood at the bifurcation of arteries. This is followed by a deposition of platelets on the damaged endothelial tissue and various neurochemical reactions which produce injury to the vessel wall. A variety of other changes results in release of lipids from damaged cells and production of atherosclerotic plaques which may cause narrowing of the lumen of the vessel, destruction of surface endothelium, and formation of a clot or thrombus. This progression of deterioration of cerebral vessels is a basic mechanism in producing cerebral infarcts, cerebral emboli, transient ischemic attacks (TIAs), and hypertensive encephalopathy. Patients with transient ischemic attacks or hypertensive encephalopathy may show any of a great number of neurological manifestations.

TIAs are acute neurological episodes which last between a few minutes and 24 hours. The patient shows clinically complete recovery between attacks. The neurological deficits may include homonymous hemianopia, hemiparesis or hemisensory loss, dysphasia, and headache (carotid system manifestations). If the vertebral-basilar system is involved, deficits and symptoms may include occipital headaches, flashing lights in the visual fields, homonymous visual field losses, diplopia, transient facial weakness, tinnitus, vertigo, nausea and vomiting, facial paresthesia, cerebellar ataxia, and sometimes physical collapse. Transient deficits of this kind are important warning signs for more serious and permanent cerebral vascular attacks.

Cerebral vascular accidents (strokes) produce focal damage of cerebral tissue and are the result of occlusion of arteries by thrombosis or embolism. These lesions may occur at any location in the cerebral vascular system and the resulting symptoms are related to the functions of the tissue specifically involved. Some patients suffer multiple cerebral infarcts resulting from multifocal reduction of local blood flow through the brain due to atherosclerosis and arteriosclerosis. The clinical diagnosis in these cases is often difficult to differentiate from primary neuronal degenerative disease, but sudden onset and focal and asymmetric neurological deficits are more characteristic in multi-infarct dementia.

Cerebral hemorrhages may also occur and destroy the brain tissue in the area where the bleeding occurs. Cerebral hemorrhage appears to be associated with long-standing hypertension which, in turn, causes degenerative changes in the muscle and elastic tissue of the blood vessel walls, resulting in the development of small aneurysms. If these aneurysms rupture, hemorrhage may occur. The blood is released into the brain substance under high pressure, causing severe destruction of tissue in the immediate area, and further dissection of brain tissue along nerve tracts. Approximately 70 to 80 percent of patients who suffer intracerebral hemorrhages expire shortly after the episode begins.

Subarachnoid hemorrhage may be due to a variety of causes and associated conditions. The most common etiology of subarachnoid hemorrhage is trauma, but the condition may also occur with ruptured cerebral aneurysms, vascular malformations, and hypertensive intracerebral hemorrhages. Vascular malformations of the cerebral vessels (aneurysms and arteriovenous malformations) are often congenital lesions which cause no particular clinical difficulty early in life and manifest themselves most frequently in the 20-40 year age range. These lesions may occur at any location of the brain blood vessels and their symptomotology is associated with their location.

Neuropsychological Correlates of Cerebral Vascular Disease

It is difficult to briefly characterize the many cerebral vascular conditions that occur in terms of neuropsychological correlates, as the conditions may produce deficits ranging from mild to severe. Considering the fact that the patient had previously developed relatively normal abilities and then sustained a rather sudden focal lesion, lateralizing signs are frequently pronounced. In patients with lateralized cerebral strokes, it is not uncommon to see very pronounced differences between Verbal and Performance intelligence measures. Conditions associated with diffuse involvement (such as hypertensive encephalopathy, generalized atherosclerosis, and arteriosclerosis) frequently manifest relatively intact I.Q. values (especially Verbal I.Q.) as well as good scores on measures dependent upon other aspects of stored information and background knowledge. In contrast, patients with cerebral vascular disease frequently have great difficulty with tests more specifically sensitive to immediate aspects of brain functions (e.g., the Category Test). Patients with aneurysms and arteriovenous malformations may also show pronounced focal and lateralizing signs, but in some instances the lesion has not bled to any considerable extent and focal signs are much less pronounced. A great deal of variability in neuropsychological test results occurs with patients having such lesions.

CASE #8

Name:	C.S.	Sex:	Male
Age:	70	Handedness:	Right
Education:	20 +	Occupation:	Admiral, U.S.N.
			(Retired)

This 70-year-old man was a retired Navy admiral. He had been in command of a submarine in Manila Harbor at the beginning of World War II and had a meritorious record. He developed a mild heart disease and retired from the Navy. C.S. was then employed by one of the major aircraft firms and worked in the development of submarine rocketry for the next 14 years.

Three years before the present examination he suffered a right hemisphere stroke and had consequent paralysis of the left extremities. The patient was referred for testing by a neurological surgeon who felt that the man was still bright and alert and had no intellectual impairment. The physician was interested in a thorough neuro-psychological evaluation because he was considering surgical procedures to improve vascularization of the patient's right cerebral hemisphere.

In reviewing the test results the reader should try to determine the nature and degree of neuropsychological deficit shown by this man. After reviewing the results, ask yourself why a neurological surgeon, who had had extensive experience evaluating persons with cerebral damage, would comment that this man's intellect "fortunately was not impaired." Is the lesion relatively stabilized at the present time? Even with improved vascularization of the right cerebral hemisphere, would this man be likely to regain enough abilites to function within the range of normal variation?

REPORT OF NEUROPSYCHOLOGICAL EXAMINATION

Three years ago this man suffered a severe stroke involving the right middle cerebral artery. The patient's wife indicated that C.S. "does not like to admit his illness" and rarely complains. He had obvious and severe impairment of his left upper extremity and some involve-

HALSTEAD-REITAN NEUROPSYCHOLOGICAL TEST BATTERY

Patient ___C.S.___ Age __70__ Sex __M__ Education __20 +__ Handedness __R__

___WECHSLER-BELLEVUE SCALE (FORM I)
_x_WAIS

VIQ	136
PIQ	78
FIS IQ	112
VWS	84
PWS	13
Total WS	97
Information	13
Comprehension	14
Digit Span	14
Arithmetic	15
Similarities	12
Vocabulary	16
Picture Arrangement	0
Picture Completion	7
Block Design	1
Object Assembly	2
Digit Symbol	3

HALSTEAD'S NEUROPSYCHOLOGICAL TEST BATTERY

Category Test _____ 130

Tactual Performance Test
Dominant hand: _____ 10.0 (2 blocks)
Non-dominant hand: _____ 10.0 (7 blocks)
Both hands: _____ 10.0 (1 block)
Total Time __30.0 +__
Memory __5__
Localization __1__

Seashore Rhythm Test
Number Correct __10__ _____ 10

Speech-sounds Perception Test
Number of Errors _____ 27

Finger Oscillation Test
Dominant hand: _____ 52 _____ 52
Non dominant hand: _____ 0

TRAIL MAKING TEST

Part A: __112__ seconds
Part B: __304__ seconds

Impairment Index __0.9__

STRENGTH OF GRIP
Dominant hand: __8.5__ kilograms
Non-dominant hand: __0.0__ kilograms

Miles ABC Test of Ocular Dominance
Right eye: __10__
Left eye: __0__

REITAN-KLØVE TACTILE FORM RECOGNITION TEST
Dominant hand: __24__ seconds; __0__ errors
Non-dominant hand: __—__ seconds; __—__ errors

REITAN-KLØVE SENSORY-PERCEPTUAL EXAM

REITAN-KLØVE LATERAL-DOMINANCE EXAM

Show me how you:

throw a ball	R
hammer a nail	R
cut with a knife	R
turn a door knob	R
use scissors	R
use an eraser	R
write your name	R

							Error Totals		
RH	LH 4	Both:RH	LH 4		RH	LH 4			
RH	LF 1	Both:RH 1	LF 1		RH 1	LF 1			
LH 4	RF	Both:LH 4	RF		RF	LH 4			
RE	LE 4	Both:RE	LE 4		RE	LE 4			
RV	LV 1	Both:RV	LV 1						
	1		2		RV	LV 4			
			1						

Record time used for spontaneous name writing:
Preferred hand __11__ seconds
Non-preferred hand __—__ seconds

TACTILE FINGER RECOGNITION
R 1 _1_ 2 _2_ 3 1 4 _2_ 5 1   R _7_ / 20
L 1 _4_ 2 _4_ 3 _4_ 4 _4_ 5 _4_   L _20_ / 20

FINGER-TIP NUMBER WRITING
R 1 _1_ 2 _2_ 3 1 4 _2_ 5 1   R _7_ / 20
L 1 _4_ 2 _4_ 3 _4_ 4 _4_ 5 _4_   L _20_ / 20

REITAN-INDIANA APHASIA SCREENING TEST

Form for Adults and Older Children

Name: ___C. S._____ Age: __70__

Copy SQUARE	Note attempt to copy over first drawing.	Repeat TRIANGLE	Speech slurred.
Name SQUARE	"Cube"	Repeat MASSACHUSETTS	Speech slurred.
Spell SQUARE		Repeat METHODIST EPISCOPAL	Speech slurred.
Copy CROSS	Drawing only on right side.	Write SQUARE	
Name CROSS		Read SEVEN	
Spell CROSS		Repeat SEVEN	
Copy TRIANGLE	Error on left side.	Repeat/Explain HE SHOUTED THE WARNING.	
Name TRIANGLE		Write HE SHOUTED THE WARNING.	
Spell TRIANGLE		Compute 85 − 27 = Answered "58" quickly before writing down problem.	
Name BABY		Compute 17 X 3 = Answered "51" quickly before writing down problem.	
Write CLOCK		Name KEY	
Name FORK		Demonstrate use of KEY	
Read 7 SIX 2	Performed slowly but correctly.	Draw KEY Note confusion, particularly on left side of key.	
Read MGW		Read PLACE LEFT HAND TO RIGHT EAR.	
Reading I		Place LEFT HAND TO RIGHT EAR	
Reading II		Place LEFT HAND TO LEFT ELBOW	

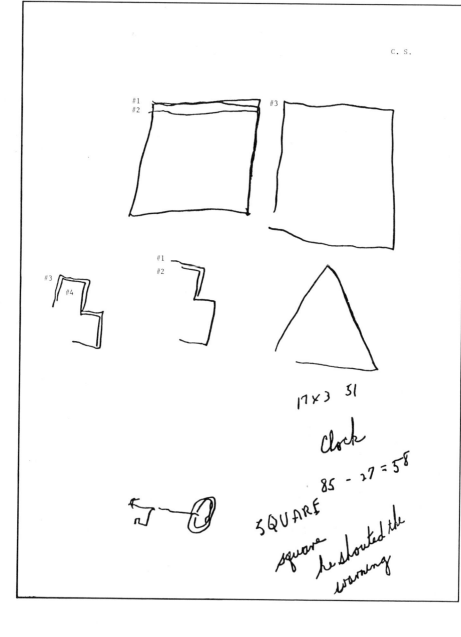

C. S.

#1
#2   #3

#1
#2

#3
#4

17 × 3   31

Clock

85 − 27 = 58

3QUARE

square   he shouted the
warning

ment of his left lower extremity. Although the patient did have pronounced enunciatory problems and was difficult to understand, the Aphasia Examination (as will be described below) showed no evidence of aphasia.

Psychological Implications

The overall set of results presents a classic picture of serious and extensive damage of the right cerebral hemisphere in a person whose previous abilities were in the superior range. The patient earned a Verbal I.Q. (136) in the Superior range (exceeding more than 99 percent of his age peers) and a Performance I.Q. (78) that was in the Borderline range (exceeding only 7 percent).

It is apparent that the patient has suffered very serious losses in his ability to deal with visuo-spatial configurations in a problem-solving context. He also showed generalized impairment of adaptive abilities, earning an Impairment Index of 0.9 (approximately 90 percent of the test scores were in the brain-damaged range). He had a great deal of difficulty on the Category Test (130 errors), indicating that he is impaired in basic reasoning ability and logical analysis skills. He also showed some difficulty in tasks that required focused attention and continued concentration. Thus, although the patient did well on the Verbal I.Q. items, he does have serious generalized impairment in other aspects of higher-level functions.

The patient also demonstrated pronounced deficits on the left side of his body in both motor and sensory-perceptual functions.

Neurological Implications

As mentioned above, the test findings present a classical picture of very severe damage of the right cerebral hemisphere. Measures of lateral dominance indicated that the patient was strongly right-handed. Because of motor impairment of his left upper extremity, we were not able to measure either grip strength or finger-tapping speed. However, his limitation was not restricted to motor functions but also involved sensory-perceptual skills. The patient had a pronounced left hypesthesia, showed difficulty perceiving auditory stimuli to his left ear when there were competing stimuli to the right ear, and showed a mild tendency toward deficits of this kind in visual perception as well. The generality of these motor and sensory-perceptual disorders, in the context of higher-level deficits described above, implicate the entire right cerebral hemisphere.

The patient also showed pronounced constructional dyspraxia, indicating his basic difficulty in dealing with visuo-spatial configurations. We see no specific evidence of damage to the left cerebral hemisphere. Although the patient had enunciatory problems, he was quick and accurate in his verbal responses and arithmetical abilities and it seems that the damage, though quite severe, is restricted to the right cerebral hemisphere.

Summary and Recommendations

Neuropsychological examination of this patient indicated severe impairment of right cerebral functions. His Verbal I.Q. was still in the superior range and the test results showed no evidence of structural damage involving the left cerebral hemisphere. C.S. showed specific deficits in motor, tactile, auditory, and visual functions on the left side of the body. The generality of impairment, including marked constructional dyspraxia, points toward extensive damage in the right cerebral hemisphere.

It seems unlikely that such a devastating loss could be compensated for adequately or regained through therapeutic procedures; the better approach may be to avoid stressing the patient unduly and assist him in settling into a retirement behavior pattern that capitalizes on his verbal abilities. Even though he does have enunciatory problems, his verbal skills are otherwise adequate.

If a therapeutic program oriented toward rehabilitation is undertaken, it is apparent that the subject needs training in all aspects of visuo-spatial relationships and temporal sequences. This kind of training would have to start with simple toys and jig-saw puzzles such as those designed for two- and three-year-old children. Since the patient does not like to admit his illness and apparently does not complain, such an approach would have to be considered carefully in order to avoid embarrassing the subject by constantly demonstrating his serious impairment and deficits. It is particularly difficult for a person who was able in the past to admit to severe selective deficits in his ability structure.

CASE #9

Name:	C.S.	Sex:	Male
Age:	70	Handedness:	Right
Education:	12	Occupation:	Loan Company Officer

Current Complaints and Pertinent History

This 70-year-old man had experienced a stroke about eight months before this neuropsychological examination was done. He reportedly sustained a mild right hemiparesis, was hospitalized, and was given a diagnosis of cerebral vascular degeneration and insufficiency involving the left internal carotid artery. The patient is also reported to have suffered from depression.

At the time of this examination the patient was undergoing evaluation as a basis for planning future activities. He was referred for neuropsychological testing by a neurological surgeon who wanted information regarding any possible impairment of brain-related abilities. The patient had spent his life developing a building and loan business. About 18 months before the present examination he had turned this business over to his son-in-law. The patient missed being involved in this business and was considering re-assuming the role of chief executive officer. If this plan was felt to be inadvisable, he wanted to get far away from the business, relocate in another part of the country and do things that were very different. Specifically, he was considering moving to Florida and purchasing and operating a marina.

Neuropsychological Test Results

The Wechsler test results indicated that this man had a Verbal I.Q. that fell in the upper part of the Average range (109). The disparity in actual level of performance on the Verbal and Performance subtests was striking, with the Performance subtests consistently well below the average level. The Verbal subtests clearly indicated that the general intellectual background of this man was above average, but it appeared that he probably had experienced some verbal impairment (Similarities score of 4).

HALSTEAD-REITAN NEUROPSYCHOLOGICAL TEST BATTERY

Patient_____C.S._____Age___70___Sex___M___Education___12___Handedness___R___

x WECHSLER-BELLEVUE SCALE (FORM I)	HALSTEAD'S NEUROPSYCHOLOGICAL TEST BATTERY

___WAIS

VIQ	109	**Category Test**	75
PIQ	101		
FIS IQ	99	**Tactual Performance Test**	
VWS	47	Dominant hand:	15.0 (3 blocks)
PWS	18	Non-dominant hand:	17.0 (6 blocks)
Total WS	65	Both hands:	18.2 (10 blocks)
		Total Time	50.2 +
Information	13	Memory	5
Comprehension	11	Localization	2
Digit Span	9		
Arithmetic	10	**Seashore Rhythm Test**	
Similarities	4	Number Correct___28___	2
Vocabulary	14		
		Speech-sounds Perception Test	
Picture Arrangement	4	Number of Errors	15
Picture Completion	6		
Block Design	1	**Finger Oscillation Test**	
Object Assembly	3	Dominant hand: 31	31
Digit Symbol	4	Non-dominant hand: 40	

TRAIL MAKING TEST   Impairment Index___0.9___

Part A:___65___seconds
Part B:___211___seconds

Miles ABC Test of Ocular Dominance
Right eye:_9_ Left eye:_1_

MINNESOTA MULTIPHASIC
PERSONALITY INVENTORY

REITAN-KLØVE SENSORY-PERCEPTUAL EXAM — No errors

			Error Totals			
				?	50	Hs 76
RH___LH___	Both:RH___LH___	RH___LH___		L	46	D 64
RH___LF___	Both:RH___LF___	RH___LF___		F	48	Hy 68
LH___RF___	Both:LH___RF___	RF___LH___		K	57	PD 46
RE___LE___	Both:RE___LE___	RE___LE___				MF 51
RV___LV___	Both:RV___LV___					Pa 52
___ ___	___ ___	RV___LV___				Pt 57
___ ___	___ ___					Sc 51
						Ma 40

TACTILE FINGER RECOGNITION

R 1___ 2___ 3_1_ 4_1_ 5___   R_2_ / 20
L 1___ 2___ 3___ 4___ 5___   L_0_ / 20

FINGER-TIP NUMBER WRITING

R 1___ 2___ 3___ 4_1_ 5___   R_1_ / 20
L 1___ 2___ 3___ 4___ 5___   L_0_ / 20

REITAN-INDIANA APHASIA SCREENING TEST

Form for Adults and Older Children

Name: _C. S._____ Age: _70_

Copy SQUARE	Repeat TRIANGLE
Name SQUARE	Repeat MASSACHUSETTS
Spell SQUARE	Repeat METHODIST EPISCOPAL
Copy CROSS Note imbalance of lateral extremities.	Write SQUARE
Name CROSS Confused at first, but named correctly.	Read SEVEN
Spell CROSS	Repeat SEVEN
Copy TRIANGLE	Repeat/Explain HE SHOUTED THE WARNING.
Name TRIANGLE Could not think of name. Wouldn't guess. Finally, said, "A masonic thing."	Write HE SHOUTED THE WARNING. Probably within normal limits.
Spell TRIANGLE	Compute 85 – 27 =
Name BABY	Compute 17 X 3 =
Write CLOCK After first attempt he was asked to write the word. Note confusion on first attempt.	Name KEY
Name FORK	Demonstrate use of KEY
Read 7 SIX 2	Draw KEY Note problems in completing symmetrical details.
Read MGW	Read PLACE LEFT HAND TO RIGHT EAR. "Place left hand at right ear."
Reading I	Place LEFT HAND TO RIGHT EAR
Reading II	Place LEFT HAND TO LEFT ELBOW

Clock
the
Clock

1.   1.   1.

Square

he shouted the warning

$$85$$
$$27$$ — 51
$$58$$

2.   2.   2.

Although some loss of ability on the Performance subtests is expected with older persons, the deficits shown by this man went beyond age-expected levels. For example, on Block Design he had a weighted score of only 1, and this corresponds with a raw score of 0; he was not able to complete even the most simple item. A performance at this level would certainly raise a question with respect to possible right cerebral damage. However, as the reader is certainly aware, the Wechsler Scale was not designed to provide a full assessment of brain-behavior relationships and only tentative observations may be made from the results on this Scale.

The four most sensitive indicators in the Halstead-Reitan Battery all showed significant impairment. The patient earned a Halstead Impairment Index of 0.9 (about 90 percent of the tests had scores in the brain-damaged range). He had significant difficulty on the Category Test (75), indicating impairment in the areas of abstraction, reasoning, and logical analysis. Studies of the tests in the Halstead-Reitan Battery related to aging have indicated that performances on the Category Test deteriorate probably more rapidly with advancing age than scores on any other measure. Nevertheless, considering the evidence of previous intellectual competence of this man, we would estimate that 75 errors goes beyond expected levels for a person of this age. The patient also had a great deal of difficulty on Part B of the Trail Making Test (211 seconds), indicating that he has experienced a considerable loss in flexibility of thought processes and the ability to keep two series of stimulus material in mind at the same time. Thus, in a general sense, it would appear that this man was somewhat more impaired than would be expected of most persons his age with his apparent prior abilities.

Inspection of the scores indicates that most of the tests in the Battery were performed poorly. Only one score stands out as being in the normal range: the Seashore Rhythm Test. C.S. made correct judgments in 28 of 30 trials, demonstrating his ability to pay attention to specified stimulus material and maintain concentration over time. In contrast, he performed much worse on tasks that required immediate adaptive abilities and analysis and definition of the nature of the problem. For example, he had great difficulty with the Tactual Performance Test and his performance could not be explained either by primary motor deficiency or tactile-perceptual impairment. C.S.'s higher level problem-solving abilities were much more impaired than were simpler tasks. The overall findings pointed toward generalized impairment of abilities dependent upon brain functions, and the good score on Seashore Rhythm suggests that the condition of the patient's brain is probably stable in a biological sense.

Lateralizing indicators implicated both cerebral hemispheres. Perhaps the most outstanding indication of left cerebral dysfunction was the impaired finger tapping speed of the right (preferred) hand (31) as compared with the left (40). The patient also performed worse with his right hand than his left on the Tactual Performance Test (5.0 minutes/block placed with the right hand as compared with 2.8 minutes/block for the left). These lateralized difficulties were probably not attributable solely to motor dysfunction on the right side.

The patient also demonstrated some difficulty in tactile finger recognition with his right hand as compared with his left. (The reader may also note that the attentional capabilities, with respect to specific and well-defined procedures, were generally adequate, as demonstrated by the scores for the tactile finger recognition and finger-tip number writing procedures. These results suggest that when observed only in well-structured situations, this man would appear to be quite capable.)

Results from the Aphasia Screening Test also supported a hypothesis of left cerebral damage. The patient demonstrated abnormal difficulty in naming (dysnomia). He was initially confused when asked to give the name of the cross and, with the triangle, was not able to give the correct name at all. Although he performed many of the items satisfactorily, these particular mistakes are not within the range of normal variation for a person with the Verbal I.Q. abilities of this man. He also demonstrated some difficulty in simple reading when asked to read PLACE LEFT HAND TO RIGHT EAR. The reader may wonder whether a minor mistake such as that made by the patient has any particular significance. Considering the care and effort requested of the patient in this testing situation, the error probably does represent some degree of difficulty dealing with verbal material for communicational purposes.

The patient's writing yields further significant information. When asked to look at the picture of a clock and to write the name of the object, this man initially started to print. He was then asked by the examiner to write the word. The error made in the first attempt (omission of the "l") almost certainly represents a further instance of abnormal verbal response. His writing of HE SHOUTED THE WARNING appears to represent the particular writing style of this man and is probably within normal limits.

His figure drawings, however, were not within normal limits, even for a 70-year-old person. He had definite difficulty with the left side of the cross and demonstrated confusion in his attempt to copy the key. Notches were made in the stem on the upper part but no corresponding notches on the lower part of the stem, the handle was very badly drawn, and the patient appeared to have great difficulty drawing the details of the teeth. These manifestations are rather typical of the drawing difficulties (constructional dyspraxia) of persons with right cerebral damage. Thus, evidence of mild constructional dyspraxia complemented the very poor performance on Block Design, as well as the much lower total score for the Performance subtests than the Verbal subtests of the Wechsler Scale, as indicators of right cerebral dysfunction.

Comparing the left and right cerebral indicators, one is impressed with the specificity of deficits (particularly in finger tapping speed with the right hand) among the left cerebral indicators. These deficiencies might be viewed as having special significance in comparing the status of the two sides of the brain. However, the more impressive information from neuropsychological testing probably concerns the generality of impairment, including evidence of right as well as left cerebral damage. This man still has stored information and the ability to pay attention to specific stimulus material, but hardly anything more. He is very seriously impaired in tasks that require analysis, definition, and novel kinds of circumstances. In addition, he has some mild difficulty in dealing with language symbols for communicational purposes. His psychomotor problem-solving abilities are severely impaired.

These are the factors that must be considered with relation to the advice sought by the patient: Should he return as chief executive officer of the building and loan association that he had developed over the years or should he buy and operate a marina in Florida? The test results indicate that an "either-or" question of this type is hardly pertinent. The answer to both of these possibilities would be "No." The patient does not have the immediate adaptive skills to run a relatively complex business and it would be a certain mistake to attempt to master even a simpler business with which the patient had no prior experience. Considering the patient's age, the neuropsychological impairment related to the generalized cerebral vascular deterioration and the residual effects from the more specific lesion involving the left cerebral hemisphere, the only meaningful recommendation for the future would relate to disengagement rather than renewal of demanding activities. The neuropsychological test results, together with the overall situation of the patient, indicate that he needs help with planning his retirement activities rather than advice about returning to stressful situations. The patient's neurological surgeon attempted to counsel him in this regard, but the patient expired about six months later from a massive stroke.

CASE #10

Name:	W.E.	Sex:	Male
Age:	63	Handedness:	Right
Education:	12	Occupation:	Business Executive

This 63-year-old man was referred for neuropsychological examination by his internist, who reported that he had been treating the patient for essential hypertension with marginal success. When questioned about his problems, the patient said that he had high blood pressure, occasional feelings of weakness, periods of feeling unsteady on his feet with an impaired sense of balance, and a slight loss of motor function of his right upper extremity. He denied any other illnesses or injuries. When asked about sensory function W.E. reported that about once every two months he had noticed a fading of vision in his left eye lasting for about 15 minutes. This almost certainly represents a manifestation of amaurosis fugax, indicating retinal ischemia due to insufficiency of the ophthalmic or carotid artery on the same side as the affected eye. The patient tended to downplay his symptoms, describing all his difficulties as only slight. His physician, however, justifiably seemed to be more concerned.

In reviewing the neuropsychological data the reader should try to determine whether this man shows any significant impairment for a person of his age. To what extent can his difficulties be explained on the basis of neuropsychological deterioration compared with emotional problems of adjustment? In his own self-assessment (Cornell Medical Index Health Questionnaire) the patient had several somatic complaints: feeling that he wears himself out worrying about his health, that he is constantly made miserable by poor health, and that he suffers from severe nervous exhaustion. He also indicated that he believes he is frequently ill.

Concerning emotional problems, W.E. did not have as many complaints, but did say that he easily becomes upset or irritated, usually feels unhappy and depressed, and gets things mixed up completely when he must do them quickly. Even though W.E. de-emphasized his symptoms when asked directly, he did admit them on the Health

HALSTEAD-REITAN NEUROPSYCHOLOGICAL TEST BATTERY

Patient _____ W.E. _____ Age _63_ Sex _M_ Education _12_ Handedness _R_

___ WECHSLER-BELLEVUE SCALE (FORM I)

_x_ WAIS

VIQ	123
PIQ	126
FIS IQ	124
VWS	63
PWS	49
Total WS	112
Information	13
Comprehension	14
Digit Span	13
Arithmetic	9
Similarities	14
Vocabulary	14
Picture Arrangement	11
Picture Completion	12
Block Design	8
Object Assembly	12
Digit Symbol	6

HALSTEAD'S NEUROPSYCHOLOGICAL TEST BATTERY

Category Test _____ 122

Tactual Performance Test
Dominant hand: _____ 15.0
Non-dominant hand: _____ 9.1
Both hands: _____ 9.4

Total Time _33.5_
Memory _8_
Localization _2_

Seashore Rhythm Test
Number Correct _28_ _____ 2

Speech-sounds Perception Test
Number of Errors _____ 2

Finger Oscillation Test
Dominant hand: _43_ _____ 43
Non-dominant hand: _36_

TRAIL MAKING TEST
Part A: _43_ seconds
Part B: _110_ seconds

Impairment Index _0.6_

STRENGTH OF GRIP
Dominant hand: _19.0_ kilograms
Non-dominant hand: _19.5_ kilograms

REITAN-KLØVE TACTILE FORM RECOGNITION TEST
Dominant hand: _9_ seconds; _0_ errors
Non-dominant hand: _13_ seconds; _0_ errors

REITAN-KLØVE SENSORY-PERCEPTUAL EXAM

				Error Totals	
RH___ LH___	Both:RH_1_ LH___			RH_1_ LH___	
RH___ LF___	Both:RH___ LF___			RH___ LF___	
LH___ RF___	Both:LH___ RF___			RF___ LH___	
RE___ LE___	Both:RE___ LE___			RE___ LE___	
RV___ LV___	Both:RV___ LV___				
				RV___ LV___	

TACTILE FINGER RECOGNITION
R 1___ 2___ 3___ 4___ 5___   R _0_ / 20
L 1___ 2___ 3 _1_ 4 _2_ 5___   L _3_ / 20

FINGER-TIP NUMBER WRITING
R 1 _1_ 2 _1_ 3___ 4___ 5 _1_   R _3_ / 20
L 1___ 2___ 3___ 4___ 5___   L _0_ / 20

Miles ABC Test of Ocular Dominance
Right eye: _10_ Left eye: _0_

MINNESOTA MULTIPHASIC
PERSONALITY INVENTORY

?	50	Hs	77
L	43	D	72
F	50	Hy	82
K	64	PD	64
		MF	69
		Pa	59
		Pt	60
		Sc	61
		Ma	55

REITAN-KLØVE
LATERAL-DOMINANCE EXAM

Show me how you:

throw a ball	R
hammer a nail	R
cut with a knife	R
turn a door knob	R
use scissors	R
use an eraser	R
write your name	R

Record time used for spontaneous name-writing:
Preferred hand _6_ seconds
Non-preferred hand _17_ seconds

Show me how you:
kick a football _R_
step on a bug _R_

REITAN-INDIANA APHASIA SCREENING TEST

Form for Adults and Older Children

Name: _____W. E._____ Age: __63__

Copy SQUARE	Repeat TRIANGLE
Name SQUARE	Repeat MASSACHUSETTS
Spell SQUARE	Repeat METHODIST EPISCOPAL
Copy CROSS Note mild degree of asymmetry of extremities.	Write SQUARE
Name CROSS	Read SEVEN
Spell CROSS	Repeat SEVEN
Copy TRIANGLE	Repeat/Explain HE SHOUTED THE WARNING.
Name TRIANGLE	Write HE SHOUTED THE WARNING.
Spell TRIANGLE	Compute 85 – 27 =
Name BABY	Compute 17 X 3 = "81" Given 13 X 4 and answered "52"
Write CLOCK	Name KEY
Name FORK	Demonstrate use of KEY
Read 7 SIX 2 "Six – 7 – six – 2"	Draw KEY Note problems with handle and notches on stem near handle.
Read MGW	Read PLACE LEFT HAND TO RIGHT EAR.
Reading I	Place LEFT HAND TO RIGHT EAR
Reading II	Place LEFT HAND TO LEFT ELBOW Attempted and said, "I don't see how."

clock

S Q U ARE

square

He shouted the warning.

85 - 27 = 58

81

52

Questionnaire. We should also note that this man was the chief executive for the regional office of a major news service and had high-level occupational responsibilities.

In interpreting W.E.'s test results, try to answer the following: (1) How do this man's abilities relate to the needs of his job? (2) Does he show deterioration that is of significance? (3) Is there evidence of any focal cerebral damage? (4) What kinds of recommendations would you make?

REPORT OF NEUROPSYCHOLOGICAL EXAMINATION

Psychological Implications

In brief, the test results for this patient are clear in their implications. The findings show that W.E. had high abilities in the past, has experienced deterioration of immediate adaptive skills dependent upon brain functions, and had many complaints related to the deterioration and undermining of his self-confidence.

Although W.E. earned both Verbal and Performance I.Q. values that were in the Superior range (exceeding about 95 percent of his age peers), he showed evidence of mild deterioration of certain aspects of general intelligence. On Halstead's tests, which are considerably more sensitive to the immediate condition of the cerebral cortex than Wechsler's Scale, the patient earned an Impairment Index of 0.6 (60 percent of the tests in the brain-damaged range). He did very well on certain tests related to background abilities and general intelligence but did poorly on tests requiring insight, logical analysis, abstract reasoning, and ability to understand the essential nature of the problem.

When required to face a problem for which he had not had prior experience, he showed considerable difficulties. He still continues to be fairly quick and alert, remembers elements of tasks to which he has been exposed, focuses his attention to specific stimulus material (Rhythm Test and Speech-sounds Perception Test), works efficiently over time, and deals capably with problems involving elements of which he is well aware. However, when it comes to analyzing a situation, identifying critical elements, getting at the heart of the problem, and organizing diverse and varied material, the patient definitely has trouble. These results make it quite clear that W.E. would be losing his self-confidence at this point and feel threatened in many ways.

In assessing the patient's own reactions, we used two techniques: a self-evaluation and a more subtle method. In his own self-evaluation, W.E. had a number of somatic complaints and it would appear that he tends to use these complaints as a recourse for emotional tensions derived from the situation described above. He also indicated that he suffers from spells of exhaustion or fatigue and that working sometimes tires him out. He reported that he usually gets up tired and exhausted in the morning and believes that he suffers from severe nervous exhaustion. He thought that he was frequently ill, that he wears himself out worrying about his health and that he is constantly made miserable by poor health.

In addition, W.E. indicated that he has difficulty sleeping, feels unsure of himself, believes that his thinking gets mixed up when he has to do things quickly and that he must proceed very slowly and carefully in order to avoid mistakes. He said that he usually feels unhappy and depressed, is easily upset and irritated, and frightening thoughts keep coming back into his mind.

Lastly, the patient noted that he usually takes two or more alcoholic drinks a day. We would postulate that this overall situation renders the patient particularly susceptible to adverse effects of alcohol, adding more confusion to that which he already feels.

The Minnesota Multiphasic Personality Inventory yielded essentially similar results. The patient's basic personality structure seems to be intact but he is anxious and concerned about his physical condition, mildly depressed, and has hysterical tendencies. This emotional pattern probably derives from or interacts with the deterioration of basic adaptive skills noted above. Thus, the patient feels threatened, has difficulties dealing with the tasks he faces in everyday living, and does not know just which way to turn to solve his problems. Under these circumstances he has gravitated toward somatic manifestations of various kinds as the most acceptable basis for the problems that he faces.

Neurological Implications

As implied above, our findings suggest that the patient has experienced some generalized deterioration of cerebral functions. Although persons in his age range often show such changes to some extent, the findings for this patient go beyond age-related expectations and are representative of mild *hypertensive encephalopathy*. It is apparent that he was an able person in the past, and continues to be very competent in many respects. However, in terms of immediate problem-solving skills dependent upon brain functions, he has shown a striking deterioration.

Some of the test results point toward left cerebral involvement and others indicate right cerebral dysfunction. We see that on complex manipulatory tasks his right (preferred) hand is not as skilled as it should be compared with his left hand. Therefore, the patient's complaint of loss of function on the right side certainly seems to be justified and is related to deterioration of brain functions. However, his language functions continue to be relatively intact.

We see no evidence of significant focal impairment of either cerebral hemisphere. Results of this kind are congruent with patients who have essential hypertension and at least a mild degree of hypertensive encephalopathy.

Summary and Recommendations

Neuropsychological examination of this 63-year-old man indicated that his I.Q. values exceeded about 95 percent of the population. Nevertheless, he was seriously impaired on some of Halstead's tests which are specifically sensitive to the organic condition of the cerebral cortex. The patient has difficulty adapting to novel types of tasks and organizing diverse stimulus material in a meaningful way. His problems appear especially when he is required to deal with new situations rather than ones with which he has had prior familiarity. He has a great deal of difficulty in abstract analysis and abstract reasoning and seeing the essential nature of new problems and situations.

These difficulties, in turn, seem to have provoked a feeling of insecurity and emotional instability in the patient. He has a definite tendency to feel that he is ill, and focuses on somatic aspects of his complaints. He also is mildly depressed and has rather definite hysterical tendencies. Thus, the overall results suggest that the patient is adapting to these problems (probably without much insight) by developing various types of somatic complaints, emphasizing these difficulties, and attempting to derive some degree of understanding or satisfaction from significant persons in his environment through this mechanism.

Since the basic problem relates to generalized deterioration of cerebral functions, we would recommend that W.E. be encouraged to gradually disengage himself from his everyday responsibilities, lessen the pressures under which he operates, and move in the direction of being able to take life easier. Following such an approach, it is likely that his feelings of stress, and emotional reactions to stress, would tend to become less pronounced. He still has the abilities to enjoy many aspects of life, continues to be competent in a general intelligence sense, and should be able to derive a great deal of enjoyment from life if he can make arrangements to become less competitive and reduce the requirments placed upon him in everyday living.

CASE #11

Name:	G.H.	Sex:	Male
Age:	34	Handedness:	Right
Education:	9	Occupation:	Factory Worker

This patient had experienced severe headaches and a stiff neck for more than four years prior to this hospitalization. He was otherwise in good health until he had a major motor seizure two days before admission to the hospital. Neurological examination at the time of admission was entirely within normal limits. However, EEG showed Dysrhythmia, Grade I, that appeared to involve both temporal areas but was clearly maximal in the left Sylvian region. An angiogram demonstrated an arteriovenous malformation in the left temporal-parietal area, being fed by the left middle cerebral artery. There was no evidence that the lesion had ruptured. Thus, the patient had a congenital vascular lesion which had progressed sufficiently far to cause a major motor seizure but no other clinical symptoms.

G.H. had both Verbal and Performance I.Q. values that were near the Average level. Although the total of the Verbal weighted scores was nearly identical with the total for the Performance weighted scores, there was a considerable degree of variability among both the Verbal and Performance subtests. Judging from the relatively low scores on Information (6) and Vocabulary (6), we would estimate that this man has never had a particularly good intellectual background in an academic sense, even though his basic verbal capabilities (Similarities score of 12) might be somewhat higher than would be inferred from the lower scores. The relatively low score on the Digit Symbol (6) subtest is not unexpected, considering that this man had a cerebral lesion. In terms of "blind" interpretation, one would necessarily have to observe the Picture Arrangement score (7), contrast it with the considerably better performance on Block Design (13), and keep in mind the possibility of some fairly discrete right anterior temporal lobe dysfunction. As is usually the case, it would be difficult to draw any firm conclusions about brain-behavior relationships from the Wechsler Scale. The results do suggest, though, that this man's prior intellectual development has been within normal limits.

HALSTEAD-REITAN NEUROPSYCHOLOGICAL TEST BATTERY

Patient _____ G.H. _____ Age __ 34 __ Sex __ M __ Education __ 9 __ Handedness __ R __

x WECHSLER-BELLEVUE SCALE (FORM I)		HALSTEAD'S NEUROPSYCHOLOGICAL TEST BATTERY

___ WAIS

VIQ	98	**Category Test** _____ 31 _____
PIQ	104	
FIS IQ	102	**Tactual Performance Test**
VWS	44	Dominant hand: _____ 14.2 _____
PWS	46	Non-dominant hand: _____ 6.4 _____
Total WS	90	Both hands: _____ 4.0 _____
		Total Time __ 24.6 __
Information	6	Memory __ 5 __
Comprehension	11	Localization __ 3 __
Digit Span	6	
Arithmetic	9	**Seashore Rhythm Test**
Similarities	12	Number Correct __ 20 __ _____ 10 _____
Vocabulary	6	
		Speech-sounds Perception Test
Picture Arrangement	7	Number of Errors _____ 11 _____
Picture Completion	9	
Block Design	13	**Finger Oscillation Test**
Object Assembly	11	Dominant hand: _____ 47 _____ 47 _____
Digit Symbol	6	Non-dominant hand: __ 49 __

TRAIL MAKING TEST   Impairment Index _____ 0.9 _____
Part A: __ 30 __ seconds
Part B: __ 120 __ seconds

Miles ABC Test of Ocular Dominance
Right eye: _7_ Left eye: _3_

MINNESOTA MULTIPHASIC
PERSONALITY INVENTORY

REITAN-KLØVE SENSORY-PERCEPTUAL EXAM — No errors

					Error Totals			?	50	Hs	65
RH___	LH___	Both:RH___	LH___	RH___	LH___		L	50	D	68
RH___	LF___	Both:RH___	LF___	RH___	LF___		F	50	Hy	64
LH___	RF___	Both:LH___	RF___	RF___	LH___		K	68	PD	64
RE___	LE___	Both:RE___	LE___	RE___	LE___				MF	53
RV___	LV___	Both:RV___	LV___						Pa	39
___	___	___	___	RV___	LV___				Pt	60
___	___	___	___						Sc	55
									Ma	53

TACTILE FINGER RECOGNITION
R 1___ 2___ 3___ 4___ 5___   R 0 / 20
L 1___ 2___ 3___ 4___ 5___   L 0 / 20

FINGER-TIP NUMBER WRITING
R 1_1_ 2_1_ 3_1_ 4_2_ 5_1_   R 6 / 20
L 1_1_ 2___ 3___ 4_1_ 5_1_   L 3 / 20

REITAN-INDIANA APHASIA SCREENING TEST

Form for Adults and Older Children

Name: ___G. H.___ Age: __34__

Copy SQUARE	Repeat TRIANGLE
Name SQUARE	Repeat MASSACHUSETTS "Massachusee"

Spell SQUARE
    "S-Q-U-R-E"
	Repeat METHODIST EPISCOPAL
	    "Methodi Episible"

Copy CROSS	Write SQUARE
Name CROSS	Read SEVEN
Spell CROSS	Repeat SEVEN
Copy TRIANGLE "Tent or 3-cornered diagram"	Repeat/Explain HE SHOUTED THE WARNING.
Name TRIANGLE	Write HE SHOUTED THE WARNING.
Spell TRIANGLE	Compute 85 – 27 =
Name BABY	Compute 17 X 3 =
Write CLOCK	Name KEY
Name FORK	Demonstrate use of KEY
Read 7 SIX 2	Draw KEY
Read MGW	Read PLACE LEFT HAND TO RIGHT EAR.
Reading I	Place LEFT HAND TO RIGHT EAR
Reading II	Place LEFT HAND TO LEFT ELBOW

□ ✚   △ tryangle clack

G. H.

~~square~~
~~Cross~~
~~seven~~

85
27

58

he shatted the morning

Although the Category Test was remarkably well done (31), the four most sensitive indicators of the Halstead-Reitan Battery overall suggested cerebral damage. Even though the Impairment Index was 0.9, one could not conclude that this man had severe impairment of higher brain functions. This finding again demonstrates the fact that the Halstead Impairment Index is a *consistency-of-impairment* index rather than a *severity-of- impairment* index. Contrasting the results on the four most sensitive indicators with the I.Q. values provides rather strong evidence for some degree of brain-related impairment.

Comparing the tests that were done well with those that showed some degree of deficit provides more information about the ability structure of this man. In most respects his scores suggested impaired brain function, generally falling at about the average level for brain-damaged subjects. In contrast, he performed extremely well on the Category Test. This score would suggest that the patient did not have an acutely or severely destructive focal lesion or a rapidly progressive condition of brain disease. The Category Test is an instrument which is especially sensitive to the status of the brain. Any recent or progressive biological embarrassment to the brain (particularly if it is very severe) will cause deficits on this measure. A major requirement in interpretation of the neuropsychological data for this man will be integration of the good Category Test score with the indications of impairment.

Next, it is necessary to review the test results with respect to lateralizing and localizing evidence. The patient showed a number of deficits that, although not strikingly pronounced, implicate the left cerebral hemisphere. G.H.'s finger tapping speed was somewhat slower with his right (dominant) hand (47) than his left (49); this is an unusual finding among normal subjects. The preferred hand is expected to be about 10 percent faster than the nonpreferred hand. In this case, then, we would have expected about an average of 54 taps with the right hand rather than 47. A deficit of this magnitude (although probably not noticeable in clinical neurological examination) has definite significance and must be considered.

The patient also had much more difficulty with his right hand than with his left on the Tactual Performance Test. Clinical observation has suggested that deficient performances on the first trial (usually using the right hand) are not quite as reliable as poor performances on the second trial (usually using the left hand). The reason for this is that occasionally a patient has great difficulty adapting to the general requirements of the Tactual Performance Test, takes a long time to get going with the task, and consequently performs poorly on the first trial. In this instance, however, the patient did so much worse with his right hand than left that we would interpret the findings as suggesting that the left cerebral hemisphere dealt with the requirements of the Tactual Performance Test much less effectively than the right cerebral hemisphere.

The Tactual Performance Test is a complex task, requiring both input (sensory) and output (motor) functions as well as problem-solving skills. Therefore, in order to compare the patient's tactile receptive and expressive capabilities, it is necessary to have additional tests which reflect receptive input. This man had no difficulty on either hand in tactile finger recognition. However, the finger-tip number writing perception measure yielded very helpful results: the patient had definitely more difficulty with his right hand than his left. There was a distinct tactile-perceptual loss on the right side of the body, complementing the motor deficit we had seen in finger-tapping speed. If we were postulating the presence of an acutely destructive lesion, we would expect to find definite and pronounced aphasic symptoms associated with these deficits.

The Aphasia Screening Test did reveal some difficulties of a pathological nature in processing verbal information, but the losses were not severe. The patient demonstrated some problems in spelling and one might wonder whether his educational background and intellectual development were responsible for these problems. Even so, it is unusual for a normal subject to leave out the "a" in spelling SQUARE. In addition, in writing HE SHOUTED THE WARNING, he wrote an "m" rather than an "n" in the word WARNING. He made other spelling errors, but these were more common among persons with limited educational training. For example, the "y" in spelling TRIANGLE and misspelling of "shouted" are not uncommon in persons with limited educational training. His spelling of "clock" may raise a question, but many people drop the line after an "O," and we would not conclude that he had actually misspelled this word. However, omission of the "a" in SQUARE and confusion of the "m" for "n" in WARNING are the kinds of mistakes that are associated with left cerebral damage.

Apparently, the patient also had some trouble naming the triangle, which suggests the presence of dysnomia. The type of mistakes G.H. made when repeating MASSACHUSETTS and METHODIST EPISCOPAL are really quite unusual but, nevertheless, strongly suggestive of left cerebral damage. As the reader will note, G.H. failed to enunciate the correct sound at the end of MASSACHUSETTS, made the same kind of mistake at the end of METHODIST, and had a little difficulty with EPISCOPAL even though the substitution of syllables did not represent as flagrant an error as in the previous instances. The overall results pointed strongly toward a lesion in the left cerebral hemisphere.

We also note that this man had some difficulty copying the cross and key. Tilting of the cross, as exhibited in this instance, is not necessarily a sign of cerebral damage, but we would be suspicious about the loss of symmetry in the lateral extremities and would raise the possibility of deficit. The drawing of the key showed a little more pronounced evidence of impairment, particularly in the loss of symmetry in the teeth. Finally, the Picture Arrangement score (7) should again be mentioned as possibly having some significance for right cerebral dysfunction. In summary then, the lateralizing indicators lean much more strongly toward left than right cerebral damage.

Next, we will jointly consider the possible type and location of the lesion because these factors often interact. First, it must be noted that except for a very good Category Test score (31) this man generally showed about the degree of impairment that would be expected from the average brain-damaged subject. Second, although there was definite evidence of involvement of the left cerebral hemisphere, the Verbal I.Q. was not significantly lower than the Performance I.Q. In fact, the distribution of Verbal subtests was more representative of a person who had not gained a very good intellectual and educational background than of one who had sustained a significant loss of pre-existing abilities.

The neuropsychologist has to consider the evidence of mild dysphasia together with motor (finger tapping speed) and tactile perceptual (finger-tip number writing) deficits of the right side of the body. The dysphasia might suggest left temporal lobe involvement; the impairment in finger tapping speed might implicate the posterior part of the left frontal lobe; and the finger-tip number writing misperception suggests some dysfunction of the left parietal lobe. In this case it is possible to postulate specific involvement of these various areas because the lesion does not appear to be sufficiently destructive to have very great "distance" effects. In fact, the lesion had not impaired left cerebral functions sufficiently to cause either difficulties in tactile finger recognition on the right hand or significantly reduce the Verbal I.Q. Finally, the lesion was not sufficiently disruptive of brain functions generally to cause a deficit on the Category Test. All of these findings suggest that the focal signs can be taken as indications of the specific areas to which they refer. Thus, the results strongly suggest a lesion in the middle part of the left cerebral hemisphere that has not caused severe tissue destruction or overall disruption of cerebral cortical functioning.

An additional question might concern the significance of mild impairment in drawing the cross and key and the relatively low score on Picture Arrangement. In many patients with arteriovenous malformations we tend to see mild dysfunction in the non-involved cerebral hemisphere in an area homologous with the area of the lesion. This does not always occur, but we have noticed this kind of difficulty pre-operatively and have seen it resolve itself after surgical repair of the lesion. The mechanism whereby this type of neuropsychological finding happens is unknown, but it may be related to reports of vascular "steal" that occur with anomalies of cerebral arteries. We might point out however, that in this instance, the patient also showed bitemporal EEG foci, with the disorder in the left Sylvian region being more pronounced.

The Minnesota Multiphasic Personality Inventory suggested that G.H. might have some emotional and affective problems but, considering the fact that the man was obviously involved in the very stressful circumstances of having a serious brain lesion, there was nothing remarkable about these findings.

In summary, then, G.H. showed a focal lesion in the middle part of the left cerebral hemisphere that (1) was not particularly destructive; (2) had not caused severe aphasia or significant reduction of Verbal I.Q.; and (3) had not impaired brain functions even generally to the point that the Category Test was involved. Conceivably, a small, very slowly growing intrinsic tumor might cause these effects, but in most cases such a lesion would have produced a poor Category Test score in association with the other findings. A meningioma in this area might well be associated with a normal Category Test score and no depression of Verbal I.Q., but a number of additional findings argue against such a lesion: the Impairment Index of 0.9, the fact that the patient generally performed about as poorly as the average brain-damaged person, and the consistency of the lateralizing indicators. A very focal head injury could possibly have produced these results, but it would be more likely that a blow coming from the outside, sufficiently strong to produce the impairment shown by this man, would also have caused a greater deficit on the Category Test. Thus, the Category Test score, in the context of the other findings shown by this patient, was of critical significance in understanding the underlying lesion.

This case well illustrates the importance of including both general and specific indicators in the Battery. Focal lesions can often be localized by a battery that includes essentially only specific indicators (most neuropsychological batteries other than the HRNB) but evaluation of the significance of these specific indicators, in the context of brain functions more generally, is also required. The converse of the results shown by this patient (poor scores on general indicators including the Category Test in the absence of specific signs) frequently occurs in other conditions such as closed head injuries, diffuse cerebral vascular disease (e.g. hypertensive encephalopathy), and even in conditions such as early primary neuronal degenerative changes. Of course, the only way in which a balance was achieved between specific and general indicators was to have developed and validated the Halstead-Reitan Battery in a large number of individual cases.

CASE #12

Name:	C.H.	Sex:	Male
Age:	30	Handedness:	Right
Education:	12	Occupation:	Farmer

Current Complaints and Pertinent History

About six weeks before neuropsychological examination, this 30-year-old farmer suddenly developed a severe headache, vomiting and aphasia while plowing his field. He did not lose consciousness, was able to seek help and was promptly taken to a local hospital. A lumbar puncture showed bloody cerebral spinal fluid. He developed a right hemiparesis shortly after the episode. His blood pressure at the time of hospital admission was 206/180.

After this initial episode C.H. gradually began to show some improvement though he still had elevated blood pressure and his fundi showed marked hypertensive changes. He had a right lower homonymous quadrantanopsia, a mild hemiparesis and right hemihypalgesia, and a mild right facial paresis. He also demonstrated dysphasia with dysnomia, dyslexia, dysgraphia, dyscalculia and mild finger dysgnosia of the right hand. His EEG showed Delta waves, Grade II, in the left temporal-parietal area. A non-functioning kidney appeared to be responsible for the elevated blood pressure.

The diagnostic impression was that this patient had experienced a focal cerebral hemorrhage involving the posterior temporal-parietal area, probably associated with the extreme elevation of blood pressure. (A substantial proportion of persons who die from other conditions show small areas of weakness in cerebral vessels which, except for the fact that they are associated with no clinical neurological manifestations, appear to be essentially similar to an aneurysm of non-clinical significance.) We would postulate that C.H. may have sustained an area of focal bleeding because of elevated blood pressure and a blood vessel weakness in the left cerebral hemisphere. There was no other evidence that the patient's brain was compromised in any clinical or pathological respect. It therefore appears that the lesion represented a very focal accident in a previously normal brain.

HALSTEAD-REITAN NEUROPSYCHOLOGICAL TEST BATTERY

Patient_____C.H._____Age__30__Sex__M__Education__12__Handedness__R__

_x_ WECHSLER-BELLEVUE SCALE (FORM I)	HALSTEAD'S NEUROPSYCHOLOGICAL TEST BATTERY

___WAIS

VIQ	88	**Category Test**	8
PIQ	117		
FIS IQ	102	**Tactual Performance Test**	
VWS	36	Dominant hand: 7.6	
PWS	59	Non-dominant hand: 5.4	
Total WS	95	Both hands: 2.4	
		Total Time 15.4	
Information	11	Memory 10	
Comprehension	7	Localization 7	
Digit Span	4		
Arithmetic	3	**Seashore Rhythm Test**	
Similarities	11	Number Correct 25	6
Vocabulary	8		
		Speech-sounds Perception Test	
Picture Arrangement	14	Number of Errors	27
Picture Completion	12		
Block Design	13	**Finger Oscillation Test**	
Object Assembly	11	Dominant hand: 60	60
Digit Symbol	9	Non-dominant hand: 56	

TRAIL MAKING TEST

Part A:__31__seconds
Part B:__106__seconds

Impairment Index__0.3__

Miles ABC Test of Ocular Dominance

Right eye:_10_ Left eye:_0_

REITAN-KLØVE SENSORY-PERCEPTUAL EXAM

					Error Totals	
RH___	LH___	Both:RH___	LH___	RH___	LH___	
RH___	LF___	Both:RH___	LF___	RH___	LF___	
LH___	RF___	Both:LH___	RF___	RF___	LH___	
RE___	LE___	Both:RE_2_	LE___	RE_2_	LE___	
RV___	LV___	Both:RV___	LV___			
___	___	___	___	RV_4_	LV___	
4		4				

MINNESOTA MULTIPHASIC
PERSONALITY INVENTORY

?	50	Hs	93
L	70	D	101
F	68	Hy	87
K	64	PD	74
		MF	61
		Pa	73
		Pt	71
		Sc	88
		Ma	53

TACTILE FINGER RECOGNITION

R 1__ 2 1 3 2 4 1 5__ R 4 / 20
L 1__ 2__ 3__ 4__ 5__ L 0 / 20

FINGER-TIP NUMBER WRITING

R 1__ 2__ 3__ 4__ 5__ R 0 / 20
L 1__ 2__ 3__ 4__ 5__ L 0 / 20

Visual Field Examination: Right lower homonymous quadrantanopsia.

REITAN-INDIANA APHASIA SCREENING TEST

Form for Adults and Older Children

Name: C. H.   Age: 30

Copy SQUARE	Repeat TRIANGLE
Name SQUARE	Repeat MASSACHUSETTS Patient couldn't comprehend the instructions; did not know what he was supposed to do.
Spell SQUARE	Repeat METHODIST EPISCOPAL (as above)
Copy CROSS	Write SQUARE
Name CROSS	Read SEVEN
Spell CROSS	Repeat SEVEN
Copy TRIANGLE	Repeat/Explain HE SHOUTED THE WARNING. Was able to repeat, but initially confused when asked to explain.
Name TRIANGLE	Write HE SHOUTED THE WARNING. Could not write the sentence.
Spell TRIANGLE	Compute 85 – 27 =
Name BABY	Compute 17 X 3 =
Write CLOCK Patient had difficulty understanding the instructions.	Name KEY
Name FORK "Talk", then self-corrected.	Demonstrate use of KEY
Read 7 SIX 2	Draw KEY
Read MGW	Read PLACE LEFT HAND TO RIGHT EAR.
Reading I	Place LEFT HAND TO RIGHT EAR
Reading II	Place LEFT HAND TO LEFT ELBOW Could not comprehend the instructions.

C. H.

$17 \times 3 = 51$

CLOCK

Clock

Square

We shout

$$8\,5^5$$
$$2\,7$$
$$\overline{5\,8}$$

$$\begin{array}{r} 39 \\ 56 \\ + 37 \\ \hline 132 \end{array}$$

Neuropsychological Test Results

The patient earned a Verbal I.Q. (88) that fell in the upper part of the Low Average range and a Performance I.Q. (117) that was in the upper part of the High Average range. It should be noted that there was a 29-point difference between these I.Q. values. The Verbal subtest scores suggest that this man had developed fairly average abilities in the past: both the Information score (11) and Similarities score (11) were slightly above the average level. In addition, C.H. had graduated from high school.

Except for Digit Symbol (9), the Performance scores were consistently higher than the Verbal scores. It is entirely possible that C.H.'s brain lesion was at least partly responsible for the Digit Symbol performance. We would also postulate that his score on the Arithmetic subtest (3) was depressed as a result of brain damage.

Of the four most sensitive indicators on the Halstead-Reitan Battery, the score on Trails B (106 seconds) was the only result in the brain-damaged range. The Impairment Index for this patient was 0.3, indicating that only about 30 percent of Halstead's tests had results in the brain-damaged range. The two tests that contributed positively to the Impairment Index were the Seashore Rhythm Test and the Speech-sounds Perception Test. The patient did not do particularly poorly on the Seashore Rhythm Test (25 correct of 30 items); however, his score on the Speech-sounds Perception Test (27 errors) was well beyond the acceptable limit. One might question whether the deficient performances on these two measures represented a deficit at the first level of neuropsychological central processing but such a hypothesis appears to be unlikely. From the scores on these two measures we would judge that his deficit was related to the content of the tasks rather than due to impaired primary attention and concentration capabilities.

The patient did extremely well on the Category Test, making only 8 errors. To obtain a score this good, a person must have more than excellent concept formation and reasoning abilities; he must be lucky as well. C.H. also had an acceptable score (7) on the Localization component of the Tactual Performance Test. Therefore, the general indicators were usually well done. The only problem in interpreting the test results relates to explaining the relatively poor performance on Trails B. Since the patient had fairly good scores on the Information and Similarities subtests, one would not postulate that this poor score was a reflection of a life-long low Verbal I.Q. It appeared likely that the patient had experienced some deficit on certain of the Verbal subtests and the mildly poor score on Trails B may have been due to impairment in dealing with verbal symbols in the context of this particular task.

A review of the patient's good and poor scores indicated that he performed quite well on a number of tests: the Category Test, the Memory and Localization components of the Tactual Performance Test, all of the Performance subtests (except Digit Symbol) and the Information and Similarities subtests. Fairly good performances were also obtained on the Tactual Performance Test–Time and the Seashore Rhythm Test.

Conversely, the patient performed poorly on a number of measures, including the Comprehension, Digit Span, Arithmetic and Vocabulary Verbal subtests; Digit Symbol; Trails B; and the Speech-sounds Perception Test. On the Aphasia Test C.H.'s performances demonstrated an impaired use of language for communicational purposes, constructional dyspraxia (cross and key), and sensory losses (right lower homonymous quadrantanopsia and difficulty perceiving an auditory stimulus to the right ear when given simultaneously with the stimulus to the left ear). These results clearly indicate a great degree of variability in performances. Although many tests were performed adequately, a sufficient number of specific signs were present to indicate definite cerebral damage.

As demonstrated by results on the Minnesota Multiphasic Personality Inventory, this man showed significant problems in the emotional and affective areas. We will not review all the possible implications of these findings except to note that C.H. appeared to be considerably distressed and disturbed. We appreciate the usefulness and significance of psychological evaluation and the contribution it can make to understanding the patient's overall clinical status; however, it is important for the investigator to realize that psychological findings of this kind do not have a limiting influence on the interpretation of neuropsychological measures.

The next step in our interpretation involves evaluation of lateralizing and localizing findings. The pattern of performances on the Tactual Performance Test was not definitive in implicating right hemisphere dysfunction. The patient was a little slow with his left hand (5.4 minutes) compared with his right (7.6 minutes), but this result, standing alone and being very mild in nature, probably is within the range of chance expectation.

C.H.'s Aphasia Test drawings cannot be considered normal. The patient had difficulty dealing with spatial configurations, exemplified by his representation of the extremities of the cross and the handle of the key. The reader should be aware that research has demonstrated that about 15 percent of persons with posterior left cerebral lesions have certain problems with drawing simple configurations (Wheeler & Reitan, 1962). We believe that the particular kinds of difficulties shown by these persons (with left cerebral lesions) are different from the confusion of spatial relationships exhibited by persons with right cerebral lesions. It is difficult to demonstrate this in a single case, but there is a definite possibility that a small proportion of persons with left cerebral lesions will exhibit impaired drawings. Since these drawing difficulties occur particularly in persons with specific structural damage of the posterior part of the language area in the left cerebral hemisphere, their presence contributes to the diagnostic impression rather than detracts from it.

All of the other lateralizing findings in this case implicated the left cerebral hemisphere. Probably the most pronounced finding was a right lower homonymous quadrantanopsia, a result implicating involvement of the geniculostriate tract in the left parietal lobe. The aphasic difficulties also point definitely to left cerebral damage. On some items of the Aphasia Test the examiner asks the subject to perform a particular task; since the subject must be able to understand verbal instructions in order to complete the task successfully, the Aphasia Test can be used to evaluate auditory comprehension skills.

C.H. had great difficulty understanding verbal instructions in several different situations. For example, when he was asked to look at the picture of a clock, avoid saying anything aloud, and write the name of what he was looking at, it was apparent that he could not figure out what he was supposed to do. Even though he had just repeated the word TRIANGLE when asked to do so, he was unable to understand the instructions to repeat MASSACHUSETTS. He also showed considerable confusion when the examiner asked him to explain HE SHOUTED THE WARNING. Eventually, the examiner was able to communicate the instructions to him in a way he seemed to understand

and the patient was able to give an explanation. However, when next asked to write the sentence HE SHOUTED THE WARNING he was scarcely able to make any progress. Dysgraphia of this nature is more often associated with acutely destructive lesions rather than lesions that have become integrated into a pattern of chronic dysfunction. The patient also had difficulty on the Speech-sounds Perception Test — his score of 27 errors definitely deviates from the normal pattern. The poor performance on this test also indicated the presence of receptive difficulty (both visual and auditory) in dealing with verbal material.

Finally, in terms of higher level functions, the patient had a much lower Verbal than Performance I.Q. value. He demonstrated some sensory-perceptual losses, making some mistakes on the right hand but none on the left hand in Tactile Finger Recognition. His perfect performance on each hand in Finger-tip Number Writing Perception is a finding that accents the significance of the four errors on the right hand in Tactile Finger Recognition. C.H. also showed some difficulty perceiving an auditory stimulus to the right ear when given in competition with a stimulus to the left ear.

In summary, we can say that despite good performances on several tests, the overall results demonstrate definite damage in the left cerebral hemisphere and show no corresponding indications of damage in the right cerebral hemisphere. The only indicator of general impairment was the poor score on Trails B. In all probability, the nature of the stimulus material used in this test was responsible for the deficit. This man was able to deal effectively with complex material if he was not required to perceive and understand verbal symbolic material. Trails B does require perception and integration of the numerical and alphabetical series, a procedure that would almost certainly be of difficulty to this man. In this instance, then, it appears that the score on Trails B was another reflection of left cerebral damage.

Next, this overall configuration of test results should be considered with relation to the independent neurological findings. The medical findings suggested that the patient had experienced a very focal area of bleeding in the posterior part of the language area of the left cerebral hemisphere. Auditory-verbal dysgnosia (pronounced difficulty in comprehension of verbal material through the auditory avenue) is one of the outstanding signs of damage in this area and was shown very strikingly by C.H. The deficit in tactile finger recognition and the homonymous right lower quadrantanopsia imply some damage in the left parietal area. The fact that finger tapping speed was uninvolved represents a factor that would incline localization away from the motor strip and toward the more posterior part of the left cerebral hemisphere. The finding of auditory imperception and the poor score on the Speech-sounds Perception Test would also be consistent with damage of the posterior temporal-parietal area of the left hemisphere. Finally, among the 15 percent of persons with left cerebral lesions who show difficulty copying the cross and key, the lesions are customarily posteriorly located. Therefore, the test results suggest that this man had sustained a discrete structural lesion in the posterior part of the left cerebral hemisphere. The measures of general cerebral status were done well, indicating that the rest of the brain was essentially uninvolved. In fact, the positive symptoms shown by this man were almost certainly a result of an accident to a discrete and restricted area of the left cerebral hemisphere resulting from weakness in a vessel wall in combination with striking elevation of blood pressure.

It may be worth noting that this man showed a remarkable recovery very shortly after a nephrectomy was done. Within two weeks following this operation we were not able to detect any dysphasic symptoms. It may well be that a generally competent brain, in a biological sense, has a much better potential for recovery of functions than a brain that is seriously or generally deteriorated. Probably the only method for obtaining this kind of information in individual subjects is in clinical neuropsychological examination and the Halstead-Reitan Battery has been shown to be particularly effective in representing both general and specific aspects of cerebral cortical functioning.

CASE #13

Name:	H.D.	Sex:	Female
Age:	61	Handedness:	Right
Education:	11	Occupation:	Homemaker

This 61-year-old right-handed woman was referred for neuro-psychological testing jointly by a cardiologist and psychiatrist. Testing was done without any detailed knowledge of the patient's illness because the referring physicians wanted an entirely unbiased assessment. It was learned later that the patient had a 60 percent occlusion of her left internal carotid artery and was scheduled for an endarterectomy shortly after the testing. The clinical plan was for neuropsychological testing to be repeated post-operatively to assess any improvement.

Our purpose for including this case, in addition to providing the reader with more experience in clinical interpretation, is to illustrate one of the important uses of neuropsychological examination — serial testing. There are many brain-related conditions that change with time, either in the direction of deterioration or improvement. Deterioration may be slow and gradual or rapid and devastating, depending upon the type of lesion involved. Improvement may be due to spontaneous recovery, surgical intervention, brain-retraining procedures, and other factors. An increasing number of physicians and psychologists are recognizing that subjective, impressionistic evaluation of change is not satisfactory. The Halstead-Reitan Battery is particularly useful for assessing changes in an individual's neuropsychological status because it has been developed to reflect both general and specific characteristics of brain function in a balanced manner. In addition, the testing procedure permits an unbiased and objective assessment.

Besides the partial occlusion of the left internal carotid artery, H.D. also had a history of severe cardiac disease. She was having progressive difficulties and felt that she had experienced a considerable degree of confusion during the past three weeks. She said that she was not able to get her thoughts straight and that everything seemed to be "topsy-turvy." Her physicians were aware of these complaints but had wondered which of her symptoms had a neurological as compared with an emotional basis. They knew that the patient was anxious and apprehensive about her physical condition and fearful of the impending surgery. In such instances an objective and valid evaluation of brain-related deficits makes an important and significant contribution to the patient's case.

Pre-operative Testing

H.D. was difficult to examine because of her slow manner of responding. She seemed to have great difficulty organizing her thoughts and when asked a question she made long pauses before answering. It seemed to the examiner that the patient had significant trouble comprehending verbal communication and it was necessary for the examiner to repeat the instructions in several different ways before the subject understood what she was being asked to do. With prompting, the patient was able to respond pertinently but needed frequent redirection to the task on which she was working for her to maintain her train of thought. General clinical observation indicated that this woman was suffering from at least a degree of dementia.

This patient's I.Q. values were within the Average range. The Verbal I.Q. (91) was at the lower limit of the Average range and the Performance I.Q. (110) was 19 points higher, falling at the lower limit of the High Average range. Inspection of the subtest scores indicated that the patient's general level of performance was not very good, and she did poorly on the Verbal subtests of Comprehension (3) and Arithmetic (3). It seems likely that on these subtests this woman had experienced some loss but whether it might be due to emotionally-determined or neurologically-determined dementia would be an open question at this point in the interpretation.

The Performance subtest scores were consistently below average, but this is not particularly surprising in a person of this age. For older subjects, the Wechsler-Bellevue Scale required an inordinate upward adjustment of Performance I.Q. with relation to actual performances on the individual subtests. Thus, we would be reluctant to conclude that the difference in the I.Q. values for this woman had any particular significance with regard to left cerebral damage, although this possibility could not be entirely ruled out.

The four most sensitive general indicators of cerebral damage all had poor scores. The patient earned a Halstead Impairment Index of

HALSTEAD-REITAN NEUROPSYCHOLOGICAL TEST BATTERY

Patient_____H.D. (I)_____Age___61___Sex___F___Education___11___Handedness___R___

x WECHSLER-BELLEVUE SCALE (FORM I)		HALSTEAD'S NEUROPSYCHOLOGICAL TEST BATTERY	
___WAIS		Category Test	Could not do

VIQ	91	**Tactual Performance Test**		
PIQ	110			
FIS IQ	96	Dominant hand:	10.0 (1 block)	
VWS	31	Non-dominant hand:	10.0 (5 blocks)	
PWS	36	Both hands:	10.0 (6 blocks)	
Total WS	67			
			Total Time	30.0
Information	8		Memory	2
Comprehension	3		Localization	2
Digit Span	9			
Arithmetic	3	**Seashore Rhythm Test**		
Similarities	8	Number Correct_____		Could not do
Vocabulary	—			
Picture Arrangement	7	**Speech-sounds Perception Test**		
Picture Completion	8	Number of Errors		5
Block Design	9			
Object Assembly	5	**Finger Oscillation Test**		
Digit Symbol	7	Dominant hand:	29	29
		Non-dominant hand:	27	

TRAIL MAKING TEST   Impairment Index___0.9___
Part A:___176___seconds
Part B:___179___seconds — Discontinued at 2-B

STRENGTH OF GRIP
Dominant hand:_____17.5 kilograms
Non-dominant hand: 18.0 kilograms

REITAN-KLØVE TACTILE FORM RECOGNITION TEST
Dominant hand:_____81_seconds;___1___errors
Non-dominant hand:_19_seconds;___1___errors

REITAN-KLØVE SENSORY-PERCEPTUAL EXAM — Patient seemed confused.

			Error Totals			
RH___LH___	Both:RH___LH___	RH___LH___				
RH___LF___	Both:RH___LF___	RH___LF___		REITAN-KLØVE		
LH___RF___	Both:LH_3_RF_1_	RF_1_LH_3_		LATERAL-DOMINANCE EXAM		

Show me how you:

RE___LE___	Both:RE_2_LE___	RE_2_LE___	throw a ball	R
RV___LV___	Both:RV___LV___		hammer a nail	R
___ ___	___ ___	RV___LV___	cut with a knife	R
___ ___	___ ___		turn a door knob	R
			use scissors	R

TACTILE FINGER RECOGNITION — Not done, patient confused.

use an eraser___R___
write your name___R___

R	1___2___3___4___5___	R___/___					
L	1___2___3___4___5___	L___/___					

Record time used for spontaneous name-writing:

FINGER-TIP NUMBER WRITING

R	1___2___3___4___5___	R 10 / 20	Preferred hand	7 seconds
L	1___2___3___4___5___	L 12 / 20	Non-preferred hand	30 seconds
	Patient confused.			

REITAN-INDIANA APHASIA SCREENING TEST

Form for Adults and Older Children

Name: H. D. (I) Age: 61

Copy SQUARE	Repeat TRIANGLE
Name SQUARE	Repeat MASSACHUSETTS
Spell SQUARE	Repeat METHODIST EPISCOPAL
Copy CROSS	Write SQUARE
Name CROSS	Read SEVEN
Spell CROSS "S-C-R-O-S-S"	Repeat SEVEN
Copy TRIANGLE	Repeat/Explain HE SHOUTED THE WARNING. OK Thought for a long time, then said, "NO". Could not explain.
Name TRIANGLE	Write HE SHOUTED THE WARNING.
Spell TRIANGLE	Compute 85 – 27 =
Name BABY	Compute 17 X 3 = "41" Given 19 X 4 = . Started to write the problem. Wrote "19" and then wrote "66" over the "19".
Write CLOCK Wrote "TIMER". Could not think of "clock".	Name KEY
Name FORK	Demonstrate use of KEY Took a pencil and was about to draw the key. Ex. repeated the instructions. Pt. turned hand, seemed confused.
Read 7 SIX 2 "SEVENTY-SIX-TWO", then corrected herself.	Draw KEY
Read MGW	Read PLACE LEFT HAND TO RIGHT EAR. "Place left hand to the right ear".
Reading I	Place LEFT HAND TO RIGHT EAR Read "He shouted the warning" from her own paper. Asked, "Is that it?" Seemed bewildered.
Reading II	Place LEFT HAND TO LEFT ELBOW "NO". Answered quickly.

timez   square

He shouted the warning

$$\begin{array}{r} 85 \\ 27 \\ \hline 58 \end{array}$$

(17×3)
41

(19×4 = 66)
58

0.9 (about 90 percent of the tests in the brain-damaged range). H.D. was not able to make any satisfactory progress on the Category Test, choosing answers essentially at random because she was not able to generate any meaningful hypotheses. Therefore, the score for the Category Test should be thought of as falling at the poor end of the distribution.

The patient had comparable difficulty on the Trail Making Test. On Part B she made an attempt to perform the test but in 179 seconds had only reached the number 2 and could not figure out where to go next. At this point the examiner discontinued the test. The patient was able to localize only two of the figures in her drawing of the Tactual Performance Test board. The deficient performances on these measures suggest that this woman had significant deterioration of brain-related abilities, but at this point in the interpretation the possibility would still exist that her impairment might be due to severe emotional distress rather than impaired brain functions.

The next step in the interpretation requires a review of all of the test performances to identify relatively good and poor scores. First, it is apparent that this woman performed poorly on most of the tests. She showed evidence of dysphasia (which will be reviewed later in this report), had very striking losses in the area of concept formation and reasoning and had some difficulties in dealing with visual-spatial tasks.

Probably the most outstanding characterization of the test results for H.D. concerns the differentiation between tasks that required immediate adaptive ability and tasks dependent on background and stored information. She had scores that approached the average level on several of the Wechsler subtests and performed remarkably well on the Speech-sounds Perception Test (5). This latter score was better than the average of 7 errors made by control subjects.

One might wonder how this woman could perform so poorly on some measures (Category Test, Tactual Performance Test, Trail Making Test) and do so well on the Speech-sounds Perception Test. The answer lies in the fact that when this woman is given highly specific stimulus material and knows exactly what is expected of her she is able to pay attention and perform the task. However, when the test is of such a nature that it requires definition through the subject's own efforts, she has a great deal of difficulty. This finding is quite characteristic of persons with dementia. If the task is well-defined and requires recapitulation of previously learned information, the patient can frequently do quite well; however, if a task is given that must be analyzed and defined before it can be answered, the patient is likely to perform poorly.

The next step in interpretation concerns evaluation of lateralizing indicators. A review of the test results revealed that there were many indicators of left cerebral damage but relatively few that pointed specifically toward right cerebral involvement. On the Tactual Performance Test this woman performed poorly on all trials, but had considerably more difficulty with her right hand than her left. She also showed reduction of grip strength in her right upper extremity as compared with her left and possibly may have been just a little slow with her left hand in finger tapping speed.

The patient's right-sided difficulty was definitely not limited to motor manifestations; on the Tactile Form Recognition Test she required much more time to identify forms with her right hand than her left. On the Sensory-perceptual Examination H.D. had no difficulty identifying unilateral stimuli but seemed to be confused when performing tests of bilateral simultaneous tactile stimulation. The occurrence of three mistakes on the left hand and one mistake on the right face seemed to the examiner to be a result of general confusion. Sometimes, in this type of patient, such confusion occurs independent of the specific test content.

The patient showed difficulty perceiving an auditory stimulus to her right ear when it was given simultaneously with a stimulus to the left ear. She had no difficulty with visual tests of bilateral stimulation. It was not possible to obtain valid information on the Tactile Finger Recognition Test or the Finger-tip Number Writing Test because of the patient's general confusion.

In addition to the above-named deficits, the patient demonstrated significant dysphasia. She was able to do many of the items on the Aphasia Screening Test satisfactorily, but when she was asked to spell CROSS she began the word with an "S." This error almost certainly represented a perseveration from her previous correct spelling of SQUARE. This type of verbal perseveration is common in persons with left cerebral damage. The patient also showed evidence of dysnomia: she was not able to think of the word CLOCK and instead wrote "timer." Her confusion in attempting to read 7 SIX 2 is also quite characteristic of persons with left cerebral damage.

The next item on which she had difficulty was the explanation of HE SHOUTED THE WARNING. The patient considered the examiner's request for a long time but finally decided that she could not explain what the sentence meant. This type of response is frequently a manifestation of auditory-verbal dysgnosia, a deficit associated with impairment of the posterior part of the language area in the left cerebral hemisphere. However, the patient did not give us a positive indication of impairment but instead merely showed that she was unable to give an explanation. As has been noted in other case interpretations of the Aphasia Test (Reitan, 1984; Reitan, 1985a), it is difficult to use a negative type of response in the same direct way as one can use a positive manifestation of impairment.

The patient also had difficulty when asked to mentally compute 17 X 3. She was given another problem, 19 X 4, and when she started to record the answer she became confused and wrote "19." Then she proceeded to write another answer, "66," over the numbers she had written previously. One could question whether this difficulty should be called dyscalculia or whether it is more closely related to the patient's general confusion. In either case, the patient's problem is likely to be a manifestation of impaired cerebral functions.

When H.D. was asked to demonstrate the use of a key she took a pencil and was about to draw the key. Noticing this, the examiner repeated the instructions. The patient had obvious difficulty understanding what she was supposed to do and seemed confused. The confusion on this item strongly suggests that the patient had trouble understanding the symbolic communicational content of verbal material through the auditory avenue and provides at least a partial confirmation of the presumption of auditory-verbal dysgnosia as a basis for the patient's inability to explain HE SHOUTED THE WARNING.

When asked to place her left hand to her right ear, H.D. did not understand the instruction and instead read the sentence she had written on the paper previously, "He shouted the warning." She asked, "Is that it?" and seemed bewildered. This inability to be in any respect pertinent to the instruction to place her left hand to her right ear almost certainly indicates the presence of auditory verbal dysgnosia over and beyond her general state of confusion.

Finally, the patient had difficulty copying the key, but she did not make the typical kinds of errors in dealing with the spatial configuration that are usually seen in persons with right cerebral damage. Instead, the multiple lines involving the nose and teeth of the key are manifestations that are more characteristic of general dyspraxia than constructional dyspraxia. We would postulate that this woman would have considerable difficulty in doing things generally of a manipulatory nature (general dyspraxia) rather than having problems specifically delimited to reproducing spatial configurations (constructional dyspraxia). Right cerebral dysfunction cannot be ruled out as a cause of her difficulty in drawing the key, but in the entire set of test results, this was the only possible indicator of right cerebral damage.

Results from the Aphasia Test were particularly useful in this case. The kinds of difficulties that the patient showed were characteristic of left cerebral involvement and would not be seen in persons with dementia associated with affective disturbances. In addition, the disparities of function on the two sides of the body (the right side demonstrating deficiencies) were consistent with these indications of dysphasia demonstrated by H.D. and provided further evidence of left cerebral damage. There is no doubt that, to a great extent, the dementia and confusional state of this woman were due to neurological involvement of the brain and the left cerebral hemisphere was more dysfunctional than the right.

The excellent score on the Speech-sounds Perception Test contributes significant additional information in the context of the serious general impairment and specific left cerebral damage indicators shown by this woman. More specifically, one must raise a question concerning the apparent disparity of positive evidence of language involvement (including auditory-verbal dysgnosia) and such a good score on a test that requires integration of auditory and verbal perception of verbal material. Admittedly, it is unusual to see disparate results of this kind, but the fact is that they happened in this case and require an explanation.

The first part of the explanation relates to the specified nature of the Speech-sounds Perception Test and the limited extent to which the task requires definition by the patient. It is not at all likely that H.D. would have been able to perform as well on the Speech-sounds Perception Test if she had an actual structural lesion in the left cerebral hemisphere. Therefore, the good Speech-sounds Perception Test score is probably related to the fact that the lesion producing the left cerebral hemisphere impairment was in the neck vessel. Also, the good score on the Speech-sounds Perception Test, in the presence of clear evidence of dysphasia and impairment of the right as compared with the left upper extremity, points toward the presence of a relatively chronic or slowly progressive type of lesion and argues against an acutely destructive or rapidly progressive lesion. In other words, in a person of this age, this particular set of results would not be likely to occur with a stroke involving the left cerebral hemisphere or a rapidly growing intrinsic tumor.

The reader may be wondering how the patient could do the Speech-sounds Perception Test so well and be completely unable to perform the Seashore Rhythm Test. The Seashore Rhythm Test is not a right hemisphere indicator, regardless of the tendency of some people to presume that it is because it involves non-verbal auditory perception. There are many reasons why individual tests may be performed poorly, but when a test is done well there is positive information with regard to the subject's ability to perform the test. We would postulate that this woman was not able to keep up with the pace of the Seashore Rhythm Test and her complete inability to do this test was probably due to procedural considerations rather than to the content of the test itself.

In summary, then, the test results clearly (1) demonstrated a significant degree of generalized impairment; (2) provided convincing evidence that the confusional state and dementia were due to impairment of cerebral functions (although this does not rule out a concomitant affective disorder); (3) provided indications that the left cerebral hemisphere was more involved than the right; and (4) ruled out a focal structural lesion in the left cerebral hemisphere. On this basis one might infer that the lesion causing left cerebral dysfunction was in the left internal carotid artery, but such a deduction would be speculative on the basis of the test results alone.

Post-operative Testing

The post-operative neuropsychological test results for this patient indicated that she had made substantial improvement in many areas and no longer demonstrated the generalized confusion or dementia. Unfortunately, the neuropsychologist who examined this patient did not give the Category Test or the Seashore Rhythm Test because

HALSTEAD-REITAN NEUROPSYCHOLOGICAL TEST BATTERY

Patient __H.D. (II) (Post-operative)__ Age __61__ Sex __F__ Education __11__ Handedness __R__

x WECHSLER-BELLEVUE SCALE (FORM I)	
___WAIS	
VIQ	117
PIQ	117
FIS IQ	116
VWS	47
PWS	42
Total WS	99
Information	14
Comprehension	10
Digit Span	10
Arithmetic	10
Similarities	3
Vocabulary	—
Picture Arrangement	7
Picture Completion	10
Block Design	11
Object Assembly	7
Digit Symbol	7

HALSTEAD'S NEUROPSYCHOLOGICAL TEST BATTERY

Category Test _____ Not done

Tactual Performance Test

Dominant hand:	18.2
Non-dominant hand:	17.4
Both hands:	12.4

Total Time __48.0__
Memory __5__
Localization __1__

Seashore Rhythm Test
Number Correct_____ Not done

Speech-sounds Perception Test
Number of Errors __6__

Finger Oscillation Test
Dominant hand: __37__   __37__
Non-dominant hand: __39__

Impairment Index_____

TRAIL MAKING TEST
Part A: __47__ seconds
Part B: __90__ seconds

STRENGTH OF GRIP
Dominant hand: __15.5__ kilograms
Non-dominant hand: __16.5__ kilograms

Miles ABC Test of Ocular Dominance
Right eye: __10__ Left eye: __0__

REITAN-KLØVE TACTILE FORM RECOGNITION TEST
Dominant hand: __9__ seconds; __1__ errors
Non-dominant hand: __8__ seconds; __2__ errors

REITAN-KLØVE SENSORY-PERCEPTUAL EXAM

				Error Totals
RH____LH____	Both:RH____LH____		RH____LH____
RH____LF____	Both:RH_1_LF____		RH_1_LF____
LH____RF____	Both:LH____RF____		RF____LH____
RE____LE____	Both:RE_2_LE____		RE_2_LE____
RV____LV____	Both:RV____LV____		
		_1_	RV_1_LV____

TACTILE FINGER RECOGNITION
R 1__ 2__ 3__ 4__ 5__ R_0_ / 20
L 1__ 2__ 3__ 4__ 5__ L_0_ / 20

FINGER-TIP NUMBER WRITING
R 1_2_2_1_3_2_4_2_5_ R_7_ / 20
L 1_2_2__3__4_1_5_2_ L_5_ / 20

REITAN-KLØVE LATERAL-DOMINANCE EXAM

Show me how you:

throw a ball	R
hammer a nail	R
cut with a knife	R
turn a door knob	R
use scissors	R
use an eraser	R
write your name	R

Record time used for spontaneous name-writing:
Preferred hand __17__ seconds
Non-preferred hand __21__ seconds

REITAN-INDIANA APHASIA SCREENING TEST

Form for Adults and Older Children

Name: _____ H. D. (II) _____ Age: __61__

Copy SQUARE	Repeat TRIANGLE
Name SQUARE	Repeat MASSACHUSETTS
Spell SQUARE	Repeat METHODIST EPISCOPAL
Copy CROSS	Write SQUARE
Name CROSS	Read SEVEN
Spell CROSS	Repeat SEVEN
Copy TRIANGLE	Repeat/Explain HE SHOUTED THE WARNING. OK "SOMEBODY SHOUTED"
Name TRIANGLE	Write HE SHOUTED THE WARNING.
Spell TRIANGLE	Compute 85 – 27 =
Name BABY	Compute 17 X 3 = "47" – changed to "41". 16 X 5 = "80"
Write CLOCK	Name KEY
Name FORK	Demonstrate use of KEY
Read 7 SIX 2	Draw KEY
Read MGW	Read PLACE LEFT HAND TO RIGHT EAR. "Place the left hand to the right ear".
Reading I	Place LEFT HAND TO RIGHT EAR
Reading II	Place LEFT HAND TO LEFT ELBOW "NO"

clock   square

He shouted the warning

$$\begin{array}{r} 85 \\ 27 \\ \hline 58 \end{array}$$
      47   41   80

the patient had been unable to complete these tasks at the first examination. Even though we did not have a quantitative score from the first examination on these measures, it would have been desirable to have had results on the second testing to assess the patient's status more completely. The Category Test is especially significant, not only for evaluating the overall biological condition of the brain but in estimating the behavioral capabilities of the patient as well.

The patient showed striking improvement on Verbal I.Q., increasing her score from 91 to 117. She also showed an improvement on Performance I.Q., increasing from 110 to 117. One might have expected a greater positive practice-effect increment on the Performance than the Verbal subtests. In this case, however, the greatest change occurred on the Verbal subtests, documenting our prior observation that when beneficial influences on brain functions occur, the areas of initial deficit show the greatest improvement (Dikmen & Reitan, 1976).

The four most sensitive general indicators continued to demonstrate a degree of impairment. Despite definite improvement, this woman had scores that still fell in the brain-damaged range on four of the five Halstead measures used to compute the Index, yielding an Impairment Index of 0.8. The Halstead Impairment Index is a consistency-of-impairment measure rather than a severity-of-impairment measure. It is not uncommon for persons with cerebral damage to do poorly on the Impairment Index even when they are not grossly or even severely impaired.

With a score of 90 seconds H.D. showed great improvement on the Part B of the Trail Making Test, indicating that her general alertness and flexibility in thinking had improved tremendously. Unfortunately, the Category Test was not done, although we would postulate that the patient would have shown improvement on that measure as well. The patient did not perform better on the Localization component of the Tactual Performance Test; as might be expected, this woman had some residual impairment of brain function and her overall postoperative results continued to show some areas of deficit.

These areas of deficit occurred particularly on measures that compared performances on the two sides of the body. The patient showed improvement of finger tapping speeds but was a little slow with her right hand compared with her left. She continued to be a little weaker on the right side of the body. She also showed very mild tactile and auditory imperception on the right side.

The present findings yielded no significant dysphasia, although the patient drew a rather simplified key which made it difficult to evaluate for specific signs of impairment. She also showed remarkable improvement in tactile finger recognition, making no mistakes on either hand. However, on the Finger-tip Number Writing Test she did make more mistakes than would normally be expected.

In summary, the test results indicate that this woman was greatly benefitted by left internal carotid endarterectomy. We would postulate that she would show continued improvement in time, although her confusional state and dementia have already essentially been overcome.

Recognizing that experiencing a state of serious impairment and confusion may be very unsettling emotionally, we would suggest that this patient be provided the opportunity for psychological counseling. In addition, we would recommend repetition of the Halstead-Reitan Battery in 6–12 months to assess the longer-term outcome of the surgery.

Clinical assessment of patients with cerebral disease or damage leads to a more complete understanding of their cognitive ability structure. Administration of the Halstead-Reitan Battery predominantly has its major value not in neurological diagnosis but in identification of deficits and disparities in intellectual and cognitive functions and their clinical significance. In the majority of persons with cerebral disease or damage, the medical diagnosis can be made accurately through use of conventional neurological diagnostic techniques, even though neuropsychological methods of evaluation are distinctly more sensitive in certain categories (e.g., closed head injuries) and nearly always make additional contributions to understanding the ability structure of the patient.

The unique contribution of neuropsychological evaluation lies in identification of areas of deficit that would otherwise be overlooked. Perhaps more than in any other area, the person with cerebral damage or disease may show neuropsychological deficits that are quite unexpected on the basis of the history or other findings.

To be able to identify such behavioral deficits, however, the psychologist must have a broad range of experience which permits recognition of various and diverse conditions. The basic and fundamental requirement, therefore, is that the neuropsychologist is familiar with the fundamentals of interpretation of the test results across a broad range of conditions. For example, the neuropsychological characteristics of conditions such as closed head injuries, multiple sclerosis, cerebral vascular disease, alcoholism, etc., can scarcely be identified by a psychologist who does not know how these conditions manifest themselves in neuropsychological measurements. These various conditions have been studied in detail using the Halstead-Reitan Battery and a review of this literature is available for the interested reader (Reitan & Wolfson, 1984).

VIII
HEAD INJURY

Mortality and morbidity resulting from head injury are major medical and neuropsychological problems. Trauma is the leading cause of death in youth and early middle age and is the third most common cause of death in the United States, being exceeded only by vascular disease and cancer (U.S. Department of Health, Education, and Welfare, 1974). In death due to trauma, head injury contributes significantly in more than half of the cases. The head is the part of the body most commonly injured in patients with multiple injuries, and in fatal road accidents injury to the brain occurs in nearly 75 percent of the cases (Gissane, 1963). Although head injury occurs principally among younger persons, it still exceeds stroke as a cause of death in males aged 45-64 years.

Studies of patients who have sustained head injuries indicate that they have many pre-existing problems and do not appear to represent a cross-section of the population. Factors over-represented in this population include low socioeconomic status, alcoholism, a history of prior head injuries (probable accident-proneness), psychiatric problems and neurological disorders.

Mechanisms of Traumatic Injuries of the Brain

The initial impact of a blow to the head results in a temporary deformation of the skull. Injury to the brain tissues is caused by compression or penetration, tension (or tearing the tissues apart), and shearing or sliding of tissues over other tissues (including bone).

In acceleration injuries the head is struck by a faster- moving object. When this happens, the slower-moving contents of the skull may be damaged by sudden contact with bony prominences or the edge of dural membranes. Contusion (bruising) of the brain may occur in many locations, including the brain stem. The poles of the frontal and temporal lobes, as well as the orbital surfaces of the frontal lobes, are particularly vulnerable to injury of this type when they move in an anteroposterior and superoinferior direction because they strike bony ridges of the inner surface of the skull. A pressure wave is also established in acceleration injuries to the head. This pressure is greatest at the point of impact but may be a factor in producing injuries on the opposite side of the brain (contrecoup injury).

Deceleration injuries occur when the head is moving and strikes a fixed and solid object. In these cases injury may occur at the point of impact and contrecoup damage may also be present. A fall on the back of the head, for example, may result in contusion of the frontal and temporal lobes. Again, a pressure wave may be established at the point of impact, with negative pressure in the area of injury and increasing pressure opposite the point of injury. Contrecoup injuries of the occipital areas are rare, probably due to the smooth contour and absence of bony projections on the inner side of the skull in this area.

A forceful impact to the head produces distortion of the skull, a change in the linear movement of the head (acceleration or deceleration), and frequently, rotation of the head. A sudden, forceful rotation of the head on the neck may produce shearing forces and tearing of tissue, a mechanism that has been implicated as the major cause of contrecoup injuries (Ommaya, Grubb, and Naumann, 1970). Other movements of the brain within the cranial cavity, in addition to rotation, may also set up shearing forces within the brain substance. These shearing forces may produce damage to blood vessels and brain tissue on a widespread basis (Tomlinson, 1970).

These comments should make it clear that a blow to a particular point of the head causes widespread damage to the underlying tissue and is not strictly associated with the point of impact. When a substantial force is delivered to a particular point on the skull the mechanisms of injury are related not only to deformation of the skull, penetration of the skull and direct tissue damage but also to compression, tension, and shearing.

Types of Head Injury

Gilroy and Meyer (1979) classify head injuries into three general categories: skull fracture, closed head injury without fracture, and penetrating wounds of the skull and brain.

Skull Fractures

Skull fractures generally fall in two categories: (1) perforation of the skull or depressed fractures, and (2) comminuted or linear fractures. About 70 percent of skull fractures are linear.

Head Injury without Skull Fracture

Many persons sustain minor head injuries, perhaps with transient impairment of consciousness but without skull fracture, that resolve in a short period of time with complete recovery. It must be remembered, however, that closed head injuries without skull fracture may result in severe and irreversible brain damage; fatal brain damage can occur even if the skull has not been fractured. The presence of a skull fracture, considered by itself, is of limited significance and the clinical significance of the injury can be determined only by evaluating the neurological and neuropsychological functions of the patient.

Autopsy studies in cases of severe closed head injuries have shown diffuse damage in the white matter with disruption of axons, apparently resulting from shearing forces caused by the impact (Strich, 1970). Although the brain may appear to be normal at autopsy, microscopic examination shows lesions not only in the white matter but in other structures as well. Careful autopsy studies of patients who had sustained severe head injuries with primary brain stem damage showed more widespread diffuse damage extending beyond the brain stem, in *every* case. A number of investigators (Mitchell & Hume-Adams, 1973; Reilly, Graham, Hume-Adams, & Jennett, 1975) reported that they were unable to find a single case of primary brain stem damage without associated diffuse damage. Oppenheimer (1968) studied patients who had suffered relatively mild head injuries resulting in cerebral concussion, recovered, and then died of unrelated causes. Neuropathological studies of these cases showed small microglial lesions diffusely distributed in the brain but not in the brain stem. It would seem possible that these residual lesions in persons who had suffered cerebral concussion are the end result of small petechial hemorrhages.

It is apparent that various mechanisms and types of head injury can cause extensive damage throughout the brain, either by direct or secondary damage of brain tissue and blood vessels. It is not surprising, therefore, that when significant neuropsychological deficit is found in persons who have sustained head injuries, the results rarely implicate only an area of specific focal, discrete damage.

Penetrating Wounds of the Brain

Many types of head injuries result in penetration of the brain and direct damage to the underlying brain tissue. In such injuries pressure waves are set up by the penetrating missile and may produce a profound change in brain stem function. The combined effects produce increased intracranial pressure and reduced systemic blood pressure. If the injury is sufficiently damaging, intracranial pressure may increase to the point that death occurs. In less severe cases brain stem centers will begin to function again and a balance is restored, although increased intracranial pressure frequently remains high because of cerebral edema (Crockard, Brown, et al., 1977).

Neuropsychological Correlates of Head Injury

As might be expected from the above description of the mechanisms of head injury, the underlying neurological damage is extremely variable and the resulting neuropsychological consequences are correspondingly variable. Head injuries may be either penetrating or closed. In both cases, pressure gradients are established which may result in widespread damage of both gray and white matter. In addition, there may be direct damage of cerebral tissue from the force of the blow, and tearing and shearing of cerebral tissues against other tissues, including bone. Contusion, caused by rupture of capillaries in the cerebral cortex and white matter, may occur and result in destruction of tissues. Movement of the brain within the calvarium may cause damage of blood vessels within the brain as well as those leading to or departing from the brain. Shearing effects may also damage cranial nerves. Autopsy studies of patients with severe head injuries have revealed that head blows may result in microglial scars, neuronal loss, axonal degeneration, loss of white matter, and long-term effects that can cause eventual formation of glial scarring or meningocerebral scar tissue formation. Many neuropsychologists, not having learned to differentiate diffuse from focal damage in cases of head injury, persist in an overly specific interpretation of individual test findings as indicators of localized damage in one area or another, often mentioning multiple focal sites. This tendency might have resulted from earlier research studies in which the focal point of damage to the skull and underlying cerebral damage was considered to be the only area of the lesion.

Considering the range of neuropathological involvement in head injury, it is not surprising that neuropsychological findings are also quite variable. However, the astute clinician can frequently recognize that results on the Halstead-Reitan Battery represent an insult to a previously normal brain and can often be relatively confident that the insult is a result of physical trauma. Severity of deficit may range from none (with extremely mild head injuries) to very severe. If there are deficits, it is not uncommon to find one cerebral hemisphere more involved than the other, but most head-trauma patients, even those with closed head injuries, show involvement of both cerebral hemispheres. In addition, when lateralizing signs are present, the general indicators also show some deficit. Most patients with head injuries demonstrate some retention of their premorbid abilities, suggesting that brain-behavior relationships have developed relatively normally up to the time of the head injury and the biological insult of the brain has resulted in losses of abilities rather than failures of acquisition. The pattern of test results — some normal scores and some showing definite impairment — also assists in evaluating the chronicity of the brain damage. Most patients who have sustained significant traumatic brain injury show at least some degree of improvement over time. The experienced neuropsychologist can often consider the total distribution of test results to estimate whether recovery is essentially complete or the deficits are sufficiently pronounced and focal so that further recovery seems to be possible. The clinician develops such ability by studying many patients with head injuries, including serial examinations of the individual patient following the injury.

CASE #14

Name:	W.B.	Sex:	Male
Age:	19	Handedness:	Right
Education:	13	Occupation:	Student

Current Complaints and Pertinent History

This 19-year-old man had been in an automobile accident six months prior to the current neuropsychological testing. He never totally lost consciousness but was in a confused state for about one week. Duration of unconsciousness alone has not been a very exact predictor of subsequent impairment in head-injured persons; duration of confusion should also be considered and usually suggests, as it did in this case, that the patient had sustained a significant head injury. Neurological examination performed after this patient recovered from the confusional state showed no significant abnormalities. Because of a badly fractured femur, however, the patient was hospitalized for about four months.

W.B. was congratulated by his neurologist for his complete neurological recovery and, upon discharge from the hospital, immediately attempted to resume his college program. He had previously been making satisfactory progress in a college known for its excellence in undergraduate education and its demanding standards. However, upon returning to classes, W.B. found that he tired easily and had difficulty concentrating. He realized that he did not have his previous capabilities and was not able to meet his expected academic responsibilities. The awareness that his intellectual competence had changed was very distressing to him, and W.B. transferred to a college that had a reputation for being less demanding academically.

Despite changing schools, W.B. continued to have difficulty with his academic work and, in addition, began developing a number of emotional problems. His parents reported that he was becoming increasingly difficult to get along with, was somewhat withdrawn, and quite irritable. These problems were sufficiently severe to warrant further medical or psychiatric help. W.B.'s parents debated whether to bring him to a psychiatrist or have further neurological evaluations performed.

HALSTEAD-REITAN NEUROPSYCHOLOGICAL TEST BATTERY

Patient_____W.B._____Age__19__Sex__M__Education__13__Handedness__R__

_x_ WECHSLER-BELLEVUE SCALE (FORM I)
___WAIS

VIQ	112
PIQ	95
FIS IQ	105
VWS	56
PWS	48
Total WS	104
Information	14
Comprehension	12
Digit Span	7
Arithmetic	9
Similarities	14
Vocabulary	12
Picture Arrangement	13
Picture Completion	9
Block Design	9
Object Assembly	7
Digit Symbol	10

HALSTEAD'S NEUROPSYCHOLOGICAL TEST BATTERY

Category Test _____ 53

Tactual Performance Test
Dominant hand: _____ 7.1
Non-dominant hand: _____ 3.5
Both hands: _____ 5.3

Total Time__15.9__
Memory__5__
Localization__2__

Seashore Rhythm Test
Number Correct____25_____6

Speech-sounds Perception Test
Number of Errors _____ 8

Finger Oscillation Test
Dominant hand: ____47_____47
Non-dominant hand: __49__

TRAIL MAKING TEST
Part A:__60__ seconds
Part B:__91__ seconds

Impairment Index__1.0__

Miles ABC Test of Ocular Dominance
Right eye:_10_ Left eye:_0_

REITAN-KLØVE SENSORY-PERCEPTUAL EXAM

Error Totals — No errors

RH____LH____	Both:RH____LH____	RH____LH____			
RH____LF____	Both:RH____LF____	RH____LF____			
LH____RF____	Both:LH____RF____	RF____LH____			
RE____LE____	Both:RE____LE____	RE____LE____			
RV____LV____	Both:RV____LV____				
____ ____	____ ____	RV____LV____			
____ ____	____ ____				

MINNESOTA MULTIPHASIC PERSONALITY INVENTORY

?	50	Hs	53
L	50	D	58
F	46	Hy	57
K	51	PD	58
		MF	51
		Pa	50
		Pt	40
		Sc	52
		Ma	50

TACTILE FINGER RECOGNITION
R 1___2___3___4___5___ R 0 / 20
L 1___2___3___4___5___ L 0 / 20

FINGER-TIP NUMBER WRITING
R 1___2___3___4___5___ R 0 / 20
L 1___2___3___4___5___ L 0 / 20

REITAN-INDIANA APHASIA SCREENING TEST

Form for Adults and Older Children

Name: _____ W. B. _____ Age: __19__

Copy SQUARE	Repeat TRIANGLE
Name SQUARE	Repeat MASSACHUSETTS
Spell SQUARE	Repeat METHODIST EPISCOPAL
Copy CROSS See mild imbalance of lateral extremities.	Write SQUARE
Name CROSS	Read SEVEN
Spell CROSS	Repeat SEVEN
Copy TRIANGLE	Repeat/Explain HE SHOUTED THE WARNING.
Name TRIANGLE	Write HE SHOUTED THE WARNING.
Spell TRIANGLE	Compute 85 – 27 =
Name BABY	Compute 17 X 3 =
Write CLOCK	Name KEY
Name FORK	Demonstrate use of KEY
Read 7 SIX 2	Draw KEY Note confusion especially at "nose" and "teeth" of key.
Read MGW	Read PLACE LEFT HAND TO RIGHT EAR.
Reading I	Place LEFT HAND TO RIGHT EAR
Reading II	Place LEFT HAND TO LEFT ELBOW

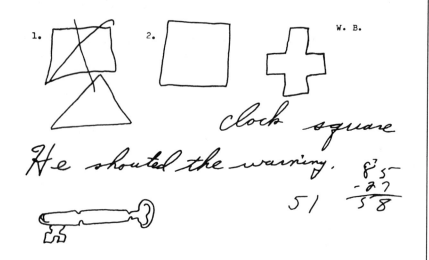

1.

2.

clock   square

He shouted the warning.

$$8'5$$
$$-27$$
$$\overline{5\,8}$$

51

First square crossed out by patient when examiner asked him
to draw it more carefully.

Finally, they decided to first contact a neurological surgeon who found that the neurological examination was entirely negative except for a mild elevation of blood pressure. EEG showed a bitemporal dysrhythmia, Grade I, judged to be non-specific in its significance. Thus, the neurological surgeon was not able to find any significant cerebral damage or dysfunction. At this point the routine procedure probably would have been to refer the patient for psychiatric evaluation. However, the neurosurgeon who had examined the patient was aware of the contribution that neuropsychological testing can make in understanding such cases and the patient was referred for testing.

Neuropsychological Test Results

The test results indicate that the subject earned a Verbal I.Q. (112) that was in the lower part of the High Average range (exceeding about 79 percent of his age peers). The subtest scores were well above average except for Digit Span (7) and Arithmetic (9). As has previously been noted, the Digit Span score is not specific for brain damage but the low Arithmetic score may possibly reflect some degree of impairment of cerebral functions.

The Performance I.Q. (95) fell in the lower part of the Average range (exceeding 37 percent). The lowest score was on Object Assembly (7), but scores on this test and Picture Completion are quite variable and difficult to interpret with respect to impaired brain functions. The score on Block Design (9), however, falls below the general level established by this subject on tests not particularly susceptible to cerebral damage, and may possibly reflect some right cerebral dysfunction. It must also be noted, though, that the score on Digit Symbol (10) was not especially low, and of the Wechsler subtests, this test is probably the most sensitive to cerebral damage. Thus, as is usually the case, results from the Wechsler Scale, considered alone, are equivocal in their significance concerning impaired brain functions.

Conversely, findings on the Halstead-Reitan Battery were unequivocal. The results definitely indicated mild to moderate impairment of adaptive abilities, particularly when the scores were evaluated with relation to the patient's I.Q. values. The subject earned a Halstead Impairment Index of 1.0 (all of the tests in the brain-damaged range), although none of the tests was particularly poorly performed. In most instances W.B.'s scores were just slightly below the cut-off point for the brain-damaged range.

These results represent an excellent example of the sensitivity of Halstead's tests to brain damage and emphasize the importance of reviewing the individual tests that contribute to the Impairment Index rather than interpreting the Index as a unitary measure. Although not a test included in Halstead's Impairment Index, Part B of the Trail Making Test (91 seconds) was also just beyond the cut-off point.

Despite contributing to the Impairment Index, W.B.'s scores on the Seashore Rhythm Test (25) and Speech-sounds Perception Test (8) were relatively good. The reader is probably aware that the cut-off score of 7 errors on the Speech-sounds Perception Test (based upon Halstead's data) does not accurately reflect impaired brain functions. Reitan's data (1955b) indicates that the average control subject makes 7 errors. W.B.'s good scores on these two tests have definite significance for interpretation. Although an Impairment Index of 1.0 might be thought to reflect serious impairment of brain functions, the scores contributing to the Impairment Index (especially the Seashore Rhythm Test and the Speech-sounds Perception Test) suggest that this patient's brain damage is relatively chronic and static. These test results are typical of persons who have had some type of insult to the brain and have recovered to a point of biological stability at the time of testing.

The lateralizing indicators will be considered next. The reader will recall that patients with closed head injuries may show more involvement of one side of the brain than the other, but that the overall results usually indicate generalized impairment. This man performed somewhat slowly with his right hand as compared with his left hand on the Tactual Performance Test. In fact, on the second trial, he required half as much time as taken on the first trial. It must be noted, however, that he did not do too poorly on either of the first two trials and, if he had been able to reduce his time to the normal range on the third trial, his scores would have fallen within the acceptable range.

This situation requires the neuropsychologist to judge whether a significant difference in performances of the two hands had occurred or whether the difference might be due to other factors (including chance). One might wonder whether the time of 7.1 minutes on the first trial was a result of difficulty adapting to the task and making initial progress. In this case, consideration of the total pattern would make it appear that the time on the first trial reflected a degree of impairment. When both hands were used, the time required to complete the task increased. It is likely that the third trial would have required less time if the patient had used only his left hand. Using both hands simultaneously caused the patient more difficulty. This is not characteristic of a normal brain and suggests left cerebral dysfunction (across from the right hand) and further describes a particular feature of deficit for this patient: a problem performing bimanual tasks.

The other significant lateralizing finding concerns the somewhat slower finger tapping speed with the right (preferred) hand (47) than the left hand (49). A performance of this kind rarely occurs among normal subjects and, together with the results of the Tactual Performance Test, suggests that the left cerebral hemisphere was more damaged than the right.

Despite the lateralizing indicators, the overall findings indicate generalized cerebral dysfunction. This conclusion would be based upon (1) the mildness of the lateralizing indicators and (2) the mild impairment shown by the general indicators. In addition, the patient had some problems copying the shape of a cross but more pronounced difficulty (especially in the configuration of the "nose") copying the key. Based on these findings, we would conclude that this man had evidence of mild constructional dyspraxia.

Unfortunately, the Reitan-Kløve Tactile Form Recognition Test had not been developed at the time this patient was examined; the results would have been valuable in terms of the overall assessment. The tests that were given to this patient involved coin differentiation using each hand. He was not able to differentiate between dimes, nickels, and pennies and, in fact, did not even believe that they were coins. By the way they felt to him, he thought they must be "slugs." This suggests that the patient did have a degree of dysstereognosis involving both hands.

Finally, results on the Minnesota Multiphasic Personality Inventory did not deviate significantly from a normal profile. Of course, this does not rule out the validity of the parents' concern about their son's emotional status. It is possible that the MMPI results did not reflect the patient's reaction to the recent stresses he had experienced but instead were a function of his previous adjustment.

In summary, this patient's test results are typical of persons with brain damage resulting from closed head injury. It is not at all uncommon for neurological examination findings to be within normal limits even though the neuropsychological results are unequivocal in their significance. Further, even without knowing W.B.'s medical history, the test results of this man would provide a definitive diagnosis of mild impairment of cerebral functions. In fact, the initial interpretation of these test results was done on a blind basis and validated (also on a blind basis) by another neuropsychologist. Both interpreters believed that the results were characteristic of persons with closed head injury. The Halstead-Reitan Battery will permit this kind of definitive and specific conclusion in many cases of head injury and this, in turn, emphasizes the validity and importance of the Battery in these cases. Results of other examinations, including computed tomography, are frequently negative.

More important, however, is the fact that the results of the Halstead-Reitan Battery relate directly to immediate adaptive abilities in everyday living. Even though this patient had a higher Verbal than Performance I.Q., his generalized impairment of adaptive abilities, together with evidence of more serious involvement of the left than right cerebral hemisphere, almost certainly would be a basis for postulating that he would have special difficulties in school. The basic adaptive skills of the left cerebral hemisphere, used principally in most college courses, was shown to be undermined by results on the Tactual Performance Test and the Finger Oscillation Test. These findings tend to overrule the Verbal I.Q., which is representative of stored and accumulated information rather than immediate competence and adaptive ability of the left cerebral hemisphere in practical situations (Reitan, Hom & Wolfson, submitted for publication).

In brief, we have consistently found that the kind of lateralizing indicators shown by this patient are of distinct and definite significance with respect to the functional competence of the left or right cerebral hemisphere, regardless of test results reflecting stored abilities gained over past years.

CASE #15

Name:	W.Bl.	Sex:	Male
Age:	21	Handedness:	Right
Education:	14	Occupation:	Student

Current Complaints and Pertinent History

The patient, a 21-year-old man in his third year of college, sustained a head injury while playing football. Although complaining of a severe headache, he was conscious and rational for about one-half hour after the injury. He then experienced a decerebrate type of seizure and lapsed into a deep coma. A lumbar puncture performed on admission to the hospital revealed blood-tinged cerebrospinal fluid. Although various diagnostic procedures did not reveal any specific lesion, W.Bl. was extremely ill for the next week. Pneumoencephalography performed one week after admission showed a shift of the ventricular system from right to left. A solid subdural hematoma, approximately 4 to 5 mm. in thickness, was surgically removed from over the entire right cerebral hemisphere.

After surgery the patient had weakness of his right limbs and right side of his face and impaired language functions and spontaneous speech. He began to gradually show improvement and one month after the injury was able to be up and about. His speech and level of consciousness appeared to be near normal. Neurological examination at this time showed a left lower quadrantic homonymous visual field defect and a slight residual right hemiparesis. Neuropsychological examination was performed the day before the patient's discharge, approximately seven weeks after the injury occurred.

Neuropsychological Test Results

The Wechsler-Bellevue Scale yielded a Verbal I.Q. of 110 (High Average), a Performance I.Q. of 88 (Low Average), and Full Scale I.Q. of 99 (Average). The patient did poorly on the Block Design subtest (7) and Digit Symbol subtest (5). Since the patient had been a successful third-year college student prior to the injury, these scores strongly suggested that he was considerably impaired at the present time.

HALSTEAD-REITAN NEUROPSYCHOLOGICAL TEST BATTERY

Patient _____ W.Bl. (I) _____ Age __ 21 __ Sex __ M __ Education __ 14 __ Handedness __ R __

x WECHSLER-BELLEVUE SCALE (FORM I)	
___WAIS	
VIQ	110
PIQ	88
FIS IQ	99
VWS	55
PWS	42
Total WS	97
Information	14
Comprehension	11
Digit Span	6
Arithmetic	10
Similarities	14
Vocabulary	12
Picture Arrangement	10
Picture Completion	14
Block Design	7
Object Assembly	6
Digit Symbol	5

HALSTEAD'S NEUROPSYCHOLOGICAL TEST BATTERY

Category Test	70

Tactual Performance Test

Dominant hand:	15.0 (1 block)
Non-dominant hand:	12.8
Both hands:	4.6

Total Time __32.4 +__
Memory __4__
Localization __4__

Seashore Rhythm Test

Number Correct_____ Could not do

Speech-sounds Perception Test

Number of Errors   Could not do

Finger Oscillation Test

Dominant hand:	31	31
Non-dominant hand:	36	

TRAIL MAKING TEST
Part A: __51__ seconds
Part B: __134__ seconds

Impairment Index __1.0__

Miles ABC Test of Ocular Dominance
Right eye: __0__ Left eye: __10__

REITAN-KLØVE SENSORY-PERCEPTUAL EXAM

					Error Totals	
RH___	LH___	Both:RH___	LH___		RH___	LH___
RH___	LF___	Both:RH___	LF___		RH___	LF___
LH___	RF___	Both:LH___	RF___		RF___	LH___
RE___	LE___	Both:RE___	LE___		RE___	LE___
RV___	LV___	Both:RV___	LV___			
___	___	___	___		RV___	LV___
___	___	___	___			

— Patient could not cooperate; he kept looking to one side or the other.

TACTILE FINGER RECOGNITION
R 1___ 2___ 3___ 4 1 5___   R_1_ / 20
L 1___ 2___ 3___ 4 1 5___   L_1_ / 20

FINGER-TIP NUMBER WRITING
R 1_3 2_2 3_2 4_2 5_2_   R_11_ / 20
L 1___ 2___ 3_1 4___ 5_1_   L_2_ / 20

REITAN-INDIANA APHASIA SCREENING TEST

Form for Adults and Older Children

Name: ___W. Bl.___   Age: ___21___

Copy SQUARE Note problem of motor control.	Repeat TRIANGLE
Name SQUARE	Repeat MASSACHUSETTS "Massachusess"
Spell SQUARE	Repeat METHODIST EPISCOPAL "Methodiss Episcopal"

Copy CROSS
   Note spatial problems in addition to
   motor control difficulty.
	Write SQUARE

Name CROSS	Read SEVEN
Spell CROSS	Repeat SEVEN
Copy TRIANGLE	Repeat/Explain HE SHOUTED THE WARNING. Patient had difficulty conceptualizing an explanation.
Name TRIANGLE	Write HE SHOUTED THE WARNING.
Spell TRIANGLE	Compute 85 − 27 =
Name BABY	Compute 17 X 3 =
Write CLOCK Motor control problem evident.	Name KEY
Name FORK	Demonstrate use of KEY
Read 7 SIX 2	Draw KEY Note spatial problems.
Read MGW	Read PLACE LEFT HAND TO RIGHT EAR. "Place the left hand to the right ear."
Reading I	Place LEFT HAND TO RIGHT EAR
Reading II	Place LEFT HAND TO LEFT ELBOW

#1

#2

Clock
square

He shouted the warning.

85
−27
─────
58

51
─

Even more pronounced deficits were shown by the scores on the four indicators in the Halstead-Reitan Battery most sensitive to cerebral dysfunction. The patient obtained an Impairment Index of 1.0, indicating that his scores on all of Halstead's tests were in the range characteristic of persons with cerebral damage. W. Bl. had difficulty alternating between numbers and letters in Part B of the Trail Making Test and required 134 seconds to complete the task. Although he performed reasonably well on certain sections of the Category Test, on other parts he demonstrated considerable confusion when trying to organize diverse stimulus material in a meaningful way, formulate hypotheses relevant to his observations of the stimulus material, and understand the essential nature of the problem situations. It was obvious by his score of 70 that he was seriously impaired in analytical reasoning and logical analysis. He performed poorly on the Tactual Performance Test and had trouble placing the blocks in their proper spaces on the board while blind-folded. It was apparent that this subject had some impairment in ability to deal with spatial configurations and in adapting to the novel aspects of this type of problem.

Additional results indicated that the patient was impaired in incidental memory: he did poorly when asked to recapitulate aspects of situations to which his attention had not been immediately directed (Memory and Localization scores of the Tactual Performance Test).

Motor and sensory-perceptual tasks also were performed poorly, especially on the right side of the body. Although the patient was definitely right-handed, his finger tapping speed (though somewhat slow in both hands) was clearly impaired in his right hand as compared with the left. He had mild difficulty in tactile finger recognition on both hands and was seriously impaired in finger-tip number writing perception on his right hand only. These various results implicated both cerebral hemispheres and, despite the fact that the subdural hematoma had been removed from the right cerebral hemisphere, suggested that the left hemisphere was more seriously damaged.

The patient was examined again three months later. At this time his Verbal I.Q. was 121, Performance I.Q. was 122, and Full Scale I.Q. was 124. It was apparent that he had made excellent progress recovering his general intelligence. The greatest improvement occurred in the areas that previously had been identified as showing the major deficits.

HALSTEAD-REITAN NEUROPSYCHOLOGICAL TEST BATTERY

Patient_____**W.Bl. (II)**_____Age___**21**___Sex___**M**___Education___**14**___Handedness___**R**___
(Re-examined 3 months after first testing)

___x___WECHSLER-BELLEVUE SCALE (FORM I)
___WAIS

VIQ	121
PIQ	122
FIS IQ	124
VWS	65
PWS	67
Total WS	132
Information	15
Comprehension	14
Digit Span	10
Arithmetic	12
Similarities	14
Vocabulary	13
Picture Arrangement	16
Picture Completion	15
Block Design	14
Object Assembly	13
Digit Symbol	9

HALSTEAD'S NEUROPSYCHOLOGICAL TEST BATTERY

Category Test	17

Tactual Performance Test

Dominant hand:	6.8
Non-dominant hand:	3.6
Both hands:	2.2
Total Time	12.6
Memory	9
Localization	7

Seashore Rhythm Test

Number Correct___26___   5

Speech-sounds Perception Test

Number of Errors   9

Finger Oscillation Test

Dominant hand:	40	40
Non-dominant hand:	35	

TRAIL MAKING TEST
Part A:___50___seconds
Part B:___150___seconds

Impairment Index___0.3___

STRENGTH OF GRIP
Dominant hand:_____37.0_kilograms
Non-dominant hand:_32.5_kilograms

REITAN-KLØVE TACTILE FORM RECOGNITION TEST
Dominant hand:_____—_seconds;__0__errors
Non-dominant hand:_—_seconds;__0__errors

REITAN-KLØVE SENSORY-PERCEPTUAL EXAM

Error Totals — No errors

RH___LH___	Both:RH___LH___	RH___LH___
RH___LF___	Both:RH___LF___	RH___LF___
LH___RF___	Both:LH___RF___	RF___LH___
RE___LE___	Both:RE___LE___	RE___LE___

Left homonymous visual field loss.

Miles ABC Test of Ocular Dominance
Right eye:__0__Left eye:__10__

TACTILE FINGER RECOGNITION
R 1___2___3___4___5___ R_0_/ 20
L 1___2___3___4___5___ L_0_/ 20

FINGER-TIP NUMBER WRITING
R 1___2___3___4___5___ R_0_/ 20
L 1_1_2___3___4___5___ L_1_/ 20

MINNESOTA MULTIPHASIC PERSONALITY INVENTORY

?	54		Hs	65
L	70		D	58
F	50		Hy	68
K	72		PD	60
			MF	49
			Pa	59
			Pt	56
			Sc	67
			Ma	43

REITAN-KLØVE LATERAL-DOMINANCE EXAM

Show me how you:

throw a ball	R
hammer a nail	R
cut with a knife	R
turn a door knob	R
use scissors	R
use an eraser	R
write your name	R

Record time used for spontaneous
name writing:
Preferred hand ____11_seconds
Non-preferred hand _21_seconds

REITAN-INDIANA APHASIA SCREENING TEST

Form for Adults and Older Children

Name: __W. Bl. (II)__   Age: __21__

Copy SQUARE	Repeat TRIANGLE "Triango"
Name SQUARE	Repeat MASSACHUSETTS "Massachusess"
Spell SQUARE	Repeat METHODIST EPISCOPAL
Copy CROSS	Write SQUARE
Name CROSS	Read SEVEN
Spell CROSS	Repeat SEVEN
Copy TRIANGLE	Repeat/Explain HE SHOUTED THE WARNING.
Name TRIANGLE	Write HE SHOUTED THE WARNING.
Spell TRIANGLE	Compute 85 – 27 =
Name BABY	Compute 17 X 3 =
Write CLOCK	Name KEY
Name FORK	Demonstrate use of KEY
Read 7 SIX 2	Draw KEY Very mild lack of apposition of notches on stem near handle.
Read MGW	Read PLACE LEFT HAND TO RIGHT EAR. "Place the left hand to the right ear."
Reading I	Place LEFT HAND TO RIGHT EAR
Reading II	Place LEFT HAND TO LEFT ELBOW

clock

Square

He shouted the warning.

$$\begin{array}{r} 85 \\ 27 \\ \hline 58 \end{array}$$

51

The patient's ability in logical analysis and analytical reasoning showed striking improvement. On retesting he performed well within the normal range on this type of task, as contrasted with severe impairment shown on the initial examination. He was able to perform the Tactual Performance Test without difficulty, and required just slightly more than one-third of the original time for completion of the task. In addition, incidental alertness and memory were now within the normal range. The patient continued to have some problems on the Trail Making Test and found it especially difficult to keep both the alphabetical and numerical series in mind at the same time as he alternated between them. Finger tapping speed was still somewhat depressed in both hands but had shown definite improvement, especially on the right side.

The overall results, although still indicating some mild impairment, were approaching the normal range. On the basis of these findings we recommended that the patient begin preparing for resumption of his college education the following fall. Even though the test results were essentially within the normal range, past experience has indicated that the intellectual and cognitive abilities of persons who have been impaired are not as capable of withstanding pressure and stress as are those of the person who has never sustained impairment. Because of this, we recommended that the patient begin studying on his own and possibly audit classes rather than immediately accept full responsibility for his academic performance. We believed that this type of preparation would enable him to resume his regular college program in the fall, approximately six months later.

In order to be sure that improvement was progressing, the patient was re-examined shortly before the beginning of the fall semester. The results indicated continued improvement. The few areas of deficit he had shown previously were now within normal limits, and the general picture of recovery appeared to be nearly complete. The subject resumed his academic training and made satisfactory progress. Neuropsychological testing was done annually for the next two years; the improvement achieved by this patient appeared to be secure. The last examination, which was within normal limits for a person of superior general intelligence, was done after the subject had successfully completed college.

In many patients with brain injuries it is difficult to correlate the exact location of the lesion with the neuropsychological deficits. Nevertheless, assessment of the initial deficits and the rate of recovery can represent important contributions. Gross observational judgments cannot accurately evaluate the patient's potential for higher-level tasks. It is entirely possible that if this man had been evaluated by the usual methods of clinical assessment, he might have been encouraged to re-enter college after missing only a single semester. Retrospectively, we believe that this would have been a mistake. Even though the patient had made good progress by this time, he showed distinct areas of deficit, and we suspect that he would have had difficulty resuming his normal academic responsibilities.

If a patient experiences failure after sustaining a brain injury, it often can seriously impair his confidence and undermine his ability to use his full potential when his recovery has been more complete. In many instances, recommendations are made on the basis of casual observations of the patient's deficits and strengths; frequently, the patient is not able to fulfill the responsibilities implicit in the task recommended to him and he consequently experiences failure. Often the next step is to recommend undertaking somewhat less demanding tasks, only to have the patient fail again. After several such experiences of failure, the patient is unable to do tasks or meet demands that in all probability should be well within his range of capability.

It is, therefore, particularly important for patients with injuries of the brain to be permitted to start with relatively simple tasks from which they can derive a sense of mastery and success and experience the positive reinforcement that is implicit in successful performance, rather than experience the sense of failure and personal inadequacy that accompanies deficient performance.

CASE #16

Name:	F.C.	Sex:	Male
Age:	62	Handedness:	Right
Education:	10	Occupation:	Telephone Line Crew Member

Current Complaints and Pertinent History

This 62-year-old man had a four-year history of major motor seizures and Jacksonian seizures, principally involving the right upper extremity. After regaining consciousness after his first major motor seizure he had a right hemiparesis that lasted for about eight hours and was completely amnestic for that period of time. Four months elapsed before he had another seizure, in which he lost consciousness, experienced a contraction of both of his feet and his toes and had residual weakness of the right arm. These episodes began to gradually increase in frequency and during the several months before this neuropsychological examination the patient was experiencing up to five attacks per day. These episodes were not considered to be severe and the patient did not lose consciousness.

At the time of the current hospital admission the patient had a mild movement disorder (especially involving his right upper extremity) and a loss in two-point discrimination on the right side of the body. Besides these lateralized motor and tactile deficits he demonstrated no other positive findings. A pneumoencephalogram showed generalized cerebral cortical atrophy, but neither this procedure nor bilateral carotid angiograms showed any evidence of a space-occupying lesion. EEG demonstrated Dysrhythmia, Grade I, in the left Sylvian area. At age 19 the patient sustained a serious closed head injury accompanied by loss of consciousness for six hours; otherwise the history was non-contributory. The complete neurological evaluation suggested that this man had generalized cortical atrophy and that his convulsive episodes were due to an irritative lesion in the middle part of the left cerebral hemisphere, possibly resulting from the head injury sustained when he was 19.

Neuropsychological Test Results

Neuropsychological examination yielded somewhat low I.Q. values, significant impairment on brain-related tests, and a number of findings that specifically implicated the left cerebral hemisphere. The Wechsler-Bellevue Scale yielded a Verbal I.Q. of 94 and a Performance I.Q. of 98, values that were in the lower part of the Average range. However, the weighted scores for the individual subtests indicated values that were consistently below average and often very considerably below this level. In older persons, the Wechsler-Bellevue Scale did not require a very high level of performance to produce fairly acceptable I.Q. values; this explains the relatively adequate I.Q. values in conjunction with the low weighted scores. Judging from the scores on the Information (8) and Comprehension (9) subtests, it would appear that this man had premorbid I.Q. values that were not grossly deficient. However, the overall distribution of scores suggests that his general intelligence level probably was never as high as the 50th percentile. The conservative procedure would be to interpret the rest of the test results for this man with an expectation that his performances might be influenced by somewhat low general capabilities (Reitan, 1985b).

The distribution of subtest scores on the Wechsler scale was not particularly revealing. There was nothing remarkable in terms of brain functions among the Verbal subtests. One might postulate that a score of 3 on Picture Arrangement reflects some difficulty but considering the fact that F.C.'s other Performance scores were not much higher, this would be open to question. Using the Wechsler Scale, it is difficult in a case of this kind to differentiate between life-long limitation of general intelligence and generalized impairment due to diffuse cerebral damage.

The four most sensitive indicators in the Halstead-Reitan Battery all showed impaired performances. The Impairment Index of 0.9 (indicating that 90 percent of the tests were in the brain-damaged range) represents a poorer performance than would be expected, even considering this man's limited general intelligence. He also performed poorly on Trails B (191 seconds) and the Tactual Performance Test — Localization Component (1). His score on the Category Test (62) was about at the average level for brain-damaged subjects. Since this man had lower general intelligence than the average brain-damaged subject, and was also considerably older, one must view the Category Test score

HALSTEAD-REITAN NEUROPSYCHOLOGICAL TEST BATTERY

Patient_____F.C._____Age__62__Sex__M__Education__10__Handedness__R__

_x_ WECHSLER-BELLEVUE SCALE (FORM I)
___WAIS

VIQ	94
PIQ	98
FIS IQ	92
VWS	33
PWS	23
Total WS	56
Information	8
Comprehension	9
Digit Span	4
Arithmetic	7
Similarities	5
Vocabulary	4
Picture Arrangement	3
Picture Completion	4
Block Design	5
Object Assembly	7
Digit Symbol	4

HALSTEAD'S NEUROPSYCHOLOGICAL TEST BATTERY

Category Test ___62___

Tactual Performance Test
Dominant hand: ___13.5___
Non-dominant hand: ___12.8___
Both hands: ___8.4___
Total Time__34.7__
Memory__6__
Localization__1__

Seashore Rhythm Test
Number Correct__24__ ___8___

Speech-sounds Perception Test
Number of Errors ___14___

Finger Oscillation Test
Dominant hand: ___33___ ___33___
Non-dominant hand:___38___

TRAIL MAKING TEST
Part A:__61__ seconds
Part B:_191_ seconds

Impairment Index___0.9___

Miles ABC Test of Ocular Dominance
Right eye:_10_ Left eye:_0_

REITAN-KLØVE SENSORY-PERCEPTUAL EXAM — No errors

				Error Totals		
RH____LH____	Both:RH____LH____			RH____LH____
RH____LF____	Both:RH____LF____			RH____LF____
LH____RF____	Both:LH____RF____			RF____LH____
RE____LE____	Both:RE____LE____			RE____LE____
RV____LV____	Both:RV____LV____			
____ ____	____ ____			RV____LV____
____ ____	____ ____			

TACTILE FINGER RECOGNITION
R 1___2_3_3_4_4_4_5___ R 11 / 20
L 1___2___3___4___5___ L 0 / 20

FINGER-TIP NUMBER WRITING
R 1___2_1_3_3_4_2_5_1_ R 7 / 20
L 1___2_1_3___4_1_5___ L 2 / 20

MINNESOTA MULTIPHASIC
PERSONALITY INVENTORY

?	50	Hs	47
L	66	D	72
F	50	Hy	64
K	55	PD	55
		MF	59
		Pa	62
		Pt	50
		Sc	53
		Ma	50

REITAN-INDIANA APHASIA SCREENING TEST

Form for Adults and Older Children

Name: _____F. C._____ Age: __62__

Copy SQUARE	Repeat TRIANGLE
Name SQUARE	Repeat MASSACHUSETTS
Spell SQUARE S-Q-U-A-R	Repeat METHODIST EPISCOPAL
Copy CROSS	Write SQUARE See two attempts
Name CROSS	Read SEVEN
Spell CROSS	Repeat SEVEN
Copy TRIANGLE	Repeat/Explain HE SHOUTED THE WARNING.
Name TRIANGLE	Write HE SHOUTED THE WARNING.
Spell TRIANGLE	Compute 85 – 27 =
Name BABY	Compute 17 X 3 =
Write CLOCK	Name KEY
Name FORK	Demonstrate use of KEY
Read 7 SIX 2	Draw KEY
Read MGW	Read PLACE LEFT HAND TO RIGHT EAR.
Reading I	Place LEFT HAND TO RIGHT EAR
Reading II	Place LEFT HAND TO LEFT ELBOW

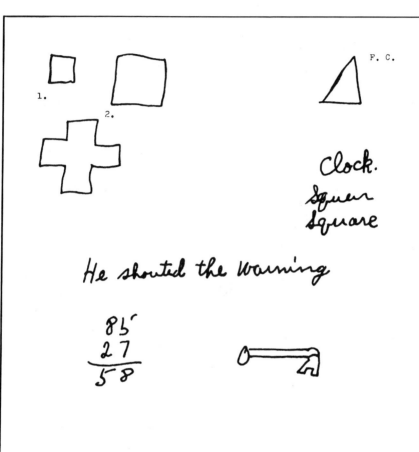

1.

2.

F. C.

Clock.

~~Squaen~~

Square

He shouted the warning

$$\begin{array}{r} 85 \\ 27 \\ \hline 58 \end{array}$$

as being relatively good for him. In general, though, it would appear that this man had experienced some degree of brain-related impairment of higher-level functions.

A review of the level of performance of the tests indicated that most of the tests were rather poorly done. In the context of this man's total cognitive ability structure, the Category Test and the Speech-sounds Perception Test (14) were relatively well done. The patient's best performances probably occurred on the Information (8) and Comprehension (9) subtests of the Wechsler Scale and the Memory component of the Tactual Performance Test (6). Overall, though, it appears that this man had fairly widespread limitations of his general intelligence and basic adaptive abilities.

Results on the Minnesota Multiphasic Personality Inventory were generally within normal limits except for a sharp elevation on the Depression scale, indicating a severe and clinically significant degree of depression. Such results usually seem to be irrelevant to interpretation of neuropsychological test findings. Our clinical observation is that even though they may be obviously depressed clinically, once these subjects develop an interest in the tasks and put forth a good effort, they frequently enjoy taking the tests and their performances are not influenced by their degree of depression.

The lateralizing and localizing findings yield definite clues to understanding the brain-behavior relationships of this man. Despite being strongly right-handed, his finger tapping speed (though slow on both sides) was distinctly slower with his right hand (33) than his left (38). Normative studies have indicated that finger tapping speed is maintained at a fairly constant level until a person reaches 55 years of age; decrements occur in the 55-59 years age interval and the 60-64 years age range. It is entirely possible, then, that the generally slow finger tapping speed for this man may be partially age-related. It should be noted, though, that the patient's poor scores on the general indicators go beyond age expectancy and most likely reflect a degree of cerebral dysfunction.

F.C. also had pronounced tactile-perceptual difficulties on the right side. Although he performed without a single error on his left hand in tactile finger recognition, he made frequent mistakes on his right hand (11 errors). By performing the test without error on his left hand the patient demonstrated that he had the attentional capability necessary to do the test well, and this strengthens the validity of the deficits shown with the right hand.

He also had more difficulty with his right hand than his left hand in finger-tip number writing perception. Clinical observation has suggested that when a greater number of errors occur in tactile finger recognition than finger-tip number writing perception (usually a more difficult task than tactile finger recognition) the validity of the errors in tactile finger recognition take on additional significance as a manifestation of cerebral damage. A comparison of the 11 errors in Tactile Finger Recognition and 7 errors in Finger-tip Number Writing Perception on the right hand adds additional credence to the tactile finger recognition errors as an indicator of left cerebral dysfunction.

In this man's case, we proceeded to extend the examination for tactile perception by writing numbers on his thighs. Even when we wrote large numbers on his thighs, drawing them slowly and deliberately, he had a great deal of difficulty on his right thigh but no difficulty on his left thigh. This finding added to the consistency of the lateralizing findings. Thus, there was strong evidence of both motor and tactile-perceptual deficits on the right side of the body. When both of these types of disorders are present the odds are strongly in favor of a lesion located at the cerebral level rather than lower in the nervous system.

In that case, then, the next question would concern a more complete review of disorders which might be associated with left cerebral damage. In general, the Aphasic Test was performed adequately. The patient omitted the "e" when spelling SQUARE orally, but this type of error is not uncommon in persons with limited educational backgrounds. However, when the patient was later asked to look at the printed letters SQUARE and write the word, he had some difficulty with the "q" (which occasionally occurs in persons with limited educational backqround), but he also again omitted the "e." Even for persons with minimal education, it is quite unusual to omit the "e" when looking directly at the printed word. With this information one might question whether there was a mild degree of impairment in dealing with language symbols, but the overall Aphasia Test results certainly do not point toward any striking loss in this regard.

The patient had some difficulty copying the cross, particularly the right lateral extremity. The key was drawn in a very simplistic manner and lacks detail. The inexperienced interpreter will sometimes postulate that drawing the key in the "wrong" direction is a sign of cerebral damage. As previously noted, we have reviewed many cases of control subjects and brain-damaged subjects with various etiologies and found that the frequency with which the key faces right instead of left is about equal in all groups. In adult subjects this kind of "reversal" appears to have no particular significance with regard to impaired brain functions. Therefore, the Aphasia Test might possibly have yielded a little information suggesting left cerebral dysfunction but essentially no indicators of specific right cerebral damage.

Other results in the Battery, however, could be cited as possible indicators of right cerebral involvement. For example, although slow with each hand, the patient showed relatively little improvement with the left hand compared with the right-handed performance on the Tactual Performance Test. And, as mentioned above, the performance on the Picture Arrangement subtest may suggest impairment. Considered within the entire context of the Battery, these findings are not very convincing of specific right cerebral dysfunction. In fact, they contribute to an impression of generalized impairment of cerebral functions of the kind seen in patients with diffuse cerebral atrophy as well as other conditions.

The test data needing additional explanation concerns the left cerebral hemisphere. The patient had very pronounced motor and tactile-perceptual losses on the right side of the body, but scarcely any aphasic difficulties. Neither did he show any striking disparity in Verbal I.Q. compared with Performance I.Q. or any tactile, auditory, or visual imperception with bilateral simultaneous stimulation. And, finally, his visual fields were full. One must ask what kind of lesion would produce such pronounced left cerebral deficits and, at the same time, not produce other kinds of associated findings? The answer would be a left cerebral lesion that was distinctly focal and not of an acutely disruptive nature. Results of this kind, for example, would not be at all likely in cases of stroke involving the left middle cerebral artery nor of an intrinsic cerebral tumor. Instead, they would be compatible with a specific focal involvement in the middle part of the hemisphere that was relatively chronic and static. In fact, it would be difficult to hypothesize a condition more compatible with the test results than scar tissue formation in the middle part of the left hemisphere together with generalized cerebral cortical atrophy.

CASE #17

Name:	G.Y.	Sex:	Male
Age:	31	Handedness:	Right
Education:	12	Occupation:	Car Salesman
			and Embalmer

Current Complaints and Pertinent History

This 31-year-old man was admitted to the hospital after having been found in a confused condition in a run-down local hotel. It appeared that the patient had been drinking and had been severely beaten; he had many lacerations and bruises. He had little recollection for the events of the previous several days. He was restless and complained of a severe headache, but the neurological examination was otherwise negative. At the time of admission a laceration oozing dark red blood was observed just anterior to the right ear. The patient was questioned about this injury but denied any knowledge of how it had occurred. X-rays of the skull showed a penetrating skull defect with indriven fragments of bone, suggesting that the laceration in front of the right ear was actually a penetrating bullet wound. The patient was referred for neuropsychological testing without knowledge on his part, or ours, that he had a bullet wound that penetrated into the anterior to middle part of the right temporal lobe. Surgical repair of this injury was done following neuropsychological testing.

Neuropsychological Test Results

The patient earned Verbal (97), Performance (98) and Full Scale (98) I.Q. values that were all very close to the Average level. Variability among the Verbal subtests was not particularly remarkable, but suggested that the patient had, in the past, acquired approximately average intelligence levels. He performed poorly on the Digit Span subtest (6), but such a score is not unusual even among hospitalized control subjects.

Although the Performance subtests yielded a Performance I.Q. of 98, there was a striking degree of variability. The patient performed poorly on Picture Arrangement (4) and Block Design (6) subtests. Research has demonstrated that Picture Arrangement is rather

HALSTEAD-REITAN NEUROPSYCHOLOGICAL TEST BATTERY

Patient_____G.Y._____Age___31___Sex___M___Education___12___Handedness___R___

_x_ WECHSLER-BELLEVUE SCALE (FORM I)

___WAIS

VIQ	97
PIQ	98
FIS IQ	98
VWS	44
PWS	44
Total WS	88
Information	10
Comprehension	8
Digit Span	6
Arithmetic	9
Similarities	11
Vocabulary	8
Picture Arrangement	4
Picture Completion	12
Block Design	6
Object Assembly	12
Digit Symbol	10

HALSTEAD'S NEUROPSYCHOLOGICAL TEST BATTERY

Category Test_____68___

Tactual Performance Test

Dominant hand:_____8.1_____

Non-dominant hand:_____10.1_____

Both hands:_____5.0_____

Total Time__23.2__

Memory___5___

Localization___1___

Seashore Rhythm Test

Number Correct____20_____10___

Speech-sounds Perception Test

Number of Errors_____13___

Finger Oscillation Test

Dominant hand:_____62_____62___

Non-dominant hand:____37____

TRAIL MAKING TEST

Part A:___58___seconds

Part B:__101__seconds

Impairment Index____0.9___

Miles ABC Test of Ocular Dominance

Right eye:_0_ Left eye:_10_

MINNESOTA MULTIPHASIC
PERSONALITY INVENTORY

?	61	Hs	70
L	53	D	72
F	58	Hy	67
K	48	PD	63
		MF	56
		Pa	50
		Pt	60
		Sc	50
		Ma	38

REITAN-INDIANA APHASIA SCREENING TEST

Form for Adults and Older Children

Name: _____ G. Y. _____   Age: _____ 31 _____

Copy SQUARE	Repeat TRIANGLE
Name SQUARE	Repeat MASSACHUSETTS
Spell SQUARE	Repeat METHODIST EPISCOPAL
Copy CROSS	Write SQUARE Patient turned paper around.
Name CROSS	Read SEVEN
Spell CROSS	Repeat SEVEN
Copy TRIANGLE	Repeat/Explain HE SHOUTED THE WARNING.
Name TRIANGLE	Write HE SHOUTED THE WARNING.
Spell TRIANGLE	Compute 85 – 27 = Patient was mildly confused.
Name BABY	Compute 17 X 3 =
Write CLOCK	Name KEY
Name FORK	Demonstrate use of KEY
Read 7 SIX 2	Draw KEY Patient turned paper around.
Read MGW	Read PLACE LEFT HAND TO RIGHT EAR.
Reading I	Place LEFT HAND TO RIGHT EAR
Reading II	Place LEFT HAND TO LEFT ELBOW

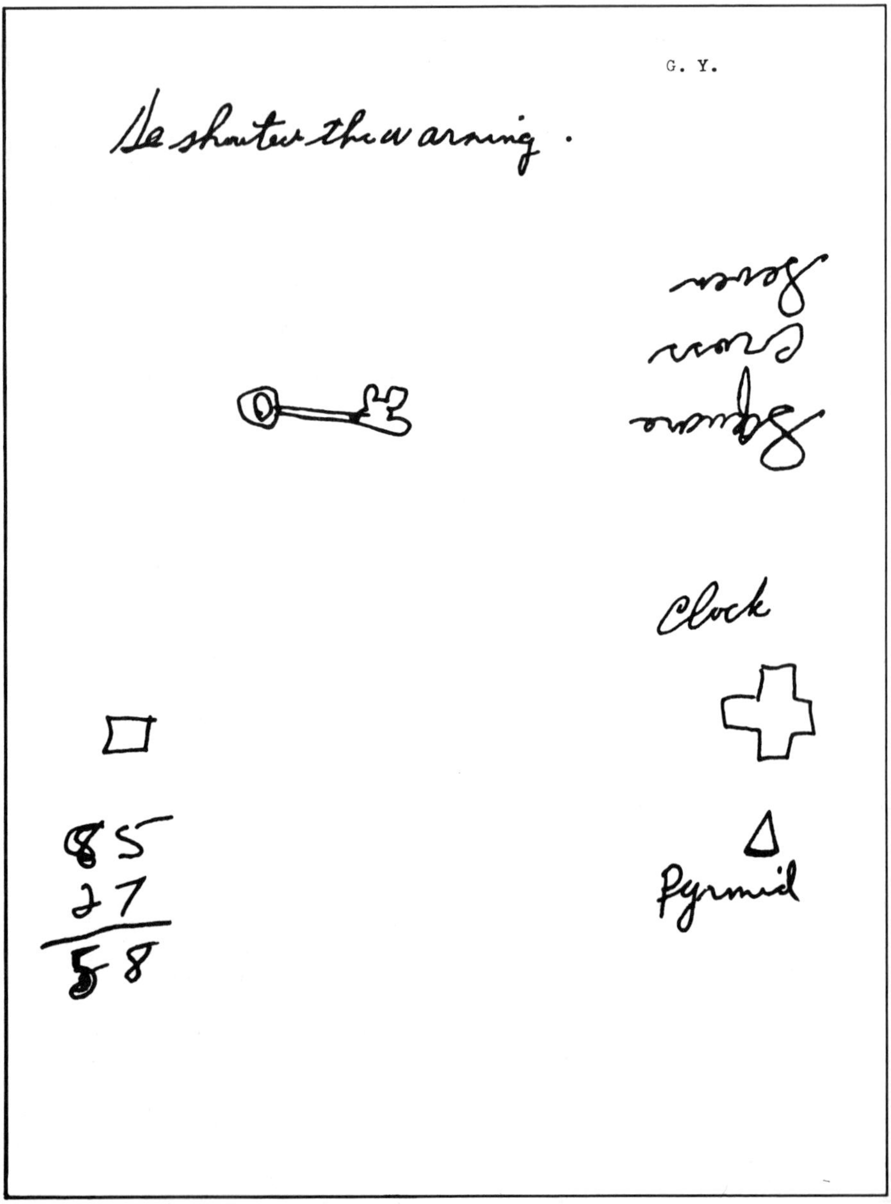

He shouted the warning .

Square
Cross
Stars

Clock

△
Pyramid

□

$$\begin{array}{r} 85 \\ 27 \\ \hline 58 \end{array}$$

specifically sensitive to the structural condition of the right anterior temporal area and Block Design is more specifically sensitive to posterior temporal, parietal and occipital damage. Thus, the pattern of Performance subtests was definitely compatible with a hypothesis of right cerebral damage. It was somewhat unusual to see a Digit Symbol score as high as this man's (10); this finding suggests that there may have been no impairment experienced on this particular subtest. This is surprising, since Digit Symbol is customarily the most sensitive of all of the subtests in the Wechsler Scale to the presence of cerebral damage, regardless of its localization. In this instance, although the Wechsler subtests suggested the possibility of right cerebral damage, other factors might conceivably be responsible for this particular pattern of results; therefore, to understand the brain-behavior relationships of this patient, it would be necessary to administer a more extensive test battery.

The four most sensitive indicators in the HRNB all had scores in the brain-damaged range. This finding, contrasted with the relatively average I.Q. values, almost certainly can be used as a basis for concluding that the patient had experienced brain damage. He earned an Impairment Index of 0.9, with only one of the seven measures (right-handed finger tapping speed) having a score in the normal range. He performed slightly worse than the average brain-damaged subject on both the Category Test (68) and Localization component of the Tactual Performance Test (1). His score on Part B of the Trail Making Test (101 seconds), although in the brain-damaged range, was his best score among these four measures.

Review of the comparative level of performance on various tests in the Battery indicated that the patient was near the average level for brain-damaged subjects on most of the tests. Therefore, although certain areas of ability were more seriously impaired than others, the results point toward generalized neuropsychological impairment. G.Y. performed at an intermediate level on Trails B and the Memory component of the Tactual Performance Test (5). His only fairly good scores occurred on certain of the Wechsler subtests and finger tapping speed with the right hand. It would appear that this man had significant impairment on a broad range of tests requiring immediate adaptive problem-solving skills, regardless of their particular content.

The Aphasia Test did not elicit any specific deficits in the use of language symbols for communicational purposes. The patient had a little difficulty and demonstrated some confusion with the problem 85−27 = , but he was finally able to solve the problem correctly. Although his performances did not suggest that his verbal and language skills had ever been very highly developed, no specific deficits were discerned.

As shown in his figure drawings, the patient probably had some difficulty in dealing with spatial configurations. This man was examined before we routinely instructed patients to make their drawings about the same size as the stimulus figures. G.Y. drew the square on the left side of the page and the cross and triangle on the right side. The cross is somewhat suspicious, particularly the disparity in the symmetry of the lateral extremities. One might postulate that the right lateral extremity was shortened because the drawing was close to the edge of the paper. This fact, in its own right, would suggest that the patient had some difficulty in dealing with spatial relationships: he should not have started drawing the figure in a position on the page that restricted his opportunity to complete the drawing correctly. The key was not drawn with as much detail as we would like to see, and from the drawing, it would be difficult to postulate that the patient had deficits of the type seen in persons with right cerebral damage. Therefore, although there might be mild pathological deviations in the drawings, they must be considered to be relatively good for a person possibly having a destructive lesion of the right cerebral hemisphere.

Next, we will review the patient's ability levels in various areas. G.Y. showed some deficits in visual-spatial and manipulatory skills, was impaired in conceptual and reasoning abilities, and showed motor impairment on the left side. This man was examined before the Sensory-perceptual Examination had been developed. As the reader can see, it would have been very helpful to have had information on these tests to effect a more complete evaluation of possible deficits on the two sides of the body.

A review of the test results with relation to lateralization and localization indicators yields findings that implicate the right cerebral hemisphere. Hardly any results were present that would specifically implicate left cerebral damage; the only possibility might be the confusion demonstrated in attempting to solve the problem 85−27 = . This finding was not indicative of unequivocal impairment inasmuch as it may have been due to a mild degree of general confusion.

Variables pointing toward right cerebral damage, however, were quite distinct. Probably the strongest indicator was obtained in measuring finger tapping speed. This man was normal with his right hand (62) but greatly slowed with his left hand (37). He demonstrated difficulty with his left hand (10.1 minutes) compared with his right hand (8.1 minutes) on the Tactual Performance Test. Although these findings can hardly be considered to be within the range of normal variation, they conceivably could be due to motor dysfunction of the left upper extremity. This possibility is minimized, though, by the general findings of impaired higher-level brain functions. Even more striking evidence was derived from Picture Arrangement and Block Design subtests of the Wechsler Scale. The overall results, then, point toward definite brain damage. The right hemisphere is implicated by the comparisons of performances with the right and left hands. The mild difficulty copying the cross would support this hypothesis, and the poor scores on Picture Arrangement and Block Design essentially make the conclusion of right cerebral damage unequivocal.

At this point, considerations may be directed to the more specific location of the lesion and its etiology. The overall results, together with the lateralizing findings, were sufficient to implicate tissue damage of the right cerebral hemisphere. The most striking right-left comparison occurred on finger tapping speed, suggesting that the lesion, if focal, might be in the vicinity of the inferior part of the motor strip. (It is difficult to understand how impairment of the left upper extremity could be missed on the physical neurological examination, but this again illustrates the limitations of this procedure.) In our experience, definite impairment of finger tapping speed is not limited to direct tissue damage in the motor strip; it also appears frequently with anterior temporal damage. This occurs particularly with the left hand and right anterior temporal involvement.

The patient also showed a definite pattern of right cerebral damage on the Tactual Performance Test, but this pattern shows up with lesions in various locations. In general, with respect to specific localization, a deficient Tactual Performance Test performance is not as helpful as an impaired finger tapping speed on one side; but the pattern of results on the TPT can aid in confirming the right cerebral lesion.

Probably the most specific information with respect to higher-level functions was derived from the low scores on Picture Arrangement and

Block Design. Picture Arrangement is rather selectively sensitive to the right anterior temporal area and, as noted earlier, Block Design tends to be more sensitive to right posterior lesions generally. The pattern in this instance would confirm the comparative relationship between finger-tapping and Tactual Performance Test measures. Therefore, the test results suggest that the major structural damage is in the right anterior temporal area and that the lesion is of such a nature that is has a somewhat generalized effect.

Finally, we should postulate what type of lesion might be responsible for the overall findings. First, one can consider the possibility of any focal lesion. These would most commonly be represented by neoplasms, vascular lesions, abscesses, and penetrating head wounds. The test findings are much more suggestive of physical trauma than of the other conditions. If either an intrinsic tumor or a focal cerebral vascular lesion had caused such specific deficits, it would be unlikely that some of the tests (particularly Trails B) would be done so well. It would be possible, however, that a congenital vascular lesion might be responsible for these test results, particularly if bleeding had occurred. We have also seen similar results shortly after surgical repair of aneurysms and arteriovenous malformations.

Based on the test results alone, we cannot be completely confident that the lesion was due to a penetrating head wound, but this certainly would seem to be the most likely explanation. Despite the contribution of Picture Arrangement and Block Design in this particular instance, the failure to find a disparity between Verbal and Performance I.Q. values would be another factor suggesting traumatic injury. Lateralized traumatic injuries tend to cause differences between Verbal and Performance I.Q. values, but not as consistently or as strikingly as lateralized intrinsic neoplastic or vascular lesions (Hom & Reitan, 1982).

The argument against a primary abscess (this patient did have an abscess secondary to the penetrating injury) is that such lesions customarily produce results very similar to intrinsic tumors. One might wonder if the test findings would be compatible with an extrinsic tumor such as a meningioma. The argument against such a lesion (extrinsic to the brain tissue but possibly causing certain focal effects) is that this man showed entirely too much generalized impairment and the focal effects (e.g., impairment of finger-tapping speed with the left hand) were too pronounced.

The reader can see that it is possible, with experience, to analyze the results in considerable detail and postulate their possible etiology. It was necessary for us to follow this procedure with thousands of cases to develop the interpretation of the tests, and to identify data with general as compared with more specific significance. In most instances using neuropsychological testing, it is not necessary to determine neurological diagnosis, because direct history information or findings on neurological diagnostic techniques provide this information. It was absolutely imperative, however, that such research studies were originally done, even to the point of permitting detailed correlation of the test results with the patient's specific neurological condition, to document the validity of the Halstead-Reitan Battery for purposes of neuropsychological interpretation. One can appreciate the problem of not having results on the Sensory-perceptual Examination in this particular case.

This patient showed evidence of some emotional difficulties of adjustment. The Hypochondriasis, Depression, and possibly the Hysteria scales were elevated, and it is probable that this man had some neurotic-like symptomatology. It was known, from other sources, that he was a relatively irresponsible person whose behavior was deviant from conventional standards.

Evaluations of interpersonal, emotional and affective aspects of behavior undoubtedly represent an important element in the overall understanding of an individual, but they seem to be of minimal significance in the interpretation of results on Halstead-Reitan Battery. This may be because (1) the biological aspects of the brain have an overriding significance in determining the results on the Battery; and (2) the tests are relatively insensitive to "personality" variables and the same set of rules may be applied to the interpretation of data regardless of the presence or absence of neurotic-like symptomatology. Of course, the reader will encounter some psychotic patients who are so disturbed that it is impossible for the examiner to establish interpersonal relationships adequate enough to be able to conduct the testing validly; however, if the patient is cooperative and able to make a consistent effort to perform well, the test findings appear to be essentially independent of personality variations.

CASE #18

Name:	J.S.	Sex:	Male
Age:	48	Handedness:	Left
Education:	3	Occupation:	Construction Worker

J.S. was examined in our laboratory before measures of grip strength and the Tactile Form Recognition Test were routinely administered. One of the reasons this case is included here is to illustrate the significance of the data these tests contribute to the Battery. Before referring to the test results it should be noted that this man had completed only three grades in school.

In evaluating this patient's test results we will refer first to the findings on the Wechsler-Bellevue Scale. The patient earned a Verbal I.Q. of 93, a Performance I.Q. of 97, and a Full Scale I.Q. of 94. Most of the results on individual subtests fell at the average level or below, suggesting that this man was probably never much above average (or perhaps never quite as high as average) in general intelligence. However, his general intelligence levels would not seem to have been the limiting factors with respect to his third-grade education. We would infer from the Wechsler results that this man had the intellectual capabilities of progressing beyond the third grade level.

In terms of identifying impaired brain functions, the I.Q. values and the results on individual subtests were not particularly revealing. Although the Arithmetic subtest of the Wechsler Scale is probably the most sensitive of the Verbal subtests to cerebral damage, it is not a particularly accurate measure of cerebral dysfunction. Considering the limited education of this man, we cannot safely infer that there has been any significant impairment of the Verbal subtests. It is possible that he had never developed any better abilities than his scores on the Arithmetic, Similarities, and Vocabulary subtests reflect.

Except for Object Assembly, the patient also performed below the average level on the Performance subtests. Some people tend to relate relatively high scores to the occupation of the subject, but we have frequently observed many deviations from postulated relationships between occupation and specific aspects of ability structure. It may be

HALSTEAD-REITAN NEUROPSYCHOLOGICAL TEST BATTERY

Patient ___J.S.___ Age __48__ Sex __M__ Education __3__ Handedness __L__

__x__ WECHSLER-BELLEVUE SCALE (FORM I)
_____ WAIS

VIQ	93
PIQ	97
FIS IQ	94
VWS	37
PWS	34
Total WS	71
Information	10
Comprehension	11
Digit Span	7
Arithmetic	3
Similarities	6
Vocabulary	6
Picture Arrangement	6
Picture Completion	4
Block Design	6
Object Assembly	12
Digit Symbol	6

HALSTEAD'S NEUROPSYCHOLOGICAL TEST BATTERY

Category Test _____ 49

Tactual Performance Test
Right hand: _____ 8.2
Right hand: _____ 7.0
Right hand: _____ 6.6
Total Time __21.8__
Memory __3__
Localization __1__

Seashore Rhythm Test
Number Correct __25__ _____ 6

Speech-sounds Perception Test
Number of Errors _____ 7

Finger Oscillation Test
Dominant hand: __28__ _____ 36
Non-dominant hand: __36__

Impairment Index __0.7__

TRAIL MAKING TEST
Part A: __54__ seconds
Part B: __113__ seconds

Miles ABC Test of Ocular Dominance
Right eye: __0__ Left eye: __10__

REITAN-KLØVE SENSORY-PERCEPTUAL EXAM

				Error Totals	
RH____LH____	Both:RH____LH _4_			RH____LH _4_	
RH____LF____	Both:RH____LF _2_			RH____LF _2_	
LH____RF____	Both:LH _4_ RF____			RF____LH _4_	
RE____LE____	Both:RE____LE____			RE____LE____	
RV____LV____	Both:RV____LV____				
____ ____	____ ____			RV____LV____	
____ ____	____ ____				

MINNESOTA MULTIPHASIC PERSONALITY INVENTORY

?	50	Hs	85
L	43	D	60
F	53	Hy	73
K	59	PD	74
		MF	47
		Pa	47
		Pt	56
		Sc	67
		Ma	68

TACTILE FINGER RECOGNITION
R 1____ 2____ 3____ 4____ 5____   R _0_ / 20
L 1 _4_ 2 _4_ 3 _4_ 4 _4_ 5 _4_   L _20_ / 20

FINGER-TIP NUMBER WRITING
R 1 _2_ 2____ 3 _2_ 4____ 5 _2_   R _6_ / 20
L 1 _4_ 2 _4_ 3 _4_ 4 _4_ 5 _4_   L _20_ / 20

REITAN-INDIANA APHASIA SCREENING TEST

Form for Adults and Older Children

Name: __J. S._____ Age: __48__

Copy SQUARE	Repeat TRIANGLE
Name SQUARE	Repeat MASSACHUSETTS
Spell SQUARE	Repeat METHODIST EPISCOPAL
Copy CROSS	Write SQUARE
Name CROSS	Read SEVEN
Spell CROSS	Repeat SEVEN
Copy TRIANGLE	Repeat/Explain HE SHOUTED THE WARNING.
Name TRIANGLE	Write HE SHOUTED THE WARNING.
Spell TRIANGLE "T-R-A-N-G-E"	Compute 85 – 27 =
Name BABY	Compute 17 X 3 =
Write CLOCK	Name KEY
Name FORK	Demonstrate use of KEY
Read 7 SIX 2	Draw KEY Note extension of "nose" of key into arithmetic problem.
Read MGW	Read PLACE LEFT HAND TO RIGHT EAR.
Reading I	Place LEFT HAND TO RIGHT EAR
Reading II	Place LEFT HAND TO LEFT ELBOW

J.S.

Clock

Square
Seven
He should the werning

$85 - 27 =$

27
55

51

that as a construction worker, this man is good at putting things together; it is more likely, though, that he was somewhat lucky on the Object Assembly items.

Considering the sensitivity of the Digit Symbol subtest to cerebral damage, this patient's comparatively low score on this subtest might be suggestive of impaired brain functions. His Picture Arrangement and Block Design scores are also relatively low in the overall subtest distribution, suggesting the possibility of some right posterior cerebral damage. An error committed frequently by neuropsychologists is to use the results of the Wechsler Scale alone and, in this case, conclude that this patient definitely has brain damage. However, all that the Wechsler findings have told us is that we should expect more from this man than might be implied by his third-grade educational level.

The next step in our interpretation is to refer to the four most sensitive indicators in the Battery. This man earned a Halstead Impairment Index of 0.7 (indicating that about 70 percent of his test results were in the brain-damaged range). This finding, considered with relation to the Wechsler values, indicates that brain damage may be present. The Category Test score of 49 is just barely in the normal range and reflects a mild degree of deficit in the area of abstraction, reasoning and logical analysis. Research data analyses have indicated that 50 errors on the Category Test is a rather liberal cut-off point and tends to increase the number of false-negatives at the expense of false-positives. The Trails B score of 113 seconds is in the brain-damaged range, but is not grossly impaired and, depending upon what other information of cerebral damage we discern from the test results, may later be used to suggest that brain damage is either mild in nature or relatively chronic and static. The patient performed poorly on the Localization component of the Tactual Performance Test, recalling the position of only one of ten blocks. Thus, the overall results on the four most sensitive indicators in the Halstead-Reitan Battery strongly implicate an impairment of brain functions.

At this point in the interpretation it is often useful to review the rest of the test results by comparing relatively good and relatively poor scores. This man scored surprising well on the Speech-sounds Perception Test, making only 7 errors. This is the mean number of errors for a normal control subject (who has an educational level and average I.Q. which are higher than this man's). This finding suggests that J.S.

is able to deal relatively well with receptive aspects of language material through the auditory and visual avenues. Obviously, the Speech-sounds Perception Test score, considered by itself, does not necessarily indicate a high level of proficiency in all areas of language functioning. Despite the fact that a score of 25 contributes to the Impairment Index, the patient also performed fairly well on the Seashore Rhythm Test. It is apparent from results on both of these measures that J.S. has good attentional capabilities and is able to maintain his concentration over periods of time to specific stimulus material. In terms of the neuro-psychological model of brain functions, then, we would postulate that any limitations demonstrated in the results of the Battery are not likely to be due to deficits at the first level of central processing.

The patient demonstrated deficits on a number of measures in the Battery. He had difficulty discerning the shapes of the blocks on the Tactual Performance Test with his left hand and it was necessary to do three trials with the right hand. His overall time (21.8 minutes) was relatively poor and his Memory score (3) and Localization score (1) reflected comparatively worse performances than the Total Time. (If the examination had included only the Wechsler Scale and the inter-pretation had suggested that the Object Assembly score was relatively good in association with the patient's employment as a construction worker, one would question why this man did so poorly on the Tactual Performance Test, even though using his "good" hand).

The patient was also slow in finger tapping speed with both hands: right hand, 36; left (dominant) hand, 28. He had some difficulty performing simple constructional tasks such as drawing a cross and key. He showed obvious impairment of tactile perception on the left side. On the Aphasia Test he demonstrated limited verbal skills, espe-cially in spelling and writing. It is entirely possible that the limited academic-type skills are related to this man's third-grade education. In fact, his writing reveals a somewhat primitive style and inadequate spelling skills. His manner of writing "warning" is sometimes seen in persons who do not spell well and never have. These persons often make marks on the paper that might possibly represent the word (almost resembling dysgraphia), but the real problem is that they do not know how to spell the word correctly and produce a general configuration that only somewhat approximates the word. It is likely that this is what happened in this case. In terms of the examination procedure, it would have been worthwhile for the examiner to challenge the subject more directly by asking him to write the word again as carefully as possible in order to discern the exact nature of the problem.

To summarize J.S.'s test results up to this point, it is apparent that this man has a number of difficulties: he does have good attentional capabilities (Speech-sounds Perception Test and Seashore Rhythm Test) but is limited in his ability to deal with language and verbal tasks (Aphasia Test); he shows evidence of impairment in ability to adapt to novel types of problem-solving situations (Tactual Performance Test — Time); he has some limitation of memory; he is impaired in dealing with even simple visual-spatial tasks (drawing figures); he has some primary motor impairment of both upper extremities (finger tapping speed); and he has definite tactile-perceptual deficits on the left side of the body (Sensory-perceptual Examination). In consideration of these results, his I.Q. values now look relatively good. At this point we can now say with certainty that the brain-related adaptive abilities of this man are generally and significantly impaired.

Results on the Minnesota Multiphasic Personality Inventory show that this man also has certain adjustmental difficulties in the emotional and affective areas. He seems to be particularly concerned about somatic difficulties and his physical condition. Overall, the results suggest that he experiences some general anxiety, a lack of self-confidence, problems in developing close personal affective relationships with others, some degree of unreality in his perception and understanding of problems, and perhaps some evidence of impulsiveness in his behavior. In addition, we would suspect that this man feels some resentment toward society and is not much concerned with observing conventional behavioral patterns.

The reader may have noted the relationships of the Hypochondriasis, Depression and Hysteria scores. This configuration has been referred to as a Conversion V and suggests that the patient has somatic complaints of a hysterical nature. A Conversion V may have this significance in a psychiatric population, but there have been no studies of patients with neurological disorders that support the validity of this configuration in this group. There appear to be consistent indications that applying psychiatric criteria to neurological patients may have serious deficiencies. Researchers should investigate the possibly limited generality of the finding before recommending any clinical application and interpretation of a particular configuration of test data. MMPI patterns have rarely been checked for their validity in neurological patients; however, the earliest validity studies with the Halstead-Reitan Battery used control groups composed principally of psychiatric patients and persons with paraplegia. Neuropsychological evaluation using the Halstead-Reitan Battery has been developed to be sufficiently specific so that conclusions can be drawn about the individual subject, regardless of the patient's general psychiatric or neurological classification.

Although the items of the MMPI may be valid in terms of how they describe the feelings and complaints of this man, we must question their validity for interpretation within a psychiatric framework. For J.S., many of the items that contribute to the Hypochondriasis scale may represent valid problems which result from his brain disorder.

The next step in interpretation should be directed toward neurological inferences. The test data have established that this man has some degree of impairment of cerebral functions; next, evidence for involvement of the left or right cerebral hemispheres must be considered. In analyzing specific measures of left cerebral involvement, only the indications of some difficulty on the Aphasic Test could possibly be considered positive findings. This man obviously became confused when trying to spell TRIANGLE; however, this is the most difficult of the spelling items on the Aphasia Test and the problem might be related to his inadequate educational training. His writing and drawings revealed further problems. He appeared to write an "m" at the end of "Seven," he misspelled "shouted" and did not clearly form the letters in "warning." However, these deficits are not perfectly characteristic of the types of disorders shown by persons with left cerebral damage and it seems more likely that they may be more of a reflection of inadequate educational background than of brain damage. Thus, the entire set of test results did not produce any specific indicators of left-sided involvement.

Conversely, there were many positive indications of right cerebral damage, some of which were quite pronounced. The most striking deficits related to impairment of tactile perception on the left side. This man had no difficulty perceiving a tactile stimulus to the left side when it was given alone, but when a competing stimulus on the right side of the body was given, he rather consistently failed to perceive the stimulus to the left side. This phenomenon occurred in all four trials of simultaneous stimuli given to the right hand and left hand or left hand and right face. However, when the left face was in competition with the right hand, the patient reported that both sides were stimulated in two of the four trials, and failed to notice the stimulus to the left face in the other trials. This is a classical picture of left tactile imperception. The face is generally more sensitive than the hand on either side and, in accordance with this observation, the left face (which was on the impaired side) competed a little more successfully with the right hand.

The patient had pronounced difficulty with tactile finger recognition on his left hand. Even though he made no mistakes on his right hand, he was unable to perform the task at all with his left hand. He had difficulty on his right hand with finger-tip number writing perception, but we would postulate that these errors stemmed from general rather than specific deficits. The patient was not able to make any progress in perceiving numbers written on the finger tips of his left hand, and the right-left comparison showed much more difficulty on the left than the right side.

The Tactile Form Recognition Test had not been developed at the time this man was examined, but we proceeded informally to test his ability to perceive objects in his right and left hands. He had distinct difficulty on the left side but demonstrated normal performances on the right side. It would have been advantageous to have had the more specific and standardized type of comparative information that can be obtained with the Tactile Form Recognition Test.

The patient was not able to perform the Tactual Performance Test with his left hand at all, and it was therefore necessary to give all three trials with the right hand. Prior clinical experience has indicated that three trials using the same hand produces approximately the same Total Time as the standard procedure.

At this point one might stop to consider the other test findings and wonder why this man was not able to use his left hand for the Tactual Performance Test. It would not appear that he had a motor deficit severe enough to preclude use of his left hand—he was able to tap an average of 2.8 times/second. (It would have been desirable to have had bilateral measures of grip strength to provide more information about any possible motor deficits.) However, considering the results that are available, we would postulate that the severe difficulty with the left hand on the Tactual Performance Test related to a tactile sensitivity loss and difficulty with form recognition. When a patient has no idea which block is in his hand, he has trouble performing this test at all. Being unable to use his left hand on the Tactual Performance Test is likely another indication of right cerebral damage in this man.

Finally, although the patient was impaired in finger tapping speed on both sides, the results still have lateralizing significance. He was considerably slower with his left (preferred) hand than his right hand, suggesting right cerebral damage. J.S. showed evidence of some degree of constructional dyspraxia, particularly in his drawing of the key. Note that the "nose" of the key extends into the arithmetic problem. It is important to be aware of the sequence in which the patient does these performances and the remaining space on the paper. The arithmetic problem was done before the key was drawn. The fact that the patient selected such a limited space for drawing the key (additional space was available at the bottom of the page) in itself suggests the presence of a problem in spatial organization. Although J.S.'s symptoms of constructional dyspraxia were relatively mild (as might be expected of a chronic-static lesion, even in the right parietal area), they were nevertheless present.

At this point the reader should note that there were striking and pronounced tactile-perceptual deficits on the left side but motor deficits on that side were not as pronounced. There was no lateralizing information from specific auditory or visual tests. In fact, this patient's visual fields were full. Findings of this type, quite pronounced but delimited with respect to types of involvement, can be associated with a highly focal lesion. In fact, considering the findings, we would postulate that this man has specific involvement in his right parietal area that extends, to a degree, to the right motor area. We find no evidence of specific involvement in other parts of the right cerebral hemisphere or the left cerebral hemisphere.

Having read the prior cases, the reader may wonder whether the findings for this patient would correspond with a right parietal intrinsic tumor. There is no doubt that J.S. has striking deficits that involve this area of the brain and the findings as stated above would not necessarily be incompatible with neoplastic involvement. To an experienced interpreter, though, the results would not be likely to suggest an intrinsic tumor. There are several reasons for this, and they all relate to the relatively good scores on some measures in the Battery.

If a patient had experienced an intrinsic tumor that had caused the pronounced deficits of the right parietal area that this man demonstrated, he most probably would have performed much worse on Trails B. In addition, even though the scores for the Speech-sounds Perception Test and the Seashore Rhythm Test do not have localizing significance in most cases, it is entirely unlikely that these tests would have been performed as well as they were if this man had had a seriously destructive right parietal neoplasm. In other words, an acutely destructive lesion of this kind (which it would have to have been, considering the intensity of the *positive* right parietal indicators) would cause more impairment at the first level of cognitive processing (attention and concentration). Also, if the positive right parietal results were due. to a recently destructive lesion, it would be improbable that J.S.'s Performance I.Q. would have been as good with relation to the Verbal I.Q. as occurred in this instance.

One might next wonder if this man has had a stroke. Two points of information argue strongly against a lesion of the right middle cerebral artery: (1) finger tapping speed was retained in the left hand; and (2) the visual fields were full.

The reader can see that there are some distinct disparities in the overall set of test results. There are strong right parietal indicators that cannot be ignored, but the level of performance on other tests and certain aspects of the test relationships are not at all compatible with a recent, acutely destructive focal lesion in the right parietal area. The alternative, in this case, is to consider other conditions that have distinct focal indicators while sparing more general brain-related abilities. Such findings can represent a chronic-static focal lesion that had permitted brain function generally to be relatively organized, even though highly specific, pronounced deficits were also present.

This man did have such a lesion. Seventeen years before this examination he had sustained a compound depressed skull fracture of the right parietal-temporal region and had been unconscious for about 1½ hours from the injury. He currently had a palpable 3 X 5 centimeter skull defect in this area. Three weeks before this neuropsychological examination he had experienced an epileptic seizure which started with numbness and twitching of the left little finger. The numbness progressed up the left arm and down the left side into his leg. After experiencing this progression, the patient lost consciousness. Since this first seizure, J.S. had experienced two similar episodes which started in the left sternocleidomastoid muscle with spasmotic contractions, became somewhat more generalized, but did not involve a loss of consciousness. A craniectomy was performed after the neuropsychological examination and meningo-cortical scar tissue and depressed bone fragments still in the brain tissue were removed. Thus, the test results corresponded almost exactly with the predicted condition.

IX
ALZHEIMER'S DISEASE

It has been estimated that up to 4.5 percent of the population over the age of 65 suffers from severe dementia: intellectual deterioration accompanied by personality disorganization and inability to carry out the normal tasks of daily living (Katzman, 1976). This estimate increases to 11 percent if mild cases are included. However, these percentages do not include the "normal" losses in memory and learning ability that seem to occur in a much larger percentage of the population after late middle age. Furthermore, among persons over 65 years of age, approximately 60 percent have been reported to have Alzheimer's disease (Tomlinson, Blessed, and Roth, 1970).

The major pathological findings in Alzheimer's disease include cortical atrophy with marked neuronal loss, intraneuronal deteriorative changes, neurofibrillary tangles, extraneuronal neuritic (or senile) plaques, and granulovacuolar degeneration. Persons aged 65 years or less having these neuropathological changes and dementia are referred to as having presenile dementia; if they are 65 years of age or older, the diagnosis is senile dementia. There are no changes in the neuropathological correlates of the dementia in accordance with this age separation, but the incidence of these neuropathological changes in normally aging persons beyond the age of 65 causes a problem of overlap in the older age group. In fact, the term *Alzheimer's disease* has been recommended for use in persons 64 and younger whereas *senile dementia of the Alzheimer type* (SDAT) has been advised for persons 65 and older.

Since motor deficits and other focal neurological signs are essentially absent during the initial stages of Alzheimer's disease, it is often clinically distinguishable from other neuronal degenerative diseases and from multi-infarct dementia. Clinically, Alzheimer's disease is defined as a progressive, generalized loss of intellectual functions, particularly involving recent memory (which is the initial or presenting complaint). General alertness is relatively preserved and in the early stages there are no positive findings on the physical neurological examination. In later stages, however, abnormal neurological signs may appear. In more advanced cases of Alzheimer's disease a relatively high incidence of incontinence and gait disturbance is present, and this makes the distinction from normal-pressure hydrocephalus difficult.

Alzheimer's disease is a condition characterized by memory loss, disorientation, agitation, dysphasia, psychotic manifestations, incontinence, general dyspraxia, hemiparesis and reflex changes, gait disturbances and other manifestations of central nervous system functions that are associated with aging (Katzman and Karasu, 1975). In individual cases these clinical deficits are often not closely correlated with pathological changes of the brain seen at autopsy. The pathological findings in patients diagnosed as having Alzheimer's disease differ in frequency rather than type from similar findings among normally aged persons. Despite these problems of scientific definition, deterioration of higher-level brain functions among the elderly is a problem of great and increasing significance.

Neuropsychological Findings in Alzheimer's Disease

As may be expected after reading the above review, the neuropsychological findings in patients with Alzheimer's disease are quite variable. The overlap between persons showing the effects of normal aging and those diagnosed as having Alzheimer's disease constitutes a considerable problem for neuropsychological study. A number of investigations have followed patients from the time of diagnosis to autopsy. Clinical diagnosis of Alzheimer's disease has not correlated very highly with autopsy findings. The reports have been variable, but, in general, they suggest that only about 50 to 60 percent of clinical diagnoses of Alzheimer's disease are confirmed by autopsy findings (pathological diagnosis).

The general neuropsychological picture in patients with clinical diagnosis of Alzheimer's disease is similar to the profile seen with normal aging except that in Alzheimer's disease the deficits are more pronounced. We have performed detailed research in the area of normal aging using the Halstead-Reitan Neuropsychological Battery and these results are briefly reviewed in a later section of this book. In brief, patients with Alzheimer's disease show particular deficits on the more demanding higher-level aspects of brain functions (Category Test, Part B of the Trail Making Test, Total Time, Memory and Localization components of the Tactual Performance Test). Primary motor difficulties (finger tapping and grip strength) are not usually affected in the early stage of the disease. These patients are usually (although not always) able to pay attention to specific stimulus material in a well-defined context (Speech-sounds Perception Test and Seashore Rhythm Test).

Aphasic deficits as well as constructional dyspraxia may be seen in these patients when the condition is more advanced. In the early stages of the illness, specific deficits of this kind are not usually prominent and I.Q. values (especially the Verbal I.Q.) are generally maintained.

There are two diagnostic categories that include patients with such serious deterioration that it often is impossible for them to perform the Halstead-Reitan Neuropsychological Battery: Alzheimer's disease and Korsakoff's syndrome. These conditions are diagnosed principally on the basis of history, clinical evaluation and observation. These assessment techniques are nowhere nearly as sensitive to deterioration of higher-level intellectual functions as the Halstead-Reitan Battery.

Since the diagnosis essentially requires severe deterioration of higher-level brain functions, the deterioration has often advanced beyond the point where the patient is still competent enough to understand instructions and be able to take the tests involved in the Halstead-Reitan Battery. In fact, when clinical deterioration has reached the point that justifies diagnosis in these conditions, the impairment is so pronounced that detailed or refined evaluation of the deficits may contribute relatively little to further clinical understanding. The significance of these observations clearly extends to the advantage of neuropsychological assessment of persons who may be showing possible age-related deficits, presently considered within the context of normal aging, rather than to wait for a clinical diagnosis of Alzheimer's disease.

CASE #19

Name:	V.C.	Sex:	Male
Age:	56	Handedness:	Right
Education:	12	Occupation:	Salesman

This 56-year-old man, who had completed high school, earned a Verbal I.Q. that fell at the upper part of the Average range (109) and a Performance I.Q. in the lower part of the Average range (95). The weighted scores for the individual subtests indicate that the patient performed relatively well on tests that depended upon stored information. He did well on the Arithmetic subtest (16), which may have been related to the fact that as a salesman for many years he had found it necessary to do mental arithmetic. Considering that his scores were still at the Average level on Information (10) and Vocabulary (10), we can presume that the general intellectual background of this man had been within the normal range.

V.C.'s scores were generally lower on the Performance than the Verbal subtests, probably reflecting the more immediate problem-solving requirements of the Performance subtests. The patient did poorly on Object Assembly (1), but we have found results on this measure to be variable with relation to neurological criteria. It appears that, to a degree, the unreliable results occurring on Object Assembly are probably related to the fact that there are relatively few items and "lucky" or "unlucky" circumstances may have a significant effect on performances.

Review of the four most sensitive indicators shows that this patient is strikingly impaired, despite having a Full Scale I.Q. at the Average level. He had an Impairment Index of 1.0 (all of the tests had results in the brain-damaged range), was unable to perform the Category Test, did very poorly on Trails B (189 seconds), and was not able to localize any of the figures in his Tactual Performance Test drawing. The fact that this man was able to do relatively simple things was shown on the Category Test. He was able to do the first two subtests, demonstrating that he understood the instructions and was able to take the test; but on the third subtest, when the complexity level of the task increased, he was completely confused and bewildered and made

HALSTEAD-REITAN NEUROPSYCHOLOGICAL TEST BATTERY

Patient ___V.C.___ Age __56__ Sex __M__ Education __12__ Handedness __R__

<table>
<tr><td>_x_ WECHSLER-BELLEVUE SCALE (FORM I)</td><td></td><td colspan="2">HALSTEAD'S NEUROPSYCHOLOGICAL TEST BATTERY</td></tr>
<tr><td>___ WAIS</td><td></td><td>Category Test</td><td>Could not do</td></tr>
</table>

VIQ	109
PIQ	95
FIS IQ	101
VWS	50
PWS	26
Total WS	76
Information	10
Comprehension	7
Digit Span	10
Arithmetic	16
Similarities	7
Vocabulary	10
Picture Arrangement	6
Picture Completion	7
Block Design	6
Object Assembly	1
Digit Symbol	6

Tactual Performance Test

Dominant hand:	15.0 (5 blocks)
Non-dominant hand:	15.0 (4 blocks)
Both hands:	15.0 (4 blocks)
Total Time	45.0 +
Memory	0
Localization	0

Seashore Rhythm Test

Number Correct __11__   __10__

Speech-sounds Perception Test

Number of Errors   Could not do

Finger Oscillation Test

Dominant hand: ____44____   __44__
Non-dominant hand: __26__

TRAIL MAKING TEST
Part A: __46__ seconds
Part B: __189__ seconds

Impairment Index __1.0__

REITAN-KLØVE SENSORY-PERCEPTUAL EXAM

					Error Totals	
RH___ LH___	Both:RH___ LH___				RH___ LH___	
RH___ LF___	Both:RH___ LF___				RH___ LF___	
LH___ RF___	Both:LH___ RF _2_				RF _2_ LH___	
RE___ LE___	Both:RE _1_ LE___				RE _1_ LE___	
RV___ LV___	Both:RV___ LV___				RV___ LV___	

TACTILE FINGER RECOGNITION
R 1___ 2___ 3___ 4___ 5___   R _0_ / 20
L 1___ 2___ 3___ 4___ 5___   L _0_ / 20

FINGER-TIP NUMBER WRITING
R 1___ 2___ 3___ 4___ 5___   R _0_ / 20
L 1_2_2_ 3___ 4___ 5___   L _2_ / 20

REITAN-INDIANA APHASIA SCREENING TEST

Form for Adults and Older Children

Name: _____V. C._____ Age: __56__

Copy SQUARE	Repeat TRIANGLE
Name SQUARE	Repeat MASSACHUSETTS "Massachusess"
Spell SQUARE	Repeat METHODIST EPISCOPAL "Methodst Epis --" Could not complete
Copy CROSS Note the asymmetry of the lateral extremities.	Write SQUARE
Name CROSS	Read SEVEN
Spell CROSS	Repeat SEVEN
Copy TRIANGLE	Repeat/Explain HE SHOUTED THE WARNING.
Name TRIANGLE	Write HE SHOUTED THE WARNING.
Spell TRIANGLE	Compute 85 – 27 =
Name BABY	Compute 17 X 3 =
Write CLOCK	Name KEY
Name FORK	Demonstrate use of KEY
Read 7 SIX 2	Draw KEY Note the poor formation of the "nose" and "teeth"
Read MGW	Read PLACE LEFT HAND TO RIGHT EAR.
Reading I	Place LEFT HAND TO RIGHT EAR
Reading II	Place LEFT HAND TO LEFT ELBOW

□ ⊹ △ clock square

He shouted the warning

$85 - 27 = 58$

51

only a chance number of correct responses. The examiner realized that the patient could not comprehend the procedure and seemed to be getting increasingly upset; therefore, the test was discontinued. In reviewing the strengths and weaknesses of this patient, it was apparent that he had poor scores on a number of measures. Besides having trouble on the Category Test, he was able to make little progress with the Tactual Performance Test. He worked for 15 minutes on each trial, but was able to place less than half the total number of blocks. Both the Speech-sounds Perception Test and the Seashore Rhythm Test were beyond the patient's capabilities, mainly because he was not sufficiently alert and quick enough to consider the stimulus material and decide on an answer in the available time. In other words, he was so slow in his mental processes that he was not able to keep up with the task. In this instance, the difficulty on these tests probably related to slowness in responses rather than ability to pay attention.

Eisdorfer and his associates have shown that the aged individual is able to perform many of the tasks that younger persons can perform, but requires a time schedule that is less pressing. (Eisdorfer, Nowlin & Wilkie, 1970; Froyer, Eisdorfer & Wilkie, 1966). The same phenomenon tends to occur in many of the older persons examined with the Halstead-Reitan Battery.

In summary, V.C. demonstrated deficits in tasks that required (1) a degree of speed in performance; (2) definition of the nature of the task (complex types of performances); and (3) immediate memory (Memory and Localization components of the Tactual Performance Test). He performed relatively well on measures of stored information (certain verbal subtests from the Wechsler Scale) and Tactile Finger Recognition. He showed no aphasic symptoms and had only a little difficulty on the left hand on Finger-tip Number Writing Perception. It is apparent from these findings that V.C. was able to pay close attention to stimulus material by recognizing the finger stimulated, remember an adequate reporting set regarding the finger that was touched, and identify and differentiate various numbers written on his fingertips. Note that in these tasks (as contrasted with the Speech-sounds Perception Test and the Seashore Rhythm Test) the subject is given the task item-by-item and is not required to keep up with a pre-determined schedule of stimulus presentation.

Intermediate performances for this man occurred on finger tapping speed with the right hand (44) and his figure drawings. Neither of these performances were in the normal range, but did represent fairly good performances for a person his age (finger tapping) and in the context of his overall performances (figure drawings). This pattern of results, in terms of good and poor scores, is characteristic of patients with a primary neuronal degenerative disease such as Alzheimer's disease.

Evaluation of specific indicators of right and left cerebral damage for this man yielded relatively little positive information. He did have some difficulty on the right side of his body with bilateral simultaneous tactile and auditory stimulation, but did not show any specific aphasic difficulties. He did have some problem enunciating METHODIST EPISCOPAL, suggesting the presence of some left cerebral damage, but in most respects he was able to deal with the simple verbal material on the Aphasia Test without difficulty. As seen in the drawings of the cross and key, he demonstrated some impairment copying simple spatial configurations. He was definitely slow in finger tapping speed with his left hand as compared with his right, and this finding was the most pronounced disparity between performances on the two sides of the body. However, considered by itself, it could hardly be a basis for postulating a specific focal lesion of the right cerebral hemisphere.

Considering the fact that the patient actually performed somewhat worse with his left hand than his right hand on the Tactual Performance Test, one might also propose that this pattern of results was suggestive of right cerebral damage. What the complete pattern indicated was that the patient did not show any improvement when using both hands (third trial). Under these circumstances it would be unsafe to draw a conclusion about comparative performances of the two upper extremities, since the overall pattern was one in which the patient just did not seem to be able to show any significant degree of improvement. Although their level of performance is not nearly as good, most persons with generalized cerebral damage demonstrate essentially the same pattern as normal subjects on the three trials of the TPT. Occasionally, though, a person seems to be so impaired in learning capability that no improvement occurs and such an observation is of definite clinical significance. One would certainly predict that this man is grossly impaired in capabilities in everyday living, despite his normal I.Q. values.

Neurological evaluation of this patient resulted in a diagnosis of

Alzheimer's disease. V.C. had a progressive history of problems and slowness of thought. On physical examination he appeared depressed and was judged to be obtunded. Otherwise, the neurological examination was considered to be within normal limits (despite the slow left-handed finger tapping shown on neuropsychological testing).

The overall pattern of test results seen here is characteristic of patients with early symptoms of Alzheimer's disease. Conventional description of this condition cites (1) a general loss of efficiency and difficulties particularly with memory; (2) relatively normal results on neurological examination; and (3) inability to perform tasks requiring immediate adaptive skills compared with better abilities on tasks requiring stored information. This pattern is far more obvious in results obtained from the Halstead-Reitan Battery than generally observed in clinical neurological examination. As noted, this man had a Verbal I.Q. that exceeded a substantial proportion of his age peers, but was so grossly impaired that he could not do the Category Test and had great difficulty with a number of other procedures. In fact, most patients with Alzheimer's disease are not able to complete the Battery because of their difficulty performing practical, meaningful problem-solving tasks; their impairment of brain function, with respect to higher level abilities, is extremely profound. Although it is customarily reported that physical neurological examination of patients with primary neuronal degenerative disease does not show any lateralizing findings, it is fairly common for mild but significant lateralizing findings to be observed on the Halstead-Reitan Battery. Deficits that have focal significance, such as hemiplegia, develop in advanced cases of Alzheimer's disease.

CASE #20

Name:	W.R.C.	Sex:	Male
Age:	51	Handedness:	Right
Education:	5	Occupation:	School Janitor

Current Complaints and Pertinent History

W.R.C., admitted to the hospital eight days before this neuro-psychological examination, had been experiencing headaches for approximately three years. For the past eight months he had been complaining of episodes of memory loss and seemed to have difficulty expressing himself verbally. The patient and his wife tended to relate his difficulties to a mild head injury he sustained about three years earlier, when he was hit on the head by an overhead door. Two years previously W.R.C. had suffered another blow when he was hit by a pipe that fell from an automobile on which he had been working. Since these injuries the patient had been having bilateral frontal headaches which occurred about two times a week. Although he had never taken any medication for it, the patient rated the pain as moderately intense.

There was some question about the relationship between the patient's head injuries and his complaints. His memory loss particularly involved recent events. His verbal expressive difficulties related to being unable to think of the words he wanted to use in speaking. The patient's wife also reported that she had noticed a personality change in her husband. He had become less sociable, did not appear to care to talk with others, and many times would just sit in a chair and say nothing at all. He had not shown any indications of irritability, destructive behavior, or decline in personal hygiene.

Physical neurological evaluation revealed principally negative findings except for the impressions of the examiner. Throughout the examination the patient seemed to forget what he was doing, wasn't sure what city he was in (although he knew it was a "big city"), and did not know the day of the week. One examiner was impressed with the patient's confusion and forgetfulness, but another neurologist felt that this was "a pleasant man who had an apologetic air and did not waste words." However, this examiner did note that the patient had a little difficulty in verbal expression, had a somewhat poor recent memory but relatively good remote memory, and was difficult to examine in terms of a sensory examination because of the patient's unreliability in remembering what he was doing. (We remind the reader that the neurological examination is relatively subjective in nature and that the impressions and opinions of one examiner may not necessarily correspond exactly with those of another.)

Electroencephalogram tracings showed mild generalized impairment with Dysrhythmia, Grade 1 and Delta waves, Grade 1 in the left Sylvian area. The electroencephalographer who interpreted the record felt that a slowly growing neoplasm or possible metastatic brain disease could not be ruled out. A pneumoencephalogram performed seven days after the neuropsychological examination showed slight symmetrical dilatation of the lateral ventricles, suggesting a generalized degenerative cerebral process. A brain biopsy from the right superior temporal gyrus resulted in a definite final diagnosis of Alzheimer's disease.

The last visit W.R.C. made to the clinic was nearly a year after this hospitalization. There appeared to be a slight worsening of his memory deficit. He also needed help dressing and undressing himself.

NEUROPSYCHOLOGICAL TEST RESULTS

Psychological Implications

As a general summary statement, we can say that this man is seriously and generally impaired. It is difficult to differentiate his general impairment from specific deficits, but, as will be noted below, some of his particular problems of performance probably do reflect specific losses related to both left and right cerebral damage.

This man had completed only five grades in school and it is difficult to determine whether he had ever developed much in the way of academic skills or general intelligence. One can often answer this question from the patient's history; however, in this instance, we knew only that W.R.C. had recently been working as a janitor and previously had done some kind of work for the railroad. All of his I.Q. values were low, falling below the lowest 1-2 percent of the general population. The fact that he earned a weighted score of 5 on the Vocabulary subtest suggests that his abilities in the past may have been somewhat

HALSTEAD-REITAN NEUROPSYCHOLOGICAL TEST BATTERY

Patient ___W.R.C.___ Age __51__ Sex __M__ Education __5 +__ Handedness __R__

x WECHSLER-BELLEVUE SCALE (FORM I)	
___WAIS	
VIQ	64
PIQ	66
FIS IQ	58
VWS	8
PWS	2
Total WS	10
Information	3
Comprehension	0
Digit Span	2
Arithmetic	0
Similarities	3
Vocabulary	5
Picture Arrangement	1
Picture Completion	0
Block Design	1
Object Assembly	0
Digit Symbol	0

HALSTEAD'S NEUROPSYCHOLOGICAL TEST BATTERY

Category Test		145

Tactual Performance Test
Dominant hand:	15.0 (3 blocks)
Non-dominant hand:	15.0 (3 blocks)
Both hands:	15.0 (2 blocks)
	Total Time 45.0 +
	Memory 0
	Localization 0

Seashore Rhythm Test
Number Correct___12___   10

Speech-sounds Perception Test
Number of Errors   40

Finger Oscillation Test
| Dominant hand: | 40 | 40 |
| Non-dominant hand: | 39 | |

TRAIL MAKING TEST
Part A: __300__ seconds
Part B: __381__ seconds — Discontinued at 3-C

Impairment Index __1.0__

STRENGTH OF GRIP
Dominant hand: __26.5__ kilograms
Non-dominant hand: __25.0__ kilograms

REITAN-KLØVE TACTILE FORM RECOGNITION TEST
Dominant hand: __—__ seconds; __1__ error
Non-dominant hand: __—__ seconds; __0__ errors

MINNESOTA MULTIPHASIC PERSONALITY INVENTORY
Patient unable to complete MMPI

Miles ABC Test of Ocular Dominance
Right eye: __5__
Left eye: __5__

REITAN-KLØVE SENSORY-PERCEPTUAL EXAM

			Error Totals
RH___ LH___	Both:RH _2_ LH _1_	RH _2_ LH _1_	
RH___ LF___	Both:RH___ LF _2_	RH___ LF _2_	
LH___ RF___	Both:LH _1_ RF _1_	RF _1_ LH _1_	
RE___ LE___	Both:RE___ LE _2_	RE___ LE _2_	
RV___ LV___	Both:RV___ LV___		
___ ___	___ ___	RV___ LV___	
___ ___	___ ___		

REITAN-KLØVE LATERAL-DOMINANCE EXAM
Show me how you:
throw a ball	R
hammer a nail	R
cut with a knife	R
turn a door knob	R
use scissors	R
use an eraser	R
write your name	R

TACTILE FINGER RECOGNITION
R 1___ 2___ 3___ 4___ 5___   R _0_ / 20
L 1___ 2___ 3___ 4___ 5___   L _0_ / 20
Patient had to point to finger touched

Record time used for spontaneous name writing:
Preferred hand __10__ seconds
Non-preferred hand __70__ seconds

FINGER-TIP NUMBER WRITING
R 1 _3_ 2 _2_ 3 _4_ 4 _1_ 5 _3_   R _13_ / 20
L 1 _3_ 2 _2_ 3 _1_ 4 _3_ 5 _1_   L _10_ / 20

REITAN-INDIANA APHASIA SCREENING TEST

Form for Adults and Older Children

Name: _W. R. C._ Age: _51_

Copy SQUARE	Repeat TRIANGLE Ok
Name SQUARE	Repeat MASSACHUSETTS "Massachusess"
Spell SQUARE	Repeat METHODIST EPISCOPAL "Methodis" "Espestica" Ex. had to give words individually to get the patient to respond.
Copy CROSS The confusion regarding spatial relationships is obvious.	Write SQUARE
Name CROSS	Read SEVEN
Spell CROSS	Repeat SEVEN
Copy TRIANGLE	Repeat/Explain HE SHOUTED THE WARNING. Repeated ok after Ex. said it twice. Expl. – "Afraid" – Could not elaborate.
Name TRIANGLE "Kind of a triangle"	Write HE SHOUTED THE WARNING.
Spell TRIANGLE "T-R-Y--" Could not finish.	Compute 85 – 27 = Wanted to add. Did not understand the minus sign.
Name BABY	Compute 17 X 3 = Cannot do. 10 X 2 = 20 3 X 5 = 15 2 X 12 = 14
Write CLOCK Patient said "Clock" aloud before writing.	Name KEY
Name FORK	Demonstrate use of KEY Negative, even with props. But Ex. noted he could stir his coffee okay when this occurred naturally.
Read 7 SIX 2 Slowly, but okay.	Draw KEY
Read MGW	Read PLACE LEFT HAND TO RIGHT EAR.
Reading I	Place LEFT HAND TO RIGHT EAR Left hand to left ear.
Reading II "He's a friendly animal of famous winners of dog shows."	Place LEFT HAND TO LEFT ELBOW Crossed hands at wrists and said, "It just won't stay there"

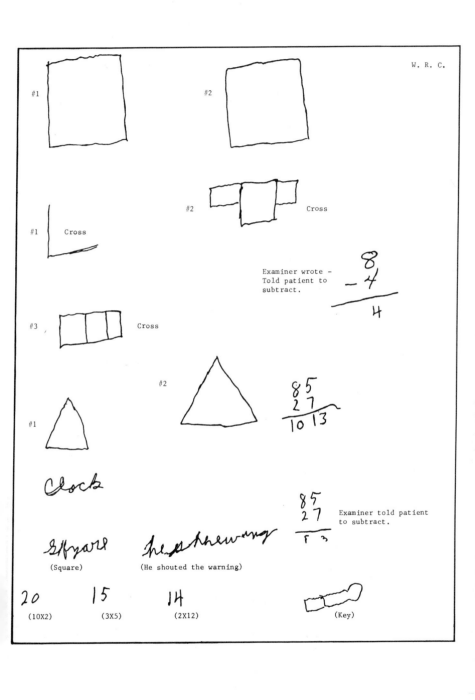

W. R. C.

#1

#2

#1 Cross

#2 Cross

#1 Cross

Examiner wrote –
Told patient to
subtract.

$$\begin{array}{r} 8 \\ -\ 4 \\ \hline 4 \end{array}$$

#3 Cross

#1

#2

$$\begin{array}{r} 8\ 5 \\ 2\ 7 \\ \hline 10\ 13 \end{array}$$

Clock

$$\begin{array}{r} 8\ 5 \\ 2\ 7 \\ \hline \end{array}$$

Examiner told patient
to subtract.

(Square)   (He shouted the warning)

20   15   14

(10X2)   (3X5)   (2X12)   (Key)

higher in general than they presently were, although such a conclusion would be difficult to draw from the Wechsler-Bellevue Scale alone. It should be noted that W.R.C. earned no credit whatsoever on the Performance subtests of the Wechsler Scale. Weighted scores of 1 on the Picture Arrangement and Block Design subtests correspond with a raw score of 0, and using Wechsler's norms for a person of this age, the Performance I.Q. of 66 corresponds with the lowest possible score attainable.

As might well be predicted from his I.Q. values, this man performed poorly on Halstead's Tests. He earned an Impairment Index of 1.0 (all of the tests had scores in the brain-damaged range). The reader should be aware that in this case a level of performance approach obviously is not sufficient to determine whether cerebral damage is present, where it might be located, or what kind of lesion might have occurred. The severity in level of performance, however, is obviously important and significant in estimating this man's capability for performances in everyday living. It is apparent that he does not have the capabilities to perform any kind of productive occupational effort and is not able to even take care of himself.

W.R.C.'s primary motor functions probably represent one of his best abilities, but more complex manipulatory skills (demonstrated on the Tactual Performance Test) show serious deficits. Although he had no difficulty whatsoever in Tactile Finger Recognition when he was permitted to point to the finger that had been touched, the patient exhibited some impairment of sensory-perceptual functions. It is apparent that this man has his major loss in higher-level aspects of brain functions (abstraction, concept formation, reasoning, visual-spatial skills, incidental memory, alertness and ability to maintain concentrated attention, and both Verbal and Performance intelligence). Such findings are not uncommon in persons with Alzheimer's disease.

Neurological Implications

As noted above, it is difficult to differentiate the severe generalized impairment shown by this man from specific deficits, particularly since he completed only five grades in school. Nevertheless, a number of findings point toward specific loss of previously acquired abilities. Deficits of left cerebral functioning include somewhat slow finger tapping speed and reduced grip strength with the right hand as compared with the left. The patient also made one mistake with his right hand on the Tactile Form Recognition Test.

In this case, it is also hard to separate language deficits on the Aphasia Test from general impairment; however, the patient's confusion with the minus sign in simple computation and his serious loss of writing ability (dysgraphia) strongly implicate damage of the left cerebral hemisphere. His right-left confusion also raises the question of cerebral dysfunction but this manifestation may be due to a low level of general competence.

Findings indicating right cerebral involvement include slightly more difficulty occurring on the left side with bilateral simultaneous tactile stimulation and, quite clearly, the patient's deficiency on the left side with bilateral auditory stimulation. He also showed striking constructional dyspraxia. Thus, the overall results clearly indicate deterioration of previously acquired abilities in association with generalized cerebral damage. Although patients with Alzheimer's disease may show a very significant degree of deterioration of higher-level abilities much earlier in the course of the disease than demonstrated by this man, his test results are fairly typical for primary neuronal degenerative disease.

X
DEMYELINATING DISEASES OF THE NERVOUS SYSTEM

There is overlap of many of the manifestations of nervous system diseases characterized by demyelination. To a varying degree, the diseases included in this category also involve other elements of the nervous system in addition to the myelin sheaths, such as neurons and axons. Understanding of etiology is insufficient at the present time to permit a more appropriate classification of these diseases, but in time it is probable that the genetic, allergic, infectious (viral), or metabolic characteristics of each disease will be identified and allow more specific classification.

Genetically determined demyelinating diseases include a category called the leukodystrophies and lipid storage diseases. Since these diseases principally involve children they will not be discussed further in this context.

A range of diseases may be due to acquired allergic disorders, viral infections, or autoimmune disorders. Although the category also includes encephalomyelitis following vaccination and encephalomyelitis and polyneuritis following other infections, the principal disease in this category is multiple sclerosis. Our current interest is principally multiple sclerosis because it is the most common demyelinating disease in adults.

Multiple sclerosis is characterized by various tactile symptoms, visual symptoms (including optic neuritis), occasional manifestations of acute dementia or acute psychosis (particularly with episodes of either euphoria or depression), dysarthric enunciation, oculomotor signs with diplopia due to involvement of the third, fourth, and/or sixth cranial nerves, ataxic gait and other signs of motor disorder which may be secondary to involvement of either the cerebellum or the posterior column of the spinal cord. These symptomatic manifestations relate principally to sensory and motor deficits, the usual areas of clinical descriptions by neurologists.

Multiple sclerosis is a disease of relatively young adults, rarely occurring in persons under the age of 20. The incidence peaks in the 30 to 35 years age range and then declines sharply. A number of theories regarding etiology have been proposed, including an allergic basis, a slow-virus infection, or an autoimmune disease.

Clinically, patients with multiple sclerosis may be classified as having one of three forms of the disease: (1) the *benign* form that affects about 30 percent of cases; (2) the *chronic relapsing* form that affects about 60 percent and is characterized by gradual progression and damage to the nervous system following each relapse; and (3) the *chronic, progressive* form, that affects about 10 percent of patients and shows an ongoing, progressive deterioration without obvious relapse or remission. It leads to severe disability and mortality of 50 percent of the patients within about 10 years of onset.

Neuropsychological Correlates of Multiple Sclerosis

In 1955 Ross and Reitan studied patients with multiple sclerosis using the Halstead-Reitan Battery and reported that besides the neurological manifestations of the disease, there were significant neuropsychological components. Since that time there have been a number of additional studies exploring the neuropsychological correlates of multiple sclerosis in further detail (Reitan, Reed, and Dyken, 1971; Goldstein and Shelly, 1974; Beatty and Grange, 1977).

A brief generalization of the neuropsychological correlates of multiple sclerosis can be described. Persons with this disease frequently maintain Verbal and Performance I.Q. values at a fairly normal level, although clinical observation has suggested that the Picture Arrangement subtest of the Wechsler Scale may often be relatively low. The Halstead Impairment Index may indicate a variable degree of impairment, ranging from mild to severe; this probably relates to the degree of cerebral deterioration that has occurred. In early stages of the disease it is not unusual to see relatively good Impairment Indexes.

Patients with multiple sclerosis have serious motor difficulty and show positive findings on tests of primary motor functions and complex psychomotor tasks (Finger Tapping and Tactual Performance Test). In addition, they frequently demonstrate scattered indications of sensory-perceptual deficits, including occasional errors in tests of bilateral sensory stimulation, tactile finger recognition and finger-tip number writing perception. These findings usually do not exhibit a pattern that would suggest focal or even lateralized cerebral dysfunction; instead, the results are scattered, sometimes involving one side of the body and sometimes the other. The clinician should be aware that it is not uncommon to find significant disparities between performances of the two hands.

In early stages of multiple sclerosis the patient may have an essentially unimpaired Category Test score. This finding, in comparison with poor performances on the Tactual Performance Test and the degree of motor and sensory-perceptual impairment, can be nearly specifically diagnostic of multiple sclerosis. Despite the inter- and intra-individual variability in this disease, it is frequently possible to identify the condition based on neuropsychological findings. It must also be noted, however, that some patients with multiple sclerosis do not fit this particular pattern even though they may show significant neuropsychological deficit.

When doing "blind" neuropsychological interpretation, the effects of multiple sclerosis may sometimes be confused with the deficits shown by patients with relatively mild or moderate closed head injuries. However, experienced neuropsychologists can differentiate these conditions fairly well. By reviewing only the Halstead-Reitan Battery results for a group of 112 neurological patients with definite but varied diagnoses, Reitan (1964) was able to identify 15 of the 16 patients with multiple sclerosis and 30 of the 32 patients with cranio-cerebral trauma.

The important point is that the neuropsychological deficits shown by patients with multiple sclerosis constitute a significant dimension of this disease in terms of practical aspects of adjustment to the requirements of everyday living. A great deal of variability occurs in the nature and severity of losses, an element of the disease that is of tremendous significance in attempting to help these patients achieve adaptations to realistic problems in everyday life.

CASE #21

Name:	W.L.	Sex:	Male
Age:	41	Handedness:	Right
Education:	16	Occupation:	Bank Officer

This patient earned a Verbal I.Q. of 134 and a Performance I.Q. of 118. In persons who depend upon relatively sophisticated language skills for both achievement and maintenance of their professional activities (writers, professors, psychologists, physicians, bankers, etc.) it is not unusual to find higher Verbal than Performance I.Q. values. Therefore, for this man, both the level and relationships of I.Q. values are within the range of expectation.

Nevertheless, he did poorly on the Digit Symbol subtest, with his score (7) being well below his level even on the next lowest subtest, Block Design (11). The score on Digit Symbol, then, appears to be defective and probably requires explanation; however, the Wechsler Scale is not definitive as an indicator of cerebral disease or damage. (Much research has documented the usefulness of the Wechsler Scales in evaluating brain-behavior relationships, but Wechsler results customarily make their contribution only in the context of a more reliable general indication of the status of the cerebral cortex.) In this case the Wechsler results tell us that this man has developed cognitive functions normally and in most respects has excellent abilities in the area of general intelligence.

The four most sensitive general indicators in the Halstead-Reitan Battery showed variable results. The patient earned a Halstead Impairment Index of 0.4 (three of seven tests were in the impaired range). This is a borderline score with regard to the integrity of the cerebral cortex. The patient performed well on the Category Test (22), had an acceptable (though not outstanding, considering his I.Q. values) score on Trails B (71 seconds) and did poorly on the Localization component of the Tactual Performance Test (0). Up to this point the patient had either excellent or acceptable scores on all measures except for Digit Symbol and the Localization component of the Tactual Performance Test. In the context of the other performances, however, these

HALSTEAD-REITAN NEUROPSYCHOLOGICAL TEST BATTERY

Patient _____ W.L. _____ Age __41__ Sex __M__ Education __16__ Handedness __R__

__x__ WECHSLER-BELLEVUE SCALE (FORM I)
___ WAIS

VIQ	134
PIQ	118
FIS IQ	128
VWS	75
PWS	55
Total WS	130
Information	12
Comprehension	18
Digit Span	13
Arithmetic	18
Similarities	14
Vocabulary	16
Picture Arrangement	12
Picture Completion	13
Block Design	11
Object Assembly	12
Digit Symbol	7

TRAIL MAKING TEST
Part A: __31__ seconds
Part B: __71__ seconds

Miles ABC Test of Ocular Dominance
Right eye: _9_ Left eye: _1_

REITAN-KLØVE SENSORY-PERCEPTUAL EXAM

						Error Totals	
RH___	LH___	Both:RH___	LH___		RH___	LH___	
RH___	LF___	Both:RH___	LF___		RH___	LF___	
LH___	RF___	Both:LH___	RF___		RF___	LH___	
RE___	LE___	Both:RE _2_	LE___		RE _2_	LE___	
RV___	LV___	Both:RV___	LV___				
___	___	_ ___	___		RV___	LV___	
___	___	___	___				

TACTILE FINGER RECOGNITION
R 1___ 2___ 3___ 4___ 5___ R_0_ / 20
L 1___ 2___ 3___ 4___ 5___ L_0_ / 20

FINGER-TIP NUMBER WRITING
R 1_2_ 2 3___ 4_1_ 5___ R_3_ / 20
L 1_1_ 2_1_ 3___ 4___ 5___ L_2_ / 20

HALSTEAD'S NEUROPSYCHOLOGICAL TEST BATTERY

Category Test	22

Tactual Performance Test

Dominant hand:	4.8
Non-dominant hand:	6.6
Both hands:	5.9
Total Time	17.3
Memory	6
Localization	0

Seashore Rhythm Test

Number Correct	28	2

Speech-sounds Perception Test

Number of Errors	2

Finger Oscillation Test

Dominant hand:	50	50
Non-dominant hand:	39	

Impairment Index __0.4__

MINNESOTA MULTIPHASIC PERSONALITY INVENTORY

?	50	Hs	72
L	43	D	58
F	46	Hy	71
K	68	PD	55
		MF	53
		Pa	53
		Pt	58
		Sc	57
		Ma	43

REITAN-INDIANA APHASIA SCREENING TEST

Form for Adults and Older Children

Name: W. L.   Age: 41

Copy SQUARE	Repeat TRIANGLE
Name SQUARE	Repeat MASSACHUSETTS
Spell SQUARE	Repeat METHODIST EPISCOPAL
Copy CROSS Note the mild asymmetry of the lateral extremities.	Write SQUARE
Name CROSS	Read SEVEN
Spell CROSS	Repeat SEVEN
Copy TRIANGLE	Repeat/Explain HE SHOUTED THE WARNING.
Name TRIANGLE	Write HE SHOUTED THE WARNING.
Spell TRIANGLE	Compute 85 – 27 =
Name BABY	Compute 17 X 3 =
Write CLOCK	Name KEY
Name FORK	Demonstrate use of KEY
Read 7 SIX 2	Draw KEY Note the difficulty with the "nose", "teeth", and stem of the key.
Read MGW	Read PLACE LEFT HAND TO RIGHT EAR.
Reading I	Place LEFT HAND TO RIGHT EAR Left hand placed to left ear – self-corrected.
Reading II	Place LEFT HAND TO LEFT ELBOW

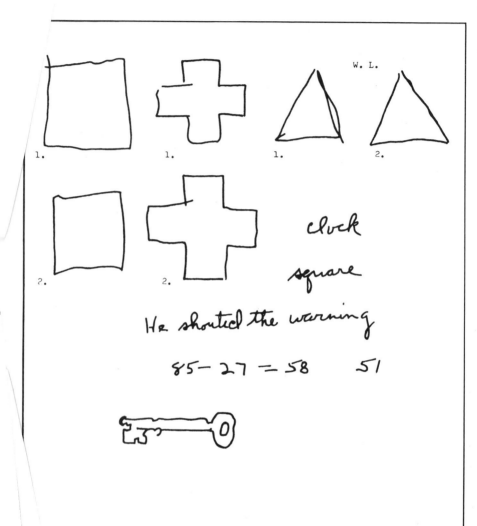

W. L.

1.　　　　1.　　　　1.　　　　2.

2.　　　　2.

clock

square

He shouted the warning

85 − 27 = 58　　　51

two defective scores almost certainly point toward an abnormal overall picture. In other words, there must be some reason that goes beyond chance or normal variation to explain the poor performances on these two measures.

The psychological or behavioral significance of the test results is best analyzed by arranging the tests into three groups: those done very well, those done adequately and those done poorly. This man had excellent scores on the Verbal I.Q. measures, the Category Test, and the Speech-sounds Perception Test. It would appear that his general intelligence is adequate, his abilities in the area of abstraction, reasoning, logical analysis and concept formation are quite good, and he has excellent capability to pay close attention to stimulus material and maintain concentrated attention. This latter conclusion is also supported by an adequate score on the Seashore Rhythm Test. These results set a standard for this man regarding his past level of achievement and also indicate that his abilities are well above average in a number of respects. Many of the other tests in the Battery were at least adequately performed, but a number of his results deviated significantly from the level of performance that would have been expected. W.L.'s time on the Tactual Performance Test (17.3 minutes) is definitely beyond the cut-off point of 15.7 minutes, and indicates that his overall performance on a test of complex manipulatory functions was inadequate.

This patient also had difficulty copying simple spatial configurations, suggesting some specific problems in this area as well. In fact, his difficulties copying the cross and key provide a clue to understanding the deficient performance on the Digit Symbol subtest. The Digit Symbol subtest requires appreciation of symbolic relationships (association of numbers and shapes), the ability to draw relatively unfamiliar shapes, and psychomotor speed with the preferred hand. As indicated by other measures, this man had good abilities in dealing with symbolic relationships and his psychomotor capability with the preferred hand (his right-handed performance on the Tactual Performance Test) was not defective. However, he did have difficulty copying simple spatial configurations, and this was probably the reason for his defective performance on the Digit Symbol subtest.

Returning to his figure drawings, we see that the first attempt to copy the cross was not seriously aberrant in its overall configuration, although the upper line representing the left lateral extremity should not have extended back into the figure. The second attempt at copying the cross again represented the general shape fairly well, but the patient had some difficulty with overlapping lines at the same point. Nevertheless, these drawings were not grossly defective. Inexperienced judges might feel that the first drawing of the triangle was also inadequate, but if one were to have observed the patient, it would have been apparent that he was merely drawing a line on the right side back in the opposite direction of the line previously drawn in order to straighten a bow on the first line.

The clearly deficient manifestation of copying spatial configurations was shown in the key. First, the patient failed to achieve symmetry in the notches of the stem near the handle; it appears that he did not even attempt to draw the notch on the lower part of the stem to represent a mirror image with the upper notch. This kind of difficulty occurs in many persons with right cerebral damage.

Second, the patient showed confusion with the notches on the lower side of the stem near the teeth of the key. In fact, he appeared to have turned the wrong way in his drawing. From this example one can see the importance of not permitting the subject to erase or cross out a mistake. The patient also did not achieve symmetry in the teeth of the key, another finding that is characteristic of right cerebral damage.

Finally, careful inspection indicates that the nose of the key was not properly drawn and the patient attempted to draw over his previous line to improve his effort. Some experience is necessary on the part of the interpreter to be able to distinguish brain-related deficiencies in these drawings from careless efforts or general inadequacy in drawing. Reitan (1984; 1985a) has provided extensive illustrative material together with comments on the types of deficits in the Aphasia Test that specifically identify brain damage.

The patient made one error on the Aphasia Test that demonstrated mild right-left confusion. The problem occurred when the patient was asked to place his left hand to his right ear. This is probably a mistake that cannot be attributed to normal variation. Evidence of right-left confusion, even mild and self-corrected errors of this type, occurs 42 percent of the time in persons with left cerebral lesions but only 5 percent of the time in persons with right cerebral damage (Wheeler & Reitan, 1962). The evidence up to this point had suggested right cerebral damage, but the finding of possible mild right-left confusion could lead us to consider some left cerebral involvement as well. The only other indicator of left cerebral damage occurred on the test for bilateral simultaneous auditory perception. On this test the patient made two mistakes on the right side when the stimuli were given simultaneously. These findings were particularly important in suggesting that cerebral damage was not strictly lateralized to the right cerebral hemisphere but instead represented a type of condition that had more general and widespread implications for both cerebral hemispheres.

Finally, in terms of areas of deficit, the patient also had some difficulties in finger-tip number writing perception on both hands, another indication that problems were present in the area of tactile perception.

Deviant psychological manifestations were shown on the Minnesota Multiphasic Personality Inventory. The pattern simulating a Conversion V was present, manifested by scores of 72 on Hypochondriasis, 58 on Depression and 71 on Hysteria. Clinical interpretation of the MMPI might lead the clinician to conclude that this patient had a hysterical tendency to experience somatic difficulties. However, this pattern may represent very legitimate and accurate statements of symptoms of brain disease, and this is especially true in patients with this diagnosis of this man: multiple sclerosis.

Lastly, it is necessary to consider the lateralizing and localizing findings. As noted above, this man had some difficulty in perception of bilateral simultaneous auditory stimulation, with the difficulty involving the right ear. This finding would point toward some degree of left cerebral dysfunction, although mild right-left confusion represented the only other indicator of possible left cerebral damage.

Right cerebral dysfunction was manifested by mild difficulty drawing the cross and definite difficulty drawing the key (as described above), distinct problems with the left hand on the Tactual Performance Test (a reduction in time of about one-third from the first trial to the second trial is expected normally), and definitely deficient finger tapping speed with the left hand.

There would seem to be no doubt that the right cerebral hemisphere is more involved than the left, but in the context of the patient's many good scores it would be extremely difficult to postulate that this man has an identifiable focal lesion of either cerebral hemisphere.

For many psychologists, the confusing issue in interpreting results for W.L. would be in effecting a meaningful integration of the poor and good scores. Obviously, this man did very well on many of the tests, including some most sensitive to cerebral damage and disease. On other tests, though, his performances were definitely abnormal and of the kind seen only in persons with cerebral dysfunction. In this case, those performances related principally to the right cerebral hemisphere, but the overall pattern of test results would not suggest the presence of a specific, focal right cerebral lesion. The overall pattern of test results is characteristic and typical for a particular condition — multiple sclerosis.

In persons with relatively mild impairment from multiple sclerosis it is not uncommon to see a good Category Test score and distinct impairment on measures of motor performances. This disparity was manifested in this particular case by definite impairment on the Tactual Performance Test (Total Time as well as a definitely deviant pattern of relationships between the two hands) and impairment of the left hand in finger tapping speed. In addition, most persons with multiple sclerosis manifest scattered difficulties on additional aspects of the Sensory-perceptual Examination (for W.L., auditory imperception with the right ear and difficulty on both hands in finger-tip number writing perception). Finally, this man also demonstrated significant evidence of impairment of brain functions in his attempt to copy simple spatial configurations.

Patients with multiple sclerosis frequently show an elevation on the MMPI of the neurotic triad (Reitan, 1955a), but it is likely that many of the complaints of these patients are legitimate manifestations of the disease and do not have the same significance as similar positive findings with psychiatric patients. This comment, however, is not intended to suggest that patients with multiple sclerosis do not have significant emotional and affective stresses and problems of adjustment; they do have serious difficulties, as would be expected from any person with a chronic and disabling nervous system disease that is generally progressive in its course.

A considerable degree of variability occurs among patients with multiple sclerosis on the Halstead-Reitan Battery, but the general pattern noted above is frequently observed. Some persons have much more deficit than was shown by W.L., but the same general pattern is present. Despite the degree of intra- and inter-patient variability in multiple sclerosis, the general neuropsychological pattern, even in the context of the full range of brain damage and disease, is still recognizable. As mentioned, this was shown by correct identification in 15 of 16 cases of patients with multiple sclerosis in a group of 112 patients whose neuropsychological results were evaluated (Reitan, 1964).

Multiple sclerosis described from a neuropsychological point of view is a rather different picture from multiple sclerosis described from a neurological point of view. Psychologists must remember that the same patients have the disease regardless of which discipline describes it, and these patients have a right to a full understanding of the consequences of their illness. We strongly recommend neuropsychological evaluation for all patients with multiple sclerosis, to identify their capabilities as well as their deficits, for integration with neurological findings in developing an overall plan for management of their condition. From a neurological point of view, the principal findings for this particular patient included bitemporal pallor of the optic discs, some evidence of nystagmus, spastic paraparesis, dysdiadokokinesis that involved the left upper extremity more than the right, and mild ataxia of the left upper extremity. Such deficits are unquestionably significant and reflect certain handicaps of the patient. It is important to correlate such problems with the neuropsychological findings in order to provide optimum care for the patient.

CASE #22

Name:	W.V.	Sex:	Male
Age:	32	Handedness:	Right
Education:	6	Occupation:	Housepainter

Current Complaints and Pertinent History

This 32-year-old man experienced his first symptoms several years before the present examination. He awoke one morning with blurred vision of his right eye; during a 10-day period his vision with this eye became so poor that he could barely perceive light. He had experienced a similar episode of visual loss in the left eye five years earlier. At that time he was hospitalized and had a normal neurological examination except for his visual problems. This was diagnosed as retrobulbar neuritis and multiple sclerosis was suspected.

Shortly before this neuropsychological evaluation the patient was hospitalized for weakness and numbness of both legs which appeared to have been progressive over a five-day period. On the day of admission W.V. felt that he had some difficulty using his right hand. The neurological examination revealed weakness of both lower extremities, a vague sensory loss in the lower part of the body, difficulty with rapid and coordinated movements of the right upper extremity, pallor of the temporal portions of the optic discs and nystagmus. A definite diagnosis of multiple sclerosis was made during this hospitalization.

Neuropsychological Test Results

Because this man had only a 6th-grade education and was employed as a housepainter, one might postulate that his general abilities might be below average. We must comment, however, that this type of inference is scarcely justified. Although there is a general correlation between education and ability levels, there are many individual exceptions.

This man earned a Verbal I.Q. that was just below the Average level (98) and a Performance I.Q. that was at the lower end of the Low Average range (80). The Verbal subtest scores suggest that the patient may have been at the Average level, or perhaps just a little lower, in

HALSTEAD-REITAN NEUROPSYCHOLOGICAL TEST BATTERY

Patient _____ **W.V.** _____ Age __32__ Sex __M__ Education __6__ Handedness __R__

__x__ WECHSLER-BELLEVUE SCALE (FORM I)
____ WAIS

VIQ	98
PIQ	80
FIS IQ	89
VWS	45
PWS	30
Total WS	75
Information	9
Comprehension	8
Digit Span	13
Arithmetic	10
Similarities	5
Vocabulary	8
Picture Arrangement	3
Picture Completion	8
Block Design	7
Object Assembly	10
Digit Symbol	2

HALSTEAD'S NEUROPSYCHOLOGICAL TEST BATTERY

Category Test _____ 21 _____

Tactual Performance Test
Dominant hand: _____ 10.0 (2 blocks) _____
Non-dominant hand: _____ 10.0 (3 blocks) _____
Both hands: _____ 11.5 (5 blocks) _____
Total Time __31.5 +__
Memory __7__
Localization __2__

Seashore Rhythm Test
Number Correct __26__ _____ 5 _____

Speech-sounds Perception Test
Number of Errors _____ 9 _____

Finger Oscillation Test
Dominant hand: _____ 43 _____ 43 _____
Non-dominant hand: __35__

TRAIL MAKING TEST
Part A: __70__ seconds
Part B: __135__ seconds

Impairment Index __0.6__

Miles ABC Test of Ocular Dominance
Right eye: _10_ Left eye: _0_

REITAN-KLØVE SENSORY-PERCEPTUAL EXAM

					Error Totals		
RH___	LH___	Both:RH___	LH___		RH___	LH___	
RH___	LF___	Both:RH___	LF___		RH___	LF___	
LH___	RF___	Both:LH___	RF___		RF___	LH___	
RE___	LE___	Both:RE _1_	LE _2_		RE _1_	LE _2_	
RV___	LV___	Both:RV___	LV___				
					RV___	LV___	

TACTILE FINGER RECOGNITION
R 1___ 2___ 3___ 4___ 5___ R _0_ / 20
L 1___ 2___ 3___ 4___ 5___ L _0_ / 20

FINGER-TIP NUMBER WRITING
R 1 _4_ 2 _3_ 3 _3_ 4 _3_ 5 _4_ R 17 / 20
L 1 _1_ 2 _1_ 3 _1_ 4 _2_ 5 _2_ L _7_ / 20

MINNESOTA MULTIPHASIC PERSONALITY INVENTORY

?	50	Hs	82
L	53	D	53
F	62	Hy	75
K	68	PD	69
		MF	45
		Pa	59
		Pt	69
		Sc	78
		Ma	50

REITAN-INDIANA APHASIA SCREENING TEST

Form for Adults and Older Children

Name: W.V.   Age: 32

Copy SQUARE	Repeat TRIANGLE
Name SQUARE	Repeat MASSACHUSETTS
Spell SQUARE	Repeat METHODIST EPISCOPAL
Copy CROSS Note that difficulty is apparent despite the tremor.	Write SQUARE
Name CROSS	Read SEVEN "Sever", then responded correctly.
Spell CROSS	Repeat SEVEN
Copy TRIANGLE	Repeat/Explain HE SHOUTED THE WARNING.
Name TRIANGLE	Write HE SHOUTED THE WARNING.
Spell TRIANGLE	Compute 85 – 27 =
Name BABY	Compute 17 X 3 = Pt. verbalized "42" then "51"
Write CLOCK	Name KEY
Name FORK	Demonstrate use of KEY
Read 7 SIX 2 "S-I-X" (pause) "7 S-I-X 2" Examiner asked pt. to repeat, then pt. responded correctly.	Draw KEY
Read MGW	Read PLACE LEFT HAND TO RIGHT EAR.
Reading I	Place LEFT HAND TO RIGHT EAR
Reading II	Place LEFT HAND TO LEFT ELBOW

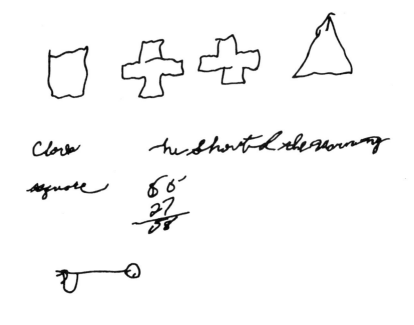

Clover

he Short d the morning

square

$$\begin{array}{r} 86 \\ 27 \\ \hline 58 \end{array}$$

his premorbid state. The lowest score was on the Similarities subtest (5) and this finding might reflect some degree of impairment. On the other hand, whenever there is a series of scores, one is going to be the lowest, and, to avoid permissive observations, a meaningful hypothesis must accompany interpretation of such data. If one were to apply the conventional interpretation to the Similarities subtest score and presume that this man had some loss in verbal abstraction and generalization capabilities, it would be necessary to explain this finding of "impairment" with relation to the excellent score on the Category Test. Our observations suggest that low scores on the Similarities subtest may be more limited by vocabulary level than by verbal abstraction skills. Thus, in this case, one can note that there was more variability among the Verbal subtests than is customarily observed and this finding might possibly be a basis for presuming that the patient had experienced some degree of loss.

The results on the Performance subtest were also variable, and in this array two of the scores were so low that a degree of impairment could be presumed. The patient did poorly on Picture Arrangement (3) and Digit Symbol (2), suggesting that some causative factor was responsible.

In summary, the overall distribution on the Wechsler Scale implied that (1) cerebral impairment might be responsible for the difference between the Verbal and Performance I.Q. values; (2) the patient might have some degree of impairment on the Similarities subtest; and (3) the patient almost certainly had suffered circumstances which led to deficits on Picture Arrangement and Digit Symbol subtests.

The four most sensitive indicators of cerebral dysfunction also yielded results that were variable. W.V. earned an Impairment Index of 0.6 (indicating that about 60 percent of the tests had results in the brain-damaged range). He also performed poorly on Trails B (135 seconds) and the Localization component of the Tactual Performance Test (2). In contrast, he did very well on the Category Test (21). Considering that the Category Test generally correlates about .5 with either the Verbal or Performance I.Q., this good performance was even enhanced in its significance. If there were deficits on subtests of the Wechsler Scale, then, one would expect the validity of such deficits to manifest itself in a poor Category Test score rather than such a good score. Nevertheless, the poor performances on the other three of the four most sensitive indicators cannot be ignored and are probably related to impairment of brain functions.

A review of the overall set of test results indicates that this man had deficient performances on several measures and had relatively average or good performances on only a few. He performed poorly on the Tactual Performance Test — Total Time (31.5 + minutes with a total of only 10 blocks placed), Localization component (2), Digit Symbol (2) and Picture Arrangement (3). He made mistakes on the Aphasia Test, had difficulty drawing the cross and key, had some sensory-perceptual deficits with bilateral simultaneous auditory stimulation and showed impairment on Trails B and finger tapping speed. He had relatively average scores on the Seashore Rhythm Test (26 correct) and Speech-sounds Perception Test (9 errors), indicating that he certainly had an adequate degree of attentional capability to perform the tests. He did well on the Category Test (21), the Memory component of the Tactual Performance Test (7), and made no mistakes in a total of forty trials in Tactile Finger Recognition. A number of errors occurred in Finger-tip Number Writing Perception.

W.V. demonstrated a marked tremor in his drawings and writing on the Aphasia Test, and this motor problem may have caused difficulty for him in performing Digit Symbol as well as certain other tests. However, primary motor difficulty was not a principal problem (note finger tapping speed). He had more problems on a complex manipulatory task (Tactual Performance Test) than he did in finger tapping.

The disparity between the total time on the Tactual Performance Test and the good score on the Category Test probably represents the greatest contrast among the entire set of test scores. One rarely sees results of this kind except in persons with multiple sclerosis.

At this point one might also note that, when asked to read "Seven" on the Aphasia Test, this man responded "sever" and then corrected himself. In all likelihood this mistake related to visual impairment (perhaps even diplopia), a type of difficulty not particularly uncommon among patients with multiple sclerosis.

The patient also demonstrated some emotional problems, as shown on the Minnesota Multiphasic Personality Inventory. His elevated scores on the Hypochondriasis and Hysteria scales and much lower score on the Depression scale simulates the Conversion V profile. However, for a person with multiple sclerosis, many of these complaints would be quite valid. It is a serious mistake to take the report of symptoms secondary to neurological disease and interpret them according to "psychiatric" norms. We would not contend that this man did not have emotional or affective difficulties; but the entire question of using psychiatric norms for assessment of possibly valid neurological symptoms must be considered more carefully.

The test results should next be evaluated specifically with relation to definite indications of left or right cerebral damage. Several positive findings occurred in this regard. The patient had much more difficulty on his right hand than his left hand in Finger-tip Number Writing Perception, a finding suggesting left cerebral dysfunction. In addition, the confusion he demonstrated when asked to read 7 SIX 2 is also typical of persons with left cerebral damage. Even on his second attempt, he still failed to recognize that SIX represented either a word or a number. Finally, when he was asked to repeat the task still another time he recognized the symbolic significance of the stimulus configuration and responded correctly. Although one could question the first letter in his writing of "square," W.V. did not demonstrate any other distinct difficulties in dealing with verbal and language symbols. The particular manifestation he did show, however, was definitely abnormal and must be used as a sign pointing toward left cerebral damage or dysfunction. His error in the initial response to 17 X 3 is questionable in its significance and not a definite indicator of cerebral damage.

The Aphasia Test was also helpful with respect to assessment of the right cerebral hemisphere. Over and beyond his obvious problem of motor control, this man had definite difficulties copying the shape of the cross. We would also judge that he had similar difficulties with the triangle and the key. The key, however, was so simply drawn that it is difficult to evaluate with relation to right cerebral damage. Undoubtedly, the strongest evidence was derived from the two attempts to copy the cross. Additionally, the very low score on the Picture Arrangement subtest and the deficiency in finger tapping speed with the left hand as compared to the right contribute to lateralizing evidence of right cerebral damage.

The overall set of test results for W.V. is typical of patients with multiple sclerosis. The customary pattern does not indicate any striking deficit on the Wechsler Scales, except that Picture Arrangement is frequently somewhat low and Digit Symbol may also be impaired (presumably due to motoric involvement). The general indicators of cerebral dysfunction are often impaired: the Impairment Index is somewhat elevated, Trails B score is in the lower part of the impaired range and some deficit on the Localization component of the TPT is customarily observed. It is not at all unusual to find a relatively good score on the Category Test and significant impairment on the TPT-Total Time. In the earlier stages of the disease, abstraction and reasoning abilities may be very well preserved; as the disease progresses, however, patients do demonstrate increasing impairment on the Category Test.

Most patients with multiple sclerosis have some degree of motoric difficulty, although not necessarily in the form of the very distinct tremor shown by this man. In the relatively early stages of multiple sclerosis specific deficits on the Aphasia Test (in terms of verbal and language deficits) are the exception rather than the rule. However, some deficit copying simple spatial configurations occurs fairly often. Scattered deficits on the Sensory-perceptual Examination are sometimes observed. This man demonstrated such a difficulty on the test of bilateral simultaneous auditory stimulation as well as in Finger-tip Number Writing Perception. It would have been very helpful to have had results on the Tactile Form Recognition Test; patients with multiple sclerosis frequently have difficulties with this task with both upper extremities, even though lateralized deficits may also extend beyond normal expectation.

Finally, patients with multiple sclerosis tend to show an elevation of the "neurotic triad" on the MMPI (Reitan, 1955a), but the validity of conventional interpretation of such findings should be subjected to further research.

XI
PARKINSON'S DISEASE

Parkinson's disease is not associated with any specific etiology. Instead, it refers to a condition characterized by motor disorders of rigidity, tremor, and bradykinesis. Although a number of etiological factors has been identified, the most common probably are postencephalitis and arteriosclerosis.

Besides occurring in many chronic nervous system diseases, symptoms of Parkinson's disease can be induced by certain drugs and toxins. Because the etiology cannot be determined, many patients with Parkinson's disease are classified as having idiopathic parkinsonism (or paralysis agitans). Parkinson's disease is a major health problem among older people, affecting about one percent of the population over the age of 50 years. Because the psychological correlates of Parkinson's disease have been studied in some detail, neuropsychologists frequently are called upon to evaluate patients with this disease.

Tremor or rigidity is the initial symptom in most patients with idiopathic parkinsonism. The tremor tends to first appear in the distal part of the limbs and may be represented by a continued rhythmic apposition of the thumb and index finger at a rate of about four movements per second. This characteristic symptom is often referred to as the "pill-rolling tremor." One limb may be affected initially and months or years may pass before the opposite side becomes involved. As the disease progresses, however, all four limbs as well as the lips, tongue, jaw and neck will probably be involved. Rigidity in movement is demonstrated when the affected limb is passively moved. The limb may move freely for about 5 to 10 degrees following which there is a tonic contraction of the stretched muscle. The "cogwheel" phenomenon is elicited as a manifestation of sequential contraction and relaxation of the muscle as the stretching continues. Rigidity is usually seen first in the shoulder, eventually followed by involvement of the forearm and hand. This problem results in a loss of normal swinging of the arm when walking and may be one of the first symptoms. Rigidity of the neck and axial muscles contribute to the characteristic flexed posture of the body which occurs when the disease is more advanced.

Patients with Parkinson's disease also suffer from weakness and fatiguability, even though there is no loss of muscle bulk or obvious weakness in testing individual muscles. Bradykinesia is a result of the rigidity of muscles and is demonstrated by slowness of finger movements and difficulty in fine motor performances such as writing and using small instruments. Frequently, the handwriting is characteristically cramped and small (micrographia). The tremor can frequently be observed in handwriting, drawing of figures, or other intentional fine-motor manifestations. In addition to the stooped posture, the gait of patients with Parkinson's disease is fairly characteristic: small steps, a tendency to fall forward, and progressive acceleration of the steps in walking.

Neurological description of Parkinson's disease has emphasized motor symptoms (dyskinesia). The neuropsychological examination, using a standard battery for overall assessment of brain functions (such as the Halstead-Reitan Battery) has shown definite sensory-perceptual deficits as well as much more generalized impairment. Computed tomography of the brain often shows ventricular dilatation and diffuse cortical atrophy, particularly in more advanced cases and in patients with obvious dementia.

Surgical intervention was previously the treatment of choice for Parkinson's disease. The surgery involved placing a small lesion in the ventrolateral nucleus of the thalamus and avoiding injury to the internal capsule. Although surgical intervention is still beneficial for some patients, it is rarely used at the present time because of the success of medical treatment with levodopa, a drug which replenishes the depleted dopamine in the brainstem and basal ganglia. In some cases levodopa therapy (particularly with overdoseage) results in a number of abnormal involuntary movements and therapy must be discontinued in about 25 to 30 percent of patients because of intolerable side-effects of this kind or lack of therapeutic results. The majority of patients, however, show a definite reduction in rigidity, tremor, and bradykinesia. Unfortunately, in most patients the favorable response to the drug gradually diminishes over time.

Neuropsychological Correlates of Parkinson's Disease

The neuropsychological correlates of Parkinson's disease have been studied by a number of investigators. In brief, the typical results for patients with Parkinson's disease show pronounced motor disorders which may be more evident on one side of the body than the other. Motor deficits, including bradykinesia in writing and drawings, are more prominent than sensory-perceptual deficits but it is not unusual to see scattered losses on the Sensory-perceptual Examination. I.Q. values are generally rather intact, although the patient may have particular difficulty on the Digit Symbol subtest of the Wechsler Scale because of motor-control problems. The remainder of the results on the Halstead-Reitan Battery indicate diffuse or generalized cerebral disease. The Category Test particularly is poorly performed, especially when considered with relation to I.Q. values. To some extent, the results resemble the pattern of impairment in higher-level abilities that is seen in association with advancing age; however, in a person with Parkinson's disease, the deficits are usually more pronounced than would be expected for the age of the subject. Considering the frequency with which serious and generalized impairment of higher-level brain functions continues to be present even after striking improvement with levodopa therapy, it is not surprising that many patients with Parkinson's disease have special difficulties in adapting to problems in everyday living. The impairment is demonstrated quite clearly by obvious difficulty on the Category Test (Reitan and Boll, 1971). It is apparent from neuropsychological studies that the typical neurological description of patients with Parkinson's disease, focusing particularly on impairment of motor functions, is inadequate in providing an overall understanding of the patient's brain-related problems. Neuropsychological evaluation can make an extremely important additional contribution in the assessment, understanding, and management of these patients.

CASE #23

Name:	E.H.	Sex:	Female
Age:	56	Handedness:	Right
Education:	13		

Current Complaints and Pertinent History

E.H. was a 56-year-old woman who had been diagnosed as having Parkinson's disease approximately three years before this neuropsychological examination. Initially, a tremor began in her left hand and progressed to involve her left foot. At the present time she sought medical evaluation and treatment because she had also developed a mild tremor of the right hand. Neurological examination revealed dyskinesia involving the left hand more than the right hand, confirming the report of the patient. Serial tracings of electroencephalograms were either normal or showed non-specific mild abnormalities.

Neuropsychological testing was done before surgical treatment. This patient was examined before chemotherapy was established as the treatment of choice in treating patients with Parkinson's Disease and following neuropsychological examination a stereotaxic thalamotomy was performed. A lesion was made in the right ventrolateral nucleus of the thalamus. Ventriculography performed in association with the surgical procedure was normal. Immediately after placing the lesion in the right ventrolateral nucleus of the thalamus there was a complete elimination of the tremor of the left hand. The patient recovered from the surgery without incident and post-operative neurological evaluation showed no left-handed tremor. The treatment was considered to have produced an excellent clinical result.

Neuropsychological Test Results

Wechsler-Bellevue scores indicated that the patient earned a Verbal I.Q. (104) that was in the upper part of the Average range (exceeding 61 percent of her age peers) and a Performance I.Q. (101) that was almost exactly at the Average level (exceeding 53 percent). These values yielded a Full Scale I.Q. (101) that was at the Average level (exceeding 53 percent) although the subtest scores suggest that the patient may

HALSTEAD-REITAN NEUROPSYCHOLOGICAL TEST BATTERY

Patient ___E.H.___ Age __56__ Sex __F__ Education __13__ Handedness __R__

x WECHSLER-BELLEVUE SCALE (FORM I)		HALSTEAD'S NEUROPSYCHOLOGICAL TEST BATTERY
___WAIS		

VIQ	104	Category Test	115
PIQ	101		
FIS IQ	101	**Tactual Performance Test**	
VWS	45	Dominant hand: 17.3	
PWS	32	Non-dominant hand: 5.5	
Total WS	77	Both hands: 5.3	

Information	11	Total Time __28.1__
Comprehension	11	Memory __7__
Digit Span	4	Localization __2__
Arithmetic	7	
Similarities	12	**Seashore Rhythm Test**
Vocabulary	13	Number Correct __24__ __8__

Picture Arrangement	4	**Speech-sounds Perception Test**
Picture Completion	10	Number of Errors __5__
Block Design	5	**Finger Oscillation Test**
Object Assembly	4	Dominant hand: 24 __24__
Digit Symbol	9	Non-dominant hand: 25

TRAIL MAKING TEST
Part A: __37__ seconds
Part B: __173__ seconds

Impairment Index __0.7__

STRENGTH OF GRIP
Dominant hand: __31.5__ kilograms
Non-dominant hand: __26.5__ kilograms

MINNESOTA MULTIPHASIC PERSONALITY INVENTORY

?	50	Hs	50
L	60	D	46
F	50	Hy	59
K	55	PD	43
		MF	49
		Pa	41
		Pt	43
		Sc	51
		Ma	35

REITAN-KLØVE TACTILE FORM RECOGNITION TEST
Dominant hand: __—__ seconds; __0__ errors
Non-dominant hand: __—__ seconds; __0__ errors

REITAN-KLØVE SENSORY-PERCEPTUAL EXAM

				Error Totals	
RH___ LH___	Both:RH___ LH___			RH___ LH___	
RH___ LF___	Both:RH_1_ LF___			RH_1_ LF___	
LH___ RF___	Both:LH___ RF___			RF___ LH___	
RE___ LE___	Both:RE___ LE_1_			RE___ LE_1_	
RV___ LV___	Both:RV___ LV___				
___ ___	___ ___			RV___ LV___	
___ ___	___ ___				

REITAN-KLØVE LATERAL-DOMINANCE EXAM

Show me how you:
throw a ball	R
hammer a nail	R
cut with a knife	R
turn a door knob	R
use scissors	R
use an eraser	R
write your name	R

TACTILE FINGER RECOGNITION

	1	2	3	4	5	
R						R 0 / 20
L						L 0 / 20

FINGER-TIP NUMBER WRITING

	1	2	3	4	5	
R	1 1	2 1	3 1	4 2	5 2	R 7 / 20
L	1 2	2 1	3	4 1	5 1	L 5 / 20

Record time used for spontaneous name writing:
Preferred hand __12__ seconds
Non-preferred hand __56__ seconds

REITAN-INDIANA APHASIA SCREENING TEST

Form for Adults and Older Children

Name: E. H.   Age: 56

Copy SQUARE Note the evidence of a fine intention tremor in her drawings.	Repeat TRIANGLE
Name SQUARE	Repeat MASSACHUSETTS "Massachusess"
Spell SQUARE "S-Q-U-A-I-R-E" Self-corrected.	Repeat METHODIST EPISCOPAL
Copy CROSS The spatial problems in her drawings go well beyond any effects of the tremor.	Write SQUARE
Name CROSS	Read SEVEN
Spell CROSS	Repeat SEVEN
Copy TRIANGLE	Repeat/Explain HE SHOUTED THE WARNING.
Name TRIANGLE	Write HE SHOUTED THE WARNING.
Spell TRIANGLE "T-R-I-N-G-L-E"	Compute 85 - 27 =
Name BABY	Compute 17 X 3 =
Write CLOCK	Name KEY
Name FORK	Demonstrate use of KEY
Read 7 SIX 2	Draw KEY Observe the serious problem with the spatial configuration.
Read MGW	Read PLACE LEFT HAND TO RIGHT EAR.
Reading I	Place LEFT HAND TO RIGHT EAR
Reading II	Place LEFT HAND TO LEFT ELBOW

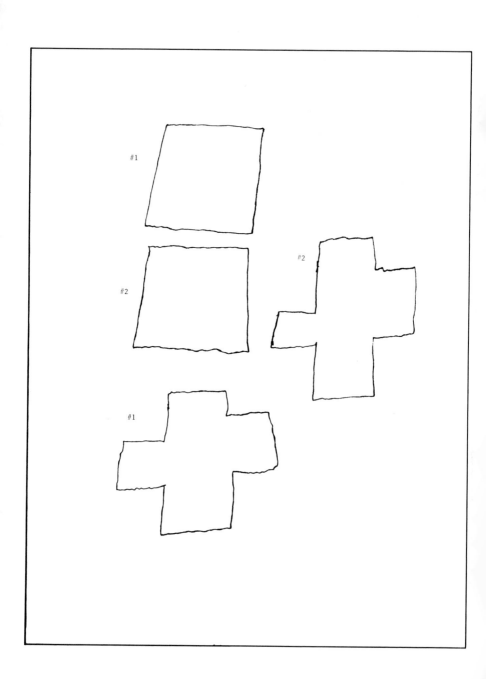

#1

#2

#2

#1

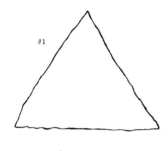

#1

#2

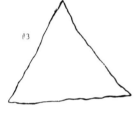

#3

Clock

Square

He shouted the warning

$$\begin{array}{r} 85 \\ -\ 27 \\ \hline 58 \end{array}$$

51 (17X3)

have experienced some deterioration. Her scores on Information (11) and Vocabulary (13) indicate that previously she had probably been somewhat above average. The low score on Digit Span (4) is not surprising in a person (with or without disease) who is hospitalized and under stress concerning what the future might bring. The score on Arithmetic (7), however, may very well reflect some brain-related deterioration.

The Performance subtests showed considerable variability. It was not surprising to see low scores on Picture Arrangement (4) and Block Design (5) because these measures are relatively sensitive to impaired cerebral functioning. Many psychologists, knowing that the patient had an intention tremor, might attribute these low scores to primary motor difficulty. However, poor scores on these measures do not often seem to be limited by motoric dysfunction but are instead due to cerebral damage involving the right hemisphere. In this case, the relatively better score on Digit Symbol (9) provided the definitive answer; even though the patient had a mild tremor involving the right upper extremity she was able to achieve an almost average score on Digit Symbol. Thus, the results suggest that the patient has probably experienced some deterioration of abilities that subserve the Performance I.Q. Although some loss in absolute level of performance is to be expected with advancing age, in this case it appears that the scores go beyond age-related expectancies.

The patient showed significant impairment on brain-related measures. A review of the four most sensitive measures indicates substantial deficit. E.H. earned a Halstead Impairment Index of 0.7, made 115 errors on the Category Test, required 173 seconds to complete Part B of the Trail Making Test, and was able to correctly localize only two of the figures in the Tactual Performance Test. Especially when considering the I.Q. values, one would conclude that the patient has striking impairment of basic adaptive abilities dependent upon brain functions.

As would be expected in a patient with Parkinson's Disease, this woman showed definite impairment of motor functions. Inspection of her drawings of the square, cross and triangle indicated that she had a distinct tremor. This problem was not as apparent in her writing, and according to the history, her right hand was not as badly affected as her left. Nevertheless, the tremor was obvious. She also had difficulties in other motor functions, as manifested by finger tapping speed with both hands and difficulty on the Tactual Performance Test with her right hand. It is equally apparent, however, that her motor problems were not as obvious as her higher-level deficits, even on tasks involving drawing and use of a pencil (note especially her attempts to copy a cross and key). Although neurological diagnosis of Parkinson's disease is dependent upon various aspects of motor function, it should be clear from the performances of this woman that neuropsychological ability goes far beyond motoric proficiency.

Further analysis of the neuropsychological data yields some findings that point toward left cerebral dysfunction and others that implicate the right cerebral hemisphere. These deficits were observed in pathognomonic signs as well as comparison of performances on the two sides of the body.

Left cerebral indicators included a poor performance with the right (preferred) upper extremity on the Tactual Performance Test (17.3 minutes). It should be noted the third trial (5.3 minutes) represented scarcely any improvement over the second (left-handed) trial (5.5 minutes), probably because the right hand was again involved. (The reader may note that the patient's tremor, both historically and clinically, involved the left upper extremity more than the right. This case serves an example that the tremor, per se, is not a basis for drawing a direct conclusion about lateralized performances on the Tactual Performance Test).

The patient's finger tapping speed also suggested left cerebral damage. E.H. was definitely slow with both hands, but just a little poorer with the right hand (24) than the left (25). She also had some difficulty perceiving a tactile stimulus to the right hand when it was given simultaneously with the left face, although this finding, considered by itself, would probably not be of significance.

On the Aphasia Screening Test the patient had some spelling difficulties that would be suspicious for a person having completed one year of college. In spelling SQUARE she inserted an "I" and in spelling TRIANGLE she failed to include the "A." Even though the first of these errors was self-corrected, they probably represent part of an overall picture of impairment of left cerebral functioning.

We should also note that the patient performed extremely well on the Speech-sounds Perception Test (5). The inexperienced neuropsychologist might be very tempted to observe this good score and use it as a basis for cancelling out the indications of left cerebral dysfunction. To achieve a complete understanding of this patient's brain-behavior relationships, though, the evidence of impaired functioning must be accepted and integrated with the good score on the Speech-sounds Perception Test. The results are telling us that the patient does not have a specific, focal lesion of the left cerebral hemisphere, but instead, a condition of involvement that is not acutely destructive.

Right cerebral indicators were also present. The most pronounced of these was a very definite and severe constructional dyspraxia. It should be of interest to the reader to observe that such difficulty drawing simple figures could occur in a person with a Performance I.Q. at the average level. (Again, the test results bear out a basis for caution in predicting the results for one test based on the findings of another.) Nearly every patient exemplifies that to comprehensively understand brain-behavior relationships, all of the tests in the Battery must be administered. Additional right hemisphere indicators might possibly include the fact that this patient's grip strength was somewhat reduced with her left upper extremity (26.5 kg) as compared with her right (31.5 kg). E.H. made one mistake perceiving an auditory stimulus to her left ear when it was given simultaneously with a stimulus to the right ear.

The distinct signs involving the left and right cerebral hemispheres were not supported by results on the Tactile Finger Recognition Test. The patient made no mistakes on either hand on this measure. In Finger-tip Number Writing, though, she made more mistakes than would be expected on each hand. With respect to implicating a focal or specific lesion of either cerebral hemisphere, however, these findings have a modulating effect. Together with the generally poor scores on some measures (such as the Category Test and Part B of the Trail Making Test) we would use these findings to translate neurologically into a condition of generalized cerebral dysfunction.

However, as is the case with most patients having Parkinson's disease, it would go beyond reasonable limits to presume from the neuropsychological findings that only thalamic nuclei were involved. In fact, recent findings have shown evidence of generalized involvement, including the cerebral cortex, in many patients with Parkinson's disease. Neuropsychological test results have supported this position for many years, long before the neurological diagnosis of this disease recognized the cerebral cortical component in many cases. Although motor disorder in patients with Parkinson's disease is certainly an important consideration, the impairment of cerebral cortical functioning probably represents by far the most critical limitation in many of these patients.

Results on the Minnesota Multiphasic Personality Inventory were essentially within the normal range. The Cornell Medical Index revealed that the patient had relatively few somatic complaints. E.H. did indicate that she has difficulty sleeping, feels a good deal of stress during examination, is unable to maintain productive work under stress, gets her thinking completely mixed up when she must do things quickly, and must constantly attempt to control herself in order to avoid going to pieces. These responses almost certainly relate to the neuro-psychological deficits shown on measures such as the Category Test and the Trail Making Test.

It is interesting to note that neurosurgical evaluation following stereotaxic surgery was judged to be clinically excellent. The patient had shown a remarkable reduction in tremor of her left upper extremity immediately after the lesion had been placed in the right ventrolateral nucleus of the thalamus. Although this improvement was undoubtedly clinically important, the neuropsychological correlates of Parkinson's disease go far beyond a matter of motor dysfunction.

At the same time that neurological evaluation was considered to represent a clinically excellent outcome, we had the opportunity to perform a post-operative neuropsychological evaluation. The patient did show somewhat better I.Q. values, but made 111 errors on the Category Test, required 224 seconds on Part B of the Trail Making Test, localized none of the figures on the Tactual Performance Test, and continued to have an Impairment Index of 0.7. In addition, she had very pronounced constructional dyspraxia. The neuropsychological picture, representing basic adaptive abilities, did not seem to be significantly changed even though the tremor had been almost eliminated. Cases of this kind make it entirely clear that the neurological criteria for particular diseases involving the nervous system have neglected the higher-level aspects of brain function and for the patient the outcome must necessarily include such considerations. In fact, this patient was very upset by the retesting; it was apparent to her that she was having essentially as much difficulty as she had before the surgery, even though she had been encouraged to believe that the surgery had been a complete success.

XII
BRAIN INFECTIONS

Brain infections include viral, bacterial, and fungal infections. The skin, muscle, bone and meninges surrounding the brain provide relatively effective protection from such infections. In addition, the blood-brain barrier aids in preventing bacteria, viruses, and toxic substances from entering into most parts of the central nervous system. When an infection does occur, though, the central nervous system does not appear to be well-equipped to fight the infections. Antibody production within the nervous system is not particularly active and passage of antibodies appears to be hindered by the blood-brain barrier. To compound the difficulties, the cerebral spinal fluid provides an excellent medium for culturing infectious agents; thus, organisms of even relatively mild pathogenicity may cause severe infections of the brain.

There are many infectious conditions involving the brain, represented principally by abscess, syphilis, meningitis, and encephalitis. At this point we will not attempt to review the many organisms which may enter the central nervous system or the principal routes of their entry. The reader should be aware, however, that meningitis is represented by an infection of the cerebral spinal fluid with inflammation of the pia-arachnoid, the subarachnoid space, and possibly the surface tissues of the brain and spinal cord. Encephalitis, on the other hand, is characterized by viral or viral-like organisms causing inflammation of the brain tissue and meninges. These various infections may be relatively focal (abscess, syphilitic gumma) or diffuse (meningitis and encephalitis).

Because encephalitis is the cerebral infection most commonly seen by neuropsychologists, we shall offer a few comments on the general characteristics of neuropsychological findings among these patients. The impairment resulting from a brain infection may range from very mild to extremely severe. Among adult subjects who have previously developed adequate levels of general intelligence, results from the Wechsler Scale may be in the average range although it is not uncommon to see a degree of variability among subtests that goes beyond the usual levels. More significant deficits customarily are shown on other tests in the Halstead-Reitan Battery. As with most conditions of generalized impairment of cerebral functioning, the four most sensitive indicators of cerebral dysfunction usually show some degree of deficit. Lateralizing indicators may be present, but are not sufficiently strong to suggest strictly unilateral involvement of either cerebral hemisphere or to identify a focal lesion. Most patients who have had encephalitis are examined neuropsychologically sometime after the acute phase of the illness has passed. Thus, one may often expect to see relatively good scores on certain measures, suggesting that the brain is fairly well stabilized in a biological sense.

In brief, patients who have encephalitic infection show (1) generalized impairment of neuropsychological functions, which may vary from mild to severe; (2) possibly more involvement in one cerebral hemisphere than the other, although the test findings are not sufficient to implicate a strictly focal lesion; and (3) some relatively good scores, suggesting that the condition is stabilized in a biological sense.

CASE #24

Name:	S.B.	Sex:	Female
Age:	35	Handedness:	Right
Education:	13	Occupation:	Typist

Current Complaints and Pertinent History

This 35-year-old woman developed symptoms of headache, back pain, blurred and double vision, malaise, and weakness of her right upper and lower extremities about three years before this neuropsychological examination. Medical evaluation at this time resulted in a diagnosis of equine encephalitis. After the acute attack she showed some improvement. Her symptoms reappeared several months later and the patient subsequently showed signs of recovery.

S.B. had a third attack just before the current hospital admission, nearly three years after her initial illness. At this time she noted difficulty with her speech, blurring of her vision, and general problems with coordination and walking. Physical neurological examination revealed that she was slow in responding and had positive neurological findings on the right side of her body. Her reflexes were generally more active on the right side and she had a lessening of sensation to pain, temperature, position, and vibration over the entire right half of her body. EEG and other objective diagnostic tests were normal. She was diagnosed as having a recurrence of her encephalitis. Such recurrences are unusual but infections of the nervous system are known to recur or, in some instances, to produce long-term symptomatic manifestations.

Neuropsychological Test Results

This right-handed woman was 35 years of age and had completed one year of college. Her physicians reported that she had shown remarkable improvement since the time of her admission to the hospital two weeks earlier.

S.B. earned a Wechsler-Bellevue Verbal I.Q. (99) that was almost exactly at the Average level (exceeding about 47 percent of her age peers) and a Performance I.Q. (105) that was in the upper part of the Average range (exceeding 63 percent). These values yielded a Full Scale

HALSTEAD-REITAN NEUROPSYCHOLOGICAL TEST BATTERY

Patient_____S.B._____Age__35__Sex__F__Education__13__Handedness__R__

_x_ WECHSLER-BELLEVUE SCALE (FORM I)
___ WAIS

VIQ	99
PIQ	105
FIS IQ	103
VWS	45
PWS	47
Total WS	92
Information	9
Comprehension	14
Digit Span	10
Arithmetic	1
Similarities	11
Vocabulary	12
Picture Arrangement	8
Picture Completion	12
Block Design	8
Object Assembly	7
Digit Symbol	12

HALSTEAD'S NEUROPSYCHOLOGICAL TEST BATTERY

Category Test_____73____

Tactual Performance Test
Dominant hand:_____7.2_____
Non-dominant hand:_____9.5_____
Both hands:_____4.3_____

Total Time__21.0____
Memory____4____
Localization___1____

Seashore Rhythm Test
Number Correct___30_____1____

Speech-sounds Perception Test
Number of Errors_____5____

Finger Oscillation Test
Dominant hand:_____46_____46____
Non-dominant hand:___44____

TRAIL MAKING TEST
Part A:__91__ seconds
Part B:__132__ seconds

Impairment Index____0.7____

Miles ABC Test of Ocular Dominance
Right eye:_10_ Left eye:_0__

REITAN-KLØVE SENSORY-PERCEPTUAL EXAM

Error Totals — No errors

RH___	LH___	Both:RH___	LH___	RH___	LH___		
RH___	LF___	Both:RH___	LF___	RH___	LF___		
LH___	RF___	Both:LH___	RF___	RF___	LH___		
RE___	LE___	Both:RE___	LE___	RE___	LE___		
RV___	LV___	Both:RV___	LV___				
___	___	___	___	RV___	LV___		
___	___	___	___				

TACTILE FINGER RECOGNITION
R 1__ 2__ 3__ 4__ 5__ R 0 / 20
L 1__ 2__ 3__ 4__ 5__ L 0 / 20

FINGER-TIP NUMBER WRITING
R 1_3 2__ 3__ 4__ 5__ R 3 / 20
L 1__ 2__ 3__ 4__ 5__ L 0 / 20

REITAN-INDIANA APHASIA SCREENING TEST

Form for Adults and Older Children

Name: _____ S.B. _____ Age: 35

Copy SQUARE
    Note fine intention tremor
    in drawing.
	Repeat TRIANGLE

Name SQUARE	Repeat MASSACHUSETTS
Spell SQUARE	Repeat METHODIST EPISCOPAL

Copy CROSS
    Note very mild imbalance
    of extremities.
	Write SQUARE

Name CROSS	Read SEVEN
Spell CROSS	Repeat SEVEN
Copy TRIANGLE	Repeat/Explain HE SHOUTED THE WARNING.
Name TRIANGLE	Write HE SHOUTED THE WARNING.
Spell TRIANGLE	Compute 85 − 27 =
Name BABY	Compute 17 X 3 = "61"
Write CLOCK	Name KEY
Name FORK	Demonstrate use of KEY
Read 7 SIX 2	Draw KEY
Read MGW	Read PLACE LEFT HAND TO RIGHT EAR.
Reading I	Place LEFT HAND TO RIGHT EAR
Reading II	Place LEFT HAND TO LEFT ELBOW

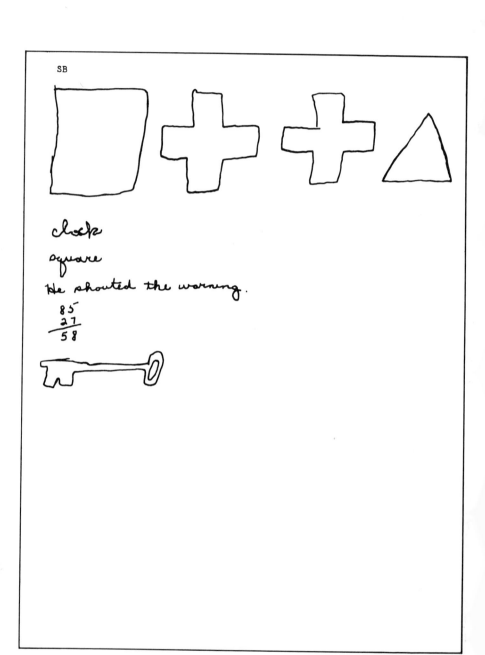

clock

square

He shouted the warning.

$$\begin{array}{r} 85 \\ 27 \\ \hline 58 \end{array}$$

I.Q. (103) that was slightly above the Average level (exceeding 58 percent).

Inspection of the subtest scores showed a considerable degree of variability among both the Verbal and Performance subtests. The patient was able to make scarcely any progress on the Arithmetic subtest (1) despite the fact that her other Verbal subtests were nearly at the average level or above. From these results, it would appear that the prior general intellectual development of this woman was adequate. It is not likely that the extremely poor score on the Arithmetic subtest is due exclusively to cerebral damage, although we are not in a position to offer an explanation for this particular score based on the Wechsler test findings alone.

Results on the Performance subtests showed some degree of variability. It is not surprising to see relatively poor scores on the Picture Arrangement (8) and Block Design (8) subtest in the context of the other Performance scores, because these tests are often performed poorly by persons with cerebral damage. The Digit Symbol subtest (12) represented one of S.B.'s best performances.

From the Wechsler-Bellevue scores one would judge that this woman has had an adequate development of intellectual abilities in the past and currently shows more variability among subtests than would normally be expected. However, an explanation for this variability may be only partly related to possible impairment of cerebral functions; as so frequently is the case, it is difficult to draw definitive conclusions regarding brain-behavior relationships from the Wechsler subtest scores alone.

More definite indications of brain dysfunction were obtained with the rest of the Battery and the scores fell in an overall context that permitted a consistent set of conclusions. The patient earned a Halstead Impairment Index of 0.7. This finding suggests the possibility of brain dysfunction, especially in light of the relatively normal intelligence levels.

On the other three most sensitive indicators, S.B. had much more difficulty than even the average brain-damaged person. Her score on the Category Test (73 errors) leaves no doubt that she has a degree of impairment in the area of abstraction, reasoning, and logical analysis; requiring 132 seconds on Part B of the Trail Making Test tells us that she is somewhat slow and not as bright and alert as she might be in dealing with tasks involving several elements simultaneously; and being able to localize only one shape on her drawing of the Tactual Performance Test board demonstrates that she has some impairment of immediate memory.

The lateralizing indicators, though not of profound significance, implicated both cerebral hemispheres. We would be inclined to discount the error in multiplying 17 X 3 because the type of mistake made by the patient occurs among a considerable number of normal subjects. Her finger tapping speed with her right hand (46) was a little slow with relation to her left hand (44), but this result, considered by itself, would also be insufficient to use as a basis for implicating left cerebral damage. Results on the Finger-tip Number Writing Perception Test were probably sufficient to complement the right-handed finger tapping speed. Thus, the left cerebral indicators were sufficient to suggest mild impairment of the left cerebral hemisphere. The excellent score on the Speech-sounds Perception Test (5) gives an indication of the prior abilities of this woman and, in addition, would suggest that at the present time she has a relatively stabilized brain condition. This assumption would also be supported by the perfect score on the Seashore Rhythm Test.

The pattern of results on successive trials on the Tactual Performance Test indicated that this woman did relatively poorly with her left hand (9.5 minutes) as compared with her right hand (7.2 minutes). We may surmise that this result probably was not due to frustration with the task or general fatigue, considering the sharp reduction in time achieved on the third trial while using both hands. It appears that the pattern provides a fair basis for comparing the two cerebral hemispheres and suggests right cerebral dysfunction.

The patient also had some difficulty copying the cross and key. Although these deficiencies were not pronounced, the disparity of the lateral extremities on both attempts to copy the cross represent a mild deviation from normal expectancy and suggests some mild degree of right cerebral damage. The key is more difficult to interpret because of the skeletal nature of the drawing, but lack of symmetry of the "teeth" of the key may represent a brain-related deficiency in performance.

In summary, the general indicators, particularly when considered with relation to the I.Q. levels, strongly suggest impairment of brain functions. The lateralizing indicators were not sufficient on either side to implicate a focal lesion; however, they complemented the overall set of test results by providing evidence of brain dysfunction derived from the methods of inference other than level of performance. Finally some of the better scores in the Battery (particularly Seashore Rhythm and Speech-sounds Perception Tests) argue strongly against a rapidly progressive condition of brain disease or damage.

The psychological implications of the test results also merit comment. Although the Wechsler subtest scores (except for Arithmetic) represent this woman as being relatively intelligent, she is much more impaired (as demonstrated by the Category Test, Part B of the Trail Making Test and Localization component of the Tactual Performance Test) than either the patient herself or others in her environment probably realize. This disparity in her ability structure is likely to cause difficulties. She will perform much more poorly on many tasks than would be expected and motivational deficiencies or interpersonal problems are likely to be considered as causative factors. Deficits of this kind often cause difficulties that are continuous, self-sustaining and even self-elaborating.

In addition to having the neuropsychological evaluation repeated (in about six months, to diminish positive practice-effects), this woman's current emotional status should be evaluated and, if difficulties arise in practical aspects of everyday living, psychological counseling would be indicated.

XIII
TOXIC AND METABOLIC
BRAIN DISORDERS

There are a number of toxic and metabolic disorders which may cause brain dysfunction. As neuropsychological correlates of these conditions have not been studied in much detail, this is an area that has great potential for further development of neuropsychological evaluation.

We shall briefly review and identify some of these conditions prior to presenting neuropsychological test results for two subjects; a young woman with carbon monoxide poisoning and a man with Wilson's disease (hepatolenticular degeneration).

The field of neurology has identified many toxic and metabolic disorders that may cause nervous system dysfunction although the higher-level and neuropsychological aspects of these conditions have not been well identified. Thus, it behooves neuropsychology to follow the lead of neurologists who have studied the neurological consequences of these conditions, and explore more fully the neuropsychological deficits that occur in these conditions. Abnormalities of water and electrolyte balance may have profound effects on brain function. Other conditions which affect cerebral functioning include potassium deficiencies, renal insufficiency, and many endocrinological disorders, e.g. diabetes mellitus and myxedema (Reitan, 1953).

Hypoxic encephalopathy is another condition which may cause either temporary or permanent damage to the brain. Hypoxia (oxygen deprivation) may result from obstruction of the airways , breathing difficulties of various causes, cardiac arrest, blood loss, or poisoning, including carbon monoxide and cyanide. When the balance of glucose or oxygen (substances which support brain metabolism) are interrupted, an adverse effect on brain function may result. Hypoglycemia, which occurs in varying degrees of severity, is representative of this type of condition.

Other conditions which are related to toxic and metabolic bases of brain dysfunction include blood dyscrasias, sickle-cell anemia, polycythemia, leukemia, Hodgkin's disease, vitamin deficiencies, heavy metals and industrial toxins, Wilson's disease, adverse reactions to antibiotics, anticholinergic drugs such as atropine, scopolamine, belladonna, tricyclic antidepressants, and phenothiazines (all of which may produce poisoning), antipsychotic drugs, barbiturates, oral contraceptives, and many other ingested substances. Alcohol consumption can also be considered to represent a toxic influence on brain functions and because of the cumulative and long-term effects seen in some cases, will be considered separately.

As one would expect, the neuropsychological manifestations of these various conditions are usually generalized rather than strictly focal. It is not unusual to occasionally see some degree of differential involvement of the two cerebral hemispheres; though the focal signs involve both cerebral hemispheres the condition is classified in a neuropsychological context as a generalized cerebral disorder.

CEREBRAL ANOXIA

Pathology and Clinical Manifestations

A great deal of variability exists in the pathological changes in the brains of persons who have suffered cerebral anoxia and anoxic encephalopathy. Even though the basic problem stems from oxygen and glucose deficiencies which impair brain metabolism, other significant factors interact to produce the resulting damage. These factors include body temperature, blood pressure, the cerebral metabolic rate for oxygen consumption, and differential susceptibility of various structures and parts of the brain to the effects of lack of oxygen. The brains of persons who have died during an anoxic episode show diffuse dilatation of blood vessels, scattered petechial hemorrhages and occasional large hemorrhages. In cases of carbon monoxide poisoning the brain is a pink color due to the carboxyhemoglobin in the blood.

The published literature reports a wide variability in the pathological changes in the brains of persons who die from the episode and patients who survive and demonstrate postanoxic encephalopathy. In the former cases some of the pathological reports have emphasized extensive necrosis in the cortical gray matter. Other reports in these patients have suggested that involvement of the white (rather than gray) matter, characterized by widespread demyelination throughout the cerebral hemispheres, is the principal pathological feature. Researchers have proposed various hypotheses of differential hypoxic damage to various parts of the brain, depending upon the metabolic rate of the tissue considered.

The clinical picture following severe anoxia is quite variable, ranging from severe impairment of consciousness (including stupor and akinetic mutism) to an apparently complete recovery. However, many patients who initially appear to recover well demonstrate clinical manifestations 48 hours to several weeks following the incident. Their symptoms typically include irritability, withdrawn behavior, apathetic behavior and general confusion. Motor deficits, including slowed movements and generalized rigidity with parkinsonian features, are often present. In patients with anoxic encephalopathy, it is not uncommon for the clinical evaluation to include reference to depression or other psychiatric disorders. In some cases the course is one of steady deterioration and death but in others a second period of recovery may begin and may, or may not, be complete.

CASE #25

Name:	B.P.	Sex:	Female
Age:	29	Handedness:	Right
Education:	13	Occupation:	Homemaker

Current Complaints and Pertinent History

Ten months before this neuropsychological examination this 29-year-old woman had attempted suicide by running the engine of her car in a closed garage. As a result, she suffered carbon monoxide poisoning and was unconscious for about five hours. Examination shortly after this incident revealed a right hemiparesis and right homonymous hemianopia. These signs suggest that the left cerebral hemisphere had been more seriously affected by the poisoning than the right.

B.P. was admitted to the hospital at the present time because of continuing weakness on the right side of her body. A detailed neurological examination showed a mild right hemiparesis, a right homonymous hemianopia, mild dysstereognosis (loss in tactile form recognition) of the right hand, a fine tremor of the right upper extremity, increased deep tendon reflexes on both sides (somewhat more pronounced on the right), and mild dysphasia. Electroencephalography showed abnormalities of the entire left cerebral hemisphere, classified as a Grade II asymmetry. Skull films and bilateral cerebral angiograms were normal. The neurological diagnosis was brain damage secondary to carbon monoxide exposure.

The patient herself noticed progressive deterioration of visual acuity. She also felt that her ability to use her right arm and hand was getting worse.

Neuropsychological Test Results

As a general summary statement, the test findings indicate generalized impairment of neuropsychological abilities with more serious involvement of the left cerebral hemisphere than the right. Some of the relatively good scores (e.g., Speech-sounds Perception Test) indicate that the dysfunction of the left cerebral hemisphere is probably not

HALSTEAD-REITAN NEUROPSYCHOLOGICAL TEST BATTERY

Patient _____ B.P. _____ Age __29__ Sex__F__ Education__13__ Handedness__R__

__x__ WECHSLER-BELLEVUE SCALE (FORM I)
____ WAIS

VIQ	76
PIQ	86
FIS IQ	80
VWS	27
PWS	38
Total WS	65
Information	9
Comprehension	6
Digit Span	4
Arithmetic	1
Similarities	7
Vocabulary	10
Picture Arrangement	14
Picture Completion	4
Block Design	6
Object Assembly	10
Digit Symbol	4

HALSTEAD'S NEUROPSYCHOLOGICAL TEST BATTERY
Category Test _____ __47__

Tactual Performance Test
Left hand: _____ 12.6 _____
Left hand: _____ 6.6 _____
Left hand: _____ 6.4 _____
Total Time __25.6__
Memory __3__
Localization __1__

Seashore Rhythm Test
Number Correct __17__ _____ 10

Speech-sounds Perception Test
Number of Errors _____ 5

Finger Oscillation Test
Dominant hand: __21__ _____ 21
Non-dominant hand: __45__

TRAIL MAKING TEST
Part A: __62__ seconds
Part B: __174__ seconds

Impairment Index __0.7__

Miles ABC Test of Ocular Dominance
Right eye: __0__ Left eye: __10__

REITAN-KLØVE SENSORY-PERCEPTUAL EXAM

MINNESOTA MULTIPHASIC PERSONALITY INVENTORY

?	50		Hs	60
L	53		D	71
F	60		Hy	68
K	60		PD	47
			MF	53
			Pa	50
			Pt	66
			Sc	66
			Ma	50

Error Totals

RH____LH____	Both:RH____LH____	RH____LH____
RH____LF____	Both:RH__4__LF____	RH__4__LF____
LH____RF____	Both:LH____RF____	RF____LH____
RE____LE____	Both:RE____LE____	RE____LE____
RV__4__LV____	Both:RV__4__LV____	
__4__ ____	__4__ ____	RV__4__LV____
__4__ ____	__4__ ____	

TACTILE FINGER RECOGNITION
R 1____ 2____ 3____ 4 2 5____ R 2 / 20
L 1____ 2____ 3____ 4 2 5____ L 2 / 20

FINGER-TIP NUMBER WRITING
R 1____ 2____ 3 2 4 4 5 3 R 9 / 20
L 1____ 2____ 3____ 4____ 5____ L 0 / 20

Visual Field Examination: Right homonymous hemianopia.

REITAN-INDIANA APHASIA SCREENING TEST

Form for Adults and Older Children

Name: _____ B. P. _____ Age: __29__

Copy SQUARE	Repeat TRIANGLE
Name SQUARE	Repeat MASSACHUSETTS
Spell SQUARE	Repeat METHODIST EPISCOPAL Confused syllables; could not enunciate.
Copy CROSS	Write SQUARE
Name CROSS	Read SEVEN
Spell CROSS	Repeat SEVEN
Copy TRIANGLE	Repeat/Explain HE SHOUTED THE WARNING. Repeated ok. Could not comprehend the meaning.
Name TRIANGLE	Write HE SHOUTED THE WARNING.
Spell TRIANGLE	Compute 85 – 27 = Confused regarding arithmetical processes or calculations.
Name BABY	Compute 17 X 3 =
Write CLOCK	Name KEY
Name FORK	Demonstrate use of KEY
Read 7 SIX 2	Draw KEY
Read MGW	Read PLACE LEFT HAND TO RIGHT EAR. Confused about right and left.
Reading I	Place LEFT HAND TO RIGHT EAR
Reading II	Place LEFT HAND TO LEFT ELBOW

clock

Square

#1

85
27
―――
6

#2

He shouted

the warning.

rapidly progressive in nature; so although many of the findings might suggest a lesion such as a glioma or vascular anamoly of the left cerebral hemisphere, with such lesions one would not expect to find an excellent Speech-sounds Perception Test score in the presence of the other deficits.

The patient earned a Verbal I.Q. (76) that was in the Borderline range (exceeding only 5 percent of her age peers) and a Performance I.Q. (86) that was in the Low Average range (exceeding 18 percent). These values yielded a Full Scale I.Q. (80) that was at the lower limit of the Low Average range (exceeding 9 percent). From these values alone it is difficult to estimate just what the premorbid intellectual abilities of this woman might have been, but from the Information (9) and Vocabulary (10) subtest scores, as well as some of the better scores on the Performance subtests, it would appear that B.P. was at least at the average level. The Verbal subtests, plotted graphically from Information to Vocabulary, show the typical V-shaped pattern so commonly seen in persons with cerebral damage. The Digit Span score (4) considered by itself, may indicate the stress surrounding the patient's present circumstances and not necessarily be a reflection of brain dysfunction. The scores on Comprehension (6) and Similarities (7) may possibly represent some degree of impairment. There can be hardly any doubt, though, that the extremely limited performance on the Arithmetic subtest (1) reflects cerebral damage.

The Performance subtest scores of the Wechsler scale show a considerable degree of variability. It is unusual to see such a good Picture Arrangement score (14) in any person with significant cerebral damage and the disparity between this score and the Block Design score (6) might be sufficient to suggest the possibility of a focal right parietal lesion. (This hypothesis was not borne out by the neurological findings or the rest of the neuropsychological test results.) The poor score on Picture Completion (4) may be due to impaired visual acuity. The low Digit Symbol score (4) is to be expected in a person with cerebral damage, regardless of whether the right or left cerebral hemisphere is principally involved.

In summary, the Wechsler subtests indicate that this woman has most likely experienced impairment of both Verbal and Performance aspects of general intelligence. The inferences were drawn from the variability among subtest scores as well as the particular subtests on which low scores were obtained. The overall pattern cannot be used to infer cerebral damage.

The patient earned a Halstead Impairment Index of 0.7 (about 70 percent of these tests in the brain-damaged range), and did especially poorly on Part B of the Trail Making Test (174 seconds) and the Localization component of the Tactual Performance Test (1). She performed surprisingly well on the Category Test, making 47 errors. The Category Test and the Speech-sounds Perception Test (5) were the only measures with scores in the normal range. The reader should be aware, however, that Halstead's cut-off point of 50 errors on the Category Test is somewhat liberal, and a score of 47 errors is probably not normal. In the interpretation of test results, each case must be evaluated individually and we must consider the I.Q. values with relation to the Category Test; for this woman 47 errors must be considered to be one of her best performances. However, the four most sensitive indicators of cerebral dysfunction clearly demonstrate that B.P. has suffered a degree of impairment of brain-related abilities.

Further analysis of the test results yields many findings that implicate the left cerebral hemisphere. Although right-handed, the patient's finger tapping speed was extremely slow with the right hand (21) as compared with the left (45). It was not possible for this woman to do the Tactual Performance Test with her right hand and, to obtain some type of overall estimate of her ability on this task, she was asked to do it three times with her left hand. We must note that her right hand was so impaired that she was not able to do the task at all, and record this finding as a possible indicator of left cerebral dysfunction. The pattern of results obtained with three trials using the left hand suggests that this woman has some difficulties in the initial aspects of complex and unique problem-solving situations, but even so, one might have expected more improvement on the third trial. Probably the best overall indicator was a Total Time on the Tactual Performance Test that was definitely in the impaired range, approximating the average time required by a person with cerebral damage.

The most significant finding related to a right homonymous hemianopia. This loss precluded our administration of tests of bilateral simultaneous visual stimulation. When tactile stimuli were used, the patient made no mistakes with unilateral stimulation but did not perceive the stimulus to the right hand in any instance in which competing stimulus was given to the left face. This is a distinctly pathological manifestation and suggests involvement of the left hemisphere, particularly in the parietal area. The patient did not make a single mistake on her left hand in Finger-tip Number Writing Perception but had pronounced difficulties on her right hand.

Tactile Finger Recognition showed mild impairment on both hands and demonstrated no lateralizing effect. The comparison between Tactile Finger Recognition and Finger-tip Number Writing Perception demonstrates the necessity of using both tests: in some cases, positive results may be obtained from one but not the other. Exactly how differential findings of this kind relate to localization of the brain lesion is not presently known; so, even though these tests often agree in the information they provide, there are instances in which the definitive positive information may be obtained from one test but not the other.

The Tactile Form Recognition Test had not been developed when this woman was tested; however, informal testing showed that she had a mild loss in tactile form recognition (mild right dysstereognosis) of her right hand.

Considering the severity of right-sided involvement in both motor and sensory-perceptual evaluations, one might very well have expected the patient to demonstrate pronounced and widespread aphasic symptoms. B.P. did show striking losses in certain respects; in general, though, she was able to complete most of the tasks without error. She had a pronounced auditory-verbal dysgnosia, being unable to comprehend or communicate any degree of understanding of the sentence HE SHOUTED THE WARNING.

She also manifested a very pronounced dyscalculia, and could not solve even the most simple arithmetic problems. She was not able to do $85-27 =$, not even realizing that she should have started by considering the numbers on the right side of the problem (5 and 7) rather than those on the left side (8 and 2). All she was able to do was subtract 2 from 8. We tried several other very simple problems for the patient to work mentally, but her response, when she was able to give one at all, was usually incorrect. Occasionally, though, she would give a correct answer to a problem that was more difficult than one she had just failed. This kind of performance is not atypical in persons with dyscalculia, and B.P.'s occasional correct responses to relatively more complex problems indicates quite clearly that at one time she had learned some basic aspects of arithmetical calculation.

The patient also demonstrated central dysarthria. She could enunciate the easier words upon command, but became totally confused when attempting METHODIST EPISCOPAL. Finally, she was completely bewildered when asked to place her left hand to her right ear. This confusion might possibly have been due in part to difficulties in auditory-verbal comprehension (auditory-verbal dysgnosia) but it seemed principally to be a manifestation of right-left confusion. In either case, the defective performance would implicate left cerebral damage (Wheeler and Reitan, 1962).

The deficiencies in this patient's drawings probably represent a problem primarily in motor control; she was impaired in the use and control of her right upper extremity. The same type of motor control problems were manifested in B.P.'s writing. However, her repetition of the "s" when she was writing SQUARE almost certainly manifests a left hemisphere-related problem in use of verbal symbols for communicational purposes.

Results on the Minnesota Multiphasic Personality Inventory suggest that this woman does have some problems of an emotional and affective nature which may be a reaction to the impairment that she has experienced or may stem from her earlier emotional condition. Many persons with significant cerebral damage, and the resulting neuropsychological impairment, manifest some evidence of emotional stress on the MMPI (Reitan, 1955a).

Cerebral damage is clearly implicated by the test results of B.P., but it is unusual to see such pronounced indications of left cerebral damage in a case of toxic poisoning of the brain. One would generally expect the results to have more widespread implications rather than show the specific kinds of deficits, such as right homonymous hemianopia, striking motor impairment, and tactile imperception usually associated with specific lateralized structural damage. The fact that the patient did not have more pronounced evidence of dysphasia would be one factor arguing against a more focal, destructive lesion of the left cerebral hemisphere in the presence of the more pronounced deficits. However, in this case, the strongest argument for a relatively chronic condition would be the excellent score on the Speech-sounds Perception Test.

Finally, the test results can be considered with relation to the patient's complaint of deteriorating visual acuity and increasing difficulty using her right hand and arm. From the test results one could say that there was no evidence to suggest the presence of organic involvement of the left cerebral hemisphere that was rapidly progressive, but it would be difficult to go beyond this without further knowledge, based on study of many patients with carbon monoxide poisoning, regarding the validity of the test results for prognostic statements.

WILSON'S DISEASE (HEPATOLENTICULAR DEGENERATION)

Wilson's disease is an inherited condition characterized by generalized neuronal degeneration. It is associated with abnormal copper metabolism and probably results from toxic effects of copper in the cerebral tissues. In this disease there is also an increase in deposition of copper in liver cells, causing at least mild cirrhosis of the liver. Deposition of excess copper (which is brownish-green) is also found in the outer limits of the cornea, next to the sclera (Kayser-Fleischer ring). The brain may appear to be grossly normal or show some degree of cortical atrophy. Microscopic examination shows diffuse neuronal degeneration throughout the gray matter with secondary gliotic changes. Widespread atrophy of the brain may be present, particularly involving tissues of the motor system.

Incidence of Wilson's disease is equal in males and females and the age of onset varies from 5 to about 40 years. In general, an early onset has a worse prognosis. The description of Wilson's disease by neurologists customarily emphasizes motor disorders (including generalized rigidity), bradykinesis, dysarthria, and a mask-like facial appearance. The patient's gait resembles that of Parkinson's disease, with a forward stoop and absence of arm swinging. Tremor may be present but it is often mild or absent entirely. In children with Wilson's disease the condition is more rapidly progressive and motor difficulties are characteristically dystonic in nature. Untreated cases show progressive impairment, including emotional lability, epileptic seizures, progressive muscular weakness, cirrhosis of the liver, and eventual dementia. Without treatment, death usually occurs within four or five years following the onset of symptoms, but ten-year survival occurs in some patients who have had a later onset of the disease. Treatment methods have been developed for inhibiting absorption of copper from the intestinal tract and promoting excretion of tissue copper into the urine.

CASE #26

Name:	W.H.	Sex:	Male
Age:	48	Handedness:	Right
Education:	12		

Current Complaints and Pertinent History

W.H.'s initial symptoms, tremors of the upper extremities, began 24 years before this neuropsychological examination. His life had been prolonged beyond the average of patients with Wilson's disease who had not had effective treatment. He had experienced a variable course over the years and complained particularly of difficulty with speech and fine movements of the hands. This was most obviously expressed when the patient attempted to write. Physical neurological examination showed gross tremors of both upper extremities, slow and deliberate speech, and a variety of other movement disorders. The typical Kayser-Fleischer ring was demonstrated by slit-lamp examination. Laboratory studies indicated a copper metabolism disorder. The electroencephalogram was normal but a pneumoencephalogram showed mild dilatation of the cerebral ventricles.

Neuropsychological Test Results

As a general summary, the test results for this man imply that (1) his general development of brain-behavior relationships was within the normal range; (2) he has experienced significant deterioration of immediate adaptive skills that involve the cerebral cortex generally; (3) motor dysfunction is prominent and involves the left side of the body slightly more than the right; (4) the neuropsychological deficits go far beyond impairment of motor functions and the I.Q. values would be misleading with respect to assessing the integrity of brain- behavior relationships; (5) the sensory-perceptual deficits complement the motor dysfunction as a basis for concluding that each stems from cerebral rather than peripheral involvement; and (6) the patient is significantly distressed emotionally.

For those clinicians interested in differential neuropsychological diagnosis, we may note that the results shown by this man are very

HALSTEAD-REITAN NEUROPSYCHOLOGICAL TEST BATTERY

Patient ____W.H.____ Age __48__ Sex __M__ Education __12__ Handedness __R__

__x__ WECHSLER-BELLEVUE SCALE (FORM I)
___ WAIS

VIQ	105
PIQ	107
FIS IQ	106
VWS	48
PWS	43
Total WS	91

Information	10
Comprehension	11
Digit Span	9
Arithmetic	9
Similarities	9
Vocabulary	10

Picture Arrangement	10
Picture Completion	12
Block Design	6
Object Assembly	10
Digit Symbol	5

HALSTEAD'S NEUROPSYCHOLOGICAL TEST BATTERY

Category Test 128

Tactual Performance Test
Dominant hand: 15.0 (8 blocks)
Non-dominant hand: 15.0 (4 blocks)
Both hands: 15.0 (5 blocks)

Total Time . 45.0 +
Memory 2
Localization 0

Seashore Rhythm Test
Number Correct 22 ——— 10

Speech-sounds Perception Test
Number of Errors ——— 10

Finger Oscillation Test
Dominant hand: 23 ——— 23
Non-dominant hand: 18

TRAIL MAKING TEST
Part A: __44__ seconds
Part B: __109__ seconds
Discontinued at H. Patient confused.

Impairment Index __1.0__

STRENGTH OF GRIP
Dominant hand: __52.5__ kilograms
Non-dominant hand: __40.5__ kilograms

REITAN-KLØVE TACTILE FORM RECOGNITION TEST
Dominant hand: __18__ seconds; __0__ errors
Non-dominant hand: __17__ seconds; __0__ errors

REITAN-KLØVE SENSORY-PERCEPTUAL EXAM

				Error Totals	
RH___LH___	Both:RH _1_ LH___	RH _1_ LH___			
RH___LF___	Both:RH___LF___	RH___LF___			
LH___RF___	Both:LH___RF___	RF___LH___			
RE___LE___	Both:RE _2_ LE___	RE _2_ LE___			
RV___LV___	Both:RV___LV___				
___ ___	___ ___	RV___LV___			
___ ___	___ ___				

TACTILE FINGER RECOGNITION
R 1__ 2 1 3 2 4 __5__ R _3_ / 20
L 1__ 2 3 3 1 4 3 5 L _7_ / 20

FINGER-TIP NUMBER WRITING
R 1 3 2 __3 2 4 1 5 2__ R _8_ / 20
L 1 2 2 __3 1 4 __5 1 L _4_ / 20

Miles ABC Test of Ocular Dominance
Right eye: __0__ Left eye: __10__

MINNESOTA MULTIPHASIC PERSONALITY INVENTORY

?	50	Hs	98
L	53	D	80
F	58	Hy	87
K	51	PD	71
		MF	59
		Pa	53
		Pt	79
		Sc	90
		Ma	60

REITAN-KLØVE LATERAL-DOMINANCE EXAM
Show me how you:
throw a ball	R
hammer a nail	R
cut with a knife	R
turn a door knob	R
use scissors	R
use an eraser	R
write your name	R

Record time used for spontaneous name writing:
Preferred hand __47__ seconds
Non-preferred hand __31__ seconds

Show me how you:
kick a football	L
step on a bug	L

REITAN-INDIANA APHASIA SCREENING TEST

Form for Adults and Older Children

Name: _____ W. H. _____ Age: __48__

Copy SQUARE Note mild problem of motor control.	Repeat TRIANGLE
Name SQUARE	Repeat MASSACHUSETTS "Massachusess"
Spell SQUARE	Repeat METHODIST EPISCOPAL "Methodiss Episcopal"
Copy CROSS Note problem of spatial relationships.	Write SQUARE
Name CROSS	Read SEVEN
Spell CROSS	Repeat SEVEN
Copy TRIANGLE	Repeat/Explain HE SHOUTED THE WARNING. Explanation – "Means to halt".
Name TRIANGLE "T–R–A–I–N"; then "T–R–A–N–G–L–E–U–R"; then "T–R–I–A–N–G–L–E–R"	Write HE SHOUTED THE WARNING. Had better motor control when printing.
Spell TRIANGLE	Compute 85 – 27 =
Name BABY	Compute 17 X 3 =
Write CLOCK	Name KEY
Name FORK	Demonstrate use of KEY
Read 7 SIX 2	Draw KEY Note spatial problems.
Read MGW	Read PLACE LEFT HAND TO RIGHT EAR.
Reading I	Place LEFT HAND TO RIGHT EAR
Reading II	Place LEFT HAND TO LEFT ELBOW

ChOCK

cloch

~give~

51

HE SHOUTED The

WARNING

8 C ~16~

2 ~Y~

similar to those obtained in many patients with Parkinson's disease. Also, these results would be similar to those seen in persons with diffuse cerebral atrophy except that the measurements of motor ability deficits (Finger Tapping and Tactual Performance Test) were performed more poorly by this patient than would be expected for most persons with diffuse cerebral atrophy. In brief, there is a pronounced cerebral cortical component to this patient's neuropsychological deficits in addition to the indications of motor impairment.

The patient earned a Verbal I.Q. (105) that fell in the upper part of the Average range (exceeding about 63 percent of his age peers) and a Performance I.Q. (107) that was also at this level (exceeding 68 percent). These values yielded a Full Scale I.Q. (106) that was in the upper part of the Average range (exceeding 66 percent).

The patient demonstrated relatively average performances on all of the subtests except for Block Design (6) and Digit Symbol (5). It is not likely that W.H.'s motor problem was a significant factor in reducing his performance on Block Design (Briggs, 1960) and this score may represent some degree of impairment on this test. However, it is possible that motor impairment of the right upper extremity may have been a factor in reducing the Digit Symbol score.

The patient consistently had difficulty on brain-sensitive tests, earning a Halstead Impairment Index of 1.0. He performed poorly on tasks that required abstraction, reasoning, logical analysis, flexibility in thought processes, adaptability to unique types of problems, and immediate memory. These deficits were demonstrated by the impairment shown on the Category Test (128 errors), Part B of the Trail Making Test (109 seconds, discontinued at "H"), and the Time (45 + minutes), Memory (2), and Localization (0) components of the Tactual Performance Test. The patient was relatively capable of paying attention to specific aspects of well-structured problems, as shown by his scores on the Speech-sounds Perception Test (10) and the Seashore Rhythm Test (22), even though he may have demonstrated a mild degree of impairment. His motor dysfunction was clearly manifested by reduced finger tapping speed, although his grip strength (especially with his preferred hand) was adequate (52.5 kg).

A more detailed review of the test results reveals evidence to implicate each cerebral hemisphere and provides a picture of generalized (rather than focal) involvement. First, the four most sensitive measures in the HRNB showed very striking impairment, suggesting that the neuropsychological deficits are relatively severe. It should be noted that after working for 109 seconds on Part B of the Trail Making Test the patient had completed only 16 of the 25 circles. At that point he was so confused that the examiner discontinued the test.

The first level of central processing (attention and concentration) was relatively intact in this man and he did not have any significant difficulties with specific aspects of language reception or production. However, it should be noted that he had difficulty spelling TRIANGLE, first responding T-R-A-I-N. When the examiner asked him to make another attempt he responded, T-R-A-N-G-L-E-U-R. Finally, when asked to try once more, his response was T-R-I-A-N-G-L-E-R.

One might wonder how this kind of confusion and deficit could occur on this particular item when the patient was able to spell other words and do simple reading satisfactorily. We have observed that a person with a brain-related deficit may occasionally manifest an instance of extreme confusion (entirely inconsistent with his usual responses) in dealing with language symbols. It would seem that brain functions suddenly lose their competence and the patient is just not able to perform adequately. We would consider these instances of spelling failure as definite manifestations of cerebral dysfunction rather than excuse them because few other mistakes were present.

The patient's enunciation of MASSACHUSETTS and METHODIST EPISCOPAL (in which he failed to emphasize the "T" sound) are within normal limits. He offered a very limited explanation of HE SHOUTED THE WARNING, and the examiner should have questioned him about this more carefully.

The patient also showed some deficits in sensory-perceptual functions, failing in one instance to perceive a tactile stimulus to his right hand when it was given simultaneously with a stimulus to the left hand and showing this tendency in two of four trials with bilateral simultaneous auditory stimulation. A single error probably cannot be counted as having special significance, but the two errors with the right ear (especially when no errors occurred with unilateral stimulation) must be taken as an indication of left cerebral dysfunction. Similarly significant results were obtained in Finger-tip Number Writing Perception: the patient made twice as many mistakes on his right hand (8) as his left (4). This suggests that there is some generalized impairment, with the results implicating the left cerebral hemisphere more than the right.

Lateralizing findings for involvement of the right cerebral hemisphere include reduced grip strength in the left upper extremity (40.5 kg.) compared with the right (52.5 kg.), a strikingly deficient performance on the Tactual Performance Test with the left hand (15.0 minutes, 4 blocks) compared with the right (15.0 minutes, 8 blocks), and, although reduced on each hand, mild reduction of finger tapping speed with the left hand (18) compared with the right (23). More errors in tactile finger recognition on the left hand (7) than the right (3) complemented the left-sided motor dysfunction.

There was definite evidence of constructional dyspraxia, especially in the patient's attempts to copy the cross. Drawings of the square, triangle, and key also showed definite impairment in the ability to deal with simple aspects of spatial configurations. This deficit probably correlates with the poor performance on the Block Design subtest of the Wechsler Scale.

The patient was given a brief examination relating to emotional and affective aspects of adjustment using one technique that inquires rather directly for the patient's self-assessment (Cornell Medical Index Health Questionnaire) and another procedure that is somewhat more subtle (Minnesota Multiphasic Personality Inventory). As might be expected, considering this patient's long history of Wilson's disease, he had a number of somatic complaints relating to pains in the heart or chest area, sometimes getting out of breath just sitting still, suffering from frequent severe headaches and spells of dizziness, experiencing twitching of the face, head or shoulders, suffering from complete exhaustion, being worn out by every little effort and constantly being too tired and exhausted even to eat, and having great difficulty sleeping.

He also had a number of emotional complaints including getting mixed up completely when required to do things quickly, and always getting directions and orders wrong. W.H. reports that it is hard for him to make up his mind, that he feels a great deal of stress during examinations or questioning, that every little thing gets on his nerves and wears him out, that he must constantly try to control himself in order to avoid going to pieces, that people often annoy and irritate him, that he often gets into a violent rage, and that he often shakes and trembles.

These responses certainly suggest that this man has difficulties that, at least in his own self-evaluation, go well beyond those of the average person. Of course, many of these complaints may be quite valid considering the patient's medical history and condition.

Results on the MMPI also indicated that this man has a number of problems. In terms of a conventional clinical interpretation, the MMPI profile might be evaluated as if the responses of the subject were valid solely in a psychiatric rather than neurological context. Many of the patient's problems and complaints may be legitimate expressions of his medical illness even though they would have significance for emotional and personality interpretation if they were made by a psychiatric patient. Nevertheless, it is probable that this man does feel considerable emotional distress and, regardless of the etiology, it should be considered a relevant and significant part of the total clinical picture. We must again emphasize that a routine, psychiatric interpretation of the MMPI profile may not be justified in patients with conditions of brain disease in which the complaints are a valid part of the neurological disorder.

ALCOHOLISM

In 1962 Fitzhugh, Fitzhugh, and Reitan described neuropsychological profiles of chronic alcoholic subjects, using comparison groups of brain-damaged subjects and non-brain damaged control subjects. The results indicated that the alcoholic subjects generally tended to simulate the performances of the control group on Wechsler-Bellevue scores but approached the deficient scores of the brain-damaged subjects on measures in the Halstead-Reitan Battery. The alcoholics performed particularly poorly on the Category Test; their scores were worse than even the brain-damaged subjects. The disparity between the alcoholics' I.Q. values (which were relatively normal) and their neuropsychological results (particularly the Category Test) were among the most pronounced that have been observed in any group comparisons. (Later studies indicated that a similar disparity occurs among patients with Parkinson's disease.) In 1965 these results on chronic alcoholic subjects were replicated using new comparison groups (Fitzhugh, Fitzhugh, & Reitan, 1965).

Prior to the time of research describing the neuropsychological deficits of alcoholics, the general opinion was that neurological deficits occurred only in some cases of severe dementia such as found in patients with Korsakoff's syndrome and Wernicke's encephalopathy. These are closely related conditions resulting from alcohol abuse in which there is severe impairment of recent memory with relatively intact remote memory and confabulatory dementia. Wernicke's encephalopathy is a term more commonly used when dementia is accompanied by abnormal eye signs including horizontal and vertical nystagmus, bilateral weakness of the lateral rectus eye muscles, internal strabismus and diplopia (double vision) as well as ataxia, particularly involving the lower extremities and accompanied by a wide-based gait or more serious involvement that makes walking nearly impossible.

These conditions of severe deterioration due to chronic alcohol ingestion had been associated with an acute thiamine deficiency. These symptoms have also been identified in persons suffering from starvation, malnutrition, pernicious vomiting, and other conditions causing a nutritional deficiency. As a result of this finding, considerable credence has been placed in the idea that nutritional deficiency is the essential factor in producing deterioration in chronic alcoholics. However, more recent research suggests that a substantial degree of cerebral deterioration may occur without the presence of nutritional deficiency. In addition, some patients developed epileptic seizures after long-term periods of alcoholism. This condition, together with delirium tremens, frequently was provoked by withdrawal of alcohol from chronic alcoholics.

Finally, it has been recognized in the neurological literature that some patients show definite, slowly progressive dementia even though they do not manifest the Wernicke-Korsakoff syndrome. Researchers have suggested that such cases of alcoholic dementia might be related to the complementary effects of alcohol abuse and the development of early stages of Alzheimer's disease, repeated instances of head trauma (suffered by many alcoholic subjects), or the insidious effects of hepatic encephalopathy. In fact, the neurological literature still tends to implicate secondary factors (as contrasted with direct effects of alcohol abuse) as a basis for impairment of brain functions. More recent studies (Fox, Ramsey, et al., 1976), however, have shown definite brain changes in chronic alcoholics. Computed tomography of the brain frequently reveals diffuse cerebral cortical atrophy with relatively less enlargement of the lateral ventricles. EEG not uncommonly shows more slowing of background activity than would be expected for the age of the subject and the presence of transient theta and delta activity in the temporal leads on both sides of the brain (Newman, 1978).

Neuropsychological Correlates of Alcoholism

The neuropsychological characteristics of chronic alcoholism are not sufficiently specific to permit accurate identification of individual subjects, as can frequently be done in cases of brain tumor, stroke, head injury, etc. The neuropsychological findings of many other conditions overlap with alcoholic deterioration, thereby precluding identification of a specific pattern of test results for alcoholics. However, as noted above, chronic alcoholics frequently have relatively adequate I.Q. values, showing little in the way of significant impairment on the Wechsler Scales. On the Halstead-Reitan Battery, though, they often demonstrate considerable impairment. The four most sensitive tests in the Battery — Impairment Index, Category Test, Trail Making Test Part B and Localization component of the Tactual Performance Test — are frequently impaired. These neuropsychological deficits occur in many chronic alcoholic subjects and are especially prominent in older persons who have abused alcohol for many years. The reader should be aware, though, that in the clinical interview, these patients often appear quite intact. In fact, the alcoholic group in the Fitzhugh, Fitzhugh, and Reitan study (1962) had a mean Full-Scale I.Q. of approximately 110 although their mean Category score was 85 errors.

CASE #27

Name:	V.H.	Sex:	Male
Age:	59	Handedness:	Right
Education:	16	Occupation:	Salesman

Current Complaints and Pertinent History

This 59-year-old man was referred by an internist who had been asked to perform a complete physical examination of the patient. The internist had found no evidence of significant physical disease except for heavy drinking (and possible alcoholism) and an electrocardiogram that was reported as "borderline normal." The patient had been an outstanding salesman for many years for a large firm. V.H. felt that his difficulties had existed for about only three weeks, and stated that he had tendencies toward forgetfulness, sometimes mumbled to himself, and often repeated himself.

Although V.H. felt that these symptoms were of recent onset, he reported that others who worked with him had noticed these difficulties before he was aware of them himself. In fact, he brought a copy of a report of a physical examination with him which was essentially within normal limits although the problems he complained of at the time of this examination were identified as having been of concern several months earlier. These complaints included difficulty with memory, poor taste in communication with his colleagues and impaired business judgment. A review of these previous records indicated that the patient had been a heavy user of alcohol for many years, but, until the past 6 or 8 months, had apparently been able to function relatively well. The internist who referred the patient for neuropsychological evaluation was concerned that the patient may have experienced some deterioration of cerebral functioning, even though objective evidence of brain disease or damage was not present in the physical or neurological examination.

Neuropsychological Test Results

This man earned a Verbal I.Q. that was in the upper part of the Average range (106) and a Performance I.Q. that was in the upper part

HALSTEAD-REITAN NEUROPSYCHOLOGICAL TEST BATTERY

Patient ___V.H.___ Age __59__ Sex __M__ Education __16__ Handedness __R__

__x__ WECHSLER-BELLEVUE SCALE (FORM I)
___ WAIS

VIQ	106
PIQ	119
FIS IQ	110
VWS	47
PWS	45
Total WS	92
Information	13
Comprehension	12
Digit Span	7
Arithmetic	9
Similarities	6
Vocabulary	14
Picture Arrangement	7
Picture Completion	13
Block Design	9
Object Assembly	9
Digit Symbol	7

HALSTEAD'S NEUROPSYCHOLOGICAL TEST BATTERY

Category Test	115

Tactual Performance Test

Dominant hand:	11.7
Non-dominant hand:	9.1
Both hands:	5.2
Total Time	26.0
Memory	7
Localization	5

Seashore Rhythm Test

Number Correct	24	8

Speech-sounds Perception Test

Number of Errors		5

Finger Oscillation Test

Dominant hand:	40	40
Non-dominant hand:	40	

TRAIL MAKING TEST
Part A: __37__ seconds
Part B: __109__ seconds

Impairment Index __0.6__

STRENGTH OF GRIP
Dominant hand: __29.5__ kilograms
Non-dominant hand: __26.5__ kilograms

REITAN-KLØVE TACTILE FORM RECOGNITION TEST
Dominant hand: __18__ seconds; __0__ errors
Non-dominant hand: __12__ seconds; __0__ errors

REITAN-KLØVE SENSORY-PERCEPTUAL EXAM

Error Totals — No errors

RH___ LH___	Both:RH___ LH___	RH___ LH___
RH___ LF___	Both:RH___ LF___	RH___ LF___
LH___ RF___	Both:LH___ RF___	RF___ LH___
RE___ LE___	Both:RE___ LE___	RE___ LE___
RV___ LV___	Both:RV___ LV___	
___ ___	___ ___	RV___ LV___
___ ___	___ ___	

TACTILE FINGER RECOGNITION
R 1__ 2__ 3__ 4__ 5__   R _0_ / 20
L 1__ 2__ 3__ 4__ 5__   L _0_ / 20

FINGER-TIP NUMBER WRITING
R 1__ 2 1 3 2 4 2 5 1   R _6_ / 20
L 1__ 2__ 3__ 4 1 5__   L _1_ / 20

Miles ABC Test of Ocular Dominance
Right eye: _10_ Left eye: _0_

MINNESOTA MULTIPHASIC
PERSONALITY INVENTORY

?	60	Hs	54
L	66	D	56
F	50	Hy	60
K	57	PD	60
		MF	61
		Pa	50
		Pt	50
		Sc	44
		Ma	48

**REITAN-KLØVE
LATERAL-DOMINANCE EXAM**
Show me how you:

throw a ball	R
hammer a nail	R
cut with a knife	R
turn a door knob	R
use scissors	R
use an eraser	R
write your name	R

Record time used for spontaneous name-writing:

Preferred hand	20 seconds
Non-preferred hand	50 seconds

Show me how you:

kick a football	R
step on a bug	R

REITAN-INDIANA APHASIA SCREENING TEST

Form for Adults and Older Children

Name: V. H.   Age: 59

Copy SQUARE	Repeat TRIANGLE
Name SQUARE	Repeat MASSACHUSETTS
Spell SQUARE	Repeat METHODIST EPISCOPAL
Copy CROSS	Write SQUARE
Name CROSS	Read SEVEN
Spell CROSS	Repeat SEVEN
Copy TRIANGLE	Repeat/Explain HE SHOUTED THE WARNING.
Name TRIANGLE	Write HE SHOUTED THE WARNING.
Spell TRIANGLE	Compute 85 – 27 =
Name BABY	Compute 17 X 3 =
Write CLOCK	Name KEY
Name FORK	Demonstrate use of KEY
Read 7 SIX 2	Draw KEY Note absence of notch on lower line of stem near the handle; note absence of "nose".
Read MGW	Read PLACE LEFT HAND TO RIGHT EAR.
Reading I	Place LEFT HAND TO RIGHT EAR
Reading II	Place LEFT HAND TO LEFT ELBOW

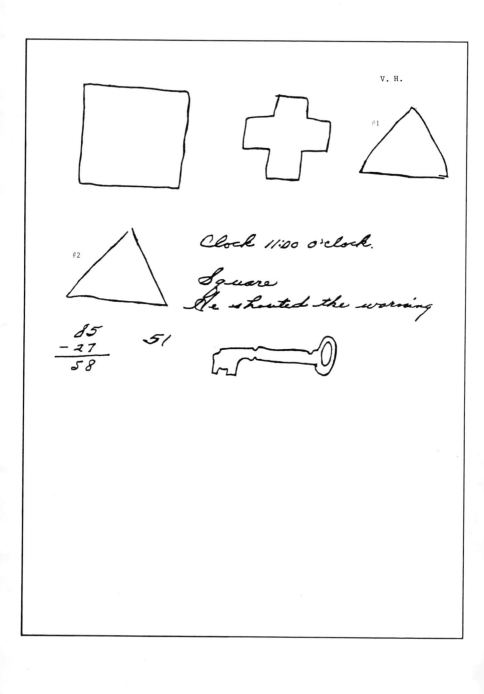

V. H.

#1

#2

Clock 11:00 o'clock.

Square

He shouted the warning

$$\begin{array}{r} 85 \\ -27 \\ \hline 58 \end{array}$$

51

of the High Average range (119). These values yielded a Full Scale I.Q. of 110, falling at the lower limit of the High Average range. The Verbal subtests showed a considerable degree of variability: the Vocabulary score was well above average and the Similarities result was well below average. It would seem likely, on the basis of the low Similarities score, that the patient had experienced some reduction of Verbal I.Q.

The distribution of scores on the Performance subtests was probably of more reliable significance with respect to impaired brain functions. The patient performed poorly on the Digit Symbol subtest, earning a score of 7. This variable is probably the most sensitive of all the Wechsler subtests to cerebral damage. In addition, the specifically poor score (7) on Picture Arrangement may well be a reflection of cerebral dysfunction. Nevertheless, on the basis of the Wechsler Scale, it would be difficult to draw any specific conclusion of cerebral damage. And, if one had done so using the Wechsler Scale alone, the full consequences of cerebral impairment would have been missed.

We see consistent evidence of cerebral impairment on the four most sensitive indicators of in the Halstead-Reitan Battery. This man earned a Halstead Impairment Index of 0.6 (about 60 percent of the tests in the brain-damaged range), but it must be recognized that higher (poorer) Impairment Indexes are expected in older persons (Reitan & Wolfson, in press). Thus, in a 59-year-old man one could not confidently postulate cerebral damage on the basis of this Impairment Index score alone.

V.H. performed very poorly on the Category Test (115 errors), especially when one considers his adequate I.Q. values. The patient's score (109 seconds) on Part B of the Trail Making Test was also in the brain-damaged range. On the Localization component of the Tactual Performance Test his score (5) was just within normal limits. These results all suggest that the patient probably has some deterioration of brain functions.

In assessing the good versus the poor performances, it is apparent that in the past this man had ability levels that were at least average or above. Some of these good scores are still reflected, especially in the Verbal subtests of the Wechsler Scale. For example, his Vocabulary score (14) was well above average. He also performed very well on the Speech-sounds Perception Test (5 errors). These values indicate that the patient has developed normally, has had good abilities in the past, and continues to have the ability to pay attention to specific stimulus material and maintain concentrated attention over time.

V.H. also showed normal results on tests of bilateral simultaneous stimulation and tactile finger recognition. These findings suggest that the patient does not have a focal destructive lesion of either cerebral hemisphere.

Despite these good scores, the patient did show evidence of pronounced deficits. His principal deficiencies occurred on the Category Test (115 errors) and the Tactual Performance Test — Total Time (26.0 minutes). As with patients who show definite evidence of dementia, many patients with alcoholic deterioration (but without dementia clinically) also have difficulty with tasks that require them to define a problem as well as solve it. Prior research results (Fitzhugh, Fitzhugh, & Reitan, 1960; Fitzhugh, Fitzhugh, & Reitan, 1965) demonstrated that chronic alcoholics performed extremely poorly on the Category Test despite having above average I.Q. values and frequently had a general pattern of results that characterized diffuse cerebral dysfunction.

Proceeding with evaluation of V.H.'s test results, one would next refer to the lateralizing and localizing indicators. This man showed positive findings implicating each cerebral hemisphere. The fact that this right-handed man was able to tap no faster with his dominant hand than his non-dominant hand suggests left cerebral dysfunction. He also had tactile-perceptual difficulties on the right side. For example, he performed slowly on the Tactile Form Recognition Test with his right hand and made significantly more errors in finger-tip number writing perception with his right hand than his left.

Findings supporting right cerebral dysfunction included a somewhat slow performance with the left hand on the Tactual Performance Test, a relatively low score on the Picture Arrangement subtest of the Wechsler Scale, and a clearly deficient performance in the attempt to copy the key. Deficits in copying the key were related particularly to a failure to represent corresponding notches on the stem near the handle and confusion about the spatial configuration of the "nose" of the key. Thus, in addition to results that pointed toward generalized involvement, the patient had positive findings to implicate each cerebral hemisphere.

The reader may wonder whether this patient might have bilateral focal lesions, but this possibility is essentially ruled out by some of the better scores, even though they may have fallen in the brain-damaged range (Trails B, Speech-sounds Perception Test and some of the scores on the Wechsler subtests). In the context of the overall results it would definitely appear that neither the left nor right indicators were sufficient to implicate a specific, focal lesion of either the left or right cerebral hemisphere. Findings of this kind are suggestive of generalized cerebral involvement and, under these conditions, the extremely poor score on the Category Test is characteristic of persons with chronic alcoholism.

The complaints of impaired memory and judgment are certainly related to basic impairment of reasoning processes and the ability to identify and organize relevant aspects of total situations. V.H.'s intact abilities, which largely represent skills acquired in the past, would be important to consider when developing an overall plan for his rehabilitation; but the best advice, certainly, would be for V.H. to discontinue use of alcohol. It is difficult to predict whether a person of this age, showing this degree of impairment, would demonstrate much spontaneous recovery, but on retesting even in 6-12 months a substantial degree of improvement sometimes occurs in persons who have totally discontinued use of alcohol.

DRUG ABUSE
(OTHER THAN ALCOHOL)

Initially the reader should be advised that Grant (1979) and Parsons and Farr (1981) have published excellent reviews of drug abuse that are considerably more detailed than this chapter will attempt to be. Grant's review is principally concerned with the clinical manifestations of drug abuse and stems from his extensive experience in both clinical and research work with these patients. Parsons and Farr have presented a comprehensive summary of neuropsychological findings in studies using the Halstead-Reitan Battery.

There is a wide degree of inter-individual variation in the history and pattern of drug abuse. Grant (1979) identifies stages of drug-taking as (1) initial or experimental; (2) occasional; (3) regular; (4) recreational; (5) functional; and (6) dependent.

Initial or *experimental* refers to the first instances of taking a drug and probably relates to wanting to imitate the behavior of others and desiring new experiences. *Occasional* users are persons who have learned the technique involved in taking a particular drug and have some familiarity with the biological and psychological effects. *Regular* use involves establishment of a routine, sometimes on a daily basis. With certain other drugs a regular pattern may be developed but there is a longer interval between the times the drug is taken. At this stage it is not unusual for a person to be a regular user of drugs (such as alcohol and marijuana), an occasional user of central stimulants, and an experimental user of heroin. *Recreational* use refers to instances in which drug use may occur in social situations or under special circumstances. Persons who use drugs to relieve anxiety or tension or hoping to improve their abilities are described as having a *functional* use of drugs. *Dependent* use or psychological dependence refers to situations in which the subject needs the drug in order to avoid tension and irritability, promote psychological coping capabilities or, in a biological sense, fulfill certain bodily needs that appear to have a physiological basis. In subjects who have a biological dependence, withdrawal phenomena usually occurs if the subject is deprived of the drug.

The use of several drugs simultaneously appears to be quite common (Grant, Adams, Carlin, Rennick, Judd, & Schooff, 1978). Grant (1979) states that the typical progression to multiple-drug use begins with alcohol between the ages of 10 and 12, marijuana between the ages of 12 and 15, and heroin between the ages of 16 and 18. Sometimes one drug succeeds another, but often the use of various drugs relates to the usage-stage described above or to the particular needs of the subject at any point in time.

Most investigators have classified drugs used non-medically in approximately similar categories. Grant (1979) separates his description of drug effects into the following classes: marijuana; sedatives and hypnotics, including barbiturates, which cause depression of central nervous system functions and include sodium amobarbital (Amytal), sodium pentobarbital (Nembutal), phenobarbital (Luminal), sodium secobarbital (Seconal), glutethimide (Doriden), methaqualone (Quaalude), ethchlorvynol (Placidyl), and certain other drugs; opiates, a group of naturally occurring and synthetic substances related to morphine which include morphine, heroin, hydromorphone, oxymorphone, levorphanol, methadone, meperidine, codeine and oxycodone; central stimulating agents, which have an excitatory effect on the central nervous system and include methylphenidate (Ritalin), methamphetamine (Desoxyn Methedrine), dextroamphetamine (Dexedrine), phenmetrazine (Preludin), phenteramine (Ionamin), and amphetamine (Benzedrine); hallucinogens, which cause marked changes in perception and thinking without corresponding changes in orientation, memory, or state of consciousness and include lysergic acid diethylamide (LSD), psilocybin, dimethyltryptamine (DMT), lysergic acid amine (which has morning glory seeds as the active ingredient), and bufotenine; mescaline (a hallucinogen derived from peyote cactus) and other drugs with a phenethylamine structure such as STP, DOM, MDA, TMA, and PMA; and phencyclidine (PCP), which may produce such serious effects as depersonalization, derealization, amnesia, and transient states with adverse reactions that are sufficiently severe to require hospitalization. In their review of neuropsychological research results Parsons and Farr (1981) classify drug groups as follows: marijuana, barbiturates, opiates, amphetamines, hallucinogens, and inhalants.

Few adverse biological effects of marijuana have been shown either as a result of immediate response or long-term consequences. Some reports from Egypt and India have suggested that dementia may develop in some chronic hashish users, but most neuropsychological studies have produced negative findings.

CNS depressants, including barbiturates and sedative hypnotics may lead to a state of physiological dependence, but the major short-term adverse effects appear to be overdose resulting in coma and possibly death. There have been reports of individual cases of hostility and combative behavior during acute intoxication. There might be some gradually developing impairment of intellectual functions which possibly is reversible after discontinuation of the drug. Case reports have appeared of persons with heavy daily usage which eventually resulted in memory impairment, a decrease in intelligence, and neurological signs, including ataxia.

The opiates, which occur naturally and can also be produced synthetically, are related to morphine, a substance derived from the sap of the poppy plant. Codeine is the most frequently used of these agents, although a large number of people in the United States have become dependent upon heroin. A danger of heroin use is overdose with fatal depression of respiratory centers in the brain. Although dependence develops more rapidly for opiates than central nervous system depressants and alcohol, the withdrawal symptoms may not be as severe. There is some evidence that long-term heroin use may be neurotoxic and cause psychological deficits, but the general conclusion is that heroin dependence, based upon need of the user, principally relates to changes in lifestyle rather than toxicological effects of the drug.

Among central stimulants, cocaine is a natural substance derived from leaves of the coca plant. Amphetamines are synthetic substances of which methamphetamine is probably the most commonly used illicitly. These substances exert excitatory effects on the central nervous system and have been reported to increase motivation and improve cognitive functioning when taken in moderate doses. They produce tolerance rather rapidly and increased doses are necessary to achieve a standard effect. Abstinence does not cause any signs or symptoms and it appears that no biological dependence develops with use. Excessive use, however, changes the initial reaction of heightened alertness to a variety of responses that may include narrowing of attention, fascination with "profound" thoughts, minute attention to details, increased suspiciousness, and sometimes frank delusions. Use of large amounts of amphetamines and habitual intoxication may change the individual's value system, interpersonal relationships, and emotional reactions and lead to social isolation. Currently available evidence (Grant & Mohns, 1975), however, does not implicate morphological changes in the brains of heavy abusers of amphetamines or cocaine.

Hallucinogens produce marked changes in perception which include increased intensity of sensations, illusions, and hallucinations. There does not seem to be a corresponding change in the individual's orientation, memory, or general alertness. Grant (1979) points out that the term "bad trip" was originally devised to describe adverse psychological experiences of hallucinogens. Questions concerning the occurrence of chromosomal damage as a result of LSD use has not been definitively answered. Chronic users, and some persons with even relatively minimal use, experience "flashbacks," which are recurrences of hallucinatory experiences previously experienced. Grant (1979) believes that hallucinogens do not cause mental illness but in certain individuals may be a precipitory factor.

Phencyclidine (PCP) may cause particularly severe adverse reactions and other agents, such as LSD, are being contaminated with PCP with increasing frequency. This drug produces disturbances in perception and thinking, general confusion, disorientation, and memory difficulties, and, sometimes, reactions that resemble delirium or schizophrenia. In some instances these reactions may last for several weeks and not clear entirely for several months. During adverse reactions to PCP the patient generally requires hospitalization, not only for pharmocological treatment of his/her symptoms but also to provide a protective environment and prevent self-harm.

A considerable number of neuropsychological studies of the effects of drug use and abuse have been done. Parsons and Farr (1981) have carefully summarized the results of 22 such studies that have reported findings related to possible neuropsychological changes with marijuana, barbiturates, opiates, amphetamines, hallucinogens, and inhalants and the general conclusion is that the results are indefinite. In this same review Parsons and Farr conclude that neuropsychological deficits may definitely result from alcohol abuse, but a number of problems have impeded drawing definite conclusions regarding other types of drug abuse. Interest was initially directed toward neuropsychological effects of alcoholism in 1962 (Fitzhugh, Fitzhugh, & Reitan) but drug abuse studies are of more recent origin. Also, the more definite evidence of neuropsychological impairment with alcoholism may possibly be due to the fact that the chronic alcoholics who have been studied had a much longer history of abuse than customarily found in the groups of drug abusers that have been evaluated. Educational and general intelligence levels appear to differ depending upon the drug used, and it is difficult to discern significant changes because of the correlation of these factors with neuropsychological measurements. Finally, as with alcoholics, it is not unusual to find associated pathology in drug abusers that may complicate the picture of assessing specific drug-related consequences.

Parsons and Farr (1981) have analyzed these 22 studies according to level of performance and patterns and relationships among the test results. Findings suggest that marijuana and hallucinogen users possibly seem to be less impaired than other drug users and that polydrug abusers seem to show the most evidence of some degree of generalized neuropsychological impairment. These researchers conclude that the available evidence does not clearly document the presence of generalized neuropsychological impairment as a result of protracted drug usage.

Another approach to this question might be to do serial investigations using drug abusers as their own controls after they have stopped using drugs. At least three such studies have been done (Adams, Rennick, Schooff, & Keegan, 1975; Grant & Judd, 1976; and Grant, Adams, Carlin, Rennick, Judd, Schooff & Reed, 1978). The results of these studies are equivocal with respect to a possible improvement gradient and the question of impairment, as inferred by eventual improvement, is still essentially unanswered.

In conclusion, I (RMR) should like to comment on my own experience in evaluating Halstead-Reitan protocols of polydrug abusers as compared with equated controls (who were medically and surgically ill but not drug abusers) and a group of persons with evidence of cerebral damage but not drug abusers. Statistical analysis of the results for these four groups (Grant, Mohns, Miller, & Reitan, 1976) showed that the control group tended to do best on neuropsychological tests, the polydrug abusers had an intermediate position, and the persons with definite evidence of cerebral disease or damage performed worst. However, Igor Grant and I were interested in more than a statistical analysis of the data and we each "blindly" evaluated the entire HRNB protocol for each of the subjects, without knowledge of the group to which any of the subjects belonged. We classified each subject as having evidence of impaired brain function or showing no such indication, according to our clinical judgment. We achieved approximately comparable results in our classifications. Nearly all of the subjects who actually had brain damage were classified in the category with impaired brain functions and nearly all of the control subjects were classified as having normal brain functions. However, we each classified about half of the polydrug abusers as having brain damage and half as having normal brain functions. When we compared our reliability in terms of the patients who fell in each classification there was little variation. Although these results are based upon an N of two (Grant and Reitan), it appears that some polydrug abusers have impaired brain functions and others do not. The next step, obviously, would be to identify the factors responsible for this dichotomous classification.

XIV
AGING EFFECTS

Biological changes of the brain associated with aging have been identified previously (Bondareff, 1959; Magladery, 1959), but it has been difficult to relate anatomical, physiological, and pharmacological changes specifically to behavioral deficits. Welford and Birren (1965) have summarized the role of the brain and nervous system in determining the types of psychological changes seen in aging. Much of this evidence strongly suggests that anatomical and physiological changes in the brain may be responsible for at least many of the psychological deficits shown by the aged.

In this context it should also be noted that there have been many studies relating to morphological and physiological changes in other organs and systems of the body and gradually progressive impairment has been associated with the aging process (Shock, 1962). Investigation of morphological and functional changes of the brain has represented an active area of study, and increasingly detailed documentation continues to be published (Cervos-Navarro, J., & Sarkander, H.I., 1983; Samuel, D., Algeri, S., Gershon, S., Grimm, V.E., & Toffano, G., 1983). The principal types of morphological changes in normal aging — neuronal loss, senile plaques, degenerative changes in the blood vessels, and neurofibrillary tangles — are sometimes difficult to differentiate from the neuropathological changes occurring in conditions such as Alzheimer's disease and the clinical manifestations of cerebral vascular disease. Such pathological changes have been related to dementia (Selkoe, 1978) and would certainly lay a basis for deterioration of higher-level neuropsychological functions dependent upon the integrity of the cerebral cortex. There probably is no possibility of perfectly differentiating the kinds of pathological changes that occur with aging from brain diseases of a vascular or degenerative nature, but in most cases of normal aging one would presume that the neuropathological changes are diffusely represented rather than to involve only focal areas of the brain.

Neuropsychological Correlates of Aging

Aging effects in both normal and brain-damaged subjects have been studied for many years using the Halstead-Reitan Neuropsychological Battery and the results of many specific research studies have been summarized (Reitan, 1967b; Reitan & Wolfson, in press). Rather than listing the details of these research studies, the findings concerning aging effects can be summarized by stating a number of principles that have been established: (1) The Impairment Index declines more rapidly than Wechsler I.Q. values in both normals and brain-damaged subjects (Reitan, 1956a); (2) The Performance subtest scaled scores decline more rapidly than Verbal subtest scaled scores in both normal and brain-damaged subjects (Reitan, 1956a); (3) Measures of reasoning, concept formation, basic problem-solving skills, and ability to solve new or unique types of problems decline more rapidly than tests of stored information, in both normal and brain-damaged subjects (Fitzhugh, Fitzhugh, & Reitan, 1964; Reed & Reitan, 1963a); (4) The Impairment Index is generally within the normal range until about the age of 45 years. At this time a progressive trend toward greater impairment is generally seen with advancing age (Reitan, 1955d; Meyerink, 1982); (5) The tests in the Halstead-Reitan Battery that are most sensitive to cerebral damage are also the tests most sensitive to advancing age among normal subjects (Reed & Reitan, 1963b); (6) The Brain-Age Quotient (developed by Reitan in 1973) reflects the individual's ability on brain-sensitive tests with relation to chronological age. It employs a normalized scale with a mean of 100 and standard deviation of 15. (Therefore, it is an I.Q. type of distribution with better scores falling above 100 and poorer scores falling below 100). The Brain-Age Quotient appears to be useful in assessing neuropsychological competence in accordance with the chronological age of the individual (Reitan & Wolfson, in press); (7) Both physiological and educational (brain-retraining) procedures appear to be of value in retarding neuropsychological deterioration among older persons (Reitan & Wolfson, in press); (8) The degree of neuropsychological deficit for normal subjects at any given age is quite variable, but definite evidence of neuropsychological impairment is routinely evident in most cases long before it is seen either in clinical assessment or routine psychological testing (Reitan & Wolfson, in press).

CASE #28

Name:	V.C.	Sex:	Male
Age:	67	Handedness:	Right
Education:	20 +	Occupation:	Physician

Current Complaints and Pertinent History

This 67-year-old man was a physician who practiced as a general surgeon. At the insistence of family members he had consulted a neurological surgeon to evaluate the possible deterioration of his abilities. The subject himself, however, told us that he felt that he had no particular difficulties. He said that others believed that he had a "memory" problem and in fairness he would not deny this contention, but he believed that he had not really changed and did not have any significant difficulties. He pointed out that he was able to continue his work as a general surgeon quite successfully. A careful and detailed neurological evaluation had been done before the referral for neuro-psychological testing. Computed tomography had shown no abnormalities and the remainder of the neurological examination was essentially negative. In this case, however, the neurological surgeon who referred the patient was familiar with neuropsychological testing and realized that additional valuable information might be gained through such an examination.

Neuropsychological Test Results

The test results indicate that this patient's I.Q. values were well above average but he performed worse than most brain-damaged subjects on a number of other tests. There was no doubt of the general nature of his impairment: tests of immediate adaptive abilities, (relatively independent of past experience) were performed more poorly than measures dependent upon stored information. In addition, the patient showed particular impairment in the areas of abstraction, reasoning, and logical analysis as well as striking deficits in performance of complex (as differentiated from primary) motor performances. He also had difficulty dealing with even very simple aspects of visual-spatial relationships.

V.C. earned a Verbal I.Q. (118) that fell in the upper part of the

HALSTEAD-REITAN NEUROPSYCHOLOGICAL TEST BATTERY

Patient _____V.C._____ Age __67__ Sex __M__ Education __M.D.__ Handedness __R__

___WECHSLER-BELLEVUE SCALE (FORM I)
_x_ WAIS

VIQ	118
PIQ	115
FIS IQ	115
VWS	57
PWS	36
Total WS	93
Information	8
Comprehension	15
Digit Span	11
Arithmetic	7
Similarities	16
Vocabulary	15
Picture Arrangement	9
Picture Completion	8
Block Design	8
Object Assembly	5
Digit Symbol	6

HALSTEAD'S NEUROPSYCHOLOGICAL TEST BATTERY

Category Test ___111___

Tactual Performance Test

Dominant hand:	15.0 (3 blocks)
Non-dominant hand:	15.0 (5 blocks)
Both hands:	15.5

Total Time __45.5 +__
Memory __2__
Localization __0__

Seashore Rhythm Test
Number Correct __26__   5

Speech-sounds Perception Test
Number of Errors   5

Finger Oscillation Test
Dominant hand: __53__   53
Non-dominant hand: __49__

TRAIL MAKING TEST
Part A: __41__ seconds
Part B: __178__ seconds

Impairment Index __0.6__

STRENGTH OF GRIP
Dominant hand: __11.25__ kilograms
Non-dominant hand: __13.5__ kilograms

REITAN-KLØVE TACTILE FORM RECOGNITION TEST
Dominant hand: __17__ seconds; __0__ errors
Non-dominant hand: __21__ seconds; __2__ errors

REITAN-KLØVE SENSORY-PERCEPTUAL EXAM

Error Totals — No errors

RH___ LH___	Both:RH___ LH___	RH___ LH___	
RH___ LF___	Both:RH___ LF___	RH___ LF___	
LH___ RF___	Both:LH___ RF___	RF___ LH___	
RE___ LE___	Both:RE___ LE___	RE___ LE___	
RV___ LV___	Both:RV___ LV___		
		RV___ LV___	

TACTILE FINGER RECOGNITION
R 1__ 2__ 3 1 4__ 5 2   R _3_ / 20
L 1__ 2__ 3 2 4__ 5 1   L _3_ / 20

FINGER-TIP NUMBER WRITING
R 1 1 2__ 3 1 4__ 5__   R _2_ / 20
L 1 2 2 1 3 1 4__ 5__   L _4_ / 20

Miles ABC Test of Ocular Dominance
Right eye: __10__ Left eye: __0__

MINNESOTA MULTIPHASIC PERSONALITY INVENTORY

?	50	Hs	47
L	56	D	60
F	53	Hy	53
K	55	PD	62
		MF	63
		Pa	59
		Pt	50
		Sc	46
		Ma	55

REITAN-KLØVE LATERAL-DOMINANCE EXAM

Show me how you:
throw a ball	R
hammer a nail	R
cut with a knife	R
turn a door knob	R
use scissors	R
use an eraser	R
write your name	R

Record time used for spontaneous name-writing:
Preferred hand	9 seconds
Non-preferred hand	17 seconds

Show me how you:
kick a football	R
step on a bug	R

REITAN-INDIANA APHASIA SCREENING TEST

Form for Adults and Older Children

Name: V. C.   Age: 67

Copy SQUARE Note the compensation required to close the figure.	Repeat TRIANGLE
Name SQUARE	Repeat MASSACHUSETTS
Spell SQUARE	Repeat METHODIST EPISCOPAL
Copy CROSS Note the disparities of the extremities.	Write SQUARE
Name CROSS	Read SEVEN
Spell CROSS	Repeat SEVEN
Copy TRIANGLE	Repeat/Explain HE SHOUTED THE WARNING. Repeated correctly. Confusion in writing the sentence.
Name TRIANGLE	Write HE SHOUTED THE WARNING.
Spell TRIANGLE	Compute 85 – 27 =
Name BABY	Compute 17 X 3 =
Write CLOCK	Name KEY
Name FORK	Demonstrate use of KEY
Read 7 SIX 2	Draw KEY Observe the general inadequacy of the drawing and the absence of the "nose".
Read MGW	Read PLACE LEFT HAND TO RIGHT EAR.
Reading I	Place LEFT HAND TO RIGHT EAR
Reading II	Place LEFT HAND TO LEFT ELBOW

#2

#1

Clock Square

He shot at the morning

$$85 - 27 = 58$$

51

High Average range (exceeding 89 percent of his age peers) and a Performance I.Q. (115) that was also in the High Average range (exceeding 84 percent). Inspection of the distribution of the subtest scores is particularly interesting. The good scores on Similarities (16) and Vocabulary (15) may well represent the premorbid intelligence levels of this subject. The Arithmetic subtest score (7) probably indicates some deterioration of brain functions, but the Information score (8), which was equivalently low, may simply indicate that this man does not stay in close touch with verbal information of specific content.

The Performance subtest scores were consistently lower than the better Verbal subtest scores, suggesting that the patient had some decline of his cognitive abilities. This pattern is quite characteristic of older persons who have experienced some degree of deterioration.

The patient showed striking deficits in brain-sensitive tests. He earned a Halstead Impairment Index of 0.6 (about 60% of the tests had scores in the brain-damaged range), but it should be noted that the tests on which he performed satisfactorily (Finger Tapping, Speech-sounds Perception, and Seashore Rhythm) are not particularly demanding of higher-level aspects of brain functions. He had great difficulties when higher-level tests were used. He performed poorly on the Category Test (111), coming close to making twice as many errors as the average person with cerebral damage. He also had problems on Part B of the Trail Making Test (178 seconds). These results suggest that this man's ability to observe simple stimulus material and draw reasonable conclusions is seriously impaired. In addition, he has trouble attending to several aspects of a situation at one time, organizing the material, and being able to work his way through to an efficient solution.

He performed poorly on the Tactual Performance Test, working for a total of 45 minutes on the three trials and placing a total of only 18 blocks. He made very little progress on the first trial with his right hand, was able to show a little improvement on the second trial, and finally completed the task on the third trial. However, the performance on the third trial alone required more time than the total of three trials for the average person with a normal brain. It is quite apparent that there is a remarkable disparity between the I.Q. values of this man and his basic adaptive abilities. His difficulty with psychomotor problem-solving performances did not appear to be due to a primary motor deficiency: his finger tapping speed was adequate in both hands. Thus, the conclusion to be drawn from the poor performance on the Tactual Performance Test was that this man had difficulty adapting to unique or novel types of problem-solving situations (having to do the task blind-folded), and when complex problem-solving elements were added to motor performances demands, this patient demonstrated a diminution in adequacy of performance.

It must be noted that this man showed specific difficulties in dealing with simple spatial configurations. In his first attempt to draw a square the lines were not strictly parallel and the subject was asked to do the task again. In this instance he drew the second line too long and found that it was necessary to compensate by drawing the third and fourth lines equivalently long and returning to complete the first line. His drawing of a cross was probably more specifically pathological. He did not leave as much room away from the margin of the paper as he should have; this observation, in its own right, indicates his problems in dealing with spatial relationships. The obvious disparity of the extremities (including the upper and lower extremities but particularly demonstrated in the lateral extremities) clearly deviates beyond normal limits. Although his triangle could be considered within normal limits, he performed poorly in drawing the key. Even though his drawing was rather primitive, failure to achieve symmetry of the teeth of the key and not being able to integrate the "nose" suggest significant impairment.

The patient did not have corresponding aphasic difficulties, a finding sometimes seen in older people. Difficulty with simple spatial relationships (as contrasted with simple verbal responses) may fall into the classification of immediate adaptive ability deficits rather than reten-tion of stored information. Although he repeated the sentence HE SHOUTED THE WARNING correctly, when he wrote the sentence he became a little confused and wrote HE SHOT AT THE WARNING.

We should note that the best performances of this man (excluding certain of the Verbal subtests of the Wechsler Scale) were the Speech-sounds Perception Test (5) and the Seashore Rhythm Test (26). On these measures the patient demonstrated that he still has the capa-bility to pay attention to specific stimulus material when it is well-defined and when he knows exactly the nature of the task.

The patient performed poorly on each of the four most sensitive measures in the Halstead-Reitan Battery, indicating that generalized impairment of adaptive abilities was quite pronounced. The patient reported that others had observed impairment of his memory abilities. Memory almost certainly was involved, perhaps directly, but also as a consequence of generalized impairment and probably particularly because of his difficulty in abstraction and reasoning (being able to relate specific elements in a reasonable and logical way to their total context).

Mild indications of left cerebral function were present: some verbal confusion on the Aphasia Screening Test and a reduction of grip strength with the right upper extremity (11.25 kg) compared with the left (13.5 kg). Indications of right cerebral dysfunction were derived specifically from the deficits in drawing the square, cross, and key and some specific difficulty in tactile form recognition with the left hand compared with the right. The patient also had two errors more with the left hand than the right in finger-tip number writing perception, but this finding could have been due to chance variation.

Results on the Minnesota Multiphasic Personality Inventory were essentially within normal limits. On the Cornell Medical Index Health Questionnaire the patient admitted to having practically no problems or difficulties. Although negative results on these procedures provide no absolute assurance of absence of emotional problems, it would not seem (judging from these instruments) that the problems of this man were emotionally based.

The lateralizing findings were not sufficiently strong to implicate a focal lesion of either cerebral hemisphere, but are of the type consistent with significant generalized involvement. Despite the extremely poor scores on certain measures, failure to find a pattern of results on the Wechsler Scale to support a focal lesion also argues for generalized involvement.

Finally, the relatively good scores on the Speech-sounds Perception Test and the Seashore Rhythm Test provide an even more convincing argument that the condition of this man's brain is relatively stable and rapid deterioration of brain functions or severe serious focal involvement (such as occurs with intrinsic tumors or strokes) is probably not part of the picture.

This man demonstrates a more striking degree of deterioration than is customarily seen in persons of his age, but the important point is that neuropsychological examination seems to be the only method that demonstrates such deficits. It may be difficult for the inexperienced psychologist to realize that there can be such striking disparities among test scores, with many scores falling toward the upper part of the reference distribution and other scores being so poorly done that they are worse than those of even the average brain-damaged person. We may note, however, that though this case goes beyond the usual expression of this type, the findings are not at all uncommon among older people.

Although it might be claimed that this man should have had a specific neurological diagnosis because of the evidence of deterioration of cerebral functions, he did have a thorough and exhaustive neurological evaluation that resulted in negative findings. In terms of conventional criteria, then, this man represents an instance of normal aging rather than of neurological disease. Although it is possible to contend that (1) neurological disease and normal aging are separate entities; and (2) neuropsychological deterioration is always a result of neurological disease, these contentions become impractical in application. In many cases there seems to be no way to differentiate presumed neuronal disease from the effects of aging and, in fact, neuropathological changes overlap in these conditions both with respect to primary neuronal degenerative disease as well as cerebral vascular disease. Neuropsychological evaluation, which appears to be more sensitive than conventional neurological diagnostic methods, is clearly needed in the area of clinical gerontology.

The practical implications of this comment are supported by the results on this particular subject. As a functioning general surgeon he was hardly a candidate for a diagnosis of Alzheimer's disease and, in fact, no positive neurological diagnosis of any kind was supported by the neurological examination and computed tomography. If these medical criteria are used to judge that the patient had no neuropsychological impairment (as contrasted with use of the Halstead-Reitan Battery), the resulting conclusion presumably would be to permit the subject to continue to impose his surgical skills on his patients. No one has evaluated gross impairment of ability to copy simple spatial configurations and extremely poor performances on the Tactual Performance Test on the expression of surgical abilities, but it is likely that they are relevant. Clearly, from the neuropsychological findings, this man is ill-equipped in terms of higher-level brain functions to continue his practice. Since neuropsychological examination is uniquely useful in cases of this kind, and since behavior is the end-result manifestation of performances in everyday life, one wonders why neuropsychological examination is not used more frequently.

XV
EPILEPSY

Epilepsy is not a disease, but a symptom of disordered brain functions associated with many kinds of underlying conditions. As a general definition, epilepsy can be described as a condition in which periodic and extreme discharge of electrical activity from neurons in the brain result in symptoms that include loss of consciousness, involuntary movements, abnormal sensory phenomena, and an increase of autonomic activity. In addition, the epileptic patient may have any of a variety of perceptions before the seizure (prodromal symptoms and/or aura) as well as postictal (after the episode) manifestations, including sleepiness, confusion, partial disorientation, headaches, paralyses, sensory losses, etc. In many patients, no evidence of neuronal damage or pathology is discernible between seizures; in others, though, the etiology can be identified, and may be extremely variable. In this book, the patients with epilepsy had varied diagnoses: intrinsic tumor, extrinsic tumor, arteriovenous malformation, penetrating head injury, closed head injury, and meningo-vascular scar. Some conditions cause epilepsy more frequently than others; however, no cause (or even probable cause) can be determined in about half of the cases. Treatment of epilepsy with antiepileptic drugs is quite effective: over 85 percent of the persons taking medication have their seizures either controlled or significantly reduced.

A number of different types of epilepsy have been identified, with the classifications based on clinical manifestations. Diagnosis may be established by clinical observation of the seizures. Electroencephalographic tracings aid in diagnosis, but it must be remembered that EEG records electrical activity principally from the superficial layers of the brain and the tracing is done through layers of tissue, including the scalp and skull. Abnormal electrical activity can almost invariably be documented when the seizure is in progress, but some patients who have epilepsy will show normal EEGs between seizures. In many cases, though, the tracing will be abnormal (although often different) at any time the EEG is taken.

The onset of epilepsy usually occurs relatively early in life with about 90 percent of epileptic patients having histories of seizures beginning in childhood. Neonatal seizures (birth to 3 months) are usually due to injuries sustained at birth, hypoxia, or hypoglycemia. Infantile epilepsy (3 months to 9 months) is more likely to be due to meningitis or encephalitis. Epilepsy beginning from 9 months to 3 years may also be due to such infections, and children in this age group frequently have febrile convulsions (convulsions associated with a fever during the course of an infectious illness). Previously, it was generally thought that febrile convulsions were merely the immature brain's response to a sudden elevation in temperature. Although the prognosis is usually excellent, recent detailed follow-up studies of these children show that many of them later have other indications of brain dysfunction. The estimate has been made that 93 percent of persons who will eventually develop epilepsy have had seizures by their young adult years. Thus, the etiology of a first seizure in adults is a cause for concern. Many different factors may be responsible, but neurologists and neurosurgeons feel that a detailed evaluation should be done to rule out a developing brain tumor.

Neuropsychology and Epilepsy

Many psychological studies of both children and adults with epilepsy have been published. In most instances, reports were based on results of only a single psychological test. It has been only during more recent years that meaningful batteries of psychological tests have been used and an understanding of epilepsy within the context of brain-behavior relationships has begun to emerge. Most studies in the literature have concentrated on intelligence tests (such as the Stanford-Binet or the Wechsler Scales). Other tests have been used, including the Mill Hill Vocabulary Test, the Raven Progressive Matrices Test, the Porteus Maze Test, the McGill Picture Anomalies Test, the Differential Language

Facility Test, the Bender Visual Gestalt Test, the Graham-Kendall Memory-for-Designs Test, the Rorschach Test, the Szondi Test, the Jung Association Test and Koch's Tree Drawing Test. A number of early studies failed to identify the particular kind of epilepsy or underlying brain disorders represented in the group. Recent research has indicated that the underlying condition, when it can be discerned, may be a fundamental factor in determining the neuropsychological deficits.

There is no doubt that the neuropsychological study of epilepsy is a complex and difficult area. However, unless information is sought and organized in research efforts concerning such factors as etiology, site of the discharge, electrophysiological abnormalities, and type of seizure, little can be learned about the differential nature of epileptic disorders. The many predisposing conditions, such as trauma, neoplasm, vascular lesions, hereditofamilial disorders, degenerative diseases, infectious and inflammatory damage, toxic factors, etc. must also be considered. It has become apparent that psychological study of epilepsy must proceed within the general framework of brain-behavior relationships and the current body of knowledge of clinical neuropsychology, as contrasted with the effect of epilepsy on a single psychological test.

Many studies have focused on intelligence levels of epileptic patients and the results generally indicate some impairment in this group of persons. Studies of patients in whom the cause of epilepsy has been diagnosed (as contrasted with patients having idiopathic epilepsy) show that greater deficits occur in persons having diagnosed brain damage. This is not particularly surprising, since such a group would include persons with intrinsic tumors, significant traumatic brain injuries, and other instances of definite cerebral tissue damage. The group with idiopathic epilepsy, though possibly showing significant impairment, also includes persons who have no evidence of morphological brain changes.

A number of studies have evaluated age at onset as an independent variable concerning degree of neuropsychological deficit (Klöve & Matthews, 1969; Dikmen, Matthews, & Harley, 1975). These studies have generally shown that greater neuropsychological impairment is related to longer duration and earlier age at onset. There is a distinct overlap in groups with early and late onset, however, and there is no doubt that many other factors, including severity of cerebral damage, are also contributory.

Neuropsychological findings have also been related to the type of seizure. Many different seizure types have been identified on the basis of clinical manifestations, including (1) generalized convulsive seizures of the tonic-clonic (grand mal) type; (2) generalized convulsive seizures that have a focal onset and spread to involve the entire nervous system; (3) generalized seizures in which clonic movements appear as repetitive generalized jerks of the entire body; (4) massive myoclonic spasms that occur in infants; (5) typical absence or petit mal epilepsy involving a brief loss of consciousness lasting from 5 to 15 seconds during which time the patient ceases activities and has a vacant expression; (6) partial motor seizures that involve a limited area of the body and do not spread; (7) partial motor seizures that begin at a particular point in the body and spread to involve larger areas (Jacksonian epilepsy); (8) partial somatosensory seizures which involve abnormal sensation and, when they spread from their point of origin, are called sensory Jacksonian seizures; (9) partial complex seizures (earlier referred to as psychomotor seizures or temporal lobe seizures); and (10) seizures induced by highly specific stimuli or activities such as listening to music, reading, observing flickering lights, or attempting to do arithmetical problems. Not all of these seizure types have been studied in neuropsychological detail. However, Matthews and Kløve (1967) demonstrated that generalized tonic-clonic seizures were generally associated with a greater degree of neuropsychological deficit than complex partial epilepsy.

Some researchers studying children with generalized absence attacks (petit mal), using only measures of general intelligence, have not found any significant differences between these children and comparison groups. However, Reitan (unpublished data) has studied a large series of individual cases of children with absence epilepsy and nearly every child showed significant neuropsychological deviation from expected findings. It is true that these children do not consistently show striking impairment in level of performance, but their overall pattern of findings on the Halstead-Reitan Battery, using the several levels of inference that have been incorporated into its design, is rarely within the normal range. There is no doubt that neuropsychological evaluation of these children can play a significant role in identifying their particular problems as well as guiding their neuropsychological remediation. Thus, it is important that the profession not be misled into believing that there are no neuropsychological abnormalities associated with generalized absence epilepsy.

Confounding of variables among epileptic patients often tends to conceal relationships. It is not uncommon, for example, to hear that persons with epilepsy are entirely normal except for the periods in which they experience seizures and that frequency of seizures has no relationship to degree of impairment. Dikmen and Matthews (1977) studied patients with generalized tonic-clonic epilepsy and compared frequency of seizures to neuropsychological deficit. These researchers demonstrated a systematic decrease in neuropsychological functioning with increasing seizure frequencies. Reitan has done serial testings over a period of several years on individuals in whom seizure control was not adequately achieved. In every case, these persons demonstrated some progression of neuropsychological deficit. Dodrill and Troupin (1976) compared identical twins, one of whom had experienced a greater frequency of seizures than the other. Performances on a number of neuropsychological tests were poorer for the patient with the greater number of seizures. However, Dodrill (1975) believes that such a trend occurs particularly in patients with generalized tonic-clonic seizures and much less frequently in patients with partial seizures.

Clinical evidence suggests that it is very important to achieve seizure control as rapidly and effectively as possible. Since failure to take antiepileptic medication is a factor in this regard, some patients (including adults) may require close supervision.

A number of studies have demonstrated relationships between EEG changes and neuropsychological test results. In general, patients show interruption of their performances or diminished capability at the time that abnormal discharges occur. Studies of patients who show EEG abnormalities during the interictal period have also had positive results. Patients in whom the EEG shows generalized discharges tend to show the greatest neuropsychological deficits; those who have only focal discharges fall at an intermediate level, and epileptics who have no signs of abnormal discharges show the least impairment. When these patients were studied with relation to the frequency of discharges per unit of time, those with more frequent discharges demonstrated greater impairment. It appears that the degree of neuropsychological deficit is associated with both the type and rate of epileptic discharges in the brain. Additional research has been done regarding the rhythm frequency of EEG tracings and most of these studies have examined variations of alpha activity. Dodrill and Wilkus (1976) found relatively little change in the normal alpha frequency range, but adequacy of neuropsychological performance was clearly decreased when rhythm frequency dropped below 8.0 Hz.

Kløve (1959) studied groups of patients who had cerebral damage with either no EEG abnormality, generalized abnormalities, abnormalities over the right cerebral hemisphere, or abnormalities over the left cerebral hemisphere. He reported results using the Wechsler-Bellevue Scale. The group with left cerebral EEG abnormalities consistently had lower Verbal than Performance subtest scores. Conversely, the group with right cerebral EEG abnormalities was consistently lower on the Performance than their own Verbal subtest scores. The group with generalized EEG abnormalities showed a degree of deficit but scarcely any difference in the level of their performances on the Verbal and Performance subtests. All groups used in the study had evidence of cerebral disease or damage. The group without EEG abnormalities consistently performed better on both Verbal and Performance subtests, although they showed no differential impairment. It must be noted, however, that types of lesions were not controlled in this study and it is possible that the lateralizing effects were due as much, if not more, to the underlying types of lesions than to the differential EEG results.

It has long been known that antiepileptic drugs may cause toxic effects, such as impairment of alertness, quickness, and ability to perform complex psychological tasks. Monitoring the amount of antiepileptic drug (serum levels) is important in clinical management of epileptic patients. Individuals who have demonstrated significant neuropsychological deficits when over-medicated showed significant clinical improvement in alertness and performed better on neuropsychological tests when properly medicated and maintaining appropriate serum levels. Repeated examinations, of course, constitute a difficult problem in terms of research design because of positive practice-effect caused by familiarity and experience with the tests. In research studies this problem can sometimes be handled (at least to some extent) by using a counterbalanced order of test administration.

Using this technique, a number of investigators have evaluated the neuropsychological effects of diphenylhydantoin (Dilantin), phenobarbital, and carbamazipine (Tegretol). Dilantin, introduced in 1938, is an effective antiepileptic drug having relatively few clinical side effects. It is particularly useful in controlling generalized seizures and is sometimes used to treat partial complex seizures. It has little effectiveness in absence epilepsy. Prior to the introduction of diphenylhydantoin, phenobarbital and the bromides were the only drugs available for treatment of epilepsy. Phenobarbital is still widely used, particularly in combination with diphenylhydantoin. It has a low incidence of toxic effects in the therapeutic dose range, is relatively inexpensive, and is often effective in all types of epilepsy. Carbamazepine (Tegretol) is generally considered to be an excellent antiepileptic drug and is effective in controlling generalized convulsive seizures as well as partial seizures of all types. Some side effects may occur but clinical observation suggests that it does not reduce alertness as much as some other medications.

There are a number of other drugs being used to control specific forms of epilesy or obtain more adequate control in the individual case. Dodrill (1975) and his collaborators (Dodrill & Troupin, 1977; Wilkus, Dodrill & Troupin, 1978) have studied these agents using an extensive battery of psychological tests, mainly representing the Halstead-Reitan Battery. Other investigators, including Hutt, Jackson, Belsham, and Higgins (1968) and Matthews and Harley (1975), have also worked on this problem. It has been possible to measure some degree of decrement resulting from therapeutic doses of diphenylhydantoin and phenobarbital. Similar studies of carbamazepine have shown perhaps a lesser impairment and some reports have also suggested that patients have improved emotionally. However, these studies have not shown dramatic effects and, neuropsychological deficits are limited when antiepileptic serum levels are within the therapeutic range and there are no clinical signs of toxicity.

Occasionally over the years there have been reports and descriptions of the typical epileptic personality. The characteristics of this personality configuration include lack of control, impulsivity, occasional rage responses, and similar behaviors. Folsom (1953) did a careful review of the neurological, neurosurgical, psychiatric, and psychological literature and concluded that there was no satisfactory evidence of either a personality type or any specific pattern of cognitive deficit. Obviously, the pattern of cognitive deficit would vary according to the location of the underlying lesion or the epileptic focus.

More recent studies have attempted to identify personality patterns associated with particular types of seizures. Complex partial seizures (temporal lobe or psychomotor epilepsy) arising from the temporal area have been studied in particular. Flor-Henry (1976) has studied the relationship of temporal lobe seizure disorders to psychosis in psychiatric patients who have epilepsy. Flor-Henry (1974) believes that schizophrenia is related to dominant (left) involvement of the temporal lobe and limbic system whereas manic-depressive psychosis is associated with non-dominant (right) involvement in the same area.

Bear and Fedio (1977) and Gur (1978) have also attempted to extend the differential functions of the left and right cerebral hemispheres into psychiatric symptomatology. Most of the evidence available at the present time does not support such differentiations (Rodin, Katz, & Lennox, 1976). Serafetinides (1965) found some evidence to support the hypothesis that an increase in aggressive behavior occurred in patients with temporal lobe epileptic foci but other investigators have found no increase in psychiatric disturbances in patients with complex partial epilepsy (Rodin, 1973; Stevens, 1966; Stevens, Milstein & Goldstein, 1972).

Finally, psychological testing may make an important contribution in the area of occupational and social adjustment of epileptic patients. There is no doubt that the majority of patients with epilepsy have problems in this respect. One instrument, the Washington Psychosocial Seizure Inventory, has recently been developed by Dodrill and his colleagues (Dodrill, Batzel, Queisser, & Temkin, 1980) to evaluate family background, emotional aspects of adjustment, interpersonal skills, vocational adjustment, financial status, the degree of acceptance of seizures, and the degree of satisfaction with medical treatment. This scale promises to be useful in assessing the complex area of psychosocial adjustment of epileptics, particularly in conjunction with neuropsychological testing.

Schwartz, Dennerll and Lin (1968) conducted a detailed study with 181 epileptic adults concerning their occupational and social adjustment. These investigators used an extensive combination of psychological tests based principally upon the Wechsler Adult Intelligence Scale and the Halstead-Reitan Neuropsychological Test Battery together with certain psychosocial measures. The subject's current employment status was used as the criterion variable to determine the relevance of the neuropsychological measures. The results indicated that the tests were significantly useful in identifying those epileptics who were currently employed compared with those who were not. These findings suggest that factors such as seizure control and employers' attitudes toward epileptic patients (often cited as critical factors) probably represent an oversimplification of the problems involved. Neuropsychological examination showed that in some instances individual epileptic subjects may be seriously impaired in intellectual and cognitive functions as well as deviant in their psychosocial reactions. Other persons with epilepsy, however, are competent and undoubtedly capable of being successful in occupational pursuits.

CONCLUSIONS

This book has concentrated on clinical evaluation of patients by using the Halstead-Reitan Neuropsychological Test Battery. Several general conclusions are supported by these clinical evaluations and the research results cited. Experimental investigations and clinical practice using the Halstead-Reitan Battery for over 30 years has led to: (1) developing an understanding of the major behavioral and psychological categories of brain functions; (2) the development of measurement strategies, incorporated into the Battery, which are basic for valid interpretation; and (3) an understanding of the data provided by the Battery for clinical evaluation and application.

The Halstead-Reitan Battery has probably been researched more thoroughly than any other set of neuropsychological tests, although more investigation of the significance of deficits for everyday behavior is needed. Through evaluation of thousands of subjects, interpretation of test results has progressed to the point that neuropsychological examination of brain-behavior relationships is routinely of clinical value. In patients with known or suspected brain disease or deficit, the test results relate directly to neurological findings and add the important dimension of the behavioral consequences of brain disease or damage. Brain functions in persons who have *not* sustained brain damage are obviously no less important, and the future trend in the field of neuropsychology is in the direction of evaluation and application of the broad differences in brain functions among normal individuals.

In addition, now that it is possible to comparatively assess the range of abilities dependent on brain function in the individual subject, and identify areas of deficit or impairment, a focused and pertinent plan can be prescribed in accordance with each person's needs for brain retraining. Reitan's brain retraining regimen, REHABIT, is correlated directly to assessment with the Halsted-Reitan Battery, and results, though variable in total, have in some instances far exceeded the range of test-score improvement seen either as a result of normal practice-effect or spontaneous recovery. Brain retraining is presently in its infancy, but is likely to represent a major role in clinical neuropsychology in the future.

GLOSSARY

GLOSSARY OF TERMS

ACOUSTIC NEUROMA. A tumor or new growth largely made up of nerve cells and nerve fibers which involves the acoustic division of the eighth cranial nerve.

AFFERENT. Conducting inward to a part or organ. In neurophysiology, a nerve impulse carried from sensory receptors in toward a synapse en route to the brain.

AGNOSIA. Denoting an absence of knowledge. In aphasia, impairment of ability to recognize the symbolic meaning of stimulus material.

AKINETIC MUTISM. Inability to speak, usually accompanied by a more general failure of ability to respond. It is frequently associated with lesions of the anterior brainstem.

ALZHEIMER'S DISEASE. Pre-senile or senile dementia with progressive mental impairment. Characterized pathologically by the presence of excessive neurofibrillary tangles and senile plaques.

AMAUROSIS FUGAX. Temporary impairment or loss of vision (blindness) in one eye due to impairment of blood supply through the internal carotid artery or the ophthalmic artery.

ANEURYSM. A sac (or bulging) of an artery or vein caused by dilatation of the walls of the vessel.

ANTERIOR. Before or toward the front.

ANTERIOR CEREBRAL ARTERY. An artery originating from the internal carotid artery serving principally the frontal lobe, corpus collosum, olfactory and optic tracts. Branches include the anterior communicating, ganglionic, commissural, and hemispheral arteries.

ANTERIOR COMMISSURE. A band of fibers that passes transversly through the lamina terminalis and connects the basal portions of the two cerebral hemispheres.

ANTERIOR COMMUNICATING ARTERY. An artery that originates from the anterior cerebral artery, supplies the caudate nucleus, and helps form the anterior part of the circle of Willis.

ANTICHOLINERGIC DRUGS. Drugs which block the passage of nerve impulses through the parasympathetic nerves.

APHASIA. Impairment, due to cerebral damage, of receptive or expressive abilities in use of language symbols for communicational purposes.

APRAXIA. Impaired ability, due to brain damage, to perform functional or purposeful acts.

AQUEDUCT OF SYLVIUS. A narrow canal, about three-quarters of an inch long, that connects the third and fourth ventricles.

ARACHNOID. The middle layer of the meninges of the brain so-named ("like a cobweb") because of its delicate network of tissue.

ARTERIOSCLEROSIS. A condition marked by loss of elasticity, thickening, and hardening of the arteries.

ARTERIOVENOUS MALFORMATION. An abnormal formation of arteries and veins. It may be only a small tangle of vessels or a large collection of abnormal vessels occupying a large area.

ARTERY. A blood vessel that carries oxygenated blood.

ASTROCYTOMA. An intrinsic tumor of the brain that arises from star-shaped cells (astrocytes) of the neuroglia.

ATAXIA. Disordered movements due to irregularity of muscular action and failure of muscular coordination.

ATHEROSCLEROSIS. A degenerative process of arteries in which there are fatty deposits and degeneration of the inner lining of the vessel which, in turn, may lead to narrowing of the lumen of the vessel.

ATHETOSIS. Involuntary, purposeless, disordered movements caused by a brain lesion, in which there is a constant recurrence of slow writhing movements of the hands and feet.

ATROPHY. A wasting away or decrease in size of a cell, tissue, organ, or part of the body due to lack of nourishment.

AUDITORY VERBAL DYSGNOSIA. An aphasic deficit characterized by impairment of ability to understand the symbolic significance of verbal communication through the auditory avenue (loss of auditory-verbal comprehension).

AUTOIMMUNE DISORDERS. Impairment of bodily processes by which immunization is effected.

AUTONOMIC NERVOUS SYSTEM. That part of the nervous system concerned with visceral and involuntary functions.

AXON. A long, slender, and relatively unbranched process of a nerve cell which conducts impulses away from the cell body.

BABINSKI RESPONSE. Extension (instead of flexion) of the toes on stimulation of the sole of the foot, occurring in persons with lesions of the pyramidal tract.

BACTERIAL INFECTION. Infection by minute, one-celled organisms which multiply by dividing in one or more directions.

BASAL GANGLIA. A group of forebrain nuclei located within the diencephalon but below the cerebral hemisphere, including all or at least parts of the thalamus, caudate nucleus, and lentiform nucleus.

BASILAR ARTERY. An artery formed by the right and left vertebral arteries which supplies blood to parts of the cerebrum and cerebellum. It supplies blood to many brainstem structures and leads to the right and left posterior cerebral arteries.

BILATERAL SENSORY STIMULATION. Stimulation of both sides of the body simultaneously, using touch, hearing, or vision, in order to determine whether an individual imperceives the stimulus on one side or the other.

BILATERAL TRANSFER. Facilitation of performance of a task by one hand as a result of having practiced the task with the other hand.

BLOOD-BRAIN BARRIER. A process whereby certain substances fail to leave the blood circulation and enter the gray and white matter of the brain. The "barrier" is more of a physiological concept than a defined anatomic structure. In addition, the barrier does not exist at certain sites in the brain, including the pituitary gland, the pineal gland, and choroid plexus.

BLOOD DYSCRASIA. Disorders that are characterized by an abnormal composition of the blood.

BODY DYSGNOSIA. A deficit, associated with aphasia, in which the subject is impaired in ability to identify body parts.

BRADYKINESIS. A motor disorder, frequently seen in Parkinson's disease, resulting from rigidity of muscles and manifested by slow finger movements and difficulty in fine motor performances such as writing.

BRAIN ABSCESS. A localized collection of pus in a cavity in the brain, formed by the disintegration of tissues.

BRAIN CONTUSION. A bruise of brain tissue in which there is capillary bleeding.

BRAIN INFECTIONS. An invasion of brain tissues by pathogenic organisms in such a way that injury of brain tissue follows with symptoms of illness.

BRAIN LESION. Any pathological or traumatic damage of brain tissue.

CALVARIUM. The cranium, or more specifically, the skull cap.

CAPILLARY. Minute blood vessels which connect the arterioles and the venules, forming a network in nearly all parts of the body that effects a transition from arterial to venous blood flow.

CARCINOGEN. Any substance which produces cancer.

CARCINOMA. A malignant new growth (cancer) that tends to infiltrate surrounding tissue and give rise to metastases.

CAROTID SYSTEM. A system of blood circulation to certain parts of the brain deriving from the internal carotid arteries.

CENTRAL DYSARTHRIA. Impairment of ability to enunciate words, characterized by an omission, addition, or transposition of syllables.

CENTRAL FISSURE (ROLANDIC FISSURE). A fissure is a deep fold in the cerebral cortex (sulcus) which involves the entire thickness of the brain wall. The central fissure is the deep fold between the frontal and parietal lobes.

CENTRAL NERVOUS SYSTEM. The part of the nervous system made up of the brain and spinal cord.

CEREBELLUM. The portion of the brain that lies behind the cerebrum and above the pons and fourth ventricle. The cerebellum is concerned particularly with coordination of voluntary movements.

CEREBRAL ANGIOGRAM. A procedure of visualization of blood vessels of the brain, using x-rays taken after injection of radiopaque material into the arterial blood stream.

CEREBRAL ANOXIA. A condition in which the cells of the brain do not have (or cannot utilize) sufficient oxygen to perform normal functions.

CEREBRAL ATROPHY. A wasting away or diminution in the size of cells or tissue structures of the brain.

CEREBRAL BLOOD FLOW. The rate of blood flow through the brain, which may be measured by various techniques and determined for various regions of the brain.

CEREBRAL CORTEX. The thin surface layer of gray matter (nerve cell bodies) that forms the outer surface of the cerebrum.

CEREBRAL EMBOLISM. A sudden blocking of an artery or vein by a clot or obstruction which has been brought to the position of blockage by the current of blood flow.

CEREBRAL HEMISPHERE. The large structure representing either half of the cerebrum.

CEREBRAL HEMORRHAGE. Bleeding of a blood vessel within the cerebrum.

CEREBRAL INFARCT. An area of coagulation necrosis in a cerebral vessel which obstructs circulation and results in pathological changes in the area deprived of blood supply.

CEREBRAL VASCULAR ACCIDENT (CVA OR STROKE). An embolism, infarct, or hemorrhage of a cerebral vessel.

CEREBRAL VASCULAR INSUFFICIENCY. Lack of a sufficient supply of blood (which can be due to many factors) for the brain to perform its normal functions.

CEREBROSPINAL FLUID. The fluid contained within the cerebral ventricles, subarachnoid sinus, and the central canal of the spinal cord. It acts as a water cushion to protect the brain and spinal cord from shock.

CEREBRUM. The main portion of the brain which occupies the upper portion of the cranium and consists principally of the two cerebral hemispheres which are united by large masses of tissue fibers (white matter) called the anterior commissure, the corpus callosum, and the posterior commissure. Some anatomists also include the anterior part of the brainstem in the cerebrum.

CHIASM. A crossing or decussation of parts. The optic chiasm refers to the crossing of fibers of the optic nerve, forming the optic tract, that lies on the ventral surface of the brain.

CHOROID PLEXUS. A highly vascularized fold of the pia matter in the third, fourth, and lateral ventricles that secretes the cerebrospinal fluid.

CIRCLE OF WILLIS. A circular system of cerebral arteries formed principally by the internal carotid, the anterior and posterior cerebral arteries, and the posterior communicating arteries.

COMPUTED TOMOGRAPHY (CT OR CAT SCAN). An x-ray procedure in which images or "slices," taken by scanners which rotate around the head, are reconstructed through computer-assisted methods. Computed tomography scanning permits identification and differentiation of many soft tissues in the body because of their absorption differences and the thin sections represented by the images in CT scanning.

CONCUSSION. A condition caused by a physical blow to the head or extreme airblast often resulting in loss of consciousness, vertigo, nausea, weak pulse, and slow respiration.

CONGENITAL LESIONS. Lesions present at or dating from birth.

CONSTRUCTIONAL DYSPRAXIA. Impaired ability to deal with spatial relationships either in a two- or three-dimensional framework. This symptom is commonly manifested by impaired ability to copy simple shapes, such as a cross.

CONTRAST RADIOGRAPHY. X-ray procedures in which a contrast substance is injected in order to enhance visualization of particular structures. Customarily a contrast substance is injected into the blood circulation of the organ before x-rays are taken.

CONTRECOUP DAMAGE. Damage to the opposite side of the brain from the point of injury.

CONVOLUTION. A rounded, elevated part of the cerebral cortex (gyrus) that is generally fairly well demarcated by fissures.

CORPUS CALLOSUM. An arched mass of white matter (nerve fibers), located at the bottom of the longitudinal fissure, made up of transverse fibers which connect the cerebral hemispheres.

CORTICAL ATROPHY. Wasting, diminution or shrinkage of the cerebral cortex.

CORTICOSTEROIDS. Crystalline steroids found in the cortex of the adrenal gland.

CRANIECTOMY. Surgical removal (excision) of a part of the skull.

CRANIUM. The skull.

DEEP TENDON REFLEXES (also called tendon reflexes and muscle stretch reflexes). Tendon reflexes or muscle stretch reflexes are contrasted with reflexes of a superficial type. In muscle stretch reflexes the tendon or insertion of a muscle is briskly tapped with a reflex hammer and the resulting contraction of the muscle is graded from 0 (no response) to 4 + (maximal response or clonus).

DELTA WAVES (ELECTROENCEPHALOGRAPHY — EEG). Random slow waves of 1 to 3 cps on EEG tracings.

DEMENTIA. Significant deterioration of intellectual and cognitive functions.

DEMYELINATING DISEASES. Diseases characterized by destruction or removal of the myelin of nerve tissue.

DENDRITE. A tree-shaped protoplasmic process from a nerve cell which receives impulses and conducts them toward the cell body.

DIABETES MELLITUS. A metabolic disorder in which there is a severe deficiency in ability to oxidize carbohydrates due to faulty pancreatic activity and consequent disturbance of normal insulin mechanism. This produces hyperglycemia with a variety of symptoms, including thirst, hunger, emaciation and weakness.

DIPLOPIA. Double vision, or seeing one object as if it were two.

DISTAL. Toward the periphery or away from the center of the body.

DOPAMINE. A neurotransmitter, produced in the neurons of the pars compacta of the substantia nigra which reaches the corpus striatum by way of the axons of the nigrostriatal pathway, and is necessary for the normal functioning of the excitatory pathways to the gamma motor neurons.

DORSAL. Pertaining to or situated toward the back of the structure.

DURA MATER. The tough and mostly fibrous outer layer of the meninges or membranes surrounding the brain.

DYSCALCULIA. An aphasic symptom characterized by impairment in the ability to appreciate the symbolic significance of numbers and the nature of arithmetical processes.

DYSDIADOCHOKINESIS. The ability to arrest one motor impulse and substitute it for one that is exactly the opposite. The clinical test for this condition is to have the patient hold out both hands and pronate and supinate them as rapidly as possible.

DYSGNOSIA. In contrast to agnosia, dysgnosia represents a partial rather than complete loss of the symbolic significance of information reaching the brain.

DYSGRAPHIA. A loss of ability to form letters when writing, resulting from a brain lesion. A symptom of dysphasia.

DYSKINESIA. A general term referring to impairment of voluntary movement which may be expressed in a number of specific ways.

DYSLEXIA. Impairment (due to a brain lesion) of reading ability and the understanding of the symbolic significance of words. A symptom of dysphasia.

DYSNOMIA. Impairment of the ability to name objects, resulting from a brain lesion. A symptom of dysphasia.

DYSPRAXIA. Impairment of ability to perform coordinated and purposeful movements, resulting from a brain lesion.

DYSRHYTHMIA (ELECTROENCEPHALOGRAPHY — EEG). A disturbance or irregularity in the rhythm of EEG tracings.

DYSSTEREOGNOSIS. Impairment of ability to recognize objects through touch.

EDEMA. Accumulation of abnormally large amounts of fluid in the intercellular tissue spaces of the body.

EFFERENT. In reference to nerve impulses, conveying impulses outward or toward an effector organ.

ENCEPHALITIS. Infection and resulting inflammation of the brain.

ENCEPHALON. A general term referring to the brain.

ENDARTERECTOMY. Surgical removal of deposits along the inner lining of arteries, intended to improve patency of the vessel.

ENDOCRINOLOGICAL DISORDERS. Any disease or disorder due to malfunction of the organs (endocrine glands) of internal secretions.

EPENDYMOMA. A tumor of the brain, classified as a glioma, which arises from adult ependymal cells.

EPILEPSY. A disorder characterized by seizures of a number of different types. It may be due to one of the many known causes but frequently is of unknown etiology.

ESSENTIAL HYPERTENSION. Elevated blood pressure of unknown etiology.

EXTRANEURONAL NEURITIC PLAQUES (SENILE PLAQUES). Areas of incomplete necrosis in the brains of patients with Alzheimer's disease and in older persons.

EXTRINSIC BRAIN TUMOR. A tumor that arises from tissue surrounding the brain and produces brain-related symptoms through compression of brain tissue.

FACIAL PARESIS. Weakness or partial paralysis of facial muscles.

FALX. The dural tissue which separates the cerebral hemispheres.

FINGER DYSGNOSIA. Impaired ability to identify individual fingers following tactile stimulation.

FISSURE. A deep fold in the cerebral cortex which involves the entire thickness of the brain wall and tends to define the limits of the lobes.

FLACCID. Relaxed, flabby or absent muscular tone.

FORAMEN. An aperture or opening.

FRONTAL LOBE. The anterior lobe in each cerebral hemisphere, bound posteriorly by the central fissure.

FUNDUS (OF THE EYE). The posterior aspect of the internal coats of the eye.

FUNGAL INFECTIONS. Infections caused by any one of a class of vegetable organisms of a low order of development, including molds.

GENERAL DYSPRAXIA. A general impairment in the ability to perform coordinated and purposeful acts.

GENERAL PARESIS (DEMENTIA PARALYTICA). A chronic syphilitic meningoencephalitis, characterized by progressive dementia and a generalized paralysis.

GENICULOSTRIATE TRACT. A tract of nerve fibers in the visual system extending from the lateral geniculate body of the thalamus to the striate cortex of the occipital lobe.

GLIA. Neuroglia cells which are part of the supporting structure of nervous tissue in the brain. This structure consists of a fine web of tissue made up of ectodermic elements in which are enclosed odd-shape branched cells known as neuroglia or glial cells. These cells are of three types: macroglia or astroglia, oligodendroglia, and microglia.

GLIOBLASTOMA MULTIFORME (ASTROCYTOMA GRADES III OR IV). A rapidly growing glioma originating from astrocytes (star-shaped cells) of the neuroglia.

GLIOMA. A brain tumor composed of tissue which represents neuroglia in any of its stages of development.

GRANULOVACUOLAR DEGENERATION. A degenerative change in neurons that occurs particularly in the hippocampal regions and a prominent finding in Alzheimer's disease.

GRAY MATTER. Cell bodies of neurons in the central nervous system composed of the cerebral cortex and various nuclei.

GYRUS (CONVOLUTION). On the surface of the brain, a convoluted ridge of cerebral cortex between sulci.

HAPTIC SENSITIVITY. Sensitivity to stimuli through touch.

HEMIANOPIA. Loss of vision in half of each eye.

HEMIHYPALGESIA. Diminished sensitivity affecting one lateral half of the body.

HEMIPARESIS. Partial paralysis or weakness of one side of the body.

HEMIPLEGIA. Paralysis of half of the body.

HEMISENSORY DEFICIT. Sensory losses, usually including tactile impairment, on half of the body.

HEPATIC ENCEPHALOPATHY. A brain disorder or dysfunction caused by liver disease or damage.

HISTOLOGICAL EXAMINATION (HISTOLOGY). An examination or study of the fine (microscopic) structure of tissues of the body.

HODGKIN'S DISEASE. A disease of unknown etiology producing painless, progressive enlargement of the lymph nodes, spleen, and general lymphoid tissues. It often begins in the neck and spreads to other parts of the body.

HOMONYMOUS HEMIANOPIA. A loss of half of the visual field for each eye with the loss being on the same side (left or right) for each eye.

HOMONYMOUS QUADRANTANOPIA. A loss of one quadrant of the visual field (either upper or lower) on the same side (either right or left) for each eye.

HYDROCEPHALUS. An excessive amount of cerebrospinal fluid or excessive pressure within the ventricular system.

HYPEROSTOSIS. Hypertrophy or excessive growth of bone tissue.

HYPERTENSION. Abnormally high blood pressure.

HYPERTENSIVE ENCEPHALOPATHY. Brain dysfunction or disease due to elevated blood pressure.

HYPESTHESIA. Impairment or lessening of tactile sensitivity.

HYPOGLYCEMIA. A below-normal concentration of glucose in the blood.

HYPOXIC ENCEPHALOPATHY. Disease or damage of the brain due to a diminished supply of oxygen.

IDIOPATHIC. A term referring to conditions of unknown cause.

IDIOPATHIC EPILEPSY. Epilepsy of unknown cause.

IMPERCEPTION (TACTILE, AUDITORY, VISUAL). Failure to perceive a sensory stimulus on one side when stimuli are delivered to both sides simultaneously, even though unilateral stimuli on both sides can be perceived correctly.

INTERNAL CAPSULE. A tract of nerve fibers passing through the corpus striatum.

INTERNAL CAROTID ARTERY. An artery that originates from the common carotid artery and supplies blood to a large portion of the brain, the orbit, internal ear, nose, and forehead.

INTRACRANIAL HYPERTENSION. Elevated pressure within the cranium or skull.

INTRACRANIAL TUMOR. A tumor that occurs within the cranium.

INTRANEURONAL DETERIORATION. Deterioration of structures within the neuron.

INTRINSIC TUMOR. A tumor arising from tissues within the brain.

ISCHEMIA. A local and temporary deficiency of blood.

JACKSONIAN SEIZURES. Epileptic seizures which begin with a small, localized group of muscles and gradually spread to involve a larger muscle group.

KINESTHESIS. A sense by which muscular motion and degree of muscular contraction permits perception of weight, bodily position, etc.

KORSAKOFF'S SYNDROME. A psychotic state, associated with chronic alcoholism, marked by disturbance of orientation, confusion, delusions, hallucinations, and inaccurate memories. Polyneuritis and wrist drop are also usually present.

LESION. Any damage to bodily tissues as a result of disease or injury.

LEUKEMIA. A disease of blood-forming organs characterized by an increase in the number of leukocytes and their precursors in the blood together with enlargement and proliferation of the lymphoid tissue of the spleen, lymphatic glands, and bone marrow.

LEUKODYSTROPHIES. A group of familial conditions occuring predominately in infancy and childhood in which there is abnormal formation of myelin.

LEVODOPA. A drug that plays an important role in treatment of Parkinsonism. The neurotransmitter dopamine is unable to pass the blood-brain barrier, but levodopa is converted to dopamine in the brain and replenishes depleted dopamine in the brainstem and basal ganglia.

LIPID STORAGE DISEASES. Diseases which involve neuronal storage of lipid and cerebromacular degeneration (an accumulation of lipid in the ganglion cells of the retina).

LUMBAR PUNCTURE. Insertion of a needle into the lumbar subarachnoid space to determine cerebrospinal fluid pressure and to withdraw cerebrospinal fluid for examination.

LYMPHOMA. A tumor made up of lymphoid tissue.

MAJOR MOTOR SEIZURES. Epileptic seizures characterized by loss of consciousness and tonic-clonic muscular activity. Also referred to as grand mal epilepsy.

MANUAL DEXTERITY. Proficiency in performances using the hands.

MEDULLA OBLONGATA. The lowest part of the brain that is continuous with the spinal cord on the lower end and the pons on the upper end. It lies below the cerebellum and the back of the medulla forms the floor of the fourth ventricle.

MEDULLOBLASTOMA. A malignant tumor in the region of the fourth ventricle, involving the cerebellum, and composed of immature neuroglial cells.

MENINGES. The three membranous tissues (dura mater, arachnoid, and pia mater) that envelop the brain and spinal cord.

MENINGIOMA. A tumor of the meninges. These tumors are classified as benign and usually are slowly growing.

MENINGITIS. Inflammation of the meninges. When the dura mater is affected the disease is referred to pachymeningitis and when the arachnoid tissue and pia mater are also involved, it is called leptomeningitis.

MENINGO-CORTICAL SCAR. Scar tissue that involves the meninges and the cerebral cortex of the brain.

METABOLIC BRAIN DISORDER. A disorder of the brain tissue that involves the physical and chemical processes by which living organized substance is produced and maintained and by which energy is made available.

METASTATIC TUMOR. A tumor that is transferred from one organ or part of the body to another organ or part not directly connected with it. In metastatic brain tumors there is a transfer of cells via the lymphatics or blood stream from the initial malignant tumor (carcinoma) to the brain.

MICROGRAPHIA. Small, cramped handwriting.

MIDBRAIN. A portion of the brain also referred to as the mesencephalon which consists of the corpora quadrigemina, tegmentum, cerebral peduncles, and cerebral aqueduct (Sylvian aqueduct). It is one of the five major divisions of the brain. Starting with the cerebral hemispheres these divisions are the telencephalon, diencephalon, mesencephalon, metencephalon and myelencephalon.

MIDDLE CEREBRAL ARTERY. One of three major arteries that serves the cerebral hemispheres. It arises from the internal carotid artery and distributes blood to the frontal, parietal, and part of the temporal lobe and the basal ganglia.

MOTOR AREA. The pre-central gyrus represented in the posterior part of the frontal lobe. This area serves primary motor functions.

MULTI-INFARCT DEMENTIA. Dementia resulting from small infarcts distributed throughout the brain due to arteriosclerosis.

MULTIPLE SCLEROSIS. A disease characterized by sclerosis (plaques) resulting from degeneration of myelin that occurs in patches throughout the brain and spinal cord.

MYELIN SHEATH. A sheath that surrounds the axis-cylinder of some nerve fibers which are then referred to as myelinized fibers.

MYXEDEMA. A condition due to hypoactivity of the thyroid gland resulting in a lowering of basal metabolism and a number of signs and symptoms.

NEPHRECTOMY. The excision or removal of a kidney.

NEUROFIBRILLARY TANGLES. Tangles of neurofibrilla, which are fibers that form a delicate network among nerve cells. These tangles are observed particularly in patients with Alzheimer's disease but are also seen in the brains of older people generally.

NEUROFIBROMA. A connective tissue tumor of the nerve fiber.

NEUROLEMMOMA. A neurofibroma.

NEUROLOGY. A branch of medical science that deals with nervous system functions and diseases.

NEURON. A nerve cell, or the structural unit of the nervous system, including the cell body and the various processes, collaterals, and terminations of the cell.

NEURONAL DEGENERATIVE DISEASE. A disease in which the primary underlying factor is degeneration of neurons.

NEURONAL LOSS. A depletion in the number of neurons which occurs with aging and many neurological diseases (e.g., Alzheimer's disease). Cell counts in the past have been done manually but now usually are done by automated procedures which use an image analyzing computer.

NEUROPATHOLOGY. A branch of medicine which deals with diseases of the nervous system and pathology of nerves and nerve centers.

NEUROPSYCHOLOGY. A branch of psychology which deals with brain-behavior relationships and measurement of the manifestations of brain functions.

NUCHAL RIGIDITY. Stiffness of the back of the neck.

NYSTAGMUS. An involuntary rapid movement of the eyeball, which may be lateral, vertical, rotatory, or a mixed combination.

OCCIPITAL LOBE. The most posterior lobe of each cerebral hemisphere.

OCCLUSION. The process of closure or the state of being closed. Vascular occulsion refers to closing of a blood vessel.

OCULOMOTOR SIGNS. Signs pertaining to abnormal movements of the eye through impaired control or coordination of the extrinsic eye muscles.

OLIGODENDROGLIOMA. A tumor of the brain that arises from oligo-dendroglial cells.

OPHTHALMIC ARTERY. An artery that arises from the internal carotid artery and supplies blood to the eye, adjacent structures, and adjacent parts of the face.

OPTIC CHIASM. The point at which there is crossing of the fibers from each optic nerve to form the optic tracts, located on the ventral surface of the brain.

OPTIC DISC. The area of the retina where the optic fibers converge to leave the back of the eye as the optic nerve.

OPTIC DISC PALLOR. An appearance of paleness in the vicinity of the optic disc.

OPTIC NEURITIS. An inflammation of the optic nerve.

OPTIC TRACT. A tract which is that part of the visual system made up of contributions of fibers from both the right and left optic nerves and extends from the optic chiasm to the point of synapse in the lateral geniculate body.

PALSY. Paralysis or weakness of muscles.

PAPILLEDEMA. Edema or swelling of the optic papilla which gives rise to an elevation of the optic disc (sometimes referred to as choked disc). Papilledema is usually a sign of increased intracranial pressure.

PARALYSIS AGITANS. Idiopathic Parkinson's disease.

PARANOID SCHIZOPHRENIA. Psychosis characterized by suspiciousness, systematized delusions of persecution, and feelings of grandeur which are often built up in logical form.

PARAPLEGIA. Paralysis of the legs and lower part of the body with sensation also often being affected.

PARESTHESIA. An abnormal tactile sensation such as numbness, burning, prickling, or tickling.

PARIETAL LOBE. One of the four lobes of each cerebral hemisphere that is bound by the frontal lobe anteriorally, the occipital lobe posteriorally, and the temporal lobe principally inferiorally.

PATHOGNOMONIC SIGNS. A sign or symptom which is specifically distinctive or characteristic of a disease or pathological condition and on which a diagnosis can be made.

PERIPHERAL DYSARTHRIA. Impaired enunciatory ability characterized by slurring of speech.

PETECHIAL HEMORRHAGE. A hemorrhage characterized by petechiae or small spots of bleeding.

PINEALOMA. A tumor of the pineal gland.

PITUITARY ADENOMA. A tumor of the pituitary gland.

PNEUMOENCEPHALOGRAPHY. A procedure in which cerebrospinal fluid is replaced with air in order to permit x-ray visualization of structures within the brain.

POLYCYTHEMIA. An excessive number of red corpuscles in the blood.

PONS. A broad, transverse band of nerve fibers which arch across the upper part of the medulla oblongata extending to the cerebellum on each side.

POSTERIOR CEREBRAL ARTERY. An artery arising from the basilar artery and supplying blood to the occipital area and parts of the temporal area.

POSTERIOR COMMISSURE. A band of nerve fibers that join nuclei of the thalamus.

POSTERIOR COMMUNICATING ARTERY. An artery that arises from the internal carotid artery, forms part of the circle of Willis, and supplies blood to the uncinate gyrus and part of the thalamus.

PRESENILE DEMENTIA. Severe deterioration of mental functions before the age of 65 years.

PRIMARY TUMORS. Tumors that develop within the affected organ rather than originating in other parts of the body.

PROXIMAL. Next to or nearest, as in a part of the limb with relation to the body.

RENAL INSUFFICIENCY. A condition in which the kidneys are unable to remove a sufficient proportion of waste matter from the blood.

RIGHT-LEFT CONFUSION. Confusion of the right and left sides of one's own body or of other persons or objects.

RIGIDITY. Abnormal or pathological stiffness or inflexibility of muscles.

ROLANDIC FISSURE (CENTRAL FISSURE). The fissure between the frontal and parietal lobes.

SAGITTAL. Pertaining to the sagittal or midline suture of the skull and in any plane that is parallel to this suture.

SCHIZOPHRENIA. A psychotic disorder manifested by a variety of symptoms depending upon the type of schizophrenia, but often characterized by withdrawal, ineffectiveness in behavior, disorientation, delusions, and hallucinations.

SENILE DEMENTIA. Severe deterioration of mental functions in persons over the age of 65 years.

SENILE PLAQUE (EXTRANEURONAL NEURITIC PLAQUE). Areas of incomplete necrosis seen in persons with primary neuronal degenerative diseases of the brain and, to a lesser degree, in older persons.

SICKLE-CELL ANEMIA. An inherited disease characterized by anemia and ulcers in which the red blood cells acquire a sickle-like or crescent shape.

SOMATIC COMPLAINTS. Complaints referring to disorders of bodily functions.

SPASTIC PARAPARESIS. Partial paralysis of the lower extremities characterized by spastic movements.

SPELLING DYSPRAXIA. Impairment of spelling ability as a result of cerebral damage. A symptom of aphasia.

STEREOTAXIC SURGERY. Surgery in which the purpose is to place a therapeutic lesion in a precise area of the brain. Mechanical equipment and x-rays are used to localize the specific area.

STERNOCLEIDOMASTOID MUSCLE. A muscle originating from the sternum and clavicle, inserting in the mastoid process and a part of the occipital bone, and used to depress and rotate the head and flex the head and neck.

STRABISMUS. Involuntary deviation of the eye from the normal position.

STROKE. A general term referring to a cerebral vascular accident.

SUBARACHNOID HEMORRHAGE. Bleeding into the subarachnoid space.

SUBCLAVIN ARTERY. The artery which arises from the brachiocephalic artery on the right side and the aortic arch on the left side and distributes blood to the brain, meninges, and other parts of the body.

SUBDURAL HEMATOMA. Bleeding into the subdural space.

SULCUS. An indentation in the cerebral cortex marking the limit of a gyrus or convolution.

SYLVIAN AREA. The area of the cerebral cortex in the vicinity of the Sylvian fissure.

SYLVIAN FISSURE. A fissure that runs along the superior surface of the temporal lobe, dividing it in its anterior portion from the frontal lobe and in the more posterior portion from the parietal lobe.

SYNAPSE. The region of contact between processes of two adjacent neurons, forming the place where a nervous impulse is transmitted from one neuron to another.

SYPHILITIC GUMMA. A soft, gummy tumor that occurs in the tertiary stages of syphilis.

SYPHILITIC INFECTION OF THE BRAIN. Syphilis is a contagious veneral disease that leads to many lesions throughout the body and, if untreated, eventually will involve the brain.

TACTILE. Pertaining to touch.

TACTILE FORM DISCRIMINATION. Ability to discriminate form or shape through the sense of touch.

TEMPORAL LOBE. One of the four lobes of the cerebral hemisphere which lies in an inferior and lateral position.

TENTORIUM. A layer of dura mater which forms a partition between the cerebrum and the cerebellum and covers the upper surface of the cerebellum.

THALAMOTOMY. A stereotaxically imposed surgical lesion in the thalamus (usually placed in the ventrolateral nucleus for relief of dyskinesia on the contralateral side of the body).

THROMBOSIS. The formation of a clot (thrombus) in a blood vessel.

TINNITUS. A noise in the ears such as ringing, buzzing, roaring, or clicking.

TOXIC BRAIN DISORDER. Damage or dysfunction of the brain as a result of toxic influences.

TRANSIENT ISCHEMIC ATTACK (TIA). A temporary manifestation of brain disorder which may last from a few minutes up to 24 hours. It usually represents focal manifestations, with a great range of symptoms, due to cerebral circulatory insufficiency.

TREMOR. An involuntary trembling or quivering.

VASCULAR MALFORMATION. A congenital abnormality of blood vessels represented by a weakness of the vessel wall with focal enlargement (such as a berry aneurysm) or a tangled mass of arteries and veins (arteriovenous malformation).

VENTRAL. Referring to the side that is toward the front, as opposed to dorsal.

VENTRICLE. A small cavity, such as the right or left ventricles of the heart or the ventricles of the brain.

VENTROLATERAL NUCLEUS OF THE THALAMUS. One of the nuclei of the thalamus is often the target in stereotaxic surgery for relief of involuntary movements.

VERTEBRAL ARTERY. One of the four major arteries (two internal carotid and two vertebral) which supplies blood to the brain. This artery arises from the subclavian artery and supplies blood to the cerebellum, muscles of the neck, vertebrae, the spinal cord and interior portions of the cerebrum.

VERTEBRAL-BASILAR SYSTEM. A system for supply of arterial blood to the brainstem and posterior part of the brain. The other system of arterial blood supply to the brain is the carotid system.

VERTIGO. A sensation of external objects revolving around the subject or the subject revolving in space. In common practice, however, this term frequently refers to a feeling of dizziness.

VIRAL INFECTIONS. Any infection of the body resulting from invasion by a virus.

VISUAL FORM DYSGNOSIA. Impairment in the ability to recognize forms or shapes through visual observation.

VISUAL LETTER DYSGNOSIA. Impairment of the ability to recognize the symbolic significance of letters of the alphabet through visual perception.

VISUAL IMPERCEPTION. Impairment of the ability to recognize stimuli presented visually on both sides simultaneously, even though the stimulus can be perceived and reported when given unilaterally. The deficit is usually contralateral to the side of cerebral damage.

VISUAL NUMBER DYSGNOSIA. Impairment of the ability to recognize the symbolic significance of numbers through visual perception.

WERNICKE'S ENCEPHALOPATHY. A syndrome due to thiamine deficiency (vitamin B1) together with other vitamins in the B complex that is frequently associated with alcoholism. The clinical features of this syndrome include ophthalmoplegia (weakness and incoordination of the eye muscles), ataxia, and dementia.

WHITE MATTER. Tissue in the nervous system that is made up of nerve fibers (contrasting with gray matter which is made up of cell bodies).

REFERENCES

REFERENCES

Adams, H., Rennick, P., Schooff, K.G., & Keegan, J.F. (1975). Neuro-psychological measurement of drug effects: Poly-drug research. *Journal of Psychedelic Drugs, 7*, 151-160.

Anderson, A.L. (1950). The effect of laterality localization of brain damage on Wechsler-Bellevue indices of deterioration. *Journal of Clinical Psychology, 6*, 191-194.

Babcock, H. (1930). An experiment in the measurement of mental deterioration. *Archives of Psychology, 18*, 5-105.

Bailey, P. & Cushing, H. (1926). *A classification of the tumors of the glioma group on a histogenetic basis with a correlated study of prognosis.* Philadelphia: J.B. Lippincott Company.

Bealty, P., & Grange, J. (1977). Neuropsychological aspects of multiple sclerosis. *Journal of Nervous and Mental Disease, 164*, 42-50.

Bear, D.M., & Fedio, P. (1977). Quantitative analysis of interictal behavior in temporal lobe epilepsy. *Archives of Neurology, 34*, 454-467.

Bender, M. (1951). *Disorders of perception.* Springfield, IL: Charles C. Thomas.

Birch, H.G., Belmont, I., & Karp, E. (1967). Delayed information processing and extinction following cerebral damage. *Brain, 90*, 113-130.

Boll, T.J., Heaton, R.K., & Reitan, R.M. (1974). Neuropsychological and emotional correlates of Huntington's chorea. *Journal of Nervous and Mental Disease, 158,* 61-69.

Bondareff, W. (1959). Morphology of the aging nervous system. In J.E. Birren (Ed.). *Handbook of aging and the individual* (pp. 136-172). Chicago, Illinois: University of Chicago Press.

Briggs, P. (1960). The validity of the WAIS performance subtests completed with one hand. *Journal of Clinical Psychology, 16,* 318-320.

Cerves-Navarro, J., & Sarkander, H.I. (Eds.). (1983). *Brain aging: Neuropathology and neuropharmacology.* Aging, Vol. 21. New York: Raven Press.

Chapman, L.F. & Wolff, H.G. (1959). The cerebral hemispheres and the highest integrative functions in man. *Archives of Neurology, 1,* 357-424.

Christenson, A.-L. (1975). Luria's neuropsychological investigation: Text, manual, and test cards. New York: Spectrum.

Cobb, C.A., & Youmans, J.A. (1982). Glial and neuronal tumors of the brain in adults. In Youmans, J.R. (Ed.). *Neurological surgery.* Philadelphia: W.B. Saunders Company.

Critchley, M. (1953). *The parietal lobes.* London: Arnold.

Crockard, H.A., Brown, F.D., et al. (1977). Physiological consequences of experimental cerebral missile injury and data analysis to predict survival. *Journal of Neurosurgery, 46,* 784-794.

Davis, L.J., Hamlett, I., & Reitan, R.M. (1966). Relationships of conceptual ability and academic achievement to problem-solving and experiental backgrounds of retardates. *Perceptual and Motor Skills, 22,* 499-505.

Davis, J., & Reitan, R.M. (1966). Methodological note on the relationships between ability to copy a simple configuration and Wechsler Verbal and Performance I.Q.s. *Perceptual and Motor Skills, 22,* 281-332.

Davis, J., & Reitan, R.M. (1967). Dysphasia and constructional dyspraxia items and Wechsler Verbal and Performance I.Q. in retardates. *American Journal of Mental Deficiency, 71,* 606-608.

Dikmen, S., & Matthews, C.G. (1977). Effect of major motor seizure frequency upon cognitive-intellectual functions in adults. *Epilepsia, 18,* 21-39.

Dikmen, S., Matthews, C.G., & Harley, J.P. (1975). The effect of early versus late onset of major motor epilepsy upon cognitive-intellectual performance. *Epilepsia, 16,* 73-81.

Dikman, S., & Reitan, R.M. (1974a). Minnesota Multiphasic Personality Inventory correlates of dysphasic language disturbances. *Journal of Abnormal Psychology, 83,* 675-679.

Dikman, S. & Reitan, R.M. (1974b). MMPI correlates of localized structural cerebral lesions. *Perceptual and Motor Skills, 39,* 831-840.

Dikmen, S., & Reitan, R.M. (1976). Psychological deficits and recovery of functions after head injury. *Transactions of the American Neurological Association, 101,* 72-77.

Dikmen, S., & Reitan, R.M. (1977a). Emotional sequelae of head injury. *Annals of Neurology, 2,* 492-494.

Dikmen, S., & Reitan, R.M. (1977b). MMPI correlates of adaptive ability deficits in patients with brain lesions. *Journal of Nervous and Mental Disease, 165,* 247-254.

Dikmen, S., & Reitan, R.M. (1978). Neuropsychological performance in post-traumatic epilepsy. *Epilepsia, 19,* 177-183.1.

Dikmen, S., Reitan, R.M., & Temkin, N.R. (1983). Neuropsychological recovery in head injury. *Archives of Neurology, 40,* 333-338.

Dodrill, C.B. (1981). Neuropsychology of epilepsy. In Filskov, S.B., & Boll, T.J. (Eds.). *Handbook of clinical neuropsychology.* New York: John Wiley and Sons.

Dodrill, C.B. (1975). Diphenylhydantoin serum levels, toxicity, and neuropsychological performance in patients with epilepsy. *Epilepsia, 16,* 593-600.

Dodrill, C.B., Batzel, L.W., Queisser, H.R., & Tempkin, N.R. (1980). An objective method for the assessment of psychological and social difficulties among epileptics. *Epilepsia, 21,* 123-135.

Dodrill, C.B., & Troupin, A.S. (1976). Seizures and adaptive abilities: A case of identical twins. *Archives of Neurology, 33,* 604-607.

Dodrill, C.B., & Troupin, A.S. (1977). Psychotropic effects of carbamazepine in epilepsy: A double-blind comparison with phenytoin. *Neurology, 27,* 1023-1028.

Dodrill, C.B., & Wilkus, R.J. (1976). Neuropsychological correlates of the electroencephalogram in epileptics: II. The waking posterior rhythm and its interaction with epileptiform activity. *Epilepsia, 17,* 101-109.

Doehring, D.G., & Reitan, R.M. (1961a). Behavioral consequences of brain damage associated with homonymous field visual defects. *Journal of Comparative and Physiological Psychology, 54,* 489-492.

Doehring, D.G., & Reitan, R.M. (1961b). Certain language and non-language disorders in brain-damaged patients with homonymous visual field defects. *AMA Archives of Neurology and Psychiatry, 5,* 294-299.

Doehring, D.G., Reitan, R.M., & Kløve, H. (1961). Changes in patterns of intelligence test performances associated with homonymous visual field defects. *Journal of Nervous and Mental Disease, 132,* 227-233.

Eisdorfer, C., Nowlin, J., & Wilkie, F. (1970). Improvement of learning in the aged by modification of autonomic nervous system activity. *Science, 170,* 1327-1329.

Falconer, M. (1961). Personal communication.

Fitzhugh, K.B., Fitzhugh, L.C., & Reitan, R.M. (1961). Psychological deficits in relation to acuteness of brain dysfunction. *Journal of Consulting Psychology, 25,* 61-66.

Fitzhugh, K.B., Fitzhugh, L.C., & Reitan, R.M. (1962a). The relationship of acuteness of organic brain dysfunction to Trail Making Test performances. *Perceptual and Motor Skills, 15,* 399-403.

Fitzhugh, K.B., Fitzhugh, L.C., & Reitan, R.M. (1962b). Wechsler-Bellevue comparisons in groups with "chronic" and "current" lateralized diffuse brain lesions. *Journal of Consulting Psychology, 26,* 306-310.

Fitzhugh, K.B., Fitzhugh, L.C., & Reitan, R.M. (1963). Effects of "chronic" and "current" lateralized and non-lateralized cerebral lesions upon Trail Making Tests performances. *Journal of Nervous and Mental Disease, 137,* 82-87.

Fitzhugh, K.B., Fitzhugh, L.C., & Reitan, R.M. (1964). Influence of age upon measures of problem solving and experiental background in subjects with long-standing cerebral dysfunction. *Journal of Gerontology, 19,* 132-134.

Fitzhugh, L.C., Fitzhugh, K.B., & Reitan, R.M. (1960). Adaptive abilities and intellectual functioning in hospitalized alcoholics. *Quarterly Journal of Studies on Alcohol, 21,* 414-423.

Fitzhugh, L.C., Fitzhugh, K.B., & Reitan, R.M. (1962). Sensorimotor deficits of brain-damaged subjects in relation to intellectual level. *Perceptual and Motor Skills, 15,* 603-608.

Fitzhugh, L.C., Fitzhugh, K.B., & Reitan, R.M. (1965). Adaptive abilities and intellectual functioning in hospitalized alcoholics: Further considerations. *Quarterly Journal of Studies on Alcohol, 26,* 402-411.

Flor-Henry, P. (1974). Psychosis, neurosis and epilepsy. *British Journal of Psychiatry, 124,* 144-150.

Flor-Henry, P. (1976). Lateralized temporal-limbic dysfunction and psychopathology. *Annals of the New York Academy of Science, 280,* 777-797.

Folsom, A. (1953). Psychological testing in epilepsy. I. Cognitive function. *Epilepsia, 2,* 15-22.

Forsyth, G.A., Gaddes, W.J., Reitan, R.M., & Tryk, H.E. (1971). Intellectual deficit in multiple sclerosis as indicated by psychological tests. Research Monograph No. 23, Victoria, B.C. (Canada): University of Victoria.

Fox, J.M., Ramsey, R.G. et al. (1976). Cerebral ventricular enlargement: Chronic alcoholics examined by computerized tomography. *Journal of the American Medical Association, 236,* 365-368.

Froyer, W., Eisdorfer, C., & Wilkie, F. (1966). Free fatty acid responses in the aged individual during performance of learning tasks. *Journal of Gerontology, 21,* 415-419.

Gilroy, J., & Meyer, J.S. (1979). *Medical neurology.* New York: Macmillan Publishing Company.

Gissane, W. (1963). The nature and causation of road injuries. *Lancet, 2,* 695-698.

Goldstein, G., & Shelly, C. (1974). Neuropsychological diagnosis of multiple sclerosis in a neuropsychiatric setting. *Journal of Nervous and Mental Disease, 158,* 280-290.

Goodglass, H., & Kaplan, E. (1979). Assessment of cognitive deficit in the brain-injured patient. In Gazzaniga, M.S. (Ed.). *Handbook of behavioral neuropsychology.* New York: Plenum Press.

Grant, I. (1979). *Behavioral disorders: Understanding clinical psychopathology.* New York: SP Medical and Scientific Books.

Grant, I., Adams, K.M., Carlin, A.S., Rennick, P.M., Judd, L., Schooff, K., & Reed, R. (1978). Organic impairment in polydrug users: Risk factors. *American Journal of Psychiatry, 135,* 178-184.

Grant, I., & Judd, L.L. (1976). Neuropsychological and EEG disturbances in polydrug users. *American Journal of Psychiatry, 133,* 1039-1042.

Grant, I., & Mohns, L. (1975). Chronic cerebral effects of alcohol and drug abuse. *International Journal of Addiction, 10,* 883-920.

Grant, I., Mohns, L., Miller, M., & Reitan, R.M. (1976). A neuropsychological study of polydrug users. *Archives of General Psychiatry, 33,* 973-978.

Gur, R.E. (1978). Left hemisphere dysfunction and left hemisphere overactivation in schizophrenia. *Journal of Abnormal Psychology, 87,* 226-238.

Halstead, W.C. (1947). *Brain and intelligence: A quantitative study of the frontal lobes.* Chicago: University of Chicago Press.

Halstead, W.C., & Wepman, J.M. (1949). The Halstead-Wepman aphasia screening test. *Journal of Speech and Hearing Disorders, 14,* 9-13.

Hathaway, S.R., and McKinley, J.C. (1967). *Minnesota Multiphasic Personality Inventory Manual.* New York: The Psychological Corporation.

Heimburger, R.F., DeMyer, W., & Reitan, R.M. (1964). Implications of Gerstmann's Syndrome. *Journal of Neurology, Neurosurgery and Psychiatry, 27,* 52-57.

Heimburger, R.F., & Reitan, R.M. (1961). Easily administered written test for lateralizing brain lesions. *Journal of Neurosurgery, 18,* 301-312.

Hom, J., & Reitan, R.M. (1982). Effect of lateralized cerebral damage upon contralateral and ipsilateral sensorimotor performances. *Journal of Clinical Neuropsychology, 4,* 249-268.

Hom, J., & Reitan, R.M. (1984). Neuropsychological correlates of rapidly vs. slowly growing intrinsic neoplasms. *Journal of Clinical Neuropsychology, 6,* 309-324.

Hutt, S.J., Jackson, P.M., Belsham, A., & Higgins, G. (1968). Perceptual-motor behaviour in relation to blood phenobarbitone level: a preliminary report. *Developmental Medicine and Childhood Neurology, 10,* 626-632.

Katzman, R. (1976). The prevalence and malignancy of Alzheimer's disease. *Archives of Neurology, 33,* 217-218.

Katzman, R., & Karasu, T.B. (1975). Differential diagnosis of dementia. In Fields, W.S. (Ed.). *Neurological and sensory disorders in the elderly.* New York: Stratton.

Kernohan, J.W., Mabon, R.F., Svien, H.J., & Adson, A.W. (1949). A simplified classification of the gliomas. *Proceedings of the Mayo Clinic, 24,* 71-75.

Kernohan, J.W., & Sayre, G.P. (1952). Tumors of the central nervous system. *Atlas of Tumor Pathology. Fascicle 35.* Washington, D.C.: Armed Forces Institute of Pathology.

Kløve, H. (1959). Relationship of differential electroencephalographic patterns of distribution of Wechsler-Bellevue scores. *Neurology, 9,* 871-876.

Kløve, H. (1974). Validation studies in adult clinical neuropsychology. In R.M. Reitan and L.A. Davison (Eds.). *Clinical neuropsychology: Current status and applications.* Washington, D.C.: V.H. Winston & Sons.

Kløve, H., & Matthews, C.G. (1969). Neuropsychological evaluation of the epileptic patient. *Wisconsin Medical Journal, 68,* 296-301.

Kløve, H., & Reitan, R.M. (1958). The effect of dysphasia and spatial distortion of Wechsler-Bellevue results. *Archives of Neurology and Psychiatry, 80,* 708-713.

Lezak, M. (1976). *Neuropsychological assessment.* New York: Oxford University Press.

Magladery, J.W. (1959). Neurophysiology of aging. In J.E. Birren (Ed.). *Handbook of aging and the individual* (pp. 173-186). Chicago: University of Chicago Press.

Matarazzo, J.D. (1972). *Wechsler's measurement and appraisal of adult intelligence.* Baltimore: Williams and Wilkins.

Matthews, C.G., & Harley, J.P. (1975). Cognitive and motor-sensory performances in toxic and nontoxic epileptic subjects. *Neurology, 25,* 184-188.

Matthews, C.G., & Kløve, H. (1967). Differential psychological performances in major motor, psychomotor, and mixed seizure classifications of known and unknown etiology. *Epilepsia, 8,* 117-128.

Matthews, C.G., & Reitan, R.M. (1961). Comparison of abstraction ability in retardates and in patients with cerebral lesions. *Perceptual and Motor Skills, 13,* 327-333.

Matthews, C.G., & Reitan, R.M. (1962). Psychomotor abilities of retardates and patients with cerebral lesions. *American Journal of Mental Deficiency, 66,* 607-612.

Matthews, C.G., & Reitan, R.M. (1963). Relationship of differential abstraction ability levels to psychological test performances in mentally retarded subjects. *American Journal of Mental Deficiency, 68,* 235-244.

Matthews, C.G., & Reitan, R.M. (1964). Correlations of Wechsler-Bellevue rank orders of subtest means in lateralized and non-lateralized brain-damaged groups. *Perceptual and Motor Skills, 19,* 391-399.

Matthews, C.G., Shaw, D., & Kløve, H. (1966). Psychological test performances in neurological and "pseudoneurologic" subjects. *Cortex, 2*, 244-253.

Meier, M.J., & French, L.A. (1966). Longitudinal assessment of intellectual functioning following unilateral temporal lobectomy. *Journal of Clinical Psychology, 22*, 22-27.

Meyerink, L.H. (1982). Intellectual functioning: The nature and pattern of change with aging. (Doctoral dissertation, University of Arizona, 1982). *Dissertation Abstracts International*.

Mitchell, D.E., & Hume-Adams, J. (1973). Primary focal impact damage to the brainstem in blunt head injuries. Does it exist? *Lancet, 1*, 215-218.

Newman, S.E. (1978). The EEG manifestations of chronic ethanol abuse: Relation to cerebral atrophy. *Annals of Neurology, 3*, 299-304.

Ommaya, A.K., Grubb, R.L., & Naumann, R.A. (1970). Coup and contrecoup cerebral contusions: An experimental analysis. *Neurology, 20*, 388-389.

Oppenheimer, D.R. (1968). Microscopic lesions in the brain following head injury. *Journal of Neurology, Neurosurgery, and Psychiatry, 31*, 299-306.

Parsons, O.A., & Farr, S.F. (1981). The neuropsychology of alcohol and drug use. In Filskov, S.B., & Boll, T.J. (Eds.). *Handbook of clinical neuropsychology*. New York: John Wiley and Sons.

Reed, H.B.C., & Reitan, R.M. (1962). The significance of age in the performance of a complex psychomotor task by brain-damaged and non-brain-damaged subjects. *Journal of Gerontology, 17*, 193-196.

Reed, H.B.C., & Reitan, R.M. (1963a). Changes in psychological test performances associated with the normal aging process. *Journal of Gerontology, 18*, 271-274.

Reed, H.B.C., & Reitan, R.M. (1963b). A comparison of the effects of the normal aging process with the effects of organic brain damage on adaptive abilities. *Journal of Gerontology, 18*, 177-179.

Reed, H.B.C., & Reitan, R.M. (1963c). Intelligence test performances of brain-damaged subjects with lateralized motor deficits. *Journal of Consulting Psychology, 27*, 102-106.

Reilly, P.L., Graham, D.I., Hume-Adams, J., & Jennett, B. (1975). Patients with head injury who talk and die. *Lancet, 2*, 375-381.

Reitan, R.M. (1953). Intellectual functions in myxedema. *AMA Archives of Neurology and Psychiatry, 69*, 436-449.

Reitan, R.M. (1955a). Affective disturbances in brain-damaged patients: measurements with the Minnesota Multiphasic Personality Inventory. *AMA Archives of Neurology and Psychiatry, 73*, 530-532.

Reitan, R.M. (1955b). Certain differential effects of left and right cerebral lesions in human adults. *Journal of Comparative and Physiological Psychology, 48*, 474-477.

Reitan, R.M. (1955c). Discussion: Symposium on the temporal lobe. *Archives of Neurology and Psychiatry, 74*, 569-570.

Reitan, R.M. (1955d). The distribution according to age of a psychologic measure dependent upon organic brain functions. *Journal of Gerontology, 10*, 338-340.

Reitan, R.M. (1955e). Evaluation of the postconcussion syndrome with the Rorschach Test. *Journal of Nervous and Mental Disease, 121*, 463-467.

Reitan, R.M. (1955f). The relation of the Trail Making Test to organic brain damage. *Journal of General Psychology, 53*, 97-107.

Reitan, R.M. (1956a). The relationship of the Halstead Impairment Index and the Wechsler-Bellevue Total Weighted Score to chronological age. *Journal of Gerontology, 11*, 447.

Reitan, R.M. (1956b). Investigation of relationships between "psychometric" and "biological" intelligence. *Journal of Nervous and Mental Disease, 123*, 536-541.

Reitan, R.M. (1958). The validity of the Trail Making Test as an indicator of organic brain damage. *Perceptual and Motor Skills, 8*, 271-276.

Reitan, R.M. (1959a). The comparative effects of brain damage on the Halstead Impairment Index and the Wechsler-Bellevue Scale. *Journal of Clinical Psychology, 15,* 281-285.

Reitan, R.M. (1959b). *The effects of brain lesions on adaptive abilities in human beings.* Tucson, Arizona: Reitan Neuropsychology Laboratories, Inc.

Reitan, R.M. (1960). The significance of dysphasia for intelligence and adaptive abilities. *Journal of Psychology, 50,* 355-376.

Reitan, R.M. (1962). The comparative psychological significance of aging in groups with and without organic brain damage. In C. Tibbitts & W. Donahue (Eds.). *Social and psychological aspects of aging* (pp.880-887). New York: Columbia University Press.

Reitan, R.M. (1964). Psychological deficits resulting from cerebral lesions in man. In J.M. Warren & K.A. Akert (Eds.). *The frontal granular cortex and behavior.* New York: McGraw-Hill.

Reitan, R.M. (1966a). Problems and prospects in studying the psychological effects of brain lesions in human beings. *Cortex, 2,* 127-154.

Reitan, R.M. (1966b). A research program on the psychological effects of brain lesions in human beings. In N.R. Ellis (Ed.). *International review of research in mental retardation: Vol. I* (pp. 153-218). New York: Academic Press.

Reitan, R.M. (1967a). Psychological assessment of deficits associated with brain lesions in subjects with normal and subnormal intelligence. In J.L. Khanna (Ed.). *Brain damage and mental retardation: A psychological evaluation.* Springfield, Illinois: Charles C. Thomas.

Reitan, R.M. (1967b). Psychological changes associated with cerebral damage. *Mayo Clinic Proceedings, 42,* 653-673.

Reitan, R.M. (1970a). Measurement of psychological changes in aging. *Duke University Council on Aging and Human Development,* Proceedings of Seminars.

Reitan, R.M. (1970b). Objective behavioral assessment in diagnosis and prediction. In A.L. Benton (Ed.). *Behavioral change in cerebrovascular disease* (pp. 155-165). New York: Medical Department, Harper & Row.

Reitan, R.M. (1970c). Sensorimotor functions, intelligence and cognition, and emotional status in subjects with cerebral lesions. *Perceptual and Motor Skills, 33,* 275-284.

Reitan, R.M. (1972). Verbal problem solving as related to cerebral damage. *Perceptual and Motor Skills, 34,* 515-524.

Reitan, R.M. (1973). Psychological testing after craniocerebral injury. In J.R. Youmans (Ed.). *Neurological surgery,* Vol. II, (pp. 1040-1048). Philadelphia: W.B. Saunders.

Reitan, R.M. (Sept. 1973). *Behavioral manifestations of impaired brain functions in aging.* Paper presented at the meeting of the American Psychological Association, Montreal, Canada.

Reitan, R.M. (1976). Psychological testing of epileptic patients. In P.J. Vinken & G.W. Bruyn (Eds.). *Handbook of clinical neurology: The epilepsies,* Vols. IX and X. New York: North Holland Publishing Company.

Reitan, R.M. (1977). Neuropsychological concepts and psychiatric diagnosis. In V.M. Rankoff, H.C. Stancer and H.B. Kedward (Eds.). *Psychiatric diagnosis* (pp. 42-68). New York: Brunner/Mazel.

Reitan, R.M. (1984). *Aphasia and sensory-perceptual deficits in adults.* Tucson, Arizona: Neuropsychology Press.

Reitan, R.M. (1985a). Aphasia and sensory-perceptual deficits in children. Tucson, Arizona: Neuropsychology Press.

Reitan, R.M. (1985b). Relationships between measures of brain functions and general intelligence. *Journal of Clinical Psychology, 41,* 245-253.

Reitan, R.M., & Boll, T.J. (1971). Intellectual and cognitive functions in Parkinson's disease. *Journal of Consulting and Clinical Psychology, 37,* 364-369.

Reitan, R.M., & Davison, L.A. (Eds.). (1974). *Clinical neuropsychology: Current status and applications.* Washington, D.C.: V.H. Winston & Sons.

Reitan, R.M., & Fitzhugh, K.B. (1971). Behavioral deficits in groups with cerebral vascular lesions. *Journal of Consulting and Clinical Psychology, 37,* 215-223.

Reitan, R.M., Hom, J., & Wolfson, D. (submitted for publication). Verbal processing by the brain.

Reitan, R.M., Reed, J.C., & Dyken, M.L. (1971). Cognitive, psychomotor, and motor correlates of multiple sclerosis. *Journal of Nervous and Mental Disease, 153*, 218-224.

Reitan, R.M., & Sena, D.A. (1983, August). The efficacy of the REHABIT technique in remediation of brain-injured people. Paper presented at the meeting of the American Psychological Association, Anaheim, California.

Reitan, R.M., & Wolfson, D. (In press). The Halstead-Reitan Neuropsychological Test Battery and aging. *The Clinical Gerontologist.*

Reitan, R.M., & Wolfson, D. (1984). The emergence of clinical neuropsychology: Practical applications for psychologists. *Texas Psychologist, 36*, 5-13.

Rodin, E.A. (1973). Psychomotor epilepsy and aggressive behavior. *Archives of General Psychiatry, 28*, 210-213.

Rodin, E.A., Katz, M., & Lennox, K. (1976). Differences between patients with temporal lobe seizures and those with other forms of epileptic attacks. *Epilepsia, 17*, 313-320.

Ross, A.T., & Reitan, R.M. (1955). Intellectual and affective functions in multiple sclerosis: A quantitative study. *AMA Archives of Neurology and Psychiatry, 73*, 663-677.

Rourke, B.P., Bakker, D.J., Fisk, J.L., & Strang, J.B. (1983). *Child neuropsychology*. New York: Guilford Press.

Russell, D.S., & Rubinstein, L.J. (1977). *Pathology of tumors of the nervous system*. Baltimore: Williams and Wilkins Company.

Samuel, D., Algeri, S., Gershon, S., Grimm, V.E., & Toffano, G. (1983). *Aging of the brain*. (Aging, Vol. 22). New York: Raven Press.

Schwartz, M.L., Dennerll, R.D., & Lin, Y.G. (1968). Neuropsychological and psychosocial predictors of employability in epilepsy. *Journal of Clinical Psychology, 24*, 174-177.

Selkoe, D.J. (1978). Cerebral aging and dementia. In H.R. Tyler & D.M. Dawson (Eds.). *Current neurology*, Vol. I (pp. 360-387). Boston: Houghton Mifflin Professional Publishers.

Serafetinides, E.A. (1965). Aggressiveness in temporal lobe epileptics and its relation to cerebral dysfunction and environmental factors. *Epilepsia, 6,* 33-42.

Shock, N.W. (1962). The physiology of aging. *Scientific American, 206,* 100-110.

Shure, G.D., & Halstead, W.C. (1958). Cerebral localization of intellectual processes. *Psychological Monographs, 72,* (12, Whole No. 465).

Stevens, J.R. (1966). Psychiatric implications of psychomotor epilepsy. *Archives of General Psychiatry, 14,* 461-471.

Stevens, J.R., Milstein, V., & Goldstein, S. (1972). Psychometic test performance in relation to the psychopathology of epilepsy. *Archives of General Psychiatry, 26,* 532-538.

Strich, S.J. (1970). Lesions in the cerebral hemispheres after blunt head injury. *Journal of Clinical Pathology, 23 (supplement 4),* 154-165.

Tomlinson, B.E. (1970). Brainstem lesions after head injury. *Journal of Clinical Pathology, 23 (supplement 4),* 154-165.

Tomlinson, B.E., Blessed, G., & Roth, M. (1970). Observation of brains of demented old people. *Journal of Neurological Sciences, 11,* 205-243.

U.S. Department of Health, Education, and Welfare: Facts of life and death. (1974). Publication number (HRS) 74-1222, National Center for Health Statistics, Rockville, MD.

Vega, A., & Parsons, O.A. (1967). Cross-validation of the Halstead-Reitan tests for brain damage. *Journal of Consulting Psychology, 31,* 619-625.

Wechsler, D. (1955). *Manual for the Wechsler Adult Intelligence Scale.* New York: The Psychological Corporation.

Wheeler, L. (1964). Complex behavioral indices weighted by linear discriminant functions for the prediction of cerebral damage. *Perceptual and Motor Skills, 19,* 907-923.

Wheeler, L., Burke, C.J., & Reitan, R.M. (1963). An application of discriminant functions to the problem of predicting brain damage using behavioral variables. *Perceptual and Motor Skills, 16,* 417-440.

Wheeler, L. & Reitan, R.M. (1962). The presence and laterality of brain damage predicted from responses to a short Aphasia Screening Test. *Perceptual and Motor Skills, 15,* 783-799.

Wheeler, L., & Reitan, R.M. (1963). Discriminant functions applied to the problem of predicting cerebral damage from behavior tests: A cross validation study. *Perceptual and Motor Skills, 16,* 681-701.

Welford, A.T., & Birren, J.E. (Eds.). (1965). *Behavior aging and the nervous system.* Springfield, Illinois: Charles C. Thomas.

Wilkus, R.J., Dodrill, C.B., & Troupin, A.S. (1978). Carbamazepine and the electroencephalogram of epileptics: A double-blind study in comparison to phenytoin. *Epilepsia, 19,* 283-291.

SUBJECT INDEX

SUBJECT INDEX

A

Acceleration injury of the brain, 238
Aging effects
  Alzheimer's disease and, 293
  Brain-age quotient, 398
  brain re-training, 398
  disparity between neurological and
    neuropsychological findings, 408
  Halstead Impairment Index, 398
  morphological changes, 397
  neuropsychological correlates, 398
  neuropsychological findings in aging, 401-409
Alcoholism
  Alzheimer's disease and, 382
  clinical symptoms, 384
  diffuse cerebral atrophy, 382
  EEG changes, 382
  head trauma, 382
  hepatic encephalopathy, 382
  Korsakoff's syndrome, 381
  neuropsychological deficits, 381, 382, 390
  neuropsychological findings for an alcoholic, 384-390
  nutritional deficiency, 382
  ventricular enlargement in, 382
  Wernicke's encephalopathy, 381
Alzheimer's disease
  definition, 292
  epidemiology, 291

H

I

J

Jung Association Test, 413

K

Kayser-Fleischer ring in Wilson's disease, 371
Koch's Tree Drawing Test, 413
Korsakoff's syndrome, 381

L

Lateral Dominance Examination, 86
Left cerebral lesions
 neuropsychological findings, 121-130, 165-174, 185-192,
  201-209, 211-219, 221-236, 261-268
Leukodystrophy, 311
Lipid storage diseases, 311

M

McGill Picture Anomalies Test, 412
Measurement strategies
 in neuropsychological assessment, 9, 97, 118, 125, 147
Memory, 6, 406
Meningioma
 neuropsychological findings in, 147-154
Mental retardation, 13
Metastatic carcinoma of the brain
 neuropsychological findings in, 155-163, 165-174
Micrographia, 334
Middle cerebral artery, 176
Middle cerebral artery lesions
 neuropsychological findings, 179-184, 185-192, 201-209
Miles ABC Test of Ocular Dominance, 88
Mill Hill Vocabulary test, 412
Minnesota Multiphasic Personality Inventory, 39
 clinical interpretation of, 137, 144, 198, 208, 216, 249, 266,
  277, 285-286, 321, 322, 330, 380

T